Fascist Femboys for No Nut November:

Sex and Sexual Minorities in Far-Right Online Spaces

Charles R. Bernard

Madness Heart Press

Madness Heart Press
2006 Idlewilde Run Dr.
Austin, Texas 78744

This is a work of fiction. Names, characters, places, and incidents either are the product of the author's imagination or are used fictitiously. Any resemblance to actual persons, living or dead, events, or locales is entirely coincidental.

Cover by Gavriel Quiroga

First Edition
ISBN: 978-1-967517-30-5
www.madnessheart.press

For every lonely queer young person out there.
You may feel alone or unloved, but you are neither.

NOTE: This book is intended for mature readers.

Contents

AUTHOR'S NOTE

I began this book before a spate of mass shootings broke out in August and September of 2025. Some of this violence was correctly or incorrectly associated with the trans community. As the introduction after this note will make clear, this book is *not* out to demonize sexual minorities. Quite the contrary. It is an attempt to understand the extremes to which the current societal moment has driven the rightmost fringe of the LGBTQIA+ community. I also seek to tell the story of how we got to this point with sex and the far-right, queer or heterosexual. I want to make my intention doubly clear, however, so I'll state it here as well as in the introduction.

My personal memory of mass shootings is long. While it doesn't stretch back to Charles Whitman's 1966 University of Texas at Austin tower shooting, *does* go back to Columbine, Colorado, in 1999. I happened to be a senior in high school in Utah, one state over, when Columbine happened. It has been in the news again recently for depressing and predictable reasons: the trailblazing duo behind that atrocity are still inspiring copycats. (1) I graduated a little two months after that mass shooting. In one way or another, my adult life from age 17 to age 44 has been punctuated by the sporadic, staccato horror of very public murders. Many of the mass shootings of the 21st century have targeted minority groups. All but a handful of them have been committed by young, white, cisgendered, heterosexual men. In particular, by sexually frustrated ones. (2) This book is *not* an argument that gender or ethnicity, i.e. white men, are at the root of mass shootings, though there are plenty of excellent books on that subject already. (3) It's simply the background data to provide context for what I'm about to say.

In fall of 2025, the far-right had a lockstep, frightening response. Very rapidly after one school shooting (out of three) and the murder of Charlie Kirk occurred (one of which was committed by a trans person and the other by a man with an alleged trans or genderqueer partner,) mass discourse of a specific type erupted online. Not just in the usual right-wing cesspits, but in a growing segment of what is now considered the mainstream media: outlets like Fox News, Newsmax, OANN, and the carefully groomed and cultivated stable of right-wing influencers the Fascist Internationale keeps on hand. The shooter was trans! No, the shooter was sleeping with a trans or genderfluid person! Being transgender is a mental illness! They're not only after your kids' bodies for sex, they're after them *FOR MURDER*!

The reaction I describe—attempting to blame a miniscule, persecuted population already at risk of harm for a spate of violence fueled in no small part by anti-trans sentiment (4)—was incredibly widespread. As is often the case with mass casualty events these days, each political faction had their own carefully scripted explanation and agenda lined up. For Democrats, it was about guns. For Republicans, the more overtly fascist party in our "two" party system, the talking points were new and nauseating. Keep in mind that this isa party that on the surface supports almost an absolute interpretation of the Second Amendment. I say on the surface, because when you peel back the mask, well...

"Trans people," these gutless pumpkin-fuckers said in fall of 2025, "are mentally ill and dangerous. Unstable, and prone to self-mutilation, violence, and self-harm. We must re-open the public insane asylums and send trans people there. At the very least, we must bar them from owning guns. It's the only way to save lives."

These messages were well-coordinated, well-financed, and prepared in advance. (5) It wasn't a groundswell of populist outrage any more than the inheritance tax being renamed the "death tax" was. Not only that, the people trying to use one of the smallest demographics of mass shooters to restrict trans peoples' rights *know* exactly what they're doing and what effect it could have on innocent people. They've read their history, and they're gloating about the chance to re-enact it. They're giddy to repeat war crimes and crimes against humanity of the past. That's what gets them off. I wish I were kidding about that last part, too. That would also just make me an asshole. Full disclosure: I'm a *bit* of an asshole, but not for fabricating or exaggerating these claims.

Behold, the well-balanced mind of a transphobe (content warning: hate speech that sounds like it was invented by Dr. Seuss):

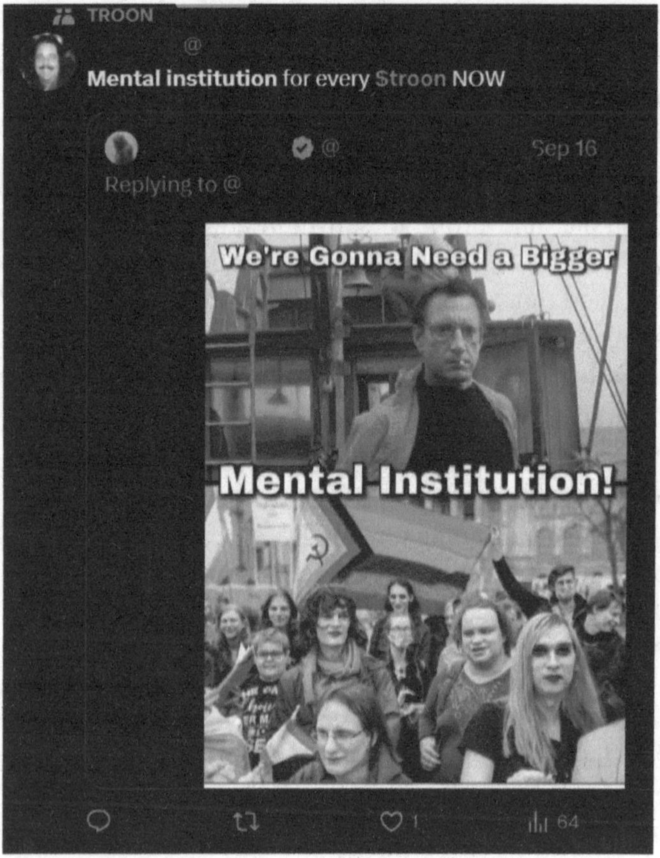

Here's another:

Aug 28

Replying to @

I agree. It's time to commit every **troon** to a **mental institution**. For their and our safety.

And another:

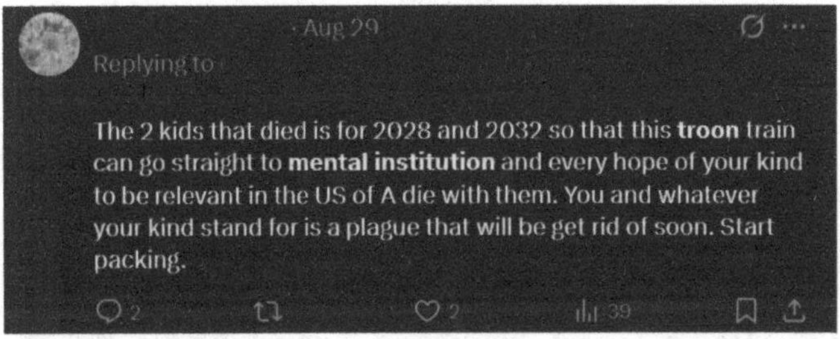
Aug 29

Replying to

The 2 kids that died is for 2028 and 2032 so that this **troon** train can go straight to **mental institution** and every hope of your kind to be relevant in the US of A die with them. You and whatever your kind stand for is a plague that will be get rid of soon. Start packing.

One more out of literally tens of thousands of posts:

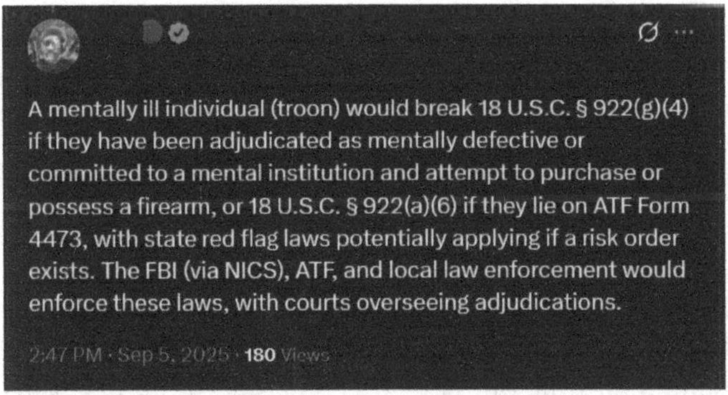
A mentally ill individual (troon) would break 18 U.S.C. § 922(g)(4) if they have been adjudicated as mentally defective or committed to a mental institution and attempt to purchase or possess a firearm, or 18 U.S.C. § 922(a)(6) if they lie on ATF Form 4473, with state red flag laws potentially applying if a risk order exists. The FBI (via NICS), ATF, and local law enforcement would enforce these laws, with courts overseeing adjudications.

2:47 PM · Sep 5, 2025 · 180 Views

This is not a "populist" or even popular movement

mind you. Hundreds of thousands or even a million people do not constitute anything like a popular majority or even a significant movement in a country of 340.1 million people. However, history teaches us that if a significant minority in any country are highly motivated, well-financed, and/or violent enough, they can wreak tremendous damage. In America right now, the most highly-motivated, well-financed, and violent movement(s) are, unfortunately, fascists. These are people whose dearest dreams are the rise of National Socialism, *Return of the Living Dead*-style, from its well-deserved place in the forgotten cemetery of history. Perceived strength excites them while perceived weakness disgusts them; the precise "authoritarian personality" Erich Fromm identified after his firsthand experience with National Socialism in the 1930s. Given that not an inconsiderable number of modern fascists read the same mystical goofball "philosophers" that the real Nazis did, this right-wing plague of defective personalities is perhaps understandable.

And yet.

And yet, I had already started work on this book by August and September of 2025. I already knew that *trans Nazis* exist. True, they are a tiny minority of a tiny minority within either the trans community *or* membership of Nazi hate cults. Given where many—not most, I cannot emphasize that enough, but a startling number of—members of sexual minorities spend their time online *, this outcome shouldn't be as surprising to normies as it was. It was as if the very purpose of the spate of shootings in August and September of 2025 were to give the "institutionalize trans people and maybe gay people too" discourse a boost to its metaphorical initial public offering. I don't necessarily believe this, but whatever the case, those months pushed the institutionalization agenda from the fringe where it has festered for untold decades to the top of online American fascism's "to do" list.

No, I do not think any of these trans-related shootings were "false flags." I think shooters in the cases of both the Minnesota Catholic school and Charlie Kirk, like most mass shooters from what I can tell, were suffering from a cornucopia of mental illnesses and spent their time self-radicalizing in very violent, very negative, very *kleine*-nihilistic spaces. Ingesting poison online may have replaced baseball as the great American pastime, but if you look into it, these murderers were consuming hate content at levels that would render an ordinary person catatonic.

The GOP's about-face on guns is jaw-dropping: the kind of thing that would get someone tarred and feathered as a commie bastard twenty short years ago. Despite a half-century of opposition to gun restrictions *including those on people with mental health issues* (6,) gun control from the right (!) was very much part of the agenda, especially after Charlie Kirk. What am I talking about?

In the wake of the Minneapolis Catholic church shooting, senior Justice Department officials are weighing proposals to limit transgender people's right to possess firearms, according to two officials familiar with the internal discussions. (7)

It's not even hypocrisy at this point. As a very well-known MAGA gaming and politics commenter on Twitter put it (which, by the way, is why I haven't edited his name or @):

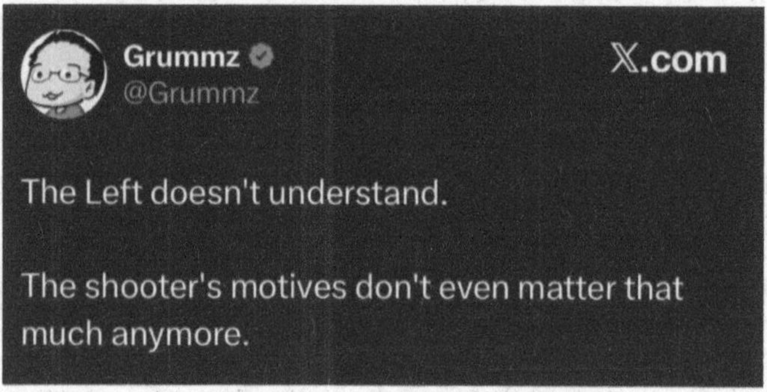

One of the first steps in exterminating any group is disarming them. If I could voyage back to 2000 and show my 18-year-old self that sentence, he would believe I'd been replaced by a Republican or libertarian pod person (*WRONG*, former Charles, it's worse: you're an anarchist now!). That's right; I used to be a big-time gun grabber! What happened? I was convinced by a combination of logical argument, evidence, practical experience, and learning more about marginalized communities.

Regarding MAGA's sudden embrace of the anti-gun nanny State, memes immediately spread specifically tailored disinformation graphics which labeled many former mass shooters trans when they were not. Calls for "reclassification" or "classification" of being trans in the DSM were driven by a group known as "TERFs" who believe that trans women suffer from something called autogynophilia, or the sexual attraction to the idea of one's self as woman. We'll touch on TERFs and a fellow named Ray Milton Blachard III in Chapters Two and Seven. The current bad-faith "take trans guns" argument from the right comes in two steps. Step one: attempt to drive trans people to self-harm or to lash out with direct action. Step two, clutch your pearls and squeal "With trans suicide rates so high, and trans mass shootings, we must take their guns away!"

Absolutely. Fucking. Not. Allow me to explain why.

In the United States of America, the police have not only no interest in protecting sexual minorities (or women, or people of color, or etc.): they actively run interference for, share intelligence with, and are on the side of fascists. (7) In some cities, the police have their own gangs (8)—and, I have to say, that just seems anti-capitalist to me and not in a cool way. If you're going to get into the dope game, cops, do it like real Americans and start as a lookout, then work your way up to corner boy, then traphouse— there's a proper order to these things!

Sexual minorities are the victims of violent crime at a horrifying rate compared to heterosexual people. (9) In most cases, when the cops become involved survivors can look forward to mistreatment and in many cases summary dismissal of any investigative effort. (10) Sexual minorities are also statistically vastly overrepresented in sex work, which in some cases is less dangerous than others, but in all cases involves interaction with potentially violent men, whether they identify as heterosexual or not. (11) For all of these reasons, due to all of these risks, and because queer folks cannot trust the police to protect them, I think it's a solid, rational choice for LGBTQIA+ people to be armed.

There are significant differences between these realities and the mindless fear that drives the larger gun industry, especially ads that target a white audience and stoke fears of everything from minorities to home invasion. In those cases, the demographic they are aiming at—white, rural, and right-wing—experience crime at a much lower rate than sexual minorities. (ibid.) Also, those white, rural people, especially if they are homeowners and can afford the type of gun collection that an average NRA member has, are among the few Americans who have a remotely reasonable chance of calling the cops and having those cops at least *pretend* to give a shit.

It seems as though after every mass shooting we hear the same outcry from the most hypocritical right-wing gun owners; "We need to screen for mental health!" If you ask for details on what they mean by this, most people are fuzzy on what exactly they think qualifies as disqualifying. Having recently heard that "liberalism is a mental disorder," "transgenderism [sic] is a mental disorder," "communists are mentally ill," etc., it's fairly clear what this has been code for all along. From day one, which I count as Ronald Reagan's efforts to disarm the Black Panthers while Governor of California, the right's cooperation with gun control has been contingent on keeping guns out of the hands out of *oppressed people*, not "the wrong people." (12)

What if the State does enact these "mental health

screenings?" Will the restrictions bar former armed forces members with PTSD and/or anxiety? Maybe. Will they bar a trans person struggling with anxiety and depression? You bet! Will they disarm a cop with a history of domestic violence? *Hell* no, are you kidding? Will they disarm a gay ANTIFA member with an expunged misdemeanor assault charge from when they were 17? You bet your sweet ass they will! In point of fact, I expect gun rights to be stripped from a great many Americans based on which political organizations they have or have not supported in the past. Never, ever trust a policy that is only meant to be selectively applied: you can be sure that it is a political weapon designed to imprison or murder opposition.

That said, gun culture has many different subcultures. Arguably the most dangerous of these are fascist, right-nihilist† spaces that promote mental illness. No, I do not mean promote *awareness* or *acceptance* of mental illness, I mean it's a community that supports and seeks to induce and/or exacerbate specific psychological processes that lead to acts of violence like mass shootings. (13) If, for example, it was possible to magically run a background check to see if a potential gun buyer has ever posted on 4Chan or 8Kun (it's not possible), someone could *feasibly* twist my arm into supporting it. Then again, that would restrict a lot of minorities—including sexual minorities—from gun ownership too. Never mind, twist away. I wouldn't even support that big, red, flapping flag.

The problem with screening for "mental health" when approaching firearms laws are multitudinous, but here are the ones I find germane to this author's note. It seems to be the case based on the sentiments I've shown examples of and the campaign that's underway to demonize trans people as "mentally ill" that one potential outcome is clear. All trans people (and nonbinary people, and genderqueer people, and the poor, poor puppygirls) will be excluded from gun ownership. These are people, members of a sexual minority, who are increasingly and as I've shown *justifiably* afraid of street violence like the kind perpetrated by Putin's "Night Wolves" and other street gangs in Russia. (The attempt to demonize trans and queer people as pedophiles is literally a step-by-step repeat of how this slow creep into forced closeting and the persecution of LGBTQIA+ people went down in Russia, incidentally.)††

2018's Small Arms Survey estimated that there are about 398 million guns rootin' and tootin' their way around America right now; more than one for every man, woman, and child who call this fair land home. In circumstances like that, should people on the left continue to try to legislate guns out of existence and show distaste for them at home? Unilateral disarmament in what is increasingly likely to be a low-grade, undeclared Civil War for the next decade-plus is a terrible idea. At least, it's a terrible idea if you want queer folks to survive, which I very much do. For my less radical, more pacifist readers, consider this question. Do you think the police—the same people who murder citizens at an exponentially higher rate than mass shooters do—will protect queer people from fascists? I don't. That leaves one option, and it isn't a rugged-individualistic, NRA-style "every person for themselves" approach. It means arming up and defending our own communities, our own loved ones, our queer friends, our immigrant neighbors, disabled comrades, and anyone else who needs protecting.

At any rate, I do not want anyone making the mistake of this being a "trans people are violent" or "trans mass shooter" book. While the Massachusetts shooter *does* fit into one of the emerging archetypes I discuss in this book, they were a mass shooter first, a National Socialist second, and a trans person last. That doesn't make a difference to grieving families, but it does to people seeking to find sense (or, at least, a set of ideas and movements driving events) in what at first blush seems an ultimately senseless, ideologically incoherent human-made catastrophe.

At any rate, in the case of the Massachusetts shooter, I can offer a few answers on what subculture they were likely part of, based on the memes and internet footprint they left. It's sad, strange stuff. There are answers, though, and "trans people are mentally ill" isn't one of them. Read on.

* This is difficult to quantify with complete accuracy, as criteria are up for debate (what constitutes a "mass shooting," for example?). That said, experts are in consensus that sexual minorities are, well, a tiny minority in shooters.

** 4Chan. I'm talking about 4Chan, which has both an /lgbt/ board and one we'll discuss later called /tttt/ that is pretty much exclusively trans femme.

A Statista Research Department. "Number of mass shootings in the United States between 1982 and August 2025, by shooter's race or ethnicity". *Statista.*

B Bowman, Emma & Michel, Martin (5/27/2021) "Why Nearly All Mass Shooters Are Men". *NPR.*

† I've used the expressions "right nihilism" and "kleine nihilism" in this introduction. In both cases, I'm referring to a sort of pop-nihilist, faux-Nietzschean creed among fascists that completely disregards the wider body of pessimist and nihilist philosophy in favor of a selective and highly action-positive reading of Nietzsche. These fools know nothing of Max Stirner, Arthur Schopenhauer, or my beloved Peter Wessel Zappfe or Philipp Mainländer.

†† Staff. "Hunting Gays For Money: How a gang of thugs in St. Petersburg has made an industry of hating and extorting homosexuals". (5/3/2016) *Meduzza.*

Brown, Chris (7/6/2019)"Extortion, violence and fear: One gay man's harrowing experience in Russia's Caucasus region". *CBS News.*

1 Paul, Jesse & Prentzel, Olivia (9/12/2025). "Evergreen High School shooter embraced Colmbune, antisemitism, and white supremacy online". *The Colorado Sun.*

2 The University of Rhode Island (1/18/2024). "New research sheds light on incel community's connection to mass violence". *Newswire.*

3 Examples include:

Anderson, Carol (2021). The Second: Race and Guns in a Fatally Unequal America. (Bloomsbury

Publishing, London).

Kimmel, Michael (2017). Angry White Men: American Masculinity at the End of An Era. (Bold Type Books, New York)

Light, Caroline (2017). Stand Your Ground: A History of America's Love Affair with Lethal Self-Defense. (Beacon Press, Boston).

Metzl, Jonathan (2024). Dying of Whiteness: How the Politics of Race Resentment is Killing America's Heartland. (Basic Books, New York).

…and many more. As LaVar Burton used to say throughout my childhood, "Ask a librarian!"

4 Staff (1/23/2025). "Nashville Shooter's Manifesto Reveals Inspiration Drawn From The Online Far Right". *Global Project Against Hate and Extremism (GPAHE)*.

Tolan, Casey et. al. (8/28/2025). "'There is no message': Journal details warning signs, violent obsessions of Minneapolis shooter". *CNN*.

Zialcita, Pablo (11/22/2022). "Colorado politicians have promoted anti-LGBTQ rhetoric and policies – from local school boards to Congress – that escalate violence, experts and advocates say". *CPR News*.

5 Riedel, Samantha (12/13/2023). "A New Report Exposes the Network of Extremist Groups Behind the Anti-Trans PR Machine". *Them*.

6 Spies, Mike (10/29/2024). "In the Land of Firearm Suicide, Republicans Ban a Policy That Might Help". *The Trace*.

LaRose, Greg (3/27/2024). "Committee rejects 'red flag' law to curb gun violence in Louisiana". *The Louisiana Illuminator*.

Kindy, Kimberly (7/18/2022). "Congress wants more red-flag laws. But GOP, states, gun groups resist". *The Washington Post*.

7 Hermes, Kris (8/26/2025). "Newly Revealed FBI Document Confirms Collaboration Between DC Police and Discredited Far-Right Group Project Veritas". *Unicorn Riot*.

Levin, Sam (2/9/2018). "California police worked with neo-Nazis to pursue 'anti-racist' activists, documents show". *The Guardian*.

German, Mike (8/27/2020). "Hidden in Plain Sight: Racism, White Supremacy, and Far-Right Militancy in Law Enforcement". *Brennan Center for Justice*.

8 Garcia, Jordy et. al. (January 2021). "50 Years of Deputy Gangs in the Los Angeles Deputy Sheriff Department". *Lloyala Law School: Center for Juvenile Law and Policy*.

Cohen, Julia (2/12/2025). "A Platform Problem: Hate Speech and Bots Still Thriving on X". *USC Viterbi School of Engineering*.

9 Wildra, Emily (7/11/2022). "New data: LGBT people across all demographics are at heightened risk of violent victimization". *Prison Policy Initiative*.

Meyer, Ilan et. al. (2/13/2025). "LGBT people five times more likely than non-LGBT people to be victims of violent crime". *UCLA School of Law:*

Williams Institute.

10 Grasso, Jordan et. al. (2024). “Policing Progress: Findings from a National Survey of LGBTQ+ People’s Experiences with Law Enforcement”. *ACLU*.

11 Blayney, Jessica et. al. (2023). “Sexual Victimization Among Sexual and Gender Minoritized Groups: Recent Research and Future Directions”. *Current Psychiatry Reports*. 4;25 (5). P183–191.

12 Large, Steve (5/2/2024). “The lasting legacy of 1967 Black Panther gun control protest at California Capitol”. *CBS News*.

Hartmann, Thom (6/8/2022). “Ronald Reagan’s moment of massive historical irony: How armed Black men led to gun control”. *Slate*.

13 Sutton, Robbie M. & Douglas, Karen M. (2022) “Rabbit Hole Syndrome: Inadvertent, accelerating, and entrenched commitment to conspiracy beliefs”. *Current Opinion in Psychology*. Vol. 48.

INTRODUCTION

THE HUGO BOSS UNDERGROUND

Does anybody remember who Milo Yiannopoulos was? No? Let me do a quick recap.

Milo is a far-right British would-have-been provocateur, raconteur, and libertine who briefly rose to fame in 2015 for coming out (so to speak) as a leader in the Gays For Trump astroturf operation. (1) From the start, Milo was an obnoxious troll who delighted in racism, misogyny, homophobia (despite the fact that he is gay), and the usual grab-bag of fascist dysfunctions that are currently Making America Great Again. When Trump rose from absolute last-pick longshot outsider candidate to fascist cult leader, Milo was ecstatic. He gloried in the far right's rise to power. He was part of the Breitbart-industrial-media complex that operated smoothly and without a conscience or a hitch during Trump's first run for office. (2)

At the time, one particularly high profile far right gathering in New York City announced a pro-Trump art show, which was intentionally, completely ridiculous. The show was called "Daddy Will Save Us" (I shit thee not). At the show, Milo and a collection of would-be fascist glitterati primped and preened for cameras, demonstrating how *outrageous!* they could be with antics including conspicuous consumption, an attempt at a fashion show of sorts, terrible faux-Andy Warhol portraits of Trump, and, finally, Milo Yiannopoulos himself, submerging his mostly-naked body in pig's blood in a very homoerotic slap at Islam. It was something to behold. (3)

Let me be straight with you; or, rather, bi*, since that's all I can be. Milo's blood bath installation, while derivative and reactionary, *was* pretty sexy. But that's in part because it wasn't really Milo's idea. It was a page torn straight from the history and modernity of leftist queer art and culture, only inverted in service of an attempt to co-opt a perceived leftist "tactic." It was pretty tame compared to Jex Blackmore's contemporaneous severed pig's head / "assassinate that motherfucker" performance while she was still a representative of the Satanic Temple of Detroit. **

Milo, as it turns out, was hiding his light beneath a bushel. He's not just pro-Trump: Milo is a Nazi. Not just far right, to be clear, an actual National Socialist whose password for Breitbart's email turned out to be "Kristallnacht." (4) While this caused a tiny, insignificant dip in support for him, some enterprising soul dredged up an old interview in which Milo talked openly and quite candidly about the benefits of young, specifically underage boys having sex with older men. (5) That did the trick! Milo had been the gay Nazi shock jock morning zoo DJ that these MAGA movement freaks loved—right up until this point. After the CSA revelation, Milo became persona non grata. He has worked seldom since then, and often begs for money on social media. Remember, though, Milo's expulsion from neo-fascist circles wasn't because he was gay, or a Nazi, or a gay Nazi. It was because in 2017, openly discussing one's taste for sex between minors and adults wasn't acceptable *yet*. That changed in 2025, but we'll get there (see: **Chapter Nine: Proud Boys, Femboys, and Towel Boys.**)

Watching Milo's Icarus reenactment was a weird experience for me, even though I was aware that queer right-wing people exist. In fact, I already knew that many more of them are out there than most might expect. But I had no idea of how deep and tangled the roots of that phenomenon were, or what was driving it today. Since at least the 1990s in America, gay right-wing culture used to hinge on small-business-owner, single-issue libertarian types. Queer politics on the right have undergone a deep, mutational shift since then.

Milo had a personal hand in that transformation. Not with his campy "art" or shitty jokes about getting topped by Black men. While he was distracting people with those antics, Yiannopoulos was acting on behalf of Steve Bannon and coaching gay right-wing billionaire Peter Thiel in the finer points of fascist philosophy via the writings of Curtis Yarvin, better known as "Mencius Moldbug" in fascist circles. (6) Yarvin is a heavy hitter in the far-right philosophical world, especially in the sphere concerned with "counter-enlightenment" theory, or, as some call it, "endarkenment thought." Thanks in part to this confluence of big MAGA money, performative queerness, and fascist ideology, there are now proud National Socialists—not just fascists, but specifically National Socialists, or NatSocs as they call themselves—who identify as lesbian, gay, bisexual, or trans. And for many of them, the era of respectability politics is dead and gone. There are far right and National Socialist furries, puppygirls, femboys, and other (from the perspective of the right) radically sexually and gender-nonconforming "degenerates" who are part of the movement.

Before I wrote this book, I was aware of isolated cases. I have a lot of friends in the furry community, so I heard about it when a Nazi furry *** got banned from a regional convention. Since then, the furry fandom has developed a bona fide Nazi problem, (7) as if it didn't have enough to deal with between zoophiles and zoo-sadists (people sexually attracted to animals and people who are sexually excited by animals in pain, respectively.) (8) Meanwhile, "Nazi play" has a history in the hard bondage / BDSM scene, including the gay portion of the scene. (9) The sexual fetishization of Nazism is as old as the "Nazi exploitation" soft porn film *Ilsa, She-Wolf of the SS*, if not older. (10)

I was tangentially aware of this strange fetishization of National Socialism, and it seemed to make a sort of sense. After all, Jean-François Lyotard established that "all politics is libidinal" in The Libidinal Economy, published more than half a century ago in 1974. However, what I knew before researching this book wasn't even the metaphorical snow atop the figurative head of the dead bird frozen to the tip of the proverbial iceberg. That iceberg itself is nearly continent-sized and bears the dread name "Semi-Secret Far Right Sex Stuff." The attitudes and ideas making up that mass are the subject of this book.

In this text, I'll be sketching out a *brief* history of sex and repression (as well as of fascism's, and the broader far-right's, perspectives on sex), and how sexual mores were both held sacred and used in a nakedly cynical way by regimes to extort and, eventually, exterminate people. We'll be going over the far right's strange peccadillos, as well as those of transphobes, members of the so-called "Gender Critical movement" (or CGs) and trans-exclusionary radical feminists (TERFs), including one of the worst people in the entire world: hack author, hatemonger, and cult leader J.K. Rowling. Her efforts to persecute trans women, one of the most persecuted groups on Earth, (11) have brushed against America, but her hate covers the contours of the United Kingdom like a sorcerous miasma. The effect has been so potent that England is now colloquially known as TERF Island. (12)

I will *not* cover the entirety of the persecution, undeserved hostility, threats, murder, rape, exploitation, fetishization, criminalization, and attempted extermination that queer people have been through in modernity, let alone throughout time. That would not just be one book, but a library. The texts in it would date back to the first stirrings of human history (see **Chapter One: Putting a Bridle on the Beast with Two Backs**). I'll mostly cover relatively new and unusual anti-trans and anti-queer movements, particularly those that exist primarily—or solely!— in online spaces. I'll touch on toxic masculinity and the far right's strange crusade against pornography, the culture of purity that often conceals a pedophilia problem, and how toxic nostalgia and dysfunctional online socialization relate to the so-called "male loneliness epidemic."

I will then talk about the history of queer communities on 4Chan, especially an overview of "4Trans" sub-board /lgbt/, better known as /tttt/. I'll share my thoughts and questions about the problems presented by such spaces (including Twitter), and what can, should, and might be done about them. That section will contain a discussion of the rare (but very real) phenomenon of fascist and even specifically National Socialist sexual minorities. Who they are, what they believe, what they want, how they feel, everything I could think of to ask or get them to answer. I'll spend a little time going over the history of sexual minorities in far-right culture, too.

Some brief interviews I conducted with members of the community of sexual minorities who hold far right views and/or spend significant amounts of time in far-right online spaces is attached as an appendix (see **Appendix A: Interviews**). I've also included a glossary in this book (see **Appendix B: Glossary**), something I failed to do with my last project and which I regret. Subjects as esoteric as these can get very jargony and strange in their language. Add layers of ironic online slang and hyper-niche references and memes to the equation and I figured that a glossary might prove helpful, although I endeavor to identify some of the most salient definitions in footnotes as we go along.

Who are You and What is this Book?

I'm Charles Bernard! I'm a couple of months shy of 44 years old at time of press, cisgendered, bi, and I'm an author. I mostly write fiction and most of it is horror. So far that includes five published novels and more than twenty published short stories, but I also write nonfiction. I have a long-running blog, but I've also penned one published nonfiction essay on religion† and one full-length nonfiction book: *Black Sunrise on Piss Earth: Nihilism, Fascism, and the 21st Century Occult*, which was a moderate success (at least, in my terms)! That made me happy, as the proceeds of the book were and are donated to Food Not Bombs. Likewise, the proceeds from this book will be donated too. Rather than distributing them to a particular pro-LGBTQIA organization, I'll be adding the funds to a queer and radically decentralized mutual aid organization that provides hormone replacement therapy (HRT) for at-risk and in-need trans people. If you have questions about what that means, I'm happy to answer them, so drop me a line or hit my perpetually-open DMs.

As I said, I'm cisgendered. I struggled with my bisexuality and remained closeted until I was well into my 30s, even as I've had lovers who were men since I was in my 20s. I kept that part of my life quiet, despite coming from an accepting family of politically left-leaning allies and having many gay and lesbian friends. The reasons for my closeting are complex, but they boil down to cowardice on my part. My "gay side," as I called it, "wasn't the real me," I thought. Therapy and self-reflection have made me a devout believer in authentic sexual self-expression. Bisexuals, in my opinion, shouldn't take the path of least resistance and live a lie of exclusive attraction to the "appropriate" gender. Yes, biphobia is a challenge, but it's one worth facing down with your bi siblings. I also think things get a little easier for queer kids over time in general, despite recent setbacks, and coming out as an adolescent is no longer quite the cataclysmic event it would have been in the early 90s.

I've been a ferocious ally of all LGBTQIA+ people since I was a young man. Many of the most important people in my young life were queer. A pair of babysitters (and couple) named Nancy and Kathy introduced me to the best music of my young life up to that point, including David Bowie and Siouxsie and the Banshees. One of my best friends since the age of seven is a guy I'll just call Max so as not to put him on blast. Max was never ashamed to be who he is, even though the two of us grew up in a blisteringly conservative community: Bountiful, Utah, a heavily white and Mormon suburb of Salt Lake City. Max always had more courage than I did, and he's a personal hero of mine. I had the pleasure of attending his wedding, and he and his husband have celebrated more than a decade and a half of anniversaries since then.

Why do I bring this up? Because, among other things, my early cowardice is something I've attempted to make up for any way I can. I'm an antifascism and extremism researcher and author, and what I like to refer to as a "gutter academic." I have zero (0) college degrees and zero (0) un/official affiliations with academic institutions or groups, although I attended enough college without graduating that I think some college somewhere owes me at least a Bachelor's in Endurance. My opinion of higher education is decidedly mixed, but I did learn to perform academic research through a Research Methods class at the University of Utah. After I dropped out (again), the knowledge was mine to do with as I saw fit. It turns out that you can just pay money for a journal archive subscription. It's expensive and you'll have to live on ramen, but anyone can do it. If you're a college student, staff, or teacher, you likely have access to at least one journal archive for free already. Consider this a call to arms. Go out and find a credible YouTube video about research methods (anything that mentions ChatGPT or Google's AI assistant is garbage, hold out for something about APA or MLS). Pick an issue that matters to you. Start studying and researching widely and take notes as you do. Read, read, read!† Notice themes and recurring patterns, and look for what is left out of certain narratives versus what is emphasized in others. Don't be quick to jump to a conclusion. Be patient. Soon, you'll have your thesis—your "what this project is about." And then you're off!

This book is something of a hybrid product. Its subject is serious, and its scholarship and synthesis are sound. On the other hand, I'm also unafraid to use filthy language, throw a WHOOP WHOOP to my Juggalo homies, make bawdy jokes, or clown on terrible people. I write in a style I call punkademic. Despite all that this text is thoroughly sourced (with

30-50 footnotes average per chapter, plus a half-dozen author notes). The sources I cite aren't nutty blogs or PragerU-quality partisan info-shops. I've relied on peer-reviewed articles as much as possible, and supplemented that with news stories, longform magazine articles, and original research in the form of interviews. A few sources I cite are non-traditional, but only when the subject matter is esoteric enough to warrant it.

This book is *not* "Queer Stuff 101." It presupposes a certain level of knowledge and allyship, albeit not that much. If you accept LGBTQIA+ people as valid people who are expressing a valid identity and trying to be themselves despite the oppression they face from the rising tide of American fascism, we're good. If you feel compelled to bark "ADAM AND EVE, NOT ADAM AND STEVE" or "TRANS WOMEN ARE CON MEN," put this book down before it slaps you. If not, we're good.

This book is also not an in-depth survey of queer history. I can recommend decent titles and resources for exactly that, and you'll find them at the end of the glossary under "Further Reading." For the most part in this book, I wanted to let the stew of sex, hate, arousal, shame, and haywire practices that define the far right speak for themselves, so I will sometimes present example screenshots.

In the interviews, I wanted to let individuals—people who were allowed to become more than just an anime profile picture on a Nazi-affiliated app—speak for themselves, as their voices are rarely (if ever) heard, let alone taken seriously or analyzed.

This is not a "come gawk at the freaks" book. I don't respect that genre of nonfiction writing. I think that communication—and, ultimately, engagement in anything approaching a productive way— starts with understanding the mindsets of those we disagree with most fractiously. To comprehend is not to condone and to understand is not to excuse. Knowledge is power, more than ever in this age of mass, instant disinformation. Gaining knowledge about some of the most violent, confused, and potentially harmful people in the world is not a waste of your time or mine.

Sophie Lewis, in an article for *Lux Magazine*, had the following to say about TERFs and the "gender critical movement":

> I'd like to suggest that there are strands of thought that are both authentically feminist and irredeemable—even fascist.

I would similarly like to suggest that there are some groups of LGBTQIA+ people who are both authentically queer and irredeemable—even fascist. "Irredeemable" is, as my father would say, a strong word. I'm not sure what other word is appropriate when we're talking about some of the people you'll meet in this book, but others who have only recently been twisted out of joint may be a different case.

I have a hard time considering any person truly irredeemable, which makes me something of a Pollyanna. I do, however, believe that certain ideas, ideologies, communities, etc., are irredeemable. 4Chan, which we'll discuss in depth, is irredeemable, as is its spicier younger sibling 8kun. National Socialism can't be redeemed. Trans-exclusionary radical feminism (TERFism) can't be redeemed. The idea some gay folks have that they can divorce gay, lesbian, and bisexual people from our trans, nonbinary, intersex, and other siblings can't be redeemed.

A Note on Imagery Citation

My editor Max Bauman (יישר כוח) has helped me wrangle this thing into a more formal structure than my previous nonfiction book. However, CSM Citation rules for images were something I didn't think I should follow with this project for a few reasons.

First, anonymity. Yes, many of these people are hateful goons, but I like to do my internet arguing the old-fashioned way rather than unleashing my readers at a specific target. Subsequently, identifying information for individuals whose posts I've screenshotted has been removed. If you think any of what I've captured is exaggerated and you have (for whatever reason) a Twitter account, you can do an app-wide search of the slur "troon" (or variations like "tr00n") and see how much of a fabulist I am.

Secondly, fascists run through accounts like ordinary people run through tissue paper. They soil them, after which they are wadded up by the threat-of-violence-detecting bots and flushed into the great septic tank of the beyond. Then they start a new account within hours and are back at it. This makes crediting a sentiment to an account with the idea of referring back to the post later pointless. The "account" is more like a burner phone used by someone far better than a fascist; someone who serves their community. Like a drug dealer.

Twitter is an openly fascist platform run by the world's richest white supremacist and populated by some of the worst people you'll find outside of the dark web. Images are incredibly important. People's minds are too worn down and their attention spans too short to read diatribes or sign their work. Things come in flashes of semiotic violence. Thus, the citation system I have employed: a screenshot with the user's handle removed but the image, that individual act of semiotic violence, stripped from the false context of a "person" who can be considered a "source."

If that disappoints you, I'm genuinely sorry. I doxx fascists regularly, but I consider that activity entirely separate from my research, as it must be. I try not to doxx anyone who isn't a far-right public figure in my work, although I made a notable exception for one fascist I had known personally in Black Sunrise. What fascist would talk to a researcher known for doxxing interview subjects and revealing their identity to the world? What fascists would talk to a researcher who is even remotely likely to draw attention to their cockroach-like existence online?

I do the best I can, and think these decisions over.

When I first put out feelers for interviews and talked to a few of my trans friends about this project, reactions were mixed. Some trans people agreed with me that the existence of sexual minorities in far-right politics and far right online spaces was noteworthy; a problem that needs to be addressed and which bears study so that we can figure out how people with such contradictory identities develop those identities and deal with what is honestly a difficult series of life choices. Am I asking you to have sympathy for a trans neo-Nazi? Absolutely not. I am asking you to ask how a trans neo-Nazi exists, and what their existence has to say about the state of politics and culture in 2025.

A few of my friends expressed concern about this book. In some cases, it was an understandable reflex. 4Trans—the community of shitposters who stew in miserable self-hatred on 4Chan's /tttt/ board all day—is one of the ugliest secrets in the LGBTQIA+ community, as are queer Nazis in general. Don't get me wrong. In my experience, the community respects a diversity of opinion within itself, provided that people express solidarity and acceptance of each other.

That last bit was the problem, in these people's opinion; like any culture, there are some members of the queer community who are the drunk uncles at Thanksgiving, the racist grandmas, or the shitty 4chan incel little brothers. But why write a book about all the worst members of a family that's already on the cultural chopping block as American fascism intensifies and solidifies its grip on the country?

Because these problematic fascist queer folks are the product of the same forces driving American fascism at large. For example, the shitty 4Chan little bro in my metaphor about the queer family is absolutely, provably a product of American fascism in the form of the expenditure of a truly awe-inspiring amount of money, billable hours, and effort (see Chapter Two: Superheavy Hate Machine). It was my fate to come of age during the transition between the high water mark of neoliberalism (the 90s, the era of Francis Fukuyama's The End of History, Bill Clinton's "Don't Ask Don't Tell" policy, and the Battle of Seattle) and the Forever Wars (Iraq and Afghanistan, defined more by Samuel Huntington's bellicose The Clash of Civilizations and the Remaking of World Order, a book in every imaginable way the opposite of Fukyama's).

All of us are shaped by the times in which we live and, especially, the years in which we experience many of life's first milestones when it comes to individuation. Two specific things—COVID and social media—have played hell with individuation and socialization with recent generations, and it shows.

Things right now are, to apocalyptically understate the case, not great. Young, cisgendered, heterosexual men are in deep shit. (14) The American cis hetero man is "in crisis," as he'll no doubt tell you given the first chance. They aren't alone in having woes. Women, whether cis or trans, are in an unenviable position. (15) Nationally, so many efforts are underway to whitewash the past that we're at the beginning of the type of cultural-historical mass extinction event that's the hallmark of a fascist regime.

(16) If cis hetero men—particularly cis hetero white men, the American demographic with the most and longest-unchallenged cultural clout (17) —feel like they're "in crisis," it strikes me as incomprehensible that they can't understand the plight of people in positions of less power.

Totalitarian systems of control (including fascism) rely on certain societal maladies to sustain them. Fear is a big one. (18) Another is a particular type of propaganda environment: one that's not so much filled with one loud, screaming voice (ala George Orwell's 1984) as they are completely reality-agnostic. This is an environment of so-called post truth. (19) Another one of fascism's load-bearing cankers is the inability of different groups of people to talk to and understand each other. That is, in fact, the reason I wrote this book. Don't mistake my meaning or intent. I do not ever plan to compromise with fascists, be they gay or straight, cis or trans or genderfluid. I do think, however, that being able to parse their language, tropes, and what drives them is valuable in combatting the ideas that cause people to embrace the swastika. Once people cross that line, it's hard to bring them back. Not impossible, but hard—and not the kind of thing an activist or even friend can plant in someone.

One of my interviews is with an extremism expert, former fascist, and former Stormfront moderator named Scott Kelley. You can find my chat with him in Appendix A, but there will be segments from it scattered throughout this book. One such pearl of wisdom seems applicable right here:

> People can't deradicalize Nazis. Only Nazis can deradicalize themselves. Do I think it is a waste of time to reach out in such a way? No. People just need to be aware that those people will only deradicalize if they want to deradicalize. (Appendix A, Interview 5)

So, let's get to it. When I described this project to one of my friends, they responded "Fascist femboys, huh? How the fuck did we wind up here?" It's a good question, and worth answering at length (albeit not the length I'd like)! Let's begin at the beginning and work our way through some of the strangest recent convolutions in fascism's unspeakable sex life, shall we?

* Parting the kimono a bit, readers should be aware that yr humble narrator identifies as bi- or pansexual. I am attracted to people regardless of their gender presentation.

** Blackmore was excommunicated by The Satanic Temple for her performance; the first of many people who would be yeeted from TST for being too Satanic for them (I earned the honor personally in August of 2021).

*** The furry fandom is made up of people who, to identify the common denominator, enjoy cartoonish depictions of anthropomorphic animals. Some people's interest is sexual, while other people simply view it as a fun, whimsical hobby. Among furries, “fursuiting” is the practice of dressing up in a suit made to resemble one’s “fursona.” The end result looks a bit like a very cuddly sports mascot.

† If possible, and this is just my opinion, entirely avoid “educational videos” and especially political streamer content to educate you on an issue. As I see it, a book is best. A longform magazine article is almost as good, but not as good as a peer-reviewed journal article. News and news magazine articles are fine. For the love of all the gods don’t cite Bad Empanada or fucking Haz.

1 Many Gays for Trump events were funded by a man named Jeff Giessa, a longtime catspaw for Peter Thiel.
Schreckinger, Ben (Jan/Feb 2017) “The Alt-Right Comes to Washington: A new generation of nationalists sees a chance to ride Donald Trump’s coattails into the capital. But first they need to do some serious re-branding.” Politico Magazine.

2 Beauchamp, Zack (2/20/2017) “Milo Yiannopoulos: Breitbart’s star provocateur and Trump champion, explained”. Vox.

3 Del Valle, Gabby (10/10/2016) “Bathing In Pig's Blood: Inside The Alt-Right's Pro-Trump Art Show”. Gothamist.

4 Kircher, Madison Malone (10/6/2017) “4 Key Takeaways From the Monster Milo Yiannopoulos Document Leak”. NY Mag: Intelligencer.

5 Hersher, Rebecca “After Comments On Pedophilia, Breitbart Editor Milo Yiannopoulos Resigns”. NPR.

6 (4) ibid.

7 Killelea, Eric (4/14/2017) "Does The Furry Community Have A Nazi Problem?" Rolling Stone.

Hicks, William (11/22/2017) "Neo-Nazi Furries are Trump's Latest and Most Puzzling Alt-Right Supporters". Newsweek.

Dunn, Cameron (November 2021) "What's Going On With Those Furry Nazis?" Slate.

8 Love, Theo (dir.) (July – August 2025) "The Furry Detectives: Unmasking a Monster". HBO.

9 Griffiths, Mark D. (6/30/2016) "Nazi Fetishism: A brief look at Nazism and sexual arousal". Psychology Today.

10 Roy, Pinaki. "Incarcerated Fantasies: Women in Nazisploitation Films". Portrayal of Women in Media and Literature. Eds. Nawale, A., S. Vashist, and P. Roy. New Delhi: Access, 2013. Pp. 23–33.

11 Mandler, C. (10/13/2022). "Murders of trans people nearly doubled over past 4 years, and Black trans women are most at risk, report finds". CBS News.

UCLA School of Law. (3/23/2021). "Transgender people over four times more likely than cisgender people to be victims of violent crime". The Williams Institute.

12 Lewis, Sophie (11/12/2024). "TERF Island: There Have Always Been Enemies Inside the Feminist Camp." Lux Magazine.

13 Waites, Matthew (2018). "Genocide and

Global Queer Politics". Journal of Genocide Research. 20 (1). P58-59.

14 Volpe, Alice (2/12/2025). “Why are young men so hopeless at dating?” Vox.

de Visé, Daniel (2/22/2023). “Most young men are single. Most young women are not.” The Hill.

Guest editor. (2/9/2023). “The toxic influence of Andrew Tate: How society has failed a generation of young men and boys”. Social Sciences Birmingham. University of Birmingham.

Parent, Mike C. et. al. (7/9/2019). “Social Media Behavior, Toxic Masculinity, and Depression”. Psychology of Men & Masculinities. 20(3). P277-287.

15 Gray, Hazel (2021). “The Age of Toxicity: The Influence of Gender Roles and Toxic Masculinity in Harmful Heterosexual Relationship Behaviours”. Canadian Journal of Family and Youth. 13(3). P41-52.

16 Vandergast, Amelia (2/18/2024). “The Silence Of Oppression: How Totalitarianism Inhibits Culture and Expression”. A&R Factory.

Levina, M. (2025). “Doing critical cultural studies in the age of totalitarian thought”. Communication and Critical/Cultural Studies. 22(1). P1–12.

Doak, Kevin M.. (2009). "Fascism Seen and Unseen: Fascism as a Problem in Cultural Representation". The Culture of Japanese Fascism, edited by Alan Tansman, Rey Chow, Harry Harootunian and Masao Miyoshi, (Duke University Press, New York). P31-55.

17 Baptiste, Bala James (5/25/2022). Ideological Hegemony: A Precursor to Institutional Racism. Black Perspectives. African American Intellectual History Society.

Solnit, Rebecca (8/8/2019). "Our forever war: how the white male hegemony uses violence to cling to power". The Guardian.

18 Neocleous, M. (2005). "Gothic fascism". Journal for Cultural Research. 9(2). P133–149.

Stone, Marla (2017). "Italian Fascism's Wartime Enemy and the Politics of Fear" in Facing Fear: The History of an Emotion in Global Perspective Michael Laffan, and Max Weiss (eds) (Princeton University Press, Princeton).

19 Berkowitz, Roger (1/14/2021). "The Fabric of Reality". The Hannah Arendt Center for Politics and Humanities. Bard College.

Graham, Daniel (1/3/2025). "The Danger of Denying Reality: Are reality deniers practicing 'expressive responding' or are they irrational?" Psychology Today.

Barrett, Elizabeth (2024). "The Psychodynamic Underpinnings of Fascism Interview With Sheldon Solomon, PhD". Eye on PSI CHI. (28)3.

Fascist Femboys for No Nut November

CHAPTER ONE

PUTTING A BRIDLE ON THE BEAST WITH TWO BACKS

In the beginning, there were creation myths. Early among those creation myths is one of my favorites, perhaps because it's the one that I was raised to believe in; the Garden of Eden. Now, we don't have the time (and no one has the patience) for me to go on a tear about all the interesting things I've learned about the differences between how that myth was conveyed to me (and, honestly, to almost every tiny Christian who has heard it) and the way the myth was originally told and what it meant. The basic moral of the story hasn't changed all that much—obey god, women evil, blah blah blah—but the set dressing has been significantly updated over the years to make the myth even remotely approachable. These changes bear a few comments.

"It was Adam and Eve, not Adam and Steve!" Okay, fucknuts, first of all it wasn't "Adam," Hebrew-European male name, at all. The Hebrew אדם is pronounced just like the name Adam, but means "man" or "mankind." It's also a little bit of an intricate, brilliant scriptural clockwork puzzle: to form humanity, the god of Genesis makes us from dust;

thus, the repetition of, to paraphrase, "from dust you come and to dust you will return" in both Genesis 3:19 and Ecclesiastes 3:20. The Hebrew "adamah" (אדמה) means "dirt" or "earth." Adam/man? Literally, etymologically a little bit of earth; a pinch of dust.

Second, it wasn't *necessarily* Adam and Eve, according to apocrypha. The Christian version of the creation myth is just a very dumbed-down version stolen wholesale from Judaism, with a much less rich history of marginalia, apocrypha, and exegesis. According to the people who wrote Exodus, Eve was either Adam's second or his third "first" wife. Initially, the god of Genesis created Adam and Lilith. I feel some eyeballs perking up— *her* you may have heard of. Rebellious? Too nonconforming to her assigned gender role to be right for that god's special boy? Kicked out for being a bra-burning radical? Fucker of fallen angels, mother of monsters? The one the music fair form the 1990s is named after? Yes, *that* Lilith. She came first.

After her, according to some Jewish stories, Adam's creator made a Lilith 2.0 for Adam. The deity, however, made the fatal error of creating her right there, live, before Adam's virgin eyes. The sight of what went into her construction—the sinew, gristle, blood, bones, and guts—horrified him. Women are just fucking *disgusting*, am I right, millennia of guys? Absolutely fucking disgusting. Hate them. Evidently, Adam's creator agreed with Adam's very Andrew Tate appraisal of Lilith 2.0, because the god uncreated her. Evidently "third time's the charm" is true of gods and men alike, because at that point the god put squeamish, fuckass Adam into an anesthetic twilight state, performed a quick sacred costectomy (removed a rib,) and used that rib to make Eve. That last version, the most easily anatomically disproven one, somehow was the "just right" of this Goldilocks tale.

Lastly, the apple that led to the Fall and humanity's expulsion from paradise? Not an apple! Apples, properly speaking, hadn't been invented yet. They only emerged as an eat-off-the-tree fruit in modernity. The fruit in the old myth most likely was a fig, based on the fact that Adam and Eve used fig leaves to cover their shame, and based on where and when Exodus was likely written down for the first time. This is a minor quibble, but it is entertaining how universally accepted this substitution of "apple" for fruit is among the laity. It reminds me of one of my other favorite weird translation and hermeneutics anachronisms that goes unremarked on by people who should know better. (Want to know how Julius Ceasar, conqueror of Gaul but not even Briton, was always talking about "corn" when it's a New World crop unknown to Europe until the Transatlantic Exchange began in the sixteenth century BCE? The answer may surprise you!)

Why do I bring up the first man and woman, according to this legend? Because this chapter is about the history of the repression of sex and sexuality—particularly among sexual minorities—and that begins with religion.

Aroace Christ, Superstar

(NOTE: Referencing this section title, let's start with a little bit of terminology. "Aroace" is a portmanteau of "aromantic" and "asexual," and is a shorthand used by and to describe people who do not experience romantic or sexual attraction as it's understood by heteronormative society. Sound like anyone you know from Sunday School?

That's right, we're going to discuss a little bit of religious history! Particularly, but not exclusively, that of Christianity. Most religions have sexual mores and taboos, and how rigidly believers conform to those mores varies wildly. For example: I was brought up very Catholic. I left the Church a little while after being confirmed, but I was also brought up strongly pro-choice and pro-LGBTQ acceptance. My folks were American Catholics more than Roman Catholics. Was this an atypical Catholic upbringing? I suppose so, if you accept the idea of a "typical [insert religion] upbringing."

One reason I start the history of control and sex with religion is that, before a certain point in history, talking broadly about left wing and right-wing politics is meaningless. Before the Enlightenment, systems of control tended toward the absolute and god-based. Whether monarchy or landed aristocracy, pharaoh or town elder, duke or rogue, our modern either didn't exist or did so in a form that was structured so differently as to render it inapplicable to today. I'm often sucked into discourse with friends about the anarchist slogan "no gods, no masters," which I endorse but only with heavy criticism. The milieu from which that slogan emerged is very different from the post-colonial one in which native religions can be liberatory when compared to the restrictive role Christianity has played in those communities— and that's just one example of how much our understanding of religion has changed just in the last two hundred years.

Before modernity, it's easier to talk about systems of control and systems of liberation than right and left. The Catholic Church, for example, was a system of control for much of history and for the most part, but certain individuals and/or sects at certain times were and are exceptions. Some sects of Christianity contain both tendencies at the same time. The Franciscan, Dominican, and Augustinian Orders all have their roots in vows of poverty, which speaks to an emphasis on Jesus' ministry to the poor and teachings critical of wealth. At the same time, those sects were all-male patriarchal societies that adhered to rigid hierarchies and repressed all sexuality, although they may also have been quiet havens for gay men and women during times when Christianity was absolutely intolerant of queerness of any kind.*

Radical sexual acceptance could be found in many heretical and excommunicated sects or movements within Catholicism throughout history. Some of them were openly tolerant of queerness. Others practiced gender nonconformity in radical and threatening ways that shook the establishment of the time. In this last category, one example I'd like to go into in depth are the *Skoptsy*, or "cutters."

Skoptsy is an Anglicization of скопцы, which translates directly from Russian as "eunuch." The sect, while referred to by the world at large as the Skoptsy, referred to themselves as either "True Christians" or "the Godly." (1) I'll be using the self-description the Godly to refer to the sect for the most part. They became infamous for the practices of self-castration and self-mastectomy, acts which the Godly believed brought them closer to the purity required of Christians. They held the belief that in the Garden of Eden, before the Fall, neither Adam nor Eve had genitals: that is to say, "[the Godly] did not conceive of the original man and woman as being differentiated by their genitalia." (2). They also found justification for their practices directly in the words of Jesus (Matthew 19:12); nor were they the first Christians to do so**. The Godly have been widely discussed in gender studies for obvious reasons. They were, after all, radically gender non-conforming subjects of a religio-political regime of total repression.

Perhaps more remarkably for a movement that engaged in acts that precluded the sole reproductive technology of the time (i.e., good, old-fashioned fuckin'), they had staying power. The Godly emerged in the late 17th century and existed into the early 20th, giving them the distinction of having been persecuted by the following tsars and well over a century of Russian Orthodox Patriarchs: Catherine the Great, Paul I, Alexander I, Nicholas I, and Nicholas II, last tsar of Russia. In short, not only did they perpetuate their sect that long through conversion alone, rather than reproduction, they survived an awe-inspiring number of rulers' attempts to stamp them out. Are the

Godly still around today? No. While Catherine the Great's priests and soldiers couldn't stop the sect from their self-mutilation and their celebration of ecstatic-religious song and dance, traditions they inherited from an earlier sect called the Khlysty, Joseph Stalin's USSR stamped them out with zeal and gusto. (3)

Examining the Godly, the problem with thinking of history in terms of "far right" or "leftist" is clearly outlined. Even the framework I suggest presents difficulties. Was the practice of removing pleasure from one's life "liberatory?" The Godly, after all, didn't drink, have sex (before ritual cutting or after), or engage in any perceived earthly pleasure, viewing only their ritual praise as a pleasure that also pleased their god. On the other hand, they shrugged off the roles assigned them by their supposed betters. They chose radical commitment to a post-gender version of Christianity, despite the threats presented to them by the great powers of their time. Ultimately, I view the Godly as a *mostly* liberatory movement for a few reasons. First, they took their reproductive rights into their own hands and did not accept the roles assigned to them by birth or station. (4) Second, they practiced radical gender nonconformity. (5) Finally, they presented a legitimate threat to both Church and State through both their recurring popularity and their radical commitment to their god and nothing else; not even the Church hierarchy so powerful in Russia then and now. Likewise with the Russian State in its various guises. They were a noteworthy enough threat that they were first attacked officially by the Russian Orthodox Church, (6) and, when that institution failed to do the job, were annihilated by the Soviet State, (7) a force more powerful than the Russian Orthodox Church had ever been.

Developing a taxonomy of sexual restrictions and practices in a liberatory versus restrictive framework is more useful than "left" versus "right," even if it still requires parsing. It is useful to examine religion—Christianity, for the purposes of this book. *** Firstly, because it is a power structure. Secondly, because it, even more than the State, has served as a means of restricting and controlling human sexuality over the majority of time. (9)

Chastity. Monogamy. Gender roles. Compulsive heterosexuality. Criminal offenses for victimless private sexual conduct. All of these were hallmarks of the reign of Christianity throughout Europe. The proto-Church, then Catholic Church, then a collection of large Protestant denominations were all gatekeepers of genital conduct and contact among the general populace. The *why* is simple. Control. Keeping men in one set of roles, entitled to one set of privileges, and women in an inferior, subservient role; a role in no small part concerned with reproduction. (10)

One way in which Christianity clamped down on this facet of human existence was through the control of sexual expression. This is curious, given that the man the faith was founded on, Jesus of Nazareth, was a sexual cipher. I started this chapter talking about the sect of the Godly in Russia for good reason. Some of Jesus' statements regarding sex (and some of the things he *didn't* say about sex) are remarkable. Take the full text of Matthew 19:11-12 in context, for example. You've heard Matthew Chapter 19 *wildly out of context* at least a hundred times, even if you don't know it. You've likely heard it even if you're not Christian!

Matthew 19 is the traditional wedding verse. It's the chapter where Jesus answers those pesky Pharisees' questions about marriage and divorce. You hear *excerpts* of Jesus' positions in this debate during most Christian weddings. Specifically, Matthew 19:5-6: "For this reason a man will leave his father and mother and be united to his wife, and the two will become one flesh So they are no longer two, but one flesh. Therefore what God has joined together, let no one separate." After hearing Jesus' answers about marriage, the disciples say, essentially, "Wow! It sounds like marriage is a pain in the ass!" Jesus responds with the following, which is what inspired acts of bodily alteration in the Godly (among others):

> "11 Jesus replied, "Not everyone can accept this word, but only those to whom it has been given. 12 For there are eunuchs who were born that way, and there are eunuchs who have been made eunuchs by others—and there are those who choose to live like eunuchs for the sake of the kingdom of heaven. The one who can accept this should accept it."

That's a remarkably strong statement if you understand Christian theology, and one that almost all sects besides Catholicism utterly ignore (Catholicism requires its priests to practice chastity). The kingdom of heaven was the primary message of Jesus' earthly mission: its purity, its justice, and above all, its imminence. While Jesus sought to curtail the fleshly attachments of his followers for the purpose of ascension (much like the Buddha did), he did not *hard-sell* restrictive sexual mores. Jesus' own sexuality is a matter of perennial scholarly and theological debate. Some scholars theorize that he married and that this was edited out of the Gospels that emerged from the fires and censors of the Councils of Nicaea, although the evidence for this is thin. (11)

Other scholars, meanwhile, speculate that Jesus was queer, but, again, there's thin and mixed evidence for that idea. The most logical conclusion in my mind, based on the life, teachings, and person of Jesus of Nazareth, is that he was asexual and aromantic. (12) Jesus, as the person whose teachings and example got the boulder of Christianity rolling, was hardly a natalist role model, since (unlike Mohammed) he never wed and had no children, and instead embraced found family and encouraged his disciples to do the same. For the inadvertent founder of a religion that would go on to become what it became, Jesus' collection of gnomic sayings, his purported miracles, and his ministry regarding the post-death, post-apocalypse kingdom of heaven, he didn't have much regard for sex, except when encouraging people not to have it, if it wasn't too much trouble (the Gospel of Matthew) but also not to be ashamed of it (the examples of Mary Magdalene and "the woman taken in adultery").

A much less cryptic figure in the history of Christianity and its role in the oppression of sexual minorities is my old friend Saul of Tarsus, who I ranted about at great length in my book *Black Sunrise on Piss Earth: Nihilism, Fascism, and the 21st Century Occult* (specifically when I talked about Christianity's early and modern attempts to distance itself from its roots as a heretical cultic sect of Judaism). Saul speaks the most in the New Testament, not Jesus. Paul, as I will refer to Saul from here on out, also often speaks in ways that seem quite at odds with Jesus' words (Paul's views on women, for example). (13) For better or, as I see it, for worse, Christianity is more Paul's religion than it is Jesus'. Suffice it to say, I'm not a fan of Paul's work.

It's hard to find many passages in the New Testament railing against sex—either contra certain practices or outraged at its very existence— that *weren't* part of one of Paul's epistles. Paul's prominence in the New Testament is the product of internecine fighting within the early Jesus Movement in which he emerged triumphant, and Paul was a controlling patriarchal asshole to his core. He made no secret of it; indeed, he stamped this worldview into the still-soft clay of the Jesus Movement in the years directly after Jesus' execution, when Jesus' actual personal opinions on many matters were regrettably unavailable. To name just one example, Paul turned Jesus' actual mystic/ascetic "render under Cesar what is Cesar's, and unto God what is God's" into the loathsome and servile formulation "slaves, obey your masters."

A big part of systems of control, both in ancient days and today, is the ways in which they control the rhetoric and ideology of sex, taboo, and most importantly, of shame. Even Paul however, sour patriarch that he was, conceded that in the kingdom of heaven all who are saved will exist as nonbinary people (Galatians 3:28). Yes, yes, the Bible is complex and contradictory, and the way I see it, many modern Christian sects operate with little or no hermeneutic knowledge or authentically deep scriptural study. The different things Jesus, Paul, and others had to say about sex, sexuality, gender, and other issues are stripped of their radical context or the interpretations given by heretic or defunct sects and movements throughout the years. More than that, material is inevitably presented in a highly cherry-picked, homogenized fashion that papers over the Christian Bible's contradictions, complexity, and internal debates. I have found it to be a religion taught, for the most part, as if its believers are much less intelligent than they are, and that's a damned shame.

Christianity is, therefore, not only an example of a 2,000-year-old system of control designed in no small part to regulate and curtail sexuality and sexual expression; it's also evidence (nonbinary angels and a nonbinary afterlife; an asexual, aromantic Jesus who encouraged asexuality) that sexual minorities have existed and, indeed, been central figures in both leadership and debate throughout human history.

Even where you'd least suspect it.

The (More Than) 120 Years of Sodomy Laws

Let's steal Doc Brown's ÐeLorean, floor it the most, and let my nugget ping off a light post†. When we hit

88 miles per hour, we'll blast into the future from our previous place among the ancient texts to take a whirlwind tour of the last century or two of sexual politics in the West. As the power of the Church has waned in many places, so the power of the State has waxed. That's no accident. In some ways, the modern State is a mask worn by the same power once wielded by a dominant Christian Church. (14) Call something by a different name, but if it operates exactly the same way, it's hard to take the distinction without a difference seriously. On the subject of "modern politics," then, let's keep the language and analysis consistent and talk about systems and mechanisms of control. Michel Foucault†† wrote about this at length in a few of his books, including *Discipline and Punish* and *The History of Sexuality*, both of which I'd recommend.

Prior to imperial conquest, it's interesting what pre-Christian, pre-colonization views of sex and its regulation were. Some tribes in the Americas accepted trans people very early in history. (15) This is an inconvenient truth for those who claim that sexual minorities are some sort of Satanic left-wing conspiracy that sprang into existence recently. This isn't just true of the Americas, either. Many areas colonized by Christianity were more accepting of queer people before being brutally reshaped by Christian colonizers. Sexual practices long considered completely normal by native populations became taboo almost overnight. As it turns out, queerphobia was as big an export of Christianity's colonial expansion as the abolition of native religions. (16)

Since the beginning, laws were (and are) the

instruments by which compulsive heterosexuality and the "traditional" (Western) family have been reinforced. Social opprobrium and extralegal violence played their part, but they never had the sheer coercive power of the State. All these tools— State, Church, and the like— have concentrated their power on confining human gender nonconformity, sex, and sexuality as if they were diseased and dangerous beasts instead of core parts of being human. Was this the case in the days of church dungeons, Joan of Arc, and even Oscar Wilde? Yes, absolutely. It was also the case more recently than you might think.

One of the reasons that the Nazis didn't win the second World War was a fellow named Alan Turing. You've probably heard of him and know where I'm going with this, but for those who don't, I'll give you the quick version of the story. During the war, both the Nazis and Allies employed complex encryption to send orders and information to and from the front. These coded messages could often easily be intercepted by one's enemies, so each nation involved in the war employed cryptography and simultaneously employed codebreakers to try to beat the foe's cryptographers.

In 1918, as the brutal, bloody, self-inflicted nightmare of World War I was drawing to humiliating end for Germany, an engineer named Arthur Scherbius had a very cool idea and started sketching it out in notebooks. By 1923, this idea became a contraption called the Enigma machine. The Enigma machine, once souped-up a bit, became one of Nazi Germany's secret weapons during World War II. Using mechanical processes more complex than any to that date, the Enigma machine was able to create a nigh-unbreakable code for the Nazis.

Enter a brilliant British polymath: a logician, mathematician, philosopher, and, importantly, one of the first modern computer scientists. Named Alan Turing, he was in his late teens and early twenties when Britain was slowly sucked into Hitler's apocalyptic, pointless war. He understandably wanted to contribute to the continued survival of the UK. Turing and mathematician Gordon Welchman took a conceptual design created by a Polish mathematician named Marian Rejewski, perfected it, and then built it. This was the birth of the amusingly-named Bombe: an automated device that performed an exhaustive key search (AKA a brute-force attack) to crack Enigma. Needless to say, having their unbreakable, ever-shifting code hacked and their secret war plans stolen by the Allies did not bode well for the Nazis. Which means it *did* bode well for humanity!

Without Alan Turing, would the Allies have won the war? Maybe. But he contributed more to the defeat of National Socialism specifically than most individual soldiers, generals, or scientists could claim. How did the Allies, those defenders of freedom, reward Turing for his service? The government of the United Kingdom harassed and psychologically tortured him for being gay and then quite possibly murdered him, according to a recent reexamination of the suicide ruling in Turing's death. (17) Thank you for your service, Alan! Turing's grim reward for saving Great Britain is a potent reminder that the State attempting to control sex and correct or extinguish queer sexuality is a running theme throughout modern history, whether that State likes to dress up in the Union Jack or swastika. (18)

There has always been resistance and public nonconformity to the State's monopoly on sexual morality. Nonconforming individuals have ranged from Saint Joan d'Arc to Oscar Wilde, nonbinary American preacher Public Universal Friend to the lost efforts of the Institut für Sexualwissenschaft in Berlin. Liberatory efforts have included some of the architects of liberal modernity itself like proto-feminist and proto-polyamorist John Stuart Mill and quasi-libertine Benjamin Franklin. Many other liberatory thinkers can be found outside liberalism in fierce left-wing critics of liberal modernity like anarcha-feminist Emma Goldman.

In terms of a single watershed moment when it comes to the establishment of rights and forms of acceptance for queer people in the modern era, a single word represents a place, a moment, a riot, a movement, and the beginning of an era: Stonewall.

A Riot, Not A Parade

How do gay enclaves develop? The short answer is that it depends on the enclave. In the case of New York City's Greenwich Village and Harlem neighborhoods, it was a process that began after World War I and continued for decades as those neighborhoods became welcoming hosts to large pockets of gay men, lesbian women, and a variety of gender nonconforming people. (19) Like the Castro in San Francisco, New

York's Village became a place where queer people could exist in relative safety. That's a load-bearing "relative," however, as all gay American neighborhoods were the subject of constant police harassment and raids, and Greenwich was no exception. (20) Near the end of the 1960s, one of the cops' regular raids in New York went exactly the way that cops are *really* scared of raids going.

Allow me to break the fourth wall for a moment. Forgive me if I sound a bit bloodthirsty or excited when I describe Stonewall. I love it when people fight the cops, especially when people win. I consider police oppression and the prison system in the United States a stain on human dignity. It takes guts to even talk back to police officers, whom Americans are programmed to simultaneously fawn over and fear. The thing about bravery is that it's contagious, and when one person kicks back against the cops, you'd be surprised how often other people—even strangers! —instinctively back their play. Yes, I'm an anarchist and a Satanist, but it's not my belief system that leads to my assertion that the essential human character is rebellious and intolerant of suppression; my belief system exists because I've observed that essential human character and admired it for my whole adult life.

At 1:20 AM on June 28, 1969, the cops thought they would bring the hammer down on the Stonewall Inn in Greenwich Village. Their mission was to put the fear of their Christian god into the godless queers congregating there, because this wasn't a pre-arranged bust; something of a sad, necessary ritual for a gay bar in 1960ss New York City. To a modern reader, it might be difficult to imagine how homophobic New York—

hell, the world—was in 1969. Maybe this will give you an insight into the attempts of civic authorities to keep the queers in line: in the year of our foul and rotting lord 1969, the Stonewall Inn was *the only gay club in New York City where dancing was allowed.* (21) Not nude dancing: dancing, period, full stop. Nobody puts Baby in a corner!

What were these raids like? In the words of the Damned, picture the scene. You're enjoying an adult beverage and, how scandalous, *dancing* with your friends at a bar. The overhead lights snap on and a series of hoarse, slur-filled shouts announce the arrival of the police. Every patron in the club is forced to line up against a wall to have their identification cards checked. ††† If you are a woman wearing "fewer than three pieces of feminine clothing," a man in full drag, or do not have ID, you are arrested on the spot. (22) The bar's employees and management are arrested as a matter of course, and all liquor is seized. To a large degree, who goes free and who gets jailed depends on police prejudice and a shitload of corruption; a shakedown, in other words. What a blast, right? Land of the free, home of the brave, free markets for all! Weren't we glad the Nazis *lost* the war?

The Stonewall Inn in 1969 (credit: Diana Davies)

The action at Stonewall started at around 1:20 AM when trans women refused to comply with the Nancy-Mace-style genital checks and gropes that were standard procedure with the Public Morals Squad (yes, that was its real name) at the time. It was also standard (if unofficial) procedure for police to sexually assault trans women, gay men, or lesbians during these encounters. (23) When the girls refused to give the Gestapo what they wanted, things began to go wrong for the cops. After that initial pushback, that human character I spoke about began to show itself. People generally began to refuse to provide ID and/or line up to be counted by the cops.

The average American cop hates very little in the world as much as it hates a good, old-fashioned failure to comply. One quite sensible (from their perspective) reason for this is that failure to comply tends to be contagious; and that's not just me speaking about my beliefs, that's backed up by hard evidence. (24) That certainly proved to be the case that warm, late night in New York City. What started as trans women refusing to be ogled and assaulted by Nancy Mace soon turned into something more, let's say, community-based.

As patrons were booted from the club one by one by the police to be transported, a crowd of both those expelled and members of the local queer community who had heard about the raid began to congregate outside. Simple acts like patrons glamorously posing and performing exaggerated, ironic salutes for the police as they left or were escorted from the bar began to garner increasingly rowdy applause. (25) A cop shoved a drag queen, who hit him on the head with her purse. He reacted by assaulting her with a truncheon. This was not received well by the crowd, and departing squad cars began to be bid a fond farewell by a hail of pennies and beer bottles. Then, shit kicked off.

A butch lesbian icon named Stormé DeLarverie did the coolest thing that anybody on Planet Earth can do: she started throwing down with the cops. After escaping an initial handcuffing and assault, DeLarverie took on *four cops at once*, earning her a place in my personal Valhalla alongside superstars like

Charles Bronson (not the actor; I'm talking about the British bare-knuckle boxer and armed robber infamous as "Britain's most violent offender," who has made his life sentence an extended series of prison riots, brutal fistfights with guards, and books about how to get yoked in solitary).

After she had kicked all four of their asses for a while, the bleeding, shamefaced cops finally forced DeLarverie back into a squad car. At that point she shouted, "Why don't you guys do something?" to the crowd of, by-then, hundreds of onlookers. Those guys (and gals and enbies) did, indeed, do something. They started to throw punches and throw bricks.

The cop cars, even one with slashed tires, immediately took off. Their hasty retreat left several police behind and unsupported. This delights me, because it proves that "the thin blue line" is really more of a cowardly excuse for misconduct than some noble code. When push came to shove, those cops straight up *bailed* on their "brothers in arms." They decided their own asses were more valuable than that thin blue line. Keep that in mind whenever you interact with the authorities: the only "solidarity" they have is in the illusion of superiority.

The cops who were left behind by their comrades resorted to brutality immediately, clubbing and laying out a few onlookers. This was not a wise decision, as there was a construction site with pallets of bricks nearby. Seeing the Stonewall crowd being beaten by the panicked cops, they began collecting bricks. The police on site then decided on a very interesting tactic—they took hostages! These included Dave Van

Ronk, a folk singer, and Howard Smith, a writer for the *Village Voice*. With their hostages secured, the police barricaded themselves inside the Stonewall Inn. (27)

According to David Carter's *Stonewall: The Riots That Sparked the Gay Revolution*, the real soldiers—the front-line risk-takers—during what happened next were what Karl Marx would call the lumpenproletariat of the gay community: street hustlers, homeless queer kids, and "flame queens:" a groovy slang term for non-straight-passing queers, who often had a hard time holding down "respectable" jobs. Sensing that the dam had burst, and seeing that the craven cops were trying to take over a queer space, these heroes fired volley after volley of garbage, garbage cans, bricks, rocks, and bottles at the barricaded cops and, unfortunately, their captives. People smashed through the plywood covering the bar's windows. The crowd uprooted a parking meter the concrete and used it as a battering ram, blasting open the Stonewall Inn's front doors. Finally, garbage and lighter fluid were strewn and squirted inside and then set alight. (ibid.)

Thus commenced six days and nights of violent clashes and confrontations with police. It wasn't all violent; the days were leavened by some very vigorous and well-organized protest. At night, things got more strenuous. Astonishingly, *nobody was killed* (unless you count a cab driver who died of a heart attack on night two). If these events had happened with the militarized and heavily armed cops of today? I can only speculate, but I think it would have been a massacre. That tells me that the refusal of police to take a punch or even get pelted by trash without opening fire is physical cowardice that costs human lives. At any rate, Stonewall was not the first, but certainly became the most visible gay uprising in modern Western history. Some scholars argue that this presents a problem, as it erases the continuity of queer folks' existence and the momentum of the nascent American gay rights movement before 1969. (28) That may be the case, but Stonewall is certainly an inflection point in LGBTQIA+ history, and one worth celebrating. Especially the part about fighting four cops at once!

Stonewall also marked the beginning of an era—and a decade—in which gay people began to make some headway. In particular, gay men, and to a lesser extent lesbians, with trans rights still lagging far behind cisgendered gay folks. What, in my opinion, queer struggles are is a set of discrete but overlapping movements for overall queer liberation. Any movement(s) have internal rifts and overall ups and downs. Unfortunately, as far back as the 1970s, a subset of cisgendered gay men and lesbians have been willing to throw their trans sisters and brothers to one side in order to secure their own happiness and perceived safety. (29) We'll meet them in a moment, but note that I say "perceived" safety, because conformity and "respectability" behavior by sexual minorities in the midst of rising fascism is a lot like the classic children's tale *If You Give A Mouse A Cookie*.

If you give the fascists your trans and nonbinary siblings, they're going to ask for your gays and lesbians. And if you give the fascists those gays and lesbians, they're going to ask for your gender-nonconforming friends. And when you give those fascists your tomboys and femboys, they're going to ask for anything they like. By that point, you will have defined "degeneracy" down to the level that not having your third child within two years of mandatory marriage might get you a visit from the Western Fertility Police (or whatever nightmarish bureaucratic name the agency might have). You fell for the first trick, which was allowing the State, or Church, or right-wing podcaster, or whomever the Big Brother of the moment is to define sex and gender for you. If you let them tell you—or if you tell others, that anyone has authority over another's bodily autonomy, you've ceded everything. ‡

Take my old friend sodomy. From BJs to butt-fuckin' and cunnilingus, just for starters, what one does for sexual pleasure with a partner or partners of one's choice (and theirs) could not possibly be less of anybody's business than your own. Despite the self-evidence of this fact, Church and State regulations of sexual conduct are practically as old as human history. Some attempts to regulate what people do with their naughty bits go so far (i.e. female genital mutilation and the stoning of homosexuals or adulterers) that, in my darker moments, it makes me wonder by what possible standard our species can be considered "sentient."

Lawrence v. Texas, the United States Supreme Court decision that officially legalized homosexuality in the United States, happened in ***2003***! Before that, most states had sodomy laws on the books. Were they regularly enforced? Not most places, but the thing about sporadically and (seemingly) randomly enforced laws is that they aren't meant to prevent crime. They're meant to spread fear of the State, and to tell a certain population in no uncertain terms to *knock it off, you.*

Sodomy was legalized in the US in ***2003 CE***. Here's an incomplete list of things mankind achieved, legislated, or developed before the United States admitted that gay people are allowed to both exist and have sex lives: space travel, desegregation (in theory if not in practice), the discovery of the structure of DNA, the legalization of interracial marriage, the discovery of quantum entanglement, the invention of lasers, the (temporary) legalization of abortion, and a federal bar on discrimination in hiring on the basis of disability. That's a sampler platter of achievements; there are paragraphs more. My point is that any gay or lesbian Americans who feel comfortable feeding trans people to the wolves to ensure their own safety aren't thinking clearly. *Gay liberation is as tenuous as trans liberation*, as is Black liberation, as is the liberation of poor, disabled, and all other people. It's all part of the same issue: self-determination in the face of the crushing weight of status quo "morality," State oppression, and hierarchy.

And if gay MAGA folks doubt me, consider this. I had to double back during the writing of this book to add the following: "conversion therapy," an abusive, (30) ineffectual, and wildly unscientific (31) way to "de-gay" gay people, banned since 2019, was back on the Supreme Court's menu! The US Supreme Court decided to hear an argument that could have invalidated conversion therapy bans on the grounds of "free speech." Thankfully, they decided in favor of the bans, but conversation therapy being allowed *at all* is indefensible. Conversion therapy (still practiced in some places in the US) is almost always inflicted on underage people by religious fundamentalist parents. That sounds like the textbook definition of sexual grooming to me, but what do I know? I'm not a parent. People don't actually have rights until they turn 18 and leave their parents' house, right? (**No, that is not right**). (31)

In the beginning, people fucked. And lo, a priestly caste was born at a later point, and this caste found some forms of fucking (especially those not given to keeping the wheels of grain surpluses and warlord-mandated military enslavement turning) *super gross*. Thus, from the priests came the sexual taboo, which was both reinforced by and fed off of successive generations of people raised in a heteronormative environment. The moral of this bummer of a story? Since the start of modern civilization, the mission of elites of Church and State has been, in part, to put a bridle on the beast with two backs. Fortunately, right now in the West being stoned to death or being jailed for homosexuality or being trans aren't on the table. Not yet. Instead, the rise of American fascism has been accompanied by a particular type of machine: the opinion-making, media-drenched machine-hammer.

* The exception to this is asexuality. While no study has been done to my knowledge, the oath of chastity that is required of many men and women of the cloth would have appealed to people who were not keen on the idea of having to produce bountiful heirs or future workers.

** This is something of a hot debate in Christian circles, in no small part because the modern, natalist, gender conforming strain of Christianity has a hard time squaring its self-image with early Church historian Eusebius' claim that when he was young, Origen either castrated himself or asked someone else to castrate him. (8)

*** I'm not just picking on Christianity here. The places where this story takes place are largely either Western or Eastern European, American, or Commonwealth Countries. Christianity is the majority religion throughout these areas, and has been since antiquity. In Christian-majority regions, thinking of historical power structures in terms of Christianity rather than, say, Buddhism, is logical.

† That one's for my Juggalo homies, and it won't be the last reference in this book. WHOOP WHOOP!

†† Foucault was a brilliant thinker and also a problematic one. Whenever I use his frameworks, I'm careful to parse Foucault-the-theorist from Foucault-the-pedophile-imperialist. This is also something I have to do with William S. Burroughs, and both of them were sex tourists in the exact same place, just separated by a decade or two. The world is a fascinating place that often sucks, and sometimes shitty people have good ideas.[a]

[a]Guesmi, Haythem (4/16/2021). Reckoning with Foucault's alleged sexual abuse of boys in Tunisia: I am not calling for Foucault to be 'cancelled', but we need to address recent reports about his predatory behaviour in Tunisia." *Al Jazeera*.

††† Please note: police were doing this to queer Americans at a rate of about one raid per bar per month at the height of anti-communist fervor: in other

words, at the exact same time that Joe and Jane Six-Pack were making "papers, please" jabs about the Soviet Union. It turns out that the Cold War was a struggle between *two* evil empires!

‡ In some cases (vaccines, for example), your choices might have an impact on others who don't interact with you out of choice. Where that line is drawn is a valid debate, but bedroom conduct is not within my Overton window for it.

1 Engelstein, Laura (1997). *Castration and the Heavenly Kingdom*. (Cornell University Press, Ithaca). P.2.

2 Wilson, Jennifer (2018). "Dostoevsky's Timely Castration". *Transgender Studies Quarterly*. 5 (4).

3 Lane, Christel (1978). *Christian Religion in the Soviet Union: a Sociological Study*. (SUNY Press, Albany)

(4 Wall, Richard (1983). *Family Forms in Historic Europe*. (Cambridge University Press, Cambridge). P.105-152

5 DeVun, Leah & Tortorici, Zeb (2018). "Trans, Time, and History". *Transgender Studies Quarterly*. 5 (4).

6 Engelstein, Laura (1997). *Castration and the Heavenly Kingdom*. (Cornell University Press, Ithaca). P29-30

7 Maltsev, Vladimir (2022). "Economic effects of voluntary religious castration on the informal provision of cooperation: the case of the Russian Skoptsy Sect". *European Economic Review*. Vol.

145.

8 Eusebius, *Historia Ecclesiastica*. VI.8.

9 Cheatham, Karen (2007). "'Let Anyone Accept This Who Can': Medieval Christian Virginity, Chastity, and Celibacy in the Latin West", in Carl Olson (ed.), *Celibacy and Religious Traditions* (Oxford Academic, Oxford).

10 Anderson, M. Christine (2004). "Negotiating Patriarchy and Power: Women in Christian Churches". *Journal of Women's History*. 16 (3).

11 Colen, B.D. (9/18/2012). "Suggestion of a married Jesus". *The Harvard Gazette*.

Sabar, Ariel (July/August 2016). "The Unbelievable Tale of Jesus' Wife". *The Atlantic*.

12 Sprayregen, Molly (5/2/2024). "Was Jesus asexual & are angels nonbinary? This history expert says absolutely." *LGBTQ Nation*.

13 For example, many of Jesus' earliest disciples were women, and supported him out of their own pockets (Luke 8:1-3). Compare that to Paul's infamous first epistle to the Corinthians, especially the verse which has been used to deny women the priesthood in many religions (including Catholicism) for most of Christianity's history. The verse I'm talking about is specifically 1 Corinthians 14:33-35:

> As in all the congregations of the Lord's people. Women should remain silent in the churches, They are not allowed to speak, but must be in submission, as the law says. If they want to inquire about

> something, they should ask their own husbands at home; for it is disgraceful for a woman to speak in the church.

14 Gryzmala-Busse, Anna (10/30/2019). “Beyond War and Contracts: The Medieval and Religious Roots of the European State”. *Annual Review of Political Science*. Vol. 23. P19-36.

15 Estrada, Gabriel (2011). "Two Spirits, Nádleeh, and LGBTQ2 Navajo Gaze". *American Indian Culture and Research Journal.* 35 (4). P167–190.

Hauser, Raymond E. & Roscoe, Will (1993). "The Zuni Man-Woman". *Ethnohistory*. 40 (1). P126.

Leland, John (10/8/2006). “A Spirit of Belonging, Inside and Out”. *New York Times*.

16 ILGA World (5/20/2023). “The impact of colonial legacies in the lives of LGBTI+ and other ancestral sexual and gender diverse persons”. *Submission to the Independent Expert on protection against violence and discrimination based on sexual orientation and gender identity*. P3-11.

17 Pease, Roland (6/26/2012). “Alan Turing: Inquest's suicide verdict 'not supportable'”. *BBC*.

Hodges, Andrew (1983). *Alan Turing: The Enigma*. (Burnett Books, London). P458.

18 Duke, Benjamin (2024). “The Imposition of Authoritarian State Sexualism: Theoretical Analysis of State Repression of Sexual Minority Groups Globally”. *Journal of Underrepresented and Minority*

Progress. (8)2.

De Orio S. (2022). "Bad Queers: LGBTQ People and the Carceral State in Modern America." *Law & Social Inquiry*. 47 (2).

19 Edsall, Nicholas (2003). *Toward Stonewall: Homosexuality and Society in the Modern Western World*. (University of Virginia Press, Charlottesville). P253-254.

20 "Anti-LGBTQ Legislation, Policing, and Harassment". *California Migration Museum*.

21 Edsall, Nicholas (2003). *Toward Stonewall: Homosexuality and Society in the Modern Western World*. (University of Virginia Press, Charlottesville). P182.

22 Duberman, Martin (1993). *Stonewall*. (Penguin Books, Westminster). P192-193.

23 Carter, David (2004). *Stonewall: The Riots that Sparked the Gay Revolution*. P141.

24 Braha, D. (2012). "Global Civil Unrest: Contagion, Self-Organization, and Prediction". *PLOS ONE*. 7 (10).

25 Teal, Donn (1971). *The Gay Militants*. (St. Martin's Press, New York City). P2.

26 Truscott, Lucian K. IV (6/282017). "The night they busted Stonewall". *Salon*.

27 Carter, David (2004). *Stonewall: The Riots that Sparked the Gay Revolution*. (St. Martin's Press, New York City). P156.

28 Armstrong, Elizabeth A. & Crage, Suzanna

M. (2006). “Movements and Memory: The Making of the Stonewall Myth”. *American Sociological Review*. (71) 5. P724-751.

29 Esposito, Veronica (6/13/2025). “In the ’70s, Gay Rights Activists Abandoned Their Trans Siblings”. *KQED*.

30 Williams, M. (5/9/2023). "Conversion Therapy on LGBTQ+ Children as a Form of Torture and the Rights of the Child in the Face of the United States Constitution's Free Speech and Religious Free Exercise Clauses". *University of Iowa*.

Staff. (2023). "It's Torture Not Therapy: A global overview of conversion therapy: practices, perpetrators, and the role of states". *International Rehabilitation Council for Torture Victims*.

31 Here is a list of American health organizations that have condemned conversion therapy as unscientific and demonstrating no efficacy over the course of 40 years of attempts (there are many, many more worldwide):

American Psychological Association
American Psychiatric Association
American Medical Association
American Academy of Pediatrics
American Association for Marriage and Family Therapy
American Counseling Association
National Association of Social Workers
American Academy of Sexuality Educators, Counselors, and Therapists

…but what do they know, right?

32 Reid, Lindsey (11/19/2018). “Children’s Rights in the United States”. *University of Alabama at Birmingham Institute for Human Rights Blog.*

CHAPTER TWO

SUPERHEAVY HATE MACHINE

As previously mentioned, queer folks have always existed. (1) This is an inconvenient fact for the Christonormative, homophobic, misogynistic, and transphobic societies that emerged from Europe after nations there embraced Christianity and then later went on to colonize and control much of the world for much of the last millennium (give or take).

Lesbian. Gay. Bisexual. Trans. Queer. Intersex. The terminology may be new to people from more conservative backgrounds, and some of these terms *are* actually new. However, none of the phenomenon they describe are new. From art in the ancient world to intentional (or unintentional) representation in some of humanity's oldest texts, myths, and religious stories, history is chockablock with examples of all of the so-called "new" forms of sexual and gender expression that have caused such a firestorm in the west recently. (2)

Anti-queer activists' and hate cults'* activity aren't new either. They have taken on surprising new forms in the 21st century. If we want to understand the phenomenon of far-right sexual minorities, it's good to start with some insights I gained from my interviews with members of that community. From trans National Socialists to gay fascists, most people I interviewed expressed self-loathing either directly or indirectly. This was often couched in half-ironic, good-natured jokes, but the use of extremely harsh, hateful language and slurs to describe their identities is noteworthy. (3)

It's true that digital natives (especially those who frequent far right spaces) engage in venomous speech toward both themselves and others, (4) but not to the degree I saw in some of my interviews. Also, when heterosexual white men use "fag" to describe themselves disparagingly, that's qualitatively different from when a queer person uses that (or more extreme) language to self-describe. I've seen, for example, "fag" used in loving, playful banter between queer people. (5) I've never seen "troon" used In playful banter among trans people—except in far-right circles; even there, the "playfulness" is edged with spite. (6) If the purpose of that is to poke fingers into eyes of alienate left-wing queer folks, it still strikes me as an act of self-harm in service of a "higher ideal," whether that ideal is slaughtering sacred cows or exercising highly selective free speech.

I grew up in the late 80s through late 90s and early 2000s, and am what is known as an "elder Millennial."** During my 40-odd years of life, I've never seen the State direct resources into homophobic and transphobic hate at as intense a level as it is does right now. (7) Coming of age at the turn of the millennium had its own (trivial) challenges, but compared to what queer young people face today when they're trying to figure their identities out, both Gen X and Millennials had it easy. Even people whose subjective (often media-influenced) opinion is that things are "better now" should acknowledge that new and noteworthy bullshit is afoot in the world of anti-queer bigotry.

To understand where far-right queer folks are coming from, we must examine the messaging, propaganda, misinformation and disinformation, and plain old hate they've been subjected to throughout their lives. This hate is no longer just a matter of peer bullying or enforcement by semi-official authority figures like clergy; that was hate as prior generations knew it. Now, people exist within a vast, febrile network of self-absorption, bombardment by negative messaging, and the measurable cognitive outcomes of that life. (8) The younger a queer person is exposed to the agitprop drumbeat of fascist hate on social media, the deeper the impact it has. That impact is deeper when queer youth are also members of an ethnic minority, (9) but the impact is there for all queer kids. (10)

Trans people are the canaries in the coal mine of human rights right now. Many of the most hateful campaigns and much of the cruel, abusive punishment dished out in the far right's *kulturkampf* has been directed at trans people. Part of this has been a deliberate divide and conquer strategy intended to break the LGBTQIA+ coalition apart and hopefully weaken it through sundered solidarity. Don't believe me? Let's have a look at the history, financing, supporters, media representation, and quasi-ideological underpinnings of two distinct, high-profile transphobic hate campaigns: TERFs (of Trans-Exclusionary Radical "Feminists") and the so-called "LGB Alliance."

The Women Who Hate

Joanne "J.K." Rowling has blood on her hands.

What would you say if I told you that one of the wealthiest and most successful authors in the world spends as much time acting like a high school mean girl on Twitter as the vapidest 15-year-old Nazi incel dipshit imaginable? Would you be surprised? Of course not, it's 2026. And, to many people, J.K. Rowling springs immediately to mind when they hear that description. These days, Joanne is better known by many people for her transphobia than for Harry Potter. If you're not a many people, allow me to break it on down for you.

There are few things that amuse me more than when the rules of an enormous system are very nakedly, transparently changed to suit the embarrassment and rage of one single individual. That's the case with Twitter's invisible likes! To explain: until Elon Musk changed the policy, Twitter users used to be able to visit a person's profile and click on a tab labeled "likes." That tab displayed every tweet that person had clicked the "like" button on. In 2018, J.K. Rowling got caught with her Klan hood on when she liked a transphobic tweet. She received some pushback for that, since a not-insubstantial portion of her fanbase prior to that point were members of the LGBTQIA+ community. (10) After that, as Ron Burgundy once remarked, things "escalated quickly." (11)

Liking a shitty tweet is one thing. Although Elon Musk's reaction to his fellow transphobe getting caught with her claws in the hate jar was hilarious – he eliminated the "view likes" feature entirely! I don't have proof that this policy change was muttered in Musk's ear by Joanne, but the timing of her getting caught and the change being made are quite suspicious, to put it mildly. At any rate, she's moved past quiet support for transphobia. These days, what Rowling does is another level of incomprehensible cruelty entirely. When folks like me mention "power dynamics" and you find yourself tempted to roll your eyes, consider the following scenario and see if you can put yourself in this person's shoes:

You're trans. It's an issue you've struggled with for your entire life, likely while also dealing with comorbidities like depression and/or any disability you may have (autism, ADHD, both). You're bullied at school. You may be bullied at home as well. Thankfully, there's the internet: a place where you can explore your true self with other isolated young people scattered across the globe. Maybe you'll even fall in love with one of them, and one or both of you will move so you can make a full-time relationship work (I have literally seen this happen multiple times with my own eyes).Or, if you're unlucky, you turn on your phone one day to discover that one of your more courageous, and perhaps forgivably outrageous, tweets has garnered the attention of a British billionaire hatemonger. She has retweeted you, mocked your appearance, and now her million-plus followers have decided to make your life a living hell.

I can only thank the dark gods that the plague upon humanity known as social media was birthed after I was an adult. As a digital native, I grew a thick skin fast online, and am, in fact, an alumnus of the exact same Awful Forums that helped spawn 4Chan, "ironic fascism," the word "troon," furry hate, and an entire cauldron's worth of bigotries and dysfunctions disguised as personality traits. Even *that* vortex of spite was better than social media.

Most movements need a figurehead, and the more socially prominent the figurehead, the better. After coming out of the closet (ho-ho, ha-ha) as a transphobic bigot in 2018, J.K. Rowling's politics rapidly began to shift rightwards and she was taken up as a saint and battle commander by a splinter group of self-proclaimed "feminists" who are nothing of the kind, but do have *one* thing in common: they really, really hate trans women. Trans men, too, but the ire of these TERFs (Trans-Exclusionary Radical Feminists) is primarily reserved for women that they've decided are men.

Rowling's output as an author has never been of any particular merit in my opinion, but both the amount and the quality of her work have taken a nosedive since her job changed from "author" to "political provocateur and right-wing activist" between 2019 and 2020 (ibid.). A little background about Just Kidding Rowling: she is a Brit, having been born in Yate, England. After her first marriage failed while she was living in Portugal, she moved to Scotland in 1993. Both the fact that Rowling is from England and the fact that she adopted Scotland as her second homeland are relevant to her development as a bigot.

Joanne's coming-out party as a transphobe in 2018 was not exactly a raging success, but it meant that she'd finally found her people: anti-trans bigots. While TERFism is an ideology that was born in the United States, it first grew from a feeble spark into a mighty blaze in the UK, especially England and Scotland. (11) My personal theory on why transphobia took off quicker there than here is that cultures whose main jest for at least a century has been "man in dress doing woman's voice badly = funny" have more issues with gender roles than ones where the national joke is, say, America's, which is basically *The Simpsons'* "Man Getting Hit By A Football" (which, if you never saw it, is just a "short film" of an old man accidentally getting slammed by a football in the groin).

By 2024, J.K. Rowling was queen of the TERFs. Her contribution to a collection of anti-trans essays by various Scottish second-wave feminists*** who were also TERFs is more than likely the sole reason the book sold so well, given the relatively niche status of the other authors compared to the globally-known author of the Harry Potter series, books so popular that they became their own fucking theme park. The anti-trans book, which has the very Scottish title *The Women Who Wouldn't Wheesht* (the Scottish version of "hush"), is a tepid anti-trans hate screed filled with disingenuous argument, disinformation, and dipshittery. It was, however, edited by two moderately prominent Scots: Luch Hunter Blackburn, an author and former civil servant, and Susan Dalgety.

TERFism plays a vital role in transphobia. As with homophobia (or biphobia), it's impossible to conjure a *rational* argument for an irrational hatred. The best one can strive for, and very seldom achieve, is to find a group willing to play the victims of the object of one's hate, thus justifying one's cause and effectively whitewashing it as bravery rather than sheer bigotry. Note that I say, "play the victims," not *be* the victims. In this case, that group turned out to be the aforementioned small group of women who wouldn't shut the fuck up about how scared of trans women they are.

Harry Potter is a cultural phenomenon and a mega-franchise that has spanned 11 feature-length films in its Wizarding World, produced four theme parks (and one affiliated tour), and launched a new HBO series so far. Multiple generations have grown up on Harry Potter now, including my cousin's kids. The Wizarding World IP, as of early 2025, was valued at about $34 billion, (12) and JK Rowling herself has an estimated net worth of £945 million ($1.21 billion) as of this writing. I'm not sure in what context J.K. Rowling feels she's being told to "wheesht." Harry Potter is a household name that probably outshines Mickey Mouse these days, and JK Rowling is arguably the best-known children's author in modern history. So, how has she used that clout?

She has used her power like a bully and a bigot. She has spent an honestly unhealthy amount of time on Twitter harassing and belittling trans people using language that has incited her fans to make death threats and engage in harassment and doxxing. (13) She donated £70,000 (about $94,000) to an anti-trans group named For Women Scotland and, in 2025, created J.K. Rowling Women's Legal Fund (JKRWLF). JKRWLF is designed to fund lawsuits against employers that fire bigots for being transphobic toward coworkers, clients, or customers: indeed, to pay for lawsuits defending bigots who denied employment and/or welfare benefits to trans women based on their gender identity. (14) In short, she has decided and declared her intention to use all the Harry Potter money possible to fight against trans rights and to exclude trans women, specifically, from public life. (15) What does one even say about a stated commitment like that? Imagine if Bill Gates declared he was dedicating the remainder of his fortune to rehabilitate the reputation of his old friend Jeffrey Epstein. That would be worse, but not by much.

Imagine growing up as a little trans girl or boy surrounded by Harry Potter paraphernalia amid this heel-turn by Rowling. Maybe your parents are even decent people, are marginally aware that you have questions about your identity, and try to keep things neutral as regards issues of gender to let you explore your own identity. Maybe you were a little "boy" who was a Hermoine at heart, or a little "girl" who was a Harry Potter at heart. You get older, you look around, and you discover that the author and creator the universe that undergirded your childhood play doesn't view you as you. Based on some of her posts and actions, it seems like she doesn't see you as a person at all, but a sexual predator and vile imposter. Indeed, she is cruel and mocking enough in her online presence to draw comparisons to Andrew Tate. These comparisons are based on her reaction on Twitter to the UK Supreme Court decision in April 2024 denying trans people protection under the Equality Act 2010:

J.K. Rowling Celebrating a Victory for Hate

Rowling posted that while on vacation, but she does

literally live in a Scottish castle these days; albeit one likely overrun by black mold based on photos she has posted with suspicious creeping tendrils in the background. I've come to believe that there's a level of both poverty and wealth at which one simply accepts and embraces the supervillain way of life. I'd like to think that I, with my rice and bean burritos and "gasolines, gunpowder, and bullets are cheap" Joker aesthetic, represent one pole on this spectrum. Rowling, with her castle, golden rings, painted claws, cigars, brandy, and net worth, represents the other, Bond-villain pole of that spectrum. Oh, and I'm not transphobic—but I *might* try to kill Batman. It's only slightly personal, Bats: it's for the love of chaos.

Anyway, back to that Andrew Tate-esque tweet. Her statement that this was "a plan coming together" wasn't just a dated reference to an American action-comedy show: it was the truth. This hate machine had been in operation with Rowling at the head for six years by 2024, and JK Rowling, Queen of the TERFs, could enjoy a Cruella De Vil moment. She'd leveraged a mix of muddled childhood innocence, transphobia, cruelty, incredible wealth, and her position of prominence—due, remember, solely to her role as a *children's author*—to maximum effect. To a hateful person like her, it was time to rub faces in the dirt and gloat.

Transphobia Is Big Business, As Are Detransitioners

I ran into a lot of surprises while researching and writing this book. One of the most startling facts I learned was the relationship between petroleum wealth and transphobia. At first, it made no sense to me. As I listened to climate and environmental health policy expert Vivian Taylor on the *Carbon Bros* podcast, it became a lot clearer what might be going on. J.K. Rowling may have blood on her hands, but the petroleum industry—and especially the American Petroleum Institute, or API—is *drenched* in blood; practically drowning in the stuff. In a move of startling perversity (and not the good kind), they've decided to cover up that blood by wallowing in even more of it. Vivian's research identified 40 groups leading the push for anti-trans legislation in the US and anti-homosexuality laws abroad. Of those 40, *32* received massive amounts of funding from the fossil fuel industry. (16)

Aside from the petroleum money, there's the money being drizzled like rich maple syrup into the anti-trans movement by individual wealthy fascists like Elon Musk. Musk is a case study in what far-right politics can do to a person's brain in a variety of ways, but his takeover of Twitter has really let his bigotry, ignorance, and menace shine in his new role as techno-fascist social media cult leader. It's well known that Musk has an estranged trans daughter who thinks he's a complete pile of shit, largely because he was incredibly transphobic, abusive, and horrible to her throughout her childhood. (17) It's not hard to tell that this estrangement eats at Musk, who has tweeted about it on and off for years. His past as an abusive, transphobic parent whose child did to him what Musk did to his own father—told him to fuck off—angers him and drives his approach to politics to an extent few understand. When Musk brought Twitter in 2022, he very quickly made it clear that his motives for the acquisition were ideological, not financial (18)—and that's a good thing for him, since his far-right, fascism-forward approach to "free speech" led to the platform hemorrhaging advertisers and profits. (19) Remember; the title of this section is "transphobia is big business," not "transphobia is profitable." Musk's white supremacist, homophobic, right-wing reign at Twitter has more or less driven the platform into the ground. Who has been there to prop up the slumping ruins of what's left? I'll give you one guess.

The first thing it's important to note about PragerU is that it's not a university. It's not an accredited learning service or school of any kind—not even a preschool! PragerU is the passion project of Dennis Prager, a 77-year-old right-wing dipshit with a pallid, punchable face, no chin, and a net worth of $20 million. PragerU, Dennis' brainchild, is a series of propaganda videos designed to indoctrinate children into believing that climate change is a hoax, slavery was a super good time for slavers' "helpers," and that fascism is a left-wing, not a right-wing, ideology—therefore, PragerU's audience can't be fascist *by definition*, silly! (20) Oh, and, just coincidentally I'm sure, PragerU receives a metric shit-ton of money (hundreds of millions of dollars over a four-year period alone) from right-wing donors, including *the petroleum industry!* (21)

In 2023, Twitter's ad revenue went into freefall as legitimate advertisers fled the site for less fascist-friendly, more politically neutral or—gasp!—"woke" platforms. Elon Musk has never admitted the consequences of his political decisions. In fact, it was only revealed by uncovered financial disclosures just how badly Elon Musk fucked Twitter up. After his takeover and into 2023, Twitter experienced a flabbergasting *63% revenue loss*. Out of every dollar of Twitter's piggybank, Elon Musk burned nearly two-thirds of it on the pyre of his fascist mission. (22) No small part of that revenue loss was due to Twitter's new political regime and Musk's far-right, white-supremacist views. (23) Never one to let a pal be hung out to dry (or, more accurately, never one to miss an opportunity to exploit weakness), PragerU purchased what's known as a "timeline takeover" in 2023. They made the buy to push their new video "Detrans." Before I explain what "Detrans" is about and why it matters so much, let me explain the changes Musk made to Twitter's level of commercialization and what a timeline takeover buys you.

One of the many reasons I hate Elon Musk is that he came along and ruined something that didn't need ruining. That's right, motherfuckers, I'm gatekeeping Elon Musk! He's a Twitter tourist! I had an account before he even signed up for the app (I was a *very* early adopter, joining in January of 2009), let alone bought it. I honestly thought he'd have gotten sick of destroying it by now, but it has become clear that it's a vanity project he intends to prop up until it costs him something even more precious than the ability to rename himself "Kekimus Maximus" and get ALL THE LULZ0RZ from the cool internet kids!

Twitter didn't have premium accounts before him. It didn't have the same number of bots it does. It certainly didn't have the number of Nazis on it, or

Klansmen, or pedophiles, or rape apologists, or any of the other hateful fuckers who clambered up out of the dark web and onto Twitter like it was an uncooked steak that inadvertently was swept beneath a garage freezer. Under that metaphorical freezer, it has nourished and made multiply the eldritch things that live there; in this metaphor, the denizens of places like 8kun. Most importantly, before Musk Twitter didn't facilitate—let alone encourage and monetize—active disinformation campaigns and propaganda through things like a timeline takeover.

During its timeline takeover, "Detrans" advertisements (which were misleading, but we'll get to that) automatically appeared at the top of everyone's timelines, and on everyone's "For You" tab. In other words, PragerU was allowed to force-feed propaganda to Twitter's then-420 to 421 million accounts†. How much did this lordly expenditure, the social media equivalent of purchasing a major advertising slot, cost PragerU? PragerU, a neofascist media organization whose foundation was worth, at the close of the 2024 fiscal year, over $95 million (now over $100m) (23) is inexplicably a nonprofit, after all. *Less than a million bucks*, considering that PragerU spent only a million bucks total on advertising for its new video. That doesn't sound like big business, but consider that this was during Elon's "fire sale" period when his advertising revenues were all but gone and he hadn't decided to just eat the loss for ideology's sake and hope Trump restored his fortunes yet.

Part of PragerU's Timeline Takeover

The ad buy was in a certain sense dark kismet. Elon Musk, a very right-wing and transphobic billionaire who'd just ruined a business, could act like he had intelligently pivoted to the right rather than blundering there in a series of profit-destroying lurches with this joining of forces. Plus, Elon's daughter just *really* pisses him off, and I'm sure he thought PragerU's video was righteous stuff and justice for his "lost son." She's not quiet about how awful and weird he is, and unlike her dad, she's really good at posting snark. In addition to shoring up and brainwashing additional young people with a film that's full of lies and misrepresentation, Elon also got to scribble a little, tiny amount of black ink in his ledger out of a clear blue sky. Transphobia helped financially shore up Twitter during one of its numerous post-purchase slumps.

For its part, what did PragerU and the broader anti-trans movement get out of the buy? A hell of a lot of eyeballs, assuming even the most damning statistics concerning active accounts versus bots are true—and let us also consider that no small part of those botnets would have been amplifying the "Detrans" signal. So, what is "Detrans?" To understand that, you have to understand who detransitioners are and how they've been turned into fetish objects by the right.

Technically speaking, detransitioning is when someone thinks they are (or are) trans, transitions for a certain period of time, then decides that their initial perceived gender is the correct one for them. There is absolutely nothing invalid about detransitioning, any more than there is discovering you're bisexual late in life, transitioning late in life, changing your religious faith, etc. All of these things fall under the header of self-discovery and identity, both of which are complex. Trying to boil them down to simpler issues than they are is a hallmark of totalistic thinking, (24) which is an important component of the psychology of fascism. (25) Our identities as humans are multilayered, ever-evolving experiments, and we're allowed to change our minds. With that said, the rate of detransition and the rate of regret for gender affirming care are both astronomically low. (26) "Astronomically" is a word you'll hear a few times in this book, by the way: as in "the number of times a trans person has actually been a mass shooter is astronomically low compared to the rate at which they are accused."

Detransitioning becomes a problem when it's done in bad faith to advance a narrative of lies and hate. As

I mentioned with TERFism, transphobia (like all queerphobia) is hate in search of a rational argument, and since one doesn't exist, one must be fabricated. Often this takes the form of what's known in the online world as "pedojacketing." This is a complex piece of modern portmanteau slang that is based on older slang††, but the gist of it is this: to pedojacket is to falsely and repeatedly accuse someone of being a pedophile for the purposes of damaging their reputation. This isn't just a "poison the well" or "shoot the messenger" tactic, It's scorched earth. Accusations like that ruin lives or potentially end them through violence, and the right is well aware of that.

If you ever wander into the wrong neighborhood online and see people shrieking *GROOMER!* at gay and trans folks, that's pedojacketing. According to these shrill accusers, queer teens and trans kids don't exist without the intervention of adults trying to "force them to transition" or "brainwash them to be gay." This is an accusation as fascinating as it is grotesque, as it implies that people who buy gender-non-neutral clothing for kids or ask their little boys about their girlfriends can be credibly accused of grooming. By their logic, believe you me: straight parents do a hell of a lot more "grooming" than queer ones.

The detransition narrative is vital because by eliding the actual number of incidences of regret and detransition, a little piece of Goebbels-esque cinema like the one cooked up by PragerU can imply that there's a vast conspiracy of sinister forces out there turning kids queer; that's simply not the case and never has been. As I stated earlier and emphatically, queer people have always existed, in all our lovely variety.

That's a very inconvenient truth for Christian Nationalists and your more traditional variety of neo-Nazis and other fascists.

A truth that too often gets left out of discussions of the right-wing propaganda machine is this: young people are poor! Hell, I'm not young, and *I'm* poor! If you're young and naïve, immature, easily swayed, relatively charismatic, and know how to massage the unspeakable apparatuses of social media to engage and/or enrage an audience, you can make a *lot of money* being a far-right influencer. Detransition-as-a-story-of-abusive-doctors is only one angle in this grift. When one deals with someone online whose output on social media is nothing but a constant, hyper-monetized stream of invective, one must always ask the question: gun for hire, a true believer, or some combination of both? In my experience, it's the latter in most cases—but in the case of "ex-gay" and "ex-trans" influencers, the ones I've come upon seem both fanatical and naïve much more than they seem like mercenaries. I strongly considered including a narrative in this book from my own circle of acquaintances, one of whom lost their fucking mind in 2025 and flipped from "pro-trans activist lawyer" and trans man to detransitioner TERF Twitter personality, but eventually I decided it wouldn't fit here. Based on tone and context clues, their situation seems to be incipient mental illness exacerbated by constant social media attention-seeking.

People going through detransition in propaganda materials like PragerU's little movie are going through intense emotional changes and are not at the most stable point in their lives. They are, after all, re-

undergoing an intense and sometimes alienating experience, one that often leaves one feeling isolated, unsure of one's self-image, and undergoing hormonal shifts with the emotional swings that hormonal changes entail. The fact that the far-right snags onto these people and convinces them to star in their propaganda is intensely predatory. Both transition and detransition are personal journeys, and ones I'll be the first to admit I know nothing about whatsoever, except from the academic literature and from talking to friends. I *do* know that if some film crew hired by an octogenarian Nazi were sticking cameras in my friend's face while they were undergoing either process, it would make me quite angry. I'd feel (quite rightly) that they were being taken advantage of, and would be cast aside once they had served their purpose.

But it's all grist for the mill to these assholes. The gristliest of this grist might be one of the strangest astroturfed hate groups I've encountered so far in the 21st century: the "LGB without the TQ" family of organizations. These include "pro-gay, anti-trans and anti-queer" groups like the LGB Alliance and LGB/TQ. Ostensibly, these are grassroots efforts led by gay, lesbian, and bisexual (hey, that's me!) people who are tired of being tarred as members of the same community as trans people, or assorted nontraditionally L, G, or B people who identify as queer. There are two faces to these groups, one of them front-facing and one of them hidden.

The front-facing aspect of these LGB groups is easy to explain, and as old as rainbow capitalism and queer small business owners or the Log Cabin Republicans, and consists of the community of small-c conservative gay men, lesbian women, and bisexual people who have been lured to the siren song of respectability politics. While I detest it and am about to talk a yard of shit about it, I should note that liberalism very much rests on respectability politics, and figures as beloved as the late Rev. Martin Luther King Jr. engaged in and promoted the doctrine. To take Dr. King as an example, he promoted the ideas that Black men should wear suits and ties to protests and never engage in even defensive violence. Respectability politics rest on the idea that by "behaving well and achieving within the system," a minority (sexual, ethnic, or otherwise) can gain approval and eventually acceptance as equals from the majority.

Sometimes, unfortunately, it works. Take the story behind the beloved American stereotype of the Irish beat cop, which was trotted out no less recently than fucking 2017 in the first half of the most recent adaptation of Stephen King's *It*. The story behind the Irish beat cop is dispiriting, and a tale of respectability politics' consequences in a nutshell. When Irish immigration to America began in earnest, the Irish were a despised group of immigrants who were considered nonwhite at the time. One might ask, "Aren't modern fascist tattoos full of Celtic knotwork?" They are!

So how did the Irish become white? Because that's literally what they did in the American mind over decades. They did it by cozying up to power and prejudice by joining the police in most major American cities. I should know! The Murphys, my dad's mom's people, produced a whole crop of cops;

an entire family of brothers who became police, in fact. Here's my ancestor, an Irish immigrant who was a beat cop in Chicago:

There he is, holding another, slightly more adorable ancestor of mine. Say "ACAB, Charles' ancestors!" My family has an extensive photographic record of all sides going back nearly to the invention of photography, and let me tell you: it never gets any less weird seeing the ghosts of your own facial features and those of your loved ones in those old and tattered photographs. History is haunted.

Unfortunately for the Irish and for everybody else, becoming white through policing often meant beating the ever-loving shit out of Black Americans. (27) Did it work? Well, the Kennedy dynasty plagues American politics to this very day. A lot of *Boondocks Saints* fans are fascists, and fake Irish is a very popular Mythic Ethnic Ancestry for racists. I'd say the Irish have become "mainstream, European" Americans—at the cost of doing so atop a pyramid of brutality and oppression. So, you be the judge!

Gay respectability politics run the range from thinking queer people should "tone it down at Pride" to conservative gay bloggers like Andrew Sullivan. Sullivan, who is considered one of the people who invented blogging in its modern sense, made an argument for same-sex marriage, but particularly gay male marriage, unlike any I had ever heard. Andrew thought that gay men were by nature promiscuous and unserious. Marriage, in his opinion, would force them to embrace stability and monogamy, own homes, vote Republican (Sullivan has since changed political persuasions), and adopt or conceive babies. The LGB Alliance promotes many of these values, as do the Log Cabin Republicans, an OG gay Republican group. The anti-trans angle is a new but depressingly predictable turn in the internal politics of the queer community. Trans people fought for gay, lesbian, and bisexual people's rights at Stonewall, and yet a tiny minority of queer people, now that anti-trans hate has increased under American neo-fascism, are willing to throw them to the wolves in the foolish hope of saving their own skin.

When confronted with the force of the superheavy hate machine of anti-queer politics, these quislings added their own strength to the machine rather than resist momentum. Maricopa County, where hell is located and the unworthy dead roast in the flames of climate change for eternity, holds a special place for these people.

Back to "gay, lesbian, and bi" hate group the LGB Alliance. It purports to be a grassroots interest group for "traditional gays" who are fed up with this trans nonsense disrupting their assimilated, square, Republican lives. However, there are very few actual gay, lesbian, or bisexual members of the LGB Alliance. It was, in fact, *not* a grassroots effort at all! In September of 2019, a transphobic letter signed by 22 more or less prominent British people (yes, an entire score of Brits) appeared in *The Sunday Times*. The letter called for an organization of gay, bi, and lesbian people to oppose "gender ideology," which is transphobic code for trans rights. One month later, the LGB Alliance was born, which speaks to an incredibly effective grassroots organizing effort tapping into a vast well of public sympathy—if you're stupid as fuck. In reality, it shortly emerged that the LGB Alliance shares an infamous street address with some very sketchy company for a "gay and lesbian rights" organization.

55 Tufton Street in London is the address of a lovely building. That address serves as the nerve center of a confluence of right-wing power in the UK. It's the headquarters of not only the LGB Alliance, but also Brexit Central, the TaxPayers' Alliance, Centre for Policy Studies, the Institute for Economic Affairs, the *Global Warming Policy Forum* (a climate change denial group funded by oil money), and New Culture Forum. (27) New Culture Forum's presence is especially interesting at that address. That group was

founded in 2006 by a fellow named Peter Robin Whittle. Whittle is best known for running as an openly gay and incredibly right-wing candidate for London mayor representing the far-right UKIP in 2016. A more successful Milo, if you will. Is it like seeing blue cars when you drive one, or are we detecting a pattern?

All of that might suggest that the LGB Alliance is a legitimate organization with 22 members, all of whom are extremely right-wing gay men. Why men? Well, according to Whittle, the vast majority of gay men are extremely right-wing—but lesbians are leftists. This is a very weird confession on Whittle's part that even the LGB "Alliance" isn't internally cohesive. (28) It might suggest the existence of a cabal of self-directed right wing gay men, except for one thing. The interest groups and think tanks at 55 Tufton, almost all of which predate the LGB Alliance, meet frequently to share agenda items and messaging and coordinate campaigns with each other. That, to me, paints the LGB Alliance as a group of useful idiots whose personal prejudices happen to align with the goals of much larger, better-funded interests who are Old Money British levels of homophobic.

The Real Miasma Theory

Speaking of Irish respectability politics and the Kennedy dynasty, here is a comforting thought to tuck you in at night: Robert F. Kennedy Junior, currently the highest-ranking health official in the US, does not believe in germs as the source of the COVID-19 pandemic or pandemics like it.

Yes, you read that right. No, I'm not shitting you. (28) Kennedy has stated that he's a believer in an esoteric (and debunked!) explanation for disease called "miasma theory." Let's not get sucked into that, but it bears some resemblance to the pre-germ-theory of toxic sewer air and malodorous winds causing disease, but with MAHA anti-seed-oil characteristics. The original miasma theory, which was less bespoke and predates RFK Jr.'s beliefs, held that the stagnant air of slums and sewers could seep upward into people's lungs and cause plague. They were sort of in the right box, even if they had the wrong corner.

I think about that idea—sewer gas rising from corruption underground to cause city-collapsing plague—more often these days when I contemplate what queer kids have to deal with growing up. Don't get me wrong, things weren't great when I was a kid, especially representation-wise. From *The Silence of the Lambs* (both book and movie) to *The Crying Game*, *Sleepaway Camp*, and *Ace Ventura: Pet Detective*, transphobia was most frequently used to label someone a monster or a punchline for being trans. Still, I do *not* remember being bombarded by the omnidirectional, high-caliber, lavishly-funded hate for trans people that I see around me today. The roots of this confluence of techbros, old oil money, shady think tanks, and the like bears further investigation as the root of the resurgence of transphobia, but this book isn't long enough for that, regrettably. Other researchers looking into this have pointed, unsurprisingly, to the strange, recurrent role that oil money has played in transphobia. Is that because oil money tends to be old, white, and conservative? Sure. But transphobia also provides a potent and divisive distraction from climate change. A potential way to keep reactionaries' eyes from seeing what is literally burning down their house because they've been bamboozled into thinking that trans people represent a threat.

This book is about the end results; the product of the mutating horrors that the far-right subjects queer people to. What *happens* to a queer kid who grows up and learns who they are while marinating in the shitty pinkish glow of 4Chan? What about the trans men and women who grow up steeped in a social media environment of competitively cruel transphobia—*even among trans youths themselves*? What about the furries who are sexually excited by both anthropomorphic animal characters and the Third Reich? What happens to them psychologically, ideologically, and politically? What movements do they join, and can they trust the people they've decided to associate with? Most importantly of all: how can we fix what is clearly a very fucked-up situation?

As I said in the introduction, whenever we examine a problem, we have to understand its history if we want to fix it. So—what does history tell us about the relationship between fascism (particularly National Socialism) and queerness?

* "Hate cult" is a term I use when referring to organizations, ideologies, cults of personality, self-help groups, etc. that are based not around shared values or a shared commitment to a cause, but based

on a shared hatred.

** I don't find generational analysis particularly helpful, except in one arena: technology. I think generations are clearly separated by tech use, and research supports that. [a]

[a]Vogels, Emily A. (9/9/2019) "Millennials stand out for their technology use, but older generations also stand out for tech use." *Pew Research Center.*

*** Most feminists do not think TERFs are feminists at all…[a]

[a]Thurlow, Claire (2022). "From TERF to gender critical: A telling genealogy?". *Sexualities*. 27 (4). P962–978.

…but there is some commonality. The tangential link between second-wave feminism, which was promoted by thinkers like Andrew Dworkin, Betty Friedan, and Gloria Steinem, and TERFism boils down to two words. Gender essentialism. *Both* several well-known second-wave feminist thinkers and trans-exclusionary radical "feminists," and so-called "gender-critical feminists" think that gender is an immutable trait that assigns certain immutable characteristics to men and others to women. Not all (or even most) second wave feminists were strict gender essentialists, but it was an unfortunate component of the ideology and a product of the time period in which it was forged. Half a century of social theory and biology have since put paid to the claims of those early thinkers.

† How many of Twitter's accounts actually are bots? It's an impossible question to answer with

absolute certainty. At the time we're writing about, 2023, the high-end estimate (from 5th Column AI) put the percentage at an impressive 64%, while on the conservative side Cybara has estimated that in the larger time between 2022 and 2025, the number has only been 11%. Anecdotal, yes, but my own experience leads me to believe that the answer is "it varies," and that the amount of activity over a certain threshold (say, 50K likes) leads to a skyrocketing preponderance of botted likes and replies.

†† Here's the long version of the slang, because I love slang history! One's "jacket" in jail, prison, or a psychiatric institution is one's record. It includes both what one is in for and the nature of one's conduct while inside. What is or isn't in your jacket can quiet literally get you killed or lauded as a hero in prison. "Fedjacketing" is the practice of correctly (or incorrectly) identifying someone as a federal informant, which, like pedojacketing, will get someone killed with extreme prejudice in prison (and elsewhere).

1 Alfonseca, Kiara (3/15/2021). "LGBTQ people have 'been around forever,' historians say" *ABC News*

Collins, Cory "Queer people have always existed – teach like it" *Learning For Justice*.

Ambrosino, Brandon (3/15/2017). "The invention of 'heterosexuality'". *BBC*

2 Academy contributor (6/12/2020). "Depictions of Queer Art throughout History" *Academy of Art University*.

Teverson, Martha (6/24/2024). "Queer Mythological Characters". *Daily Art Magazine.*

3 Thurlow, Crispin (2001). "Naming the 'outsider within': homophobic pejoratives and the verbal abuse of lesbian, gay, and bisexual high-school pupils". *Journal of Adolescence*. Vol 24. P25-38.

Li, Y., & Samp, J. A. (2018). "Internalized Homophobia, Language Use, and Relationship Quality in Same-sex Romantic Relationships." *Communication Reports*. 32 (1). P15–28.

4 Cinelli, Matteo et. al. (11/112021). "Dynamics of online hate and misinformation." *Nature*.

Morales, Esteban et. al. (7/11/2025). "Online toxic speech as positioning acts: Hate as discursive mechanisms for othering and belonging." *New Media and Society*. Article 14614448251338493 (Advance online publication). P1-19.

5 Wheeler, André (3/9/2020). "Why I'm reclaiming the homophobic slur I used to fear." *The Guardian.*

6 Like everything horrible, it originally came from the Something Awful Forums (I'm very glad Rich "Lowtax" Kyanka is dead!). An SA forums user was and is known as a "goon" in forums slang. It escaped its intended audience who got the in-joke. After that:
"This usage became far more targeted and derisive on Kiwi Farms, a notorious anti-trans online forum known for mass-organized stalking, doxxing, stealing, and harassment, including prompting the

suicides of three trans people targeted by members." GLAAD (11/1/2023). "Troon: Definition, Meaning, and Origin in Anti-LGBTQ Hate"

7 Jones, T. (2025). "Trans Bans Expand: Anti-LGBTIQ+ Lawfare and Neo-fascism." *Sexuality Research and Social Policy*. Vol. 22. P69–84.

Hummel, Callan et. al. (9/10/2025). "Antitransgender Legislation and Needs of Transgender Floridians, 2018-2024." *American Journal of Public Health.*

Christiansen, Sophie (06/2025). "State Legislature Demographics and Anti-Transgender Legislation." *Undergraduate capstone project, Utah State University*.

8 Samari, Elaisha et. al. (2022). "A qualitative study of negative experiences of social media use and harm reduction strategies among youths in a multi-ethnic Asian society." *PLoS One*. 17 (11).

Smith, Molly (5/16/2023). "The impacts of social media on youth self-image." *Loma Linda University Health.*

Jacobson, Rae & Emanuele, Jill (8/27/2025). "Social Media and Self-Doubt." *Child Mind Institute*.

9 Bridges, Emily (2007) "The Impact of Homophobia and Racism on GLBTQ Youth of Color." *Advocates For Youth.*

Poteat, Paul et. al. (2011) "The Effects of General and Homophobic Victimization on Adolescents' Psychosocial and Educational Concerns: The Importance of Intersecting Identities and Patient Support." *Journal of Counseling Psychology*. 58 (4). P597 – 609.

10 Limbong, Andrew (12/20/2019). "Why Author J.K. Rowling is Facing Backlash From LGBTQ Activists." *NPR*.

Gordon, Eden Ariella (6/29/2023). "For Many Queer Harry Potter Fans, J.K. Rowling's Transphobia Feels Like a Betrayal." *PopSugar*.

11 Hines, Sally (2020). "Sex wars and (trans) gender panics: Identity and body politics in contemporary UK feminism". *The Sociological Review*. 68 (4).

12 "List of highest-grossing media franchises" (dynamic list). *Wikipedia*.

13 Dec 18 2022: @jessegender "Calls for my death, insinuations that I'm a pedophile, dehumanizing comments about my supposed masculine features. Calling me a creature. All this because I said "maybe don't buy Rowling's stuff going forward in protest". *Twitter*.

14 Monteil, Abby (5/27/2025). "J.K. Rowling's New Org Will Fund Cis Women Fighting To Exclude Trans Women From Public Life." *Them*.

15 Adamczeski, Ryan (5/28/2025). "J.K. Rowling uses Harry Potter wealth to fund anti-transgender organization." *Advocate*.

16 Penny, Daniel & Westervelt, Amy (8/22/2025). "Why Is the Fossil Fuel Industry Funding Anti-Trans Politics?". *Carbon Bros Podcast*.

17 Ingram, David (6/25/2024). "Elon Musk's

transgender daughter, in first interview, says he berated her for being queer as a child”. *NBC News*.

18 Bond, Shannon & Allyn, Bobby (10/26/2024). “2 years in, Trump surrogate Elon Musk has remade X as a conservative megaphone”. *NPR*.

19 Sweney, Mark (9/4/2024). “Advertiser exodus from X gathers pace with 26% planning to cut spending”. *BBC*.

20 Ecarma, Caleb (8/172023). "PragerU: Coming to a Public School Near You?". *Vanity Fair*.

Anderson, Drew (8/6/2019). "BACKGROUNDER: PragerU's Ties to White Supremacy, Horrific Anti-LGBTQ Record". *GLAAD*.

McCarthy, Joseph (12/182018). "A Course in Climate Misinformation: How Prager U. Is Propagating Climate Misinformation". *The Weather Channel*.

21 Stone, Peter (9/6/2023). “US ‘university’ spreads climate lies and receives millions from rightwing donors: PragerU is not accredited but has become a key tool in pushing false claims to youngers – and raked in $200m from 2018 to 2022”. *The Guardian*.

22 Noran, Beatrice (4/16/2025). “X just revealed a glimpse of how dramatic its revenue drop was after Elon Musk’s $44 billion takeover and rebrand from Twitter.” *Fortune*.

23 Staff. (9/22/2025). “Prager University Foundation[a]” *Propublica*. Nonprofit Explorer –

California.

[a]: Again, PragerU is *not* a university, legally speaking. Yet they have a university foundation?

24 Anthony, Dick, et. al. (2011). "Reciprocal Totalism: The Toxic Interdependence of Anticult and Cult Violence" in James R. Lewis (ed.), *Violence and New Religious Movements*. (Oxford Academic, Oxford):
"Religio-ideological totalism entails an absolute division of humanity into dual categories such as saved/damned, human/subhuman, and godly/demonic."

25 Traverso, Enzo (2017). "Totalitarianism Between History and Theory". *History and Theory*. 56 (4). P97–118.

26 Gershon, Livia (5/27/2025). "How Stereotypes of the Irish Evolved From 'Criminals' to Cops: One immigrant group's journey from outsiders to shaping 20th-century law enforcement." *History.com*.

27 Stone, Gemma (12/19/2022). "Revealed: LGB Alliance has secret office at UK's libertarian think tank hub". *OpenDemocracy*.

28 Stone, Jon (10/24/2015). "Gay people tend to be right-wing, says Ukip's candidate for Mayor of London: Peter Whittle said lesbians were the exception and tended to be left-wing." *The Independent*.

29 O'Brien, Sara Ashley (9/25/2025). "RFK Jr. Is Dismantling Public Health. A Fringe Theory May Explain Why." *Wall Street Journal*.

Wu, Katherine J. (9/19/22025). "RFK Jr.'s Miasma Theory of Health Is Spreading". *The Atlantic*.

Dinerstein, Chuck M.D. (7/11/2025). "Secretary Kennedy's War on Miasma". *American Council on Science and Health*.

CHAPTER THREE

ERNST GOES TO JAIL

There is a book that this book hates. It's called *The Pink Swastika.* One of the most egregious, laugh-out-loud shoddy pieces of fabricated history ever foisted on Evangelical Christianity (1) (and that is a *crowded* field, beloveds), it was released in 1995 in the same sense that a long-pent-up deviled egg fart might be "released." Penned by right-wing Christian Nationalist asshats Scott Lively and Kevin Abrams, the latter mainly there because Lively is a charismatic weirdo in real life but is functionally illiterate, *The Pink Swastika* makes the provably untrue, provably *anti*-true* claim that the Nazi Party was a homosexual conspiracy of Satanic sodomites and not, in fact, a right-wing phenomenon at all.

Lively's unlively opus wasn't even the first bite at this bad apple. The Gay Nazi Myth (proper nouns—it has its own Wikipedia page!) originated with a *1945* book. Written by an American homophobe and right-wing crank Samuel Igra, *Germany's National Vice* was the first in a long series of "hey, look over there!" efforts by conservative and right-wing figures to somehow, in some way, differentiate National Socialism from what it is: a reactionary, right-wing authoritarian movement; one that frankly had more in common with the government of the United States of America in the 1930s and 1940s than our postwar society was willing to admit. Each of these efforts to project fascism onto something other than the political far-right (from the Gay Nazi Myth to Jonah Goldberg's 2008 rib-tickler *Liberal Fascism*) has gotten successively weaker and sillier as the far right in Europe, the Commonwealth, and the United States has grown more comfortable identifying with their goosestepping forebears. Suddenly, now that being a Nazi isn't politically radioactive anymore due to our nation's chronic historical illiteracy, it turns that out the Nazis *were* right-wing!

Even so, *The Pink Swastika* holds a special place in my heart as one of the stupidest books ever written, let alone foisted off as "scholarship." Maybe it's because the knockoff is seldom as good as the original, or maybe it's because a solid half-century of "vulgarization" passed between the two, but *Pink* is far, far stupider than *Vice*. At any rate, both are attempting to spin gold from purest bullshit so it's really a question of awarding style points rather than accuracy.

The thesis of both books is that the defining feature of National Socialism is "sexual degeneracy," especially (though not only) of the gay BDSM variety. Yes, that's right, instead of executing several different classes of gay people just like they did to other groups of undesirables including Jews, the disabled, Romani people, communists, and various other ethnicities, the

Nazis were *actually* running around naked but for oil and crotchless, assless leather uniforms, plotting the destruction of Christendom. For those of you not already terminally poisoned by exposure to right-wing rewrites of history performed on quite this audacious a scale, I'll give you a moment to take it in. As Lord Summerisle says to Sgt. Neil Howie in the 1973 film *The Wicker Man*, "Sit down. Shocks are best absorbed with the knees bent."

Let's make no bones about it: Lively is as full of shit as his porn browsing history probably is. *The Pink Swastika*, ironically enough, was a salvo (albeit a low blow) in America's own *kulturkampf*. Excuse me, I mean "culture war." That probably sounds more familiar to my American readers. The weird thing? The term *kulturkampf*, which refers to a pre-WWI period in Germany long before Hitler's entrance into politics, but which was pivotal to his political thinking, (2) *means fucking culture war in fucking German!* The *kulturkampf* was, for the curious, a time when the Kingdom of Prussia (the Reich) briefly went a-scrappin' with that winner and heavyweight champion, the Catholic Church.

I honestly think Lively is too stupid for this to have been intentional. Nowadays, I wouldn't put it past a character like Stephen Miller as a subtle "fuck you" to eggheads like me. But Lively? That dude just has rocks for brains. Call it kismet, then, that an attempt to invert National Socialism (from homo-eradication to homo-eroticism) was part of an American *kulturkampf* of its own; one started on American soil by American (and a few Canadian and British) inheritors of the Third Reich.

The Gay Nazis Myth has gone too far and lived for far too long. Long enough, in fact, that now it's attempting to extrude itself into the minds of real queer people. It's time to clear the air regarding the Nazis' relationship with sexuality—or, at least, to do so in a chapter here. If you want to know more than can be contained in a chapter, whole books have been devoted to this topic. (3) I'll cut right to the chase, so spoiler alert: was National Socialism a radical homosexual movement? No. *God*, no. Was National Socialism *accepting* of gays? No, but a more complex no that involves a lot of "buts" and "ands." Were there *any* openly homosexual members of the NSDAP, the official Nazi Party in Germany? Yes, there were! However, remember when I said "no, but a more complex no?" There *were* gay Nazis, past tense, by the time World War II was well underway. *Were* because they'd all been executed for their homosexuality by their fellow Nazis (who knew about it all along) by that point. The NSDAP's brief quasi-tolerance of people having unconventional sex was followed by a murderous course-correction.

The thing about Adolf Hitler (well, just one of many things, really) is that he was an almost uniquely fucked up human being. I say "almost uniquely" because I know all dictators get to this point at some stage in their trajectory, but *wow* was Hitler hypocritical, inconsistent, unnecessarily angry, cryptic, mocking, manic, maudlin, and always. always self-obsessed. (4) There seemed to be as many things he passionately didn't care about at any given point in time as there were things he obsessively fixated on. These shifts in mood had one exception, of course: his eternally white-hot, pathologically intense, and utterly baseless hatred of Jews. That was, as *Mein Kampf* accurately put at least one thing, the "red thread" running through his life.

Did Hitler consider homosexuality immoral? By 1934 he certainly did. The invasion of Poland took place in 1939, and by 1941, before America even entered the war in December, he was saying things in public like "homosexuality is actually as infectious and as dangerous as the plague." (5) Throughout his reign, he seemed to consider a personal sex life of any kind a potential PR disaster and projected a public image of celibacy and total dedication to the Nazi project. (6) At any rate, Hitler's one great, lifelong love wasn't Eva Braun: it was National Socialism. Well, that and a (thankfully) unrequited crush on his much younger niece. He did take time out of his exceptionally deep commitment to Nazi world domination to harass and, well, dominate his baby niece. (7) A major part of the NSDAP's public rhetoric— and domestic action —was dedicated to a decidedly familiar vision of the "ideal family," at least for someone like me who hails from Utah. (8)(9) Mormon Utah, Nazi Germany: it's always the same cultic hyper-natalist claptrap. Such sentiments should always be a big, red, flapping flag whenever a group or organization dabbles in it. Like natalists past and future, the Nazi regime promoted a gender binary focused on war, procreation, and State service and expansion.

With all of that considered, I don't find Hitler's long-time friendship with Ernst Röhm strange at all, despite the fact that Röhm was openly—even, in some senses, radically—gay, especially for his time. I also don't find Hitler's utterly coldblooded murder of that friend and turn to ferocious homophobia when gay allies were no longer politically expedient surprising. Röhm knew and loved the fact that Adolf Hitler was pure poison from the moment that the two made common cause.

Queer Inside the Reich

To understand Ernst Röhm, one must understand that there was a period between 1919 and 1934 when the idea of gay Nazis wasn't just plausible—it was a fully lived reality. Now, as I've repeatedly stated, *The Pink Swastika* is absolute bullshit. However, I think that we can cover some ground that Scott Lively covered while being better people than Scott Lively. That isn't hard, honestly. I mean I haven't spearheaded an "execute the gays" bill in a developing nation in, oh, ever. Scott cannot make that claim. (10) We can both acknowledge that in its infancy the NSDAP was unusually accepting of a certain type of homosexual man, while acknowledging that this was never true of any other group within the LGBTQIA+ coalition. (11) Even when it was true for homosexual men in the Nazi Party, it was only true until 1934, after which the Nazi policy on queer people was quite literally to murder each and every single one.

Let's not get ahead of ourselves. What about that honeymoon period for gay Nazi men? Imagine it: a time when a kinder, gentler, *woker* Nazi Party existed, right? I mean, "unit cohesion" or "fags can't aim" or some stupid shit was the reason the United States military denied openly gay people enlistment until fucking ***2011***. Surely it had *something* to do with manly vigor and combat readiness like all of the 20th and 21st century politicians from both major US political parties said, right?

Evidently not. Gay Nazis were, for the most part, members of the SA—the famed "stormtroopers" who were some of the most brutal, absurdly violent, bloodthirsty, and (by those standards) "manly" men in the early National Socialist movement. The Sturmabteilung (SA, or Stormtroopers) are even considered by some to be the "first Nazis" (11) and both their leader, Ernst Röhm, and a core but not majority group of members were gay. It's an uncomfortable truth for antifascist allies and the LGBTQIA+ community alike: some of the Stormtroopers and Brownshirts, the most violent anti-Jew and anti-communist street fighters who painted Berlin's streets with blood, probably went home and fucked each other afterwards.

It's a bitter pill that must be swallowed so that we can move on to the larger, much more defining issues of Nazi Germany's crushing, leaden heteronormative and natalist moralism and the loathsome, cowardly nature of Adolf Hitler's character. It's also an excellent illustration of a point I will hammer over and over and over again until our fascist-curious LGBTQIA+ friends get wise (so, likely until death's sweet release finally breaks my shackles). Being in the Inner Party can insulate you from scrutiny and protect you if you're a member of a class the Inner Party has a public stance against—*for a while*. Whether it's Milo or

Röhm, Caitlyn Jenner or "let's find common ground with MAGA" Democratic trans influencer Brianna Wu, being LGBTQIA+ *inside* the Reich is a thrill ride that only ever can or does end one way, and it's not a pretty ending.

If there's anyone in history who had reason to think he was insulated from the whirlwind he helped sow, it was probably Ernst Röhm. Röhm was one of the original group of "Young Germans" (as identified by fascist theorist Julius Evola) who fought tooth and nail in World War I and came back with a bottomless pit of hate inside them which they filled with a thirst for blood and a sense of aggrieved humiliation. In this sense, Röhm and Hitler were two peas in a pod. Röhm was one of Nazism's earliest adopters. Besides that, Röhm was one of Adolf Hitler's oldest, dearest friends by the time the Nazis rose to power. He was so close to Hitler that up until Röhm's death, he was allowed to address Hitler by the informal *du* for "you" instead of the more formal *Sie*, as everyone else did. Not only that, Röhm was literally the only human being on Earth allowed to call Adolf Hitler not only "Adolf" instead of "mein Fuhrer," but even the diminutive Adi. (12) Maintaining or cultivating this sort of intimacy with a murderous tyrant known for unpredictable fits of manic rage (13) is something of a risk, as any number of dead former dictators' best friends throughout the centuries would testify in ghostly chorus. Röhm was able to keep hold of the tiger's tail for far longer than most, and achieved a remarkable amount of terrible, shitty things for his friend Hitler.

Ernst Röhm, Munich, 1924

I don't intend to go through Ernst Röhm's career in depth, but it was long and storied. Some of the highlights include his participation in the Beer Hall Putsch (14)***, his co-founding of the Nazis' original paramilitary wing, and his reorganization and term as director of the reorganized and vastly expanded SA Stormtroopers, after which their highest group leaders reported directly only to Röhm or Hitler. Hitler acted as formal head of the organization while Röhm ran day-to-day operations. (15) He served in this role from 1930, until, well...

I have a hard time putting myself in the shoes of someone as shitty as Ernst Röhm, but had I been him, I would have started getting nervous right around 1931. 1931 and 1932 marked years when Röhm's homosexuality was given greater publicity via the domestic and foreign press, which caused scandal for the NSDAP. (16) At the time, the Nazi Party was attempting to reposition itself as a more socially conservative party to court broader electoral appeal and win more votes. This was in sharp contrast to Röhm's vision of National Socialism. In his autobiography, whimsically titled *The Story of an Arch-Traitor*, Röhm wrote:

> The struggle against the cant, deceit and hypocrisy of today's society must take its starting point from the innate nature of the drives that are placed in men from the cradle ... If the struggle in this area is successful, then the masks can be torn from the dissimilation in all areas of the human social and legal order. (17)

Not only that, Röhm blamed this moralistic, bourgeois deceit and hypocrisy for causing suicides, (18) leading me to the stomach-churning conclusion that there is at least one thing I agree with Ernst Röhm about. Fucking *gross*. Whatever Röhm's personal vision was, it didn't matter in the least. The NSDAP was tacking socially much further right. After the press exposure, Röhm was removed from the limelight a bit, as was his SA.

The SA was still used as the Nazis' primary streetfighters against anarchists, communists, and representatives of other political movements. They no longer served as the personal bodyguards of the Nazi elite, however, which pushed the SA from a high-profile, somewhat glamorous role into one more alleyway- and gutter-based. (19) This wasn't surprising and probably was decided in part by burgeoning Nazi elitism as the Party gained momentum and respectability of a sort within bourgeois German society. The SA stormtroopers were, on average, from a more working-class background than Party leadership. The SA, like Röhm, had expected a radical transformation of the social order via participation in NSDAP putsches. (20) Instead, they were about to experience a radical transformation of their faction's previously high status in the Nazi Party's hierarchy.

More broadly, the Party itself made a series of statements and took a series of steps by then to make it clear they viewed homosexuality as a degenerate sexual perversion. Whatever Hitler's quiet, close-held feelings on the matter, as early as 1928 the NSDAP responded to a questionnaire by stating that "Anyone who even thinks of homosexual love is our enemy." (21) There were exceptions to this view of homosexuality (as we've seen), but there was a big difference between being gay within the Reich and being gay outside of it. While Hitler might have made exceptions to this policy for longtime friends, his first, highest, and primary loyalty was to National Socialism, his creation and the sole object of his daily obsessions. As I see it, if Adolf had found it convenient for the Nazi cause to have Eva Braun drawn and quartered at a Nuremberg rally, he would have done it.

Was Röhm getting nervous in those days? It's hard to tell. It's subjective, but having read about what happened in 1934, I can't help but think that the purge came as a surprise to the men swept up in it. They may have had *some* inkling that a change was coming, especially as Heinrich Himmler's rival SS (*Schutzstaffel*) fought for dominance with Röhm's SA. It doesn't seem as though anyone at the SA thought that change would take the form of a sudden, savage purge. Weren't there Jews to worry about, not to mention Romani people, the disabled, communists, etc.? Hadn't they proved their utter, unquestioning loyalty to the Fuhrer by shedding the blood of his enemies early and often? Hadn't they delighted in the destruction of the degenerate transgender institute (more on that in a second) and the enemies of the NSDAP?

It's hard to argue with any of that. The gay rank-and-file members of the SA had proven that they were under Hitler's sway as much as any straight Nazis had—more than most, in fact. But they'd served their purpose. The SA had always drawn most of its membership from working class street brawlers. While brutal thuggery would still be required after 1934, the days of National Socialism's ludicrous version of respectability politics had arrived. (22) Working class and *especially* gay Nazis never stood a chance. They, like most participants in the mass politics of Germany in the 1930s, were taken in by Hitler's charismatic rhetoric and forceful, brutal style. The uniforms, marches, parades, brawls, proud bodyguard gigs, flapping banners, and crisp salutes—they create something commonly referred to as a milieu, and one's milieu can have profoundly negative impact on critical thinking and discernment. (23) Cults—political *and* religious—count on that.

Ernst Röhm didn't have that excuse. Not only had he known Hitler intimately for longer than just about anybody, he was also almost uniquely unaffected by Hitler's forceful charisma compared to other high-ranking members of the NSDAP. (24) It appears Röhm was immune to Hitler's weird, megalomaniacal spell, perhaps because he knew Hitler before he was *der Führer*. That might be why Hitler allowed *du*, Adolf, and even Adi to cross Röhm's lips without evident rancor; it's just a personal theory, but I think people like Adolf Hitler have contempt for those taken in by their personas. However (and this is, again, just me speculating), it's the last position you want to be in during the rise of an *authentically* megalomaniacal leader. Would-be gods (or epoch-making God-Men) don't have longtime friends, let alone gay ones. Certainly not ones who call them Adi. Well Ernst, in the parlance of the proletariat, fuck around and find out.

The Night of the Long Knives took place from the night of July 30th to July 2nd, 1934. It marked the consolidation of Hitler's absolute control over the Nazi Party and the elimination of any remaining perceived challenge to the Reich, including Röhm's theoretical, sometimes-muttered-about "second revolution." During the Night of the Long Knives, there were over 1,000 arrests and almost all of them were Nazis themselves. Estimates of the death toll range from 85 to 1000. (25) Why is that remarkable? I mean, the Nazis kicked down doors left and right. It's remarkable because this was an *internal purge*. All 85 to 1,000 of those murdered people? Nazis who weren't the right type of Nazi, murdered by other Nazis. Again, I am fucking begging my LGBTQIA+ fascist readers (and I know there's at least *one* of you reading this, hello!) to think about this at length. The Night of the Long Knives was officially known as Operation Hummingbird, and colloquially as *the Röhm Purge*. If that doesn't give you an idea of how things went for Ernst Röhm, it would be my absolute pleasure to go into detail.

Operation Hummingbird was planned in response to a supposed, planned Röhm Putsch that would have used the SA to drive Hitler from power (Himmler's evidence of this "planned putsch" was largely fabricated). The reality of the Röhm Purge was a complex changing of the guard and consolidation of legal and extrajudicial power. Don't take my word for it: Hitler bragged about it in a radio address afterward. (26) In addition to consolidating power, the Night of the Long Knives acted as a chance for Hitler to eliminate two hated factions: Röhm's gay inner circle at the SA (called the "Röhm cult" by Himmler) and the Strasserists, a group of vocal internal dissenters led from outside the NSDAP by a former Nazi named Gregor Strasser who'd resigned in 1932. (27) Other victims of the purge included conservative, old-guard government officials whom Hitler viewed as obstacles to the new phase of his project.

The SA Brownshirts, those venerable breakers of communist jaws, were out. Himmler's SS was in, and it was primarily the SS that carried out the rapid mass murder (excuse me— "extrajudicial executions") required to make that happen. These weren't gunfights or street fights, for the most part. They were sneak attacks: late-night arrests followed by firing squads. Sometimes, it was just a surprise bullet in the brain. Himmler didn't pull it off alone. Before Operation

Hummingbird was launched, he and Reinhard Heydrich (more or less Himmler's second in command and co-conspirator) fabricated evidence of the supposed Röhm Putsch and presented it to other high-ranking Nazi officials, including the Fuhrer. (28) Röhm was not given a chance to make his case or contest the "evidence." After a brief perusal, Germany's supreme leader—AKA Adolf or Adi to his dear friend—drew up a death list of SA members and other victims to be executed, and the gears of Röhm's doom began turning. I can only imagine that Himmler broke into a brief, scuttling dance of joy at the way everything was coming up Henrich.

On June 30th, 1934, Hitler and a large group of SS troops (the *new* face of hardcore Hitler loyalism) flew to Munich to surprise Röhm and other senior SA leaders at a hotel where they were ensconced. They arrived early enough that the SA men were still in bed—in one case, two of the men were caught in bed together. (29) Hitler personally arrested Ernst Röhm and turned him over to two goons holding pistols. Röhm was denounced and demonized at a furiously demagogic meeting of high Nazi brass. Hitler didn't dissolve the group completely; a few fortunate, surviving SA members were present at the meeting. But Himmler's SS was the paramilitary group now in the Fuhrer's good graces. (30) In some ways the change would have been inevitable regardless or Röhm, given Hitler's changing political stance and situation.

SA stormtroopers had alienated the army and had so terrorized the German populace that there were widespread demands for their curtailment. (31) By

1934, there were roughly *three million* SA members. Not only that, they were also the sort of rubes who believed the "socialism" part of National Socialism (making them about as bright as your average conservative blogger). Röhm's most ardent supporters believed in a radical anti-capitalist restructuring of the German State—a so-called "second revolution" that would be more overtly socialistic, (32) although this change would have kept Hitler as the head of state. This was not the direction Hitler or the Party were headed, however, and Röhm's more vocal working-class supporters were a bad look for a party that was by then courting millionaire backers. Regardless of what these SA Stormtroopers discussed in beer halls, Hitler slapped this possibility down vigorously when talking to German industrialists. (33)

With the Night of the Long Knives' arrests carried out, the NSDAP's internal structure shifted. The process was almost complete, and only one thing remained to be done. The relatively newly created (1933) *Leibstandarte SS Adolf Hitler*, a Waffen-SS division answering to Adolf Hitler alone, was instructed to form "execution squads" and march the prisoners into the courtyard of the prison where they were being held and shoot them dead— with one notable exception. (34)

On some level, even a man as deeply pathological, treacherous, and ridiculous as Adolf Hitler knew that this was a supremely fucked up way to treat Ernst Röhm, his oldest friend and one of his most loyal supporters. Still, he couldn't let Röhm go free after the evidence presented by the SS and his own public condemnations of Röhm as a traitor—something he by then likely personally believed, based on the preponderance of Inner Party whispers. Whatever to do? He did the most Hitler thing imaginable; he delegated like a chickenshit. Hitler dispatched two men, Theodore Eicke and Michael Lippert, to visit Röhm in his cell. They presented him with an ultimatum. He could kill himself with a pistol they'd provide or they would shoot him. Saying perhaps the only cool thing in a brutal, miserable life of treachery and wanton hate, Ernst Röhm replied "If I am to be killed, let Adolf do it himself." Ten minutes later, Eicke and Lippert revisited Röhm to find him bare-chested, daring them to shoot him. They obliged. (35)

Und du, Adi?

Queer Outside the Reich

That was one type of gay experience in Nazi Germany. If one *wasn't* Ernst Röhm or one of his SA golden boys, one's life as a queer person under the Third Reich was nasty, brutish, and all too often short. It's difficult to talk about Nazi "policy" before they got the chance to govern. Certainly, they had rhetoric— and more importantly, they had their actions. Let's start the vicious history of Nazi treatment of LGBTQIA+ people with the group that is so often the canary in the coal mine of authoritarian meddling in sexuality: the trans community.

Germany *wasn't* a queerphobic hellscape before the NSDAP took control. Weimar Germany had a thriving gay scene, especially in cities like Berlin.

Magnus Hirschfeld, a pioneering figure in the new field of sexology, established a world-renowned sexology institute in Berlin in 1919. The Weimar period also gives Germany the distinction of having one of the first gay rights movements in the world. None of this tolerance or learning survived contact with National Socialism. (36) By 1933, the tide had turned in such a reactionary typhoon that the Institute for Sexual Science (as Hirschfeld's research and science group's headquarters was called) was looted. Before that point, the Institute was home to a vast library of theoretical writing and studies, many of which were about trans people and were among the earliest Western scientific studies of trans identity. (37) All of that learning was dragged into Bebelplatz (then called the Opernplatz) in Berlin by a Hitler-worshiping youth group and burned. Hirschfeld's life's work was destroyed. (38) The Nazis were robustly anti-gay, anti-bisexual (which they classified as a subtype of homosexuality), anti-lesbian, anti-transgender (which they labeled transvestitism and therefore a subtype of homosexuality)—anti-queer from wall-to-wall.

As I covered above, Hitler tolerated some gay men within the ranks of the SA, particularly if they were violent brawlers and effective strongarm soldiers. Once the NSDAP started gaining momentum, however, Hitler and his party had to appeal to more conservative, wealthy, and traditional sectors of German society in order to cement their hold on power and fuel a war of conquest and expansion. This meant policy statements, propaganda, and actual government action to legitimize themselves. For the purposes of this book, two of those rhetorical and policy combinations were particularly important once the Nazis became the German State.

First, there was the Nazi expansion of Paragraph 175. In 1871, the then-extant German Empire's King Wilhelm I and Chancellor Otto Bismarck oversaw the enactment of a revised penal code that included (in Paragraph 175) criminal penalties for "unnatural sexual acts" between men. (39) After Hitler cleaned house, purging gay Nazis and executing Ernst Röhm, the Third Reich waded even deeper into the morass of legislating sexual morality. In 1935, they radically expanded the definitions of acts that would get a person arrested under Paragraph 175. This led to LGBTQIA+ people becoming victims of the Nazi death camps. Between 5,000 and 6,000 queer folks were sent to them, where about 60% of them died. Outside the camps, other queer people were sentenced to jail, publicly denounced, and generally persecuted. (40)

Did Nazis hate gay people? Absolutely, as they demonstrated, but they framed it as a warped expression of their hatred of Judaism. To Nazis, then and now, there's literally only one explanation for anything in society being undesirable: the Jews. Thus, after assuming power in 1933 and especially after 1935, the NSDAP denounced homosexuality loudly and frequently as a Jewish conspiracy to destroy Western society. (41) I'm going to take a break from history here to point out that it's not just a straight line from these ideas to modern talk about "globalists" and "cultural Marxism." *These are quite literally the same ideas that were at the heart of National Socialism and the Holocaust*, only with a paper-thin veneer of modern reframing. (42) When you hear Ron DeSantis use the term "cultural Marxism" in a speech at Liberty University or read former National Security Council member Richard Higgins use the term in 2017 in a memo to then- and now-President Trump, I think it's safe to say that this live-action role play of the Third Reich is sticking to the script. I have no idea how gay and trans neo-Nazis can possibly think they're safe.

Henrich Himmler, who successfully ousted and executed Ernst Röhm, was a notorious and vicious homophobe. It would not be a stretch to say that Himmler was obsessed with purging Germany of queer people. He viewed German queers as a destructive and degenerative presence within the nation, even in the civilian population outside the Party. Himmler devoted a frankly asinine amount of public time and money to persecuting homosexual men. In the two years between 1937 and 1939 alone, the Gestapo (and sometimes original-recipe police) arrested 95,000 men for homosexuality. (43) That's 130 men per day. Those arrested in the earliest years of the anti-queer campaign in Nazi Germany were almost certain to receive jail sentences, often with judges howling at them from the bench in terms straight out of National Socialist ideology rather than actual German law. After 1937, one particular part of the Nazi expansion of Paragraph 175 became of note. The clause concerned "seducing someone into homosexuality," which was a very subjective and shifting accusation—a bit like "grooming," which is the term favored by modern Nazis. In Russia, the favored term is, loosely translated, "propaganda of non-traditional sexual relations" (пропаганда нетрадиционных сексуальных отношений). In Germany from1937 to 1945, anyone convicted of "seduction" was sent straight to a concentration camp. (44)

The Nazis didn't understand queer people. By burning the Institute for Sexual Science's library and papers and then banning any study of the subject, they guaranteed that they *couldn't* understand queer people. As a result, it's difficult to break down which specific groups of gay people, in today's terms, were included in the broad category "homosexual" by the Nazis. For example, as I mentioned before, trans women were classified as "transvestites" in the terminology of the Reich and therefore homosexual men. (45) Touching base with our present, neofascist moment, there was certainly no LGB Alliance in Weimar or Nazi Germany, nor any Nazi smokeshow trans femmes fatales. The only categories the early Nazis recognized among queer folks were "masculine gay men willing to fight for Hitler" and "degenerates." After 1934, it wasn't even safe for the highest-ranking Nazis to be masculine gay men. Had any masculine gay Nazi tried to make the case for "gay without the degenerates" in the style of the LGB Alliance, they would have been sent to the camps—right alongside everyone that they'd denounced.

As for Nazi views on gender nonconformity, they were essentially of the "real men, real women, and everyone else are degenerates" school of thought. A man who dressed in drag (*even a kawaii maid skirt!*) was considered a homosexual. Trans women were considered homosexual men, whether they dyed their hair blue or happily tried to assume the role of a tradwife married to a man. I cannot emphasize this enough: presentation and respectability didn't matter. National Socialism's crude, bio-mythic, and antiscientific understanding of humanity and *especially* human sexuality is at the core of Nazi thought. (46) There's no place for an "accept my femboy tradwife" school of thought within the movement. There never has been, and because of far-right beliefs about gender roles and natalism, there never can be.

With strict definitions of gender come ironclad definitions of gender roles. In the Third Reich, such training started in infancy, but the Nazis also sought to retrain grown men to meet the Nietzschean physical standards the Reich thought fitting of a nation in pursuit of its Aryan destiny. In 1933 the NSDAP promoted gender roles associated with fertility and emphasized natalism by asking women to drop out of college en masse to spray out babies. (47) That sounds exactly backwards to my way of thinking, but it also sounds like something that the Trump Reich might propose as policy.

Fascism is not a normal ideology. Everyone knows that as times change, good ideas change with them. While the most useless communists ever to walk Lucifer's black beach are currently rehashing 19th century arguments on Twitter, Reddit, TikTok, and YouTube, there is also a vast canon of vibrant, forward-looking Marxist work†. There are progressive strains of Islam, Christianity, Judaism, Buddhism, Hinduism—*all* of those supremely ancient pageants. There are, of course, regressive, reactionary versions, but my point is that forward-looking elements exist within all of these tradition-worshiping belief systems. *There is not and can never be a forward-looking fascism*

"That's a pretty bold statement, Juffy!" I hear you exclaim††. Bear with me.

Fascist masculinity is necessarily and always restrictive. Although we're coming up on a century since fascism's emergence in the early 20th century, the *same exact shit* is being sold this time around. Admittedly, this time it's with the most eye-blisteringly awful, neon repackaging imaginable. Inasmuch as neo-Nazis are likely to accept anything their forebears wouldn't have, it's the worst shit you can possibly imagine (see **Chapter Nine: Proud Boys, Femboys, and Towel Boys**). Trans rights and gay rights are not on the neo-Nazi menu; at least, not in a way that even gay Nazis would find palatable. While liberals might dream of finding common ground with MAGA on a restricted set of gay rights, I don't see that happening. A national bill to decriminalize pedophilia passing the same muster? *That* I can see.

Don't believe me? Turn the page!

* Did I just invent the term anti-true? Maybe! I mean it in the following sense, which is a similar sense to the difference between disinformation and misinformation. An untrue statement is one which lacks truth-value: "Steak is a vegetable." An *anti*-true statement is one which inverts truth value and weaponizes it: "Steak is a vegetable, and vegans are trying to hide that fact from you because they're

carnivores."

** I'm just fucking with you. The real saying is, "A Nazi in the streets winds up in a coroner's sheet"

*** The 1923 Beer Hall Putsch was Hitler's first and very premature power grab, and most of the participants were jailed. That included Röhm, although he was released on a suspended sentence and continued to organize the nascent movement and Party outside. Meanwhile Hitler, the putsch's leader, stayed locked up. Hitler used the time in prison to begin writing Volume 1 of *Mein Kampf*. Two world's shittiest best pals!

† Those who know how critical of Marxism I am know that it was physically painful to type this, but credit where credit is due, comrades.

†† I warned you there'd be more Juggalo slang ahead! Show me your butthole!

1 The best summary of thoroughly worthless the book is comes in two parts. First, the book that debunks *The Pink Swastika* is damn near as long as its subject matter. There's that much to debunk. The text is an online, interactive book called *The Annotated Pink Swastika*.

Secondly, Fordham University's *Internet History Sourcebook* entry for "the Holocaust" states, and I quote,

> …no serious historian takes the Lively/Abrams book seriously as anything other than evidence about the modern American far-right [and its fixations].

2 Weir, Todd H. (2018). "Hitler's Worldview and the Interwar Kulturkampf". *Journal of Contemporary History*. (33) 3. P597-621.

3 *Sexuality and German Fascism* edited by Dagmar Herzog (2004)

Sex and Society in Nazi Germany by Hans Peter Bleuel (1972)

Sexual Violence against Jewish Women during the Holocaust by Sonja M. Hedgepeth and Rochelle G. Saidel (2010)

Ilse Koch on Trial by Tomaz Jardin (2023), to name a few

4 Dormer, Dietrich & Glass, C. (3/4/2011). *Review of General Psychology*. (15) 1. P37-49

Mankelwicz, John & Kane, Robert (2022). "Hitler as a Narcissistic Leader". *The Journal of Psychohistory.* (50) 2.

Hyland, Philip et. al. (2011) "Psycho-Historical Analysis of Adolf Hitler: the Role of Personality, Psychopathology and Development". *Psychology and Society*. (42) 2. P. 58-63.

5 Evans, Richard J. (2008). *The Third Reich at War*. (Penguin Group, New York). P535.

6 Brikhof, Tim (1/31/2022). "Adolf Hitler's girlfriends: What was it like to date the German dictator?" Big Think.

> "Joachim C. Fest's authoritative biography of the Führer, Hitler, presents him as an aloof and deeply serious individual who,

from early childhood on, was enamored above all with his own ideas; when his peers started discussing girls, Hitler showed interest only in opera and architecture."

7 Kershaw, Ian (2008). *Hitler: A Biography*. (W. W. Norton & Company, New York). P219.

8 Helen L. Boak, (1999). "Book Review: Nazi Family Policy, 1933–1945". German History (17) 3. P445.

9 The First Presidency of the Church of Jesus Christ of Latter-Day Saints (9/23/1995). "The Family: A Proclamation to the World". *General Conference 1995*.

10 Okeowo, Alexis (8/16/2013). "An Anti-Gay Pastor Takes On Uganda and Russia". *The New Yorker*.

11 Willard, Jeremy (11/17/2016). "Homosexual Nazis and The Night of the Long Knives: Hitler used homophobia to justify murder and pave the way for further state violence". *Xtra**.

12 Gunther, John (1940). *Inside Europe*. (Harper & Brothers, New York). P6.

Manvell, Roger & Fraenkel, Heinrich (2010). *Goebbels: His Life and Death*. (Skyhorse Publishing, New York). P135.

13 Doyle, D. (2005). "Adolf Hitler's medical care". *Journal of the Royal College Physicians Edinbugh*. 35 (1). P75-82.

14 Childers, Thomas (2017). *The Third Reich: A History of Nazi Germany*. (Simon & Schuster, New

York). P57.

15 McNab, Chris (2013). *Hitler's Elite: The SS 1939–45*. (Osprey Publishing, Oxford). P16.

16 Marhoefer, Laurie (2015). *Sex and the Weimar Republic: German Homosexual Emancipation and the Rise of the Nazis*. (University of Toronto Press, Toronto). P156.

17 Hancock, Eleanor (1998). "'Only the Real, the True, the Masculine Held Its Value': Ernst Röhm, Masculinity, and Male Homosexuality". *Journal of the History of Sexuality*. 8 (4). P616–641.

18 ibid., P623

19 Cook, Stan & Bender, Roger James (1994). *Leibstandarte SS Adolf Hitler: Uniforms, Organization, & History*. (James Bender Publishing, San Jose). P17, 19.

20 Frei, Norbert (1993). *National Socialist Rule in Germany: The Führer State, 1933–1945*. (Wiley-Blackwell, Cambridge). P10-11.

21 (16 ibid.) P151-152.

22 Gopnik, Adam (3/13/2024). "The Forgotten History of Hitler's Establishment Enablers". *The New Yorker*.

Attar, Rob (9/9/2019). "Hitler's millionaire backers: how Germany's elite facilitated the rise of the Nazis". *BBC History Magazine*.

23 Hartman, John J. (11/23/2023). "The emotional appeal of shared fantasies in Nazi propaganda: A psychoanalytic view". *Applied*

Psychoanalytic Studies. 21 (1).

Griffin, R. (2008). "Fatal Attraction: Why Nazism Appealed to Voters". In: Feldman, M. (eds) *A Fascist Century*. (Palgrave Macmillan, London).

24 Moulton, Jon (1999). "Röhm, Ernst (1887–1934)". In David T. Zabecki (ed.). *World War II in Europe: An Encyclopedia*. Vol. 1. (Garland Publishing Inc., London and New York). P469.

25 Larson, Erik (2011). *In the Garden of Beasts: Love, Terror, and an American Family in Hitler's Berlin*. (Broadway Paperbacks, New York). P314.

26 Hitler, Adolf (1941). *My New Order*. (Reynal & Hitchcock, New York). P266.

27 Spielvogel, Jackson J. (1996). *Hitler and Nazi Germany: A History*. (Prentice Hall, New York). P78-79.

28 Wheeler-Bennett, John (2005). *The Nemesis of Power: The German Army in Politics 1918–1945* (2nd ed.). (Palgrave Macmillan, London). P319-320.

29 Kempka, Erich (1948). "Erich Kempka interview". *Library of Congress: Musmanno Collection-Interrogations of Hitler Associates – Kempka. Erich* Box1FF33 23.

30 Evans, Richard (2005). *The Third Reich in Power*. (Penguin Group, New York). P30.

31 Shirer, William L. (1960). *The Rise and Fall of the Third Reich*. (Simon & Schuster, New York).

32 McDonough, Frank (1999). *Hitler and Nazi*

Germany. (Cambridge University Press, Cambridge & New York). P26.

33 Bendersky, Joseph W. (2007). *A Concise History of Nazi Germany*. (Rowman & Littlefield, Lanham).

34 Cook, Stan & Bender, Roger James (1994). *Leibstandarte SS Adolf Hitler: Uniforms, Organization, & History*. (James Bender Publishing, San Jose)

35 Kershaw, Ian (2008). *Hitler: A Biography*. (W. W. Norton & Company, New York). P312.

36 Beachy, Robert (2014). *Gay Berlin: Birthplace of a Modern Identity*. (Knopf Doubleday Publishing Group, New York). P160-161

37 Green, Jamison (2020). "History, Societal Attitudes, and Contexts". In Schechter, Loren S. (ed.). *Gender Confirmation Surgery: Principles and Techniques for an Emerging Field*. (Springer Nature Publishing, London & Berlin). P1–22.

38 Bracher, Karl Dietrich (1970). *The German Dictatorship*. Translated by Jean Steinberg. (Penguin Books; New York). P325.

39 1872, *Imperial Penal Code of Prussia*

40 "Paragraph 175". Holocaust Encyclopedia. *United States Holocaust Memorial Museum*.

41 Longerich, Peter (2011). *Heinrich Himmler: A Life*. (Oxford University Press, Oxford). P231.

42 Jamin, Jérôme (2014). "Cultural Marxism and the Radical Right". In Shekhovtsov, Anton &

Jackson, Paul (eds.). *The Post-War Anglo-American Far Right: A Special Relationship of Hate*. (Palgrave Macmillan, London). P84–103.

Jay, Martin (2010). "Dialectic of Counter-Enlightenment: The Frankfurt School as Scapegoat of the Lunatic Fringe". *Salmagundi*. Vol. 168/169. P30–40.

43 Giles, Geoffrey J. (2010). "The Persecution of Gay Men and Lesbians During the Third Reich". *The Routledge History of the Holocaust*. (Routledge, New York). P395.

44 Zinn, Alexander (2020) "'They are enemies of the state': The Nazi persecution of homosexuals 1933–1945". *Bulletin des Fritz Bauer Instituts*. (in German). P6–13.

45 Sutton, Katie (2012). ""We Too Deserve a Place in the Sun": The Politics of Transvestite Identity in Weimar Germany". *German Studies Review*. 35 (2). P348.

46 Newsome, William Jake (2022). *Pink Triangle Legacies: Coming Out in the Shadow of the Holocaust*. (Cornell University Press, Ithaca). P26-27.

47 Moser-Verrey, Monique (1991). "Les femmes du troisième Reich". *Recherches féministes*. 4 (2). P25–44.

CHAPTER FOUR

FIELD NOTES ON THE MATING HABITS OF THE MASTER RACE: THE MANSCAPE

You're reading this book, so I figure you know more or less what you're in for. Still, I'm going to take a moment here to warn you that this chapter will contain discussions of child abuse (including sexual abuse), incest, and pretty much anything else that can trigger somebody. You have been warned, but I encourage you to keep reading, as it's worth noting that queer Nazis are, arguably, some of the *least* sexually dysfunctional people on the far-right.

The conventional wisdom about events like 9/11 is that people can tell you exactly where they were and what they were doing when they got the news and experienced a moment of jarring personal trauma. For my part, I will never, until the day I die laughing, forget the first time that I saw the phrase "Hyperborea Is Your Sister's Womb." Where was I? In my suite of rooms near Miskatonic University, reading an ancient tome about... no, I'm kidding. It was in the cellars of the internet, of course. The characters in the meme are certainly appropriate to the message, I suppose! Here, feel free to take a look:

For those who don't enjoy digital self-harm, those are Andrew and Ashley (or "Leyley") Graves, the protagonists (?) of a niche, retro-style PC game called *The Grave of Andy and Leyley.* In it the player, as the titular siblings, murders and cannibalizes their way to Satanic, demon-fueled success. Oh, and this is germane to the meme: Andy and Leyley fuck each other's brains out, Lannister-style (or kill each other, based on the storyline you choose). (1) Hey, there's a Black Sun in the background of that meme and a swastika around Leyley's neck! Is the game pro-Nazi? No! It's just a very fucked up, niche, 8bit-style psychological horror game! This isn't a leftist meme taking the piss out of fascists—we don't use Esoteric Hiterlist symbols. This is a half-ironic encapsulation of a very real belief, expressed through the lens of a niche group within fascism with incredible power over the most violent elements within the movement. Buckle up.

“Hold up,” I can hear you say. “A fucked-up edgelord video game from Japan—that I can understand. But Nazis? And *what* is my sister’s *what*?”

Hyperborea! The mythical, ancient land of the prehistoric, high-tech, utopian civilization (?) of the primordial race of eight-foot Aryan giants who fathered the modern peoples of the capital-w White race! (2) “That sounds like some absolutely crazy bullshit,” you might reply. Yep! I wrote a whole book about it and other esoteric fascist beliefs! * Hyperborea is at least half-ironically believed in by all manner of neo-Nazis and Nazi-adjacent conspiracy theorists. As a literal place it is 100% believed in by the most googly-eyed and deeply down the rabbit hole among their ranks. To all of them, Hyperborea is thought of as at least a metaphor and myth based on kernels of ancient truth.

“Okay,” you could say, nodding. “But Hyperborea is in my sister’s *what* again, exactly?”

In 2024, a post by a fascist on 4Chan (but I repeat myself) went viral. The image attached to the post was, of course, art of Andy and Leyley. The post read, in part:

> People say “don’t fuck your sister, it will fuck up your genes” but actually it’s the opposite, and in this post I will explain why.

Ok, off to one *hell* of a start as far as posts go. Proceed.

> Let's start with the conventional view. Genes can break because of mutations. However normally if we have one family gene copy, the other healthy gene copy can compensate. This situation is known as a recessive gene because the healthy copy will "dominate" the unhealthy copy. Not all genetic diseases are recessive but it's the most common one [sic]. Now imagine if your dad had one healthy gene G and a very rare broken gene g. Your mom had two healthy genes...

I'm going to stop Doctor Science right there and point out that neither my mother nor father are type 1 (insulin-dependent) diabetics. Type 1 diabetes is genetic, so I'm good, right? Wrong. Both me and my little sister have it. It's a recessive, genetic disorder—and not even a rare one. It's one of the many reasons eugenics are bullshit that no actual geneticist (other than probably Richard Dawkins) supports. Where Doctor Science goes with his thesis is the meat of the unspeakable matter, however:

> Now imagine yourself fucking your cute sister. If the healthy genes combine then the broken gene has been fixed—success! [Ed.—No. As I pointed out above, recessive genes can run for multiple generations and not manifest for generations.] If the broken genes are

> passed on and the child has issues, then the child will be less able to pass the broken gene on! Partial success! ... This is why fucking your sister leads to better genes in the long term!

Incidentally, I should hire that asshole to write the first sentences of my chapters. That's another first sentence that really *grabs* the reader: "Now imagine yourself fucking your cute sister." No, creepy anon! I will not picture that, thank you very much!

Meanwhile, other corners of the vast and sweaty online fascist sexual unconscious have birthed other schemes to "fix sex." Some are busy promoting the conspiracy theory that "pornography addiction" is eating the West alive, the latest and most successful Jewish plot to sabotage good old-fashioned heterosexual monogamy. Masturbation, after all, thwarts the *Völkisch* goal of twelve to fourteen white kids per household, to serve the regime. (3) Others have deeper pathologies that *really* ought to make them a higher priority for organizations like the FBI on grounds of criminally predatory behavior (if the FBI weren't too busy hunting imaginary ANTIFA cells). (4) But hey, what Nazis? The Department of Justice has been busy not fighting fascist terror, but *removing reports* on right-wing domestic threats from the DoJ website (I'm sure that's nothing to worry about). (5)

If we're going to understand the roles and fate of sexual minorities within far-right spaces online (and off), it makes sense to start with what those sexual minorities are a deviation *from*: What are "normal" fascists up to when it comes to slap and tickle? If LGBTQIA+ fascists are a tiny minority who has never had real clout within the Fascist Internationale as I demonstrated last chapter, what then of the majority of fascists? What are they up to, when the lights go out? This isn't just for compare-and-contrast purposes. Some of the same dysfunctions that afflict sexual minorities in far-right spaces take luxurious root in the fertile, shitty hearts of hetero Nazis, too. If we understand the net background sexual weirdness of fascism, ** it helps us to understand how someone raised in an increasingly fascist media and cultural environment might turn out the way they do.

Allow your dear tour-clown to take you by the trembling elbow and lead you on a curated walk along the pathways of the fever swamp of neofascist sexuality in the 2020s. This is a two-chapter tour (♪a TWO-CHAPTER TOUUUUR♫), because we have a bit of ground to cover that hasn't received enough attention. At the end of the tour, the Great Egress will present a summary of one thing that is predictably, depressingly normal (for the right) about the Fascist Internationale: it's a roiling, filth-infested cesspit of homo-, trans, and queerphobia.

As forlorn and misguided as gay men's attempts at assimilation into National Socialism always turn out to be, the "trans tradwife," the Milo-esque modern homofascist, and other current 4Chan-poisoned queer Nazis may be even more misguided. It makes me wonder, when I read the self-hating screeds of trans fascists, if they know just what they're trying so desperately to assimilate *into*. I suspect not. Fascism is a dark, miserable place, and trying (and mostly failing) to join that club must be even *more* dark and miserable. These chapters also serve as a warning, though it will probably go unheeded. This is the fascist sexual milieu these outcasts *want to be a part of.*

Let's start with the Great Masculinity Crisis, shall we?

Are We Not Men?

This isn't a book primarily about patriarchy, although there are several excellent books along those lines which I'd recommend to anyone seeking to understand our world. I'd even recommend them to devout men's rights dingbats who want to sound less asinine when they talk about what feminists believe. *** That said, we can't really talk about fascism in any sense without talking about patriarchy and the reactionary conception of masculinity and men. (6) Given that this is a book about what fascism does to sex, and sex is what happens between 1-? people, all of whom have gender of some kind (even if it's none), talking about sexual issues always means talking about gender. In terms of our social reality, gender is largely defined by how it stands in affirmation of or contradiction of the patriarchal norm, (7) so it makes sense that it would be a perennial and divisive part of modern politics.

I say "modern politics" because before the last few centuries in law (and arguably the last century in fact), women were property. Just like goats, sheep, camels, or horses. That makes sense, since livestock was the currency usually exchanged in antiquity to unite two families in matrimony, the better to produce heirs, laborers, or both (as times and customs varied slightly). This has always been truer for BIPOC women (and still is) than their white sisters, (8) but the fact remains that even rich white women couldn't own property until 1842, and even then, only if they were married and had their husband's say-so. (9)

I'm old enough to remember when discussing facts like "women couldn't own property until recently" actually came as news to people, and shocking news at that. Who could believe what had been denied to women, and so recently: let alone what was still denied? Admittedly, the more reactionary people I'd mention it to didn't find it gross, necessarily. They'd just furrow their brows in what I mistook for irritation and grumble "that was thousands of years ago" (not true, it hasn't even been two centuries!). I took those furrows for irritation because I can't read minds and, despite the stuff I write, I remain remarkably optimistic about human nature most of the time. If I had been able to read minds, I'd have known that those proto-chuds hearing this in the 1990s were furrowing their brow in *frustration.* When they grumbled "that was thousands of years ago," it was them complaining that it's been far too long since women knew their place! Think I'm exaggerating?

Within my lifetime—which isn't even a full average human lifespan yet!—I've seen a rapid, alarming regression in male views of female autonomy and rights. Not just in the US, but worldwide as well. (10) This brave new world isn't being driven only by pockets of obnoxious Christian assholes who nobody likes. Those folks have ever been with us, grumping in the background. No, there is such a plague of regressive, childish views of women on the part of men that it is one of the aspects of the 2020s I find most shocking. I've been strapped down now, Ludovico-technique-style, and made to watch as *four generations* of men have been presented with the option to treat women like human beings. Instead, by and large we've acted like poisonous brutes instead.

Baby Boomer men (including prolific rape monsters like Donald Trump, Bill Clinton, Jefferey Epstein, etc.), Gen X men (including Louis CK, Neil Gaiman, Bryan Singer, Joe Rogan, etc.), Millennials (Andrew fucking Tate, Sneako, Myron Gaines, etc.): *all* of us have been exposed to feminist ideas and writing, meaning we've been given the choice to be good. *Every* one of us. Even the most Bible-sick, blighted, third generation homeschooled cult member probably snuck off and saw a Marvel movie at least once (and no, feminist allies, I'm not saying Marvel is a feminist cinematic universe, but most of the movies are "woke" enough to get the essential idea of girlbossing from, which is at least enough to point a mind in the right direction). None of us have any excuse.

To an extent, I don't hold Gen Z and Gen Alpha men equally responsible for their failure to learn these values— and they *have* failed, dismally (11)—as I do previous generations. One reason for that is that Gen X and my cohort (elder Millennials) have aggressively brainwashed younger men; much more aggressively than we were or could have been brainwashed ourselves. There were no "influencers" when we were growing up, let alone a "manosphere." We decided to take the creepy, selfish "pickup artist" ideas that barely survived the 1970s intact and sow them where they could truly thrive. That wasn't television, print, radio, or movies. Those were too busy pushing the more mainstream, John Wayne masculine-man ideal to bother overmuch with seedy sex shit, with the exception of print and VHS pornography, the inexplicably popular 1996 film shitshow *Swingers*, and the reason you know who Adam Carolla is: an at-the-time satirical-seeming meat-fest called *The Man Show*.

This is all a very roundabout way of introducing the following concept: the "masculinity crisis" that has been in the news for the last few elections is a manufactured crisis, not a real one, and not the first imaginary crisis to assail masculinity. (12) The most recent "crisis" has been ginned up as a reaction to certain events which we can point to directly. One was #MeToo, which led to an uptick in celebrity rapists getting their shit proverbially kicked in. This sparked a predictable, but still obnoxious, pushback from some men. (13) Another event was Hillary Clinton's run for President. No, I was not Team Hillary (I detest her more than almost any other modern Democrat). I thought she was an elitist, entitled jackass with a lot of the wrong kind of job experience and that too many people forget that she took point in helping the Iraq War happen. Even so, the Hillary vs. Trump contest really brought something ugly out in a lot of Americans. Her candidacy didn't create it, but brought it to the surface where it wasn't rephrased, prettied up, or euphemized away. The same thing happened in 2008 with Barack Obama and white America's relationship to Black people; the normally polite, country-club-racist sections of society fucking *werewolfed*, seemingly overnight.

All of these moments have something in common. They were moments when reactionaries tried to reframe equality as privilege, and treated their *own* privilege like a literally God-given right. Being asked to share an overabundance is treated like deprivation, and being asked to compete with other groups is treated like an unfair advantage given to those groups. Most importantly, being asked to *earn* respect or face the same discourtesy one routinely inflicts on others is treated as an attack. An elite group's attempts to retain privilege and promote bigotry is compared to the Civil Rights Movement.

Thus, using this same upside-down logic, when some encouraging things started happening for feminism in the late 1990s through the 2000s and the 2010s, it was treated as an attack on "manhood." Specifically, the way that boys were educated in public schools and by culture at large in the West throughout those years has been treated as an attack on masculinity. (14) Not a metaphorical attack: a *literal* attempt to emasculate Western men so that, as part of a grand conspiracy, they can be rendered serfs by women who would then throw themselves at the swarthy foreigners who'd cuck those men, impregnate the Rose of England (or the Cornflower of Kansas), and bring down capitalism, apple pie, and America. You've heard this absurd garbage before; the conspiracy is referred to as "the Great Replacement."

It was my exact cohort— Millennials and people

one to three years older than us— who turned this childish, shallow, silly, unsubstantial, frankly embarrassing conspiracy theory into the makings of a cultural tsunami of fascist radicalization. (15) Reality check; have little white boys ever, in America or any other white-majority nation or culture in history, grown up actually "being taught to hate themselves" for being little white boys? No. (16) What kind of monster would teach that to *any* child or *any* race? The answer to that is public education in America throughout history when dealing with Black children. (16) There has never been any sort of "conspiracy" to undermine the cultural majority, however. Likewise, has there ever been an attempt— *ever*—to brainwash and torture a straight kid into being gay? No. Not once. Did the Supreme Court recently re-legalize Gay Torture Camp? Yes, they did. (17)

In this perverse, inverted narrative, promoting women and girls in STEM fields in which they are usually underrepresented is an attack on masculinity. Teaching about women's contributions to the course of history is an attack on masculinity. Teaching consent culture to combat the likelihood of frats drugging women, pouring liquor into them, and raping them is *definitely* an attack on masculinity. (18) Rei Skywalker, a Star Wars heroine? The worst attack on masculinity since the invention of the cup check. More female protagonists, authors, gamers, Warhammer 40K players? YOU'RE RUINING THE FUCKING HOBBY! It's hardly surprising that queer people's representation in spaces traditionally monopolized by heteronormativity has also been viewed as an attack on both straight people and masculinity. Of course, "heteronormativity" is the type of word that draws guffaws when you pull it out in conversation with a member of the right, let alone the far-right. If you tried to explain water to a fish, they'd laugh the same way.

The "masculinity crisis" narrative as represented in far-right media goes something like this: our boys have been raised by a generation of radicalized leftist communists in education and popular culture who hate America. Either consciously or as useful idiots, these teachers serve the interests of Jews by forcing sex change surgery on little boys and making them write "being a white boy is a sin" on the board while the girls in class laugh at them and pelt them with rainbow butt plugs. When they turn on the TV, little boys are the villain of every show and little girls are the heroes. Same with movies. In these conditions, how can you expect a boy to become a man—a real man, a *really* real man— like our dying White nation needs?

Smash that like button if you agree and hit subscribe to learn how to fight this menace!

And that's *literally* what's fueling this. Andrew Tate, Joe Rogan, the entire Manosphere exists precisely because of and to perpetuate this farcically baseless panic. One researcher calls this "manufactured outrage and instructed victimhood... fueled by anti-feminist agendas," (19) which is the best encapsulation that I've ever read. This instructed victimhood, fascinatingly, has led to a very *real* (but different kind of) masculinity crisis in the West. It's not boys under attack for being boys. It's an environment in which toxic masculinity is touted as a virtue by vile pseudo-authority figures. Toxic masculinity has predictable consequences for men who suffer from it. Credulous or toxic men have encouraged boys to turn to figures that will feed them the same poison. This is indescribably irresponsible, especially when those boys face quite ordinary insecurities for anyone coming of age in the era of an omnidirectional panopticon of social media and an increasingly encroaching State. Not that there's much difference between the two these days: the Trump Reich has made it a top priority to expand that dystopian confluence. (20)

Even the phrase "toxic masculinity" has been used as a tool to trick men and boys. The far right treats the phrase "toxic masculinity" as if it's an actual condemnation of any and all masculinity. There are tiny schools of fringe feminist thought that adhere to this point of view, (21) but they certainly aren't the ones being taught or talked about in culture and education and never have been. These masculinist maggots refuse to engage with the term "toxic masculinity" in good faith as a critique of the most extreme, violent, and damaging expressions of the cultural construct of masculinity. The truth is that people like Andrew Tate pretend that women hate men to sell them video courses on how it wouldn't hurt if they were to pop their wife around a time or two every so often.

Here's the blunt, basic truth that Andrew Tate will obviously never admit: listening to him, and those like him, makes young men unfit to date and undesirable to others, both as a potential romantic partner and as a potential friend.

These "solutions" to the problems many young men face connecting with the opposite (or same) sex (22) are *causing the problems*. Of *course* you're going to be single in your twenties indefinitely if you've grown up believing that Andrew fucking Tate or Joe fucking Rogan know how to interact with other humans appropriately. It's as though figures like Tate are the snake oil salesmen of yore. They pull up to town in their wagon, claiming that they have a cure for throat and stomach pain. The actual cure is hydrofluoric acid labeled TOUGHEN UP, THROAT! A few people in town try it and complain to Dr. Tate. What's that? TOUGHTEN UP, THROAT! is causing you excruciating pain and tissue damage? You're just not drinking enough of it, you pussy! If you keep chugging that corrosive acid for long enough, that THROAT will TOUGHEN UP! As outlandish as my metaphor sounds, it's apter than you might think. There's an almost unbelievable level of cognitive dissonance at work in young right-wing men that I've been watching unfold in real time.

Presented with evidence that, with men shifting further right, more women are avoiding their company, (23) a one-man brain trust chimed in to this discourse with the following meme. This is a very smart, very likely prediction from Sam Costner (@samuel_costner), who says, "My prediction on the left/right gender divide IF young men hold the course."

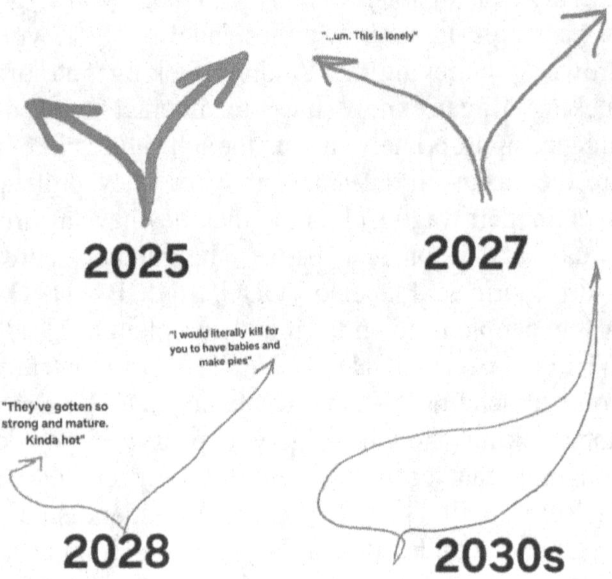

It's okay to laugh at Sam. Speaking personally, "They've gotten so strong and mature. Kinda hot" makes me giggle, but maybe that's because I know what these men are *actually* like: weak and childish. We can laugh, but this type of highly profitable ass-brained content has created a very real problem. Part of that problem is political. While some polling data shows a rightward shift in voting habits among young men, (24) a loss for the wretched shitbag Dems is not the political problem I'm talking about. Lonely men tend to drift toward the far-right, and that causes a cascading series of other societal problems. (25)

Major risks of this rightward shift include an

increased likelihood of what fascists themselves would label "degeneracy" in others, but which I'll just call an affinity for the extreme. Extreme politics don't just bring the expected political baggage: street fighting, tiki torch parades, hate crimes, or synagogue vandalism. Some of the spaces in which the far-right recruits these days are well off the beaten track by deliberate design. Even when members are recruited through more traditional or non-creepy ways, the price of entry to some of the most exciting (read: extreme and violent) fascist groups in the world is steeper than you think, and you don't pay it in Bitcoin.

Neo-Nazi Terror Organizations and Child Sexual Abuse Material (CSAM)

QAnon is not an overtly Nazi or neo-Nazi movement, although based on their core set of beliefs and cast of villains I would argue that they qualify as a fascist new religious movement (and I'm not alone). (26) Despite ostensibly being about freeing children from some sort of world (or intergalactic, it depends on whom you ask) trafficking ring, the QAnon new religious movement is closely associated with harming children through acts like kidnapping, bomb threats, etc., (27) but not necessarily with CSAM. I bring them up at the beginning of this section simply to prove that once you cross a certain threshold on the right, you're often required to pay a toll you might not even be aware of. You'll be asked to share space with, cover for, apologize or stand up for, and all too often aid and abet pedophiles. This is true, to a lesser but similar extent, in any power structure that encourages sexual secrecy—the Catholic Church, the USSR's Communist Party, the Nazi Party, the Reverend Jim Jones' People's Temple; the examples are practically endless. This is even true of QAnon, a movement ostensibly founded on an almost religious obsession with the evils of child exploitation and abuse. The road to the plague sewers of right-wing politics are sometimes paved with good intentions, but the outcomes are what matter in the end.

At a certain point in the development of QAnon the conspiracy cult was based out of 8kun (and is to this day, to an astonishing extent). (28) 8kun, a more extreme breakaway dark web board from 4Chan, has previously physically lived on servers located outside of international jurisdictions, but now is back on US soil. The site tends to switch host nations based on which way the political wind blows. (29) This now-you-see-us, now-you-don't server movement, coupled with the same anonymity that powers 4Chan, previously attracted a bustling marketplace of CSAM (30) that ran alongside—but separate from—the boards where Qanon did their thing. At a certain point researching Qanon for my previous book and this one, a chicken-and-the-egg question developed in my mind. Ponder it with me, if you dare.

Did QAnon start out obsessed with CSAM and child abuse and gravitate to 8kun out of some sick fascination? Or did rubbing up against the most fucked-up people on Planet Earth (the dark web creeps swapping pictures and videos of children being abused on 8kun) lead the cult to its apocalyptic fixations? Either way, it's a little like the local Catholic priest's living in an apartment over the only adult theater in town. It's weird, for an alleged moral crusader? Wait, scrap that. Adult theaters are treasured establishments in the communities lucky enough to host them. 8kun is a cesspit that shouldn't exist full of ruined human beings.

As I said, however, QAnon isn't closely associated with CSAM—they just so happen to have located their hub on a notorious CSAM site for years. So, let's talk about the price of entry into the most violent, secretive, and esoteric white supremacist and neo-Nazi groups online. Entry into such circles requires a more personal investment in CSAM, even if you aren't a practicing pedophile or excited in the least by the material. In fact, as far as I can tell from my research, the worse it is for a potential recruit to think about or witness CSAM, the better for the initiation process. I hope you liked my Jim Jones reference up top, because I'll be mentioning him a few times in this next bit as I discuss the State Socialist-founded practice of coerced self-recrimination. (31) It seems a bit ironic for these fascist commie-hating fucks but, well, the more you know about State Socialism, the less ironic it is.

Generally, forced self-incrimination or confession consists of a written confession or blackmail material coerced out of a person to be used against them in case of defection, as was the case with the Reverend Jim Jones making members of Peoples Temple sign documents claiming they'd molested their own children, been unfaithful to their spouses, were drug users, or whatever sick whim took Jones that day. (32) If a member turned on Jones, he'd produce the documents to discredit them. In the case of the USSR, it was usually a confession to crimes against the State one did not commit. In the case of hardcore neo-Nazi would-be revolutionaries, the self-compromise is much, much worse.

From a very excellent write-up of this phenomenon in *Vice:* (33)

> [In June of 2022], according to court documents, Jared Boyce crammed himself into the back of a U-Haul with his fellow members of Patriot Front, a white supremacist group, to protest an LGBTQ pride event in Idaho and slur attendees as "groomers." ...
>
> Once the group pulled up to the event, they were all promptly arrested and charged with conspiracy to commit a riot. Less than a month later, police seized Boyce's phone. While they weren't actively searching for illegal sexual material on it, they found 22 photos of child sexual abuse material, or CSAM. According to court documents, these photos "involve children from toddlers to prepubescents performing sexual acts on adults or other children, as well as images of children exposing their genitals." The 28-year-old had also, police found, sent a picture of his penis to a 16-year-old girl.

Let's note that Boyce was only sentenced to a year in

prison for a *lot* of incredibly incriminating material. Good thing for him he was busted for creeping on a minor twelve years his junior and possessing pictures of the sexual abuse of toddlers while residing in the great state of Idaho, former home of the Aryan Nations National Compound and current home of that compound's modern-day replacement. (31) What's that you ask? Am I saying that a man of color might have done more poorly in the Idaho courts were he in Boyce's shoes? Yes, I fucking am. But wait, there's more— this wasn't just *one* creepy member of Patriot Front. The article goes on to list dozens of cases involving the distribution of CSAM (and even the manufacturing of it by some neo-Nazis). What gives?

Blackmail, that's what gives. *Vice* goes on to helpfully explain the practice of forced self-incrimination as practiced by these groups:

> There is reason to think, though, that in at least some circles [CSAM] serves as an integral part of initiation into some of the most extreme and fringe corners of neo-Nazism, with the taboo material desensitizing recruits to a point of no return and binding them to others who know—and share—their secret.

We then get another peek into the fetid, secret life of an organization I've written about before: (34) Satan-worshiping neo-Nazi terror cult the Order of Nine Angles.

While the group has undoubtedly had a large impact on the current far right, it's intentionally sensationalistic and obtuse in a way that makes reporting on it incredibly difficult. In an explainer about the group, the Institute for Strategic Dialogue writes "several O9A texts promote rape and pedophilia as a way to transgress against civilized norms." *[Note: in O9A's religious theory and practice, this transgression of all societal norms is known as 'the Sinister Path.' If you want to know more, check out my previous nonfiction title Black Sunrise on Piss Earth: Fascism and Nihilism in the 21st Century Occult, available through this publisher.]*

"O9A followers are more likely than other neo-fascists to be found with this sort of material because of their doctrinal willingness to embrace taboo, immoral, and violent practices," an analyst for the Institute for Strategic Dialogue told VICE News—they did not want their name used out of fear of retaliation due to the extreme nature of the group. "While some of these practices have ritual purposes, others simply desensitize practitioners to suffering and violence in a way that creates rigid points of no

> return. There are many opportunities to back out of participating in a violent extremist group or movement, but there is a threshold of trauma, both received and inflicted, after which those opportunities all but stop."

Who's afraid of O9A? Evidently, that unnamed source with the Institute for Strategic Dialogues. O9A's taste for CSAM lines up nicely with what I described as their "uncritical antinomianism," which is a fancy way of saying that they always do what society thinks is evil as a matter of religious doctrine, without bothering to stop and think about whether that taboo is rational or not. It's essentially a form of oppositional defiance as religious fundamentalism, and the results are pretty much what you'd expect. Yet, for a bunch of CSAM-enjoying, Satan-worshiping pedophiles, they are *astonishingly* popular with some sections of the "restore Western Civilization" right! They've been involved with neo-Nazi terror groups like Atomwaffen SS, the 764 Network, and others. It's not just O9A, however! *Vice* continues:

> [The widespread nature of this phenomenon] was evident in Germany recently after the country made the decision to kill Frankfurt police's tactical team after it was then found that over 20 officers in the unit were engaging in far-right chats where they shared neo-Nazi imagery. The probe into the unit came

> after one 38-year-old member was found to be involved in a massive CSAM ring and authorities found evidence of the racist chats while investigating his phone.

Police, incidentally, have a long, sordid history of giving aid and comfort to white supremacists and neo-Nazis. (35) Good thing those are the good guys, the ones on the correct side of that fabled Thin Blue Line, right?

There are many possible explanations for this. First, there's the O9A/antinomian explanation. If you've already done *one* thing that the compassionate, Sesame Street society we like to think of as our best, most tolerant version of a country considers "the worst things you can do"— become a Nazi and call for violence, genocide, and hate—why not do the *other* thing society deems just as bad? Why not commit rape (like Andrew Hazelton, a member of neo-Nazi organization NSC-131, who raped a 10-year-old child)? Why not commit murder (like Wade-Michael Page, James Alex Fields Jr., Brandon Clint Russel, or the faceless, forgettable, but numberless horde or neo-Nazis who commit murder)? And, hell, while you're at it, why not enjoy some CSAM if that's to your disgusting taste?

But *why* would it be to these people's disgusting taste? Why is there such a significant overlap between fascists and those who victimize children? I have a theory regarding why sex creeps might be more prominent on the right, especially the far-right. It doesn't just apply to fascists, either, but the political right more broadly. The fellow whose story helped me distill and crystalize my thoughts on this matter isn't the type you'd find worshiping Satan with O9A. In fact, he made a career out of being the self-described "Ten Commandments Judge," although I'd wager it's been a while since you've heard about him, if you ever followed his career.

Sing, muse, of Roy Moore, Flip Benham, and the search for chaste maidens.

Putting The 'Cult' In Purity Culture

Roy Moore, for the mercifully uninitiated, is an Alabama dipshit (recognized globally as one of the finest varieties of dipshit on the market—ask for them by name!). He served as an Alabama Supreme Court justice, which is an elected position, for years before trotting forward on his hind legs to run for an open Alabama Senate seat in a 2017 special election. Moore's opponent was a vaguely non-Republican Democrat named Doug Jones, but Jones is unimportant to the story here.

What *is* important are allegations that came out against Roy Moore during that race. It seems like ever since Bill Clinton served his second term, shitty white southern men with sexual skeletons in their closets have felt invincible. Few realize that it was a combination of the right time (the freewheeling, libertine 1990s) and the right place (Arkansas, whose rape culture is distinct from that of Alabama) which let Clinton get away with assaulting women. 2017 in

Alabama was definitely *not* the 1990s in Arkansas. Very soon, all of Roy Moore's skeletons came prancing out of the proverbial closet in a veritable kick line.

It turns out that back in the late 1970s, Roy Moore roamed the cursed earth of Alabama in search of prey. What was Yung Roy up to? Why, using his credentials as a 30-something-year-old assistant DA to try to pick up underage girls, one as young as 14 at the time. (36) When questioned about this questionable behavior Moore denied everything, despite evidence including his signature on an at-the-time young girl's yearbook. Signing a young girl's yearbook was a weird move for a 30-something DA with no ordinary fucking reason to do that. (37) As such evidence of his past behavior emerged, Moore began to crater in the polls leading up to the race and started to shed donors left and right. One of Moore's close supporters, a pastor named Flip Benham, emerged with a defense that struck me like a thunderbolt. For me, it was like Flip's words were the secret key that unlocked all the discourse that would later come along regarding "body count," marrying young, the tradwife lifestyle, and so forth. Here was Flip's defense for Roy hitting on a 14-year-old girl:

> Judge Roy Moore graduated from West Point and then went on into the service, served in Vietnam and then came back and was in law school. All of the ladies, or many of the ladies that he possibly could have married, were not available then, they were already married, maybe,

> somewhere. The lady that he's married to now, Ms. Kayla, is a younger woman. He did that because there is something about a purity [sic] of a young woman, there is something that is good, that's true, that's straight and he looked for that. (38)

It has emerged since then that Moore's taste for "young girls" (shades of Trump talking about Jeffrey Epstein) was well known to Alabamans, *including the fucking police* who knew that Moore cruised for girls *at high school football games* as an adult man. Did the cops do anything? Hell no, Moore was Assistant DA! They "sir, yes sir"-ed that pedophile and never would have dreamed of considering him a sex criminal. In the memorable words of retired detective Faye Gray, a 37-year veteran of the Gadsden police, "we were also told to make sure he didn't hang around the cheerleaders." (39) To protect and serve, indeed!

Time for a little bit of full disclosure here on my part: purity culture completely grosses me out. I have never, in my life, had sex with a virgin and I find the very idea sort of off-putting. The male impulse to deflower a virgin (40) has absolutely never made sense to me even one time in my entire fucking life. Make no mistake, when Flip (which is a dog's name, not a person's) says that Roy Moore was looking for purity, truth, good, and straightness, what all of that is code for is "white virgin." It's honestly that simple and that disgusting. While Lord Roy of House Moore was galloping around Alabama trying to find a constitutional justification for taking the right of *jus primae noctis* with the virignal brides of newly married country galloots and yoeman farmers, his cohorts in the less Christed-up quadrants of the Fascist Internationale have also been hard at work on the same predatory pursuit.

The fetishization of supposed sexual "purity" has only ever had ruinous consequences. In sex ed it leads to disease, pregnancy, and other preventable outcomes. (Yes, I just called teen pregnancy a "preventable outcome" and I'm all for abortion, too.) (41) It always has. Fun piece of family history; during some of the hot years of the HIV/AIDS crisis in the 80s and 90s, my beloved grandparents on my mother's side became HIV/AIDS counsellors and sex education specialists. My grandma used to tote around a gunny sack of condoms and toss them at everyone she could. She was a wonderful woman, as was my grandfather, who moved from a career in the military to retirement then a second career spent doing good works. Even some members of the Greatest Generation did not have their heads up their asses about purity culture. Boomers, Gen X, Millennials, and younger folks have no excuse.

In our culture, the fixation on "purity" has given America a national Maddona/whore complex, although I'd add a third role. Women can be sacred virgins, worthless harlots, or servile tradwives (42) whose province is the mommyblog and the production of a household full of white children and probably baked goods. Maybe yarn, depending on how cottagecore the tradwife gets. If the husband takes up P90X and a carnivore diet, expect the wife to get into yarn.

One obvious result of purity culture is the normalization of pedeophilia ("ephebophilia," if you want to get all 4Chan about it, or attraction to adolescent girls instead of children—still gross, still unjustifiable on the grounds that non-adults cannot consent). I was presented with an extraordinarily surreal example of this on my favorite fascist slurry trough these days, Twitter, where a remarkable man came to everyone's attention and became the internet's main character for a day or two.

The character in question is (still, as of right now!) a professor of economics at George Mason University and an incredibly influential blogger who started as a "libertarian" and now has gone full fascist. *** Here's Professor Tyler Cowen talking about his desire to "see a virgin on-screen:"

My Favorite Actress Is Not Human

Tilly Norwood doesn't need a hairstylist, has no regrettable posts, and if you wish to see a virgin on-screen, this is one of your better chances. That's because she's AI.

"NOT EVERYONE IS HAPPY ABOUT THIS GORGEOUS INNOVATION," WRITES TYLER COWEN. (@TILLYNORWOOD VIA INSTAGRAM)

By Tyler Cowen

PREVIEW

Lest you think that's Tyler's only dip into the territory of desifing to use his XXX-ray vision to spot maidensheads, he's been writing on the subject since 2009. He's 63 years old, by the way:

MARGINALREVOLUTION

Where to find virgins: go to urban churches

by Tyler Cowen *September 24, 2009 at 7:26 am in* Education

The Man Who Would be Thursday opines:

> ...look for someone at
> a church in an urban area. For example, evangelicals in downtown
> Toronto are there because they really believe, while those in rural
> Alberta perhaps less so.

He also adds (and explains why):

> ...find yourself a cute but not spectacular 22 year old with a bachelor's degree.

P.S. The biggest indicator that a girl is a virgin is her insistence that she wants a guy who is a virgin himself.

Hat tip goes to Robin Hanson, who discusses Thursday more generally.

22 Comments

marginalrevolution.com

As Roy Moore's wingman Flip put it, "there is something about a purity of a young woman, there is something that is good, that's true, that's straight," and I have no doubt Tyler Cowen is drooling over just those qualities whenever he can: both on-screen and, I'd wager, at any middle or high schools within a few square miles of his primary residence. The far right is, on the one hand, perversely libidinal: see Jesse Watters calling Stephen Miller a "sexual matador" on Fox News in September 2024, and the title resurfacing on Fox in September 2025, for example. Libidinal not just in the sense of horny, for those new to the theory of Libidinal Economy, but representative of repressed desires whose fulfillment is sought out in misdirected ways. Through mechanisms of political power and capital accumulation, for example. On the other hand, the right is also sick with woman-hatred, and that even applies to right-wing women. (43) Purity culture is—and always has been—undershot with a deep vein of violence and threat.

Purity culture is also part of rape culture. (44) Specifically, purity culture promotes the idea that by dressing certain ways, acting certain ways, having certain beliefs, being of certain races or sexual orientations, etc., women are "asking for rape." This isn't just an American sense of entitlement to others' bodies on the part of men— *god* is it not just Americans. It's universal and despicable. (45) How can it be both, you ask? Once upon a time, people used to beat children to death in public streets or sell them into slavery. Those practices were (and are) both universal and despicable, and still exist, albeit not on the scale tha they once did.

If the objectifictation and sexualization of adult women by capital in the West has had the profound effect that both conservatives and feminists think it has (and I don't disagree), that doesn't leave many madonnas fit for marriage and child-rearing as potential tradwives, does it? How does our society treat women who are "unfit to marry," but marry regardless? This was exemplified in the very gross outrage over the wedding of Riley Reid.

Riley Reid is the screen name of an adult film actress— a prolific, well-known adult film star, in fact. Many people reading this probably know her work, even if they won't admit it (it's just between you and me, tender reader, and I won't judge you). Some time in the early 2020s (accounts differ but the generally accepted year is 2021), Riley Reid married her partner Pasha Petkuns. The marriage went viral (a few times), and each time it did, it garnered attention for the same reason: "Can you *believe* this shit?! What kind of *CUCK* would want a *WHORE* like her! Bro, look at this scene where Riley fucks a bunch of Black dudes! You want to wife *THAT* up? *CUCK*." The outrage went so far that some jackass who goes by the name of Dr. Clown World online † started a petition-cum-movement to annul the marriage, which indicates to me how little the good doctor understands about how marriage works. (46)

Utterly disgusting. Call me a liberated soul if you must, but I don't give a tin shit what someone does for a living unless it's *actually* unethical (for example, police officers and judges). If Riley Reid had worked for, say, Raytheon or Turning Point USA, I would have wished her nothing but a happy visit to Orem, Utah. However, as far as I know Riley Reid has only ever done good works; fucking on camera for money so horny strangers can crank it. She gives (or gave) the world the gift of orgasms! And, yes, arguably the problematic continuation of fantasies that degrade women and decenter their personhood, but I'd argue that fucking on camera for money (or just fucking for money— any kind of sex work, really) is more moral than what 55% of people do for a living.

This is where the Manosphere discourse of "body count" comes in. Body count is slang among the worst people you know for how many people a person has had sex with. Here's how out of touch with the insecure little snowflakes coming of age as young men these days *I* am. When I first heard the phrase "body count," I thought it referred to the number of abortions a woman had received: *and I was still at a loss as to why it was anybody's fucking business, or why anyone would care about that in a romantic partner*. How did the mainstreaming of such a fetid, trifling conern come about? The culture that's been indoctrinating young men, that's how. As their fathers freak out about a "masculinity crisis" that is self-produced and fall victim to a "male loneliness epidemic" of their own making, these young men are all too often left to learn the lessons of masculinity from the least trustworthy source possible: right-wing, imsogynistic influencers.

Dehumanizing and devaluing women, refusing to listen to their conerns, dismissing them, arguing about what "body count" is acceptable, outdoing previous generations in your infantile fixations and name-calling— all of these are actions that will ensure a man remains lonely in 2026. Hell, they'll keep him single in *2050*. No matter how much American fascism tries to turn back the clock, even women within the fascist movement show surprising signs of self-determination when push comes to shove (47). While *public* disagreements with the household patriarch might not be countenanced, not all is as it seems behind the scenes—even within those supposed bastions of white virtue, the neo-Nazi community.

Nazis tend to beat the shit out of those they perceive as having nontraditional family values, when all too often the state of their own family and "moral" life is abysmal. As I pointed out in the last chapter, the ideology driving these dipshits is centered on an austere, almost monkish (or cultish) dedication to The Cause— and that cause includes having children, in wedlock, with people one is married to and who are of the same race, religion, and creed. That creed, of course, is the brilliance of Adolf Hitler, the superiority of the white "race," and an arcane prophecy of an gibbous Southern rising bneath the banner of the elder god Y'all.

Speaking of southern risings, let's get to the weirdest shit in the far right mainstream; a thing well outside the scope of patriarchy or toxic masculinity. I would be doing my readers a disservice by confining a description of the modern hetero right to just one chapter. Buckle up for two scoops of whoop † and one more loop around the rollercoaster of ambient far right and National Socialist sexual baggage and gaggage; fixations which have poisoned the atmosphere of sexual discourse and produced multiple crops of terrible right wing men, women, and closeted enbies.

* *Black Sunrise on Piss Earth: Nihilism, Fascism, and the 21st Century Occult* by known miscreant Charles R. Bernard, available from this fine press (Gutter Mystic, Austin); Chapter Seven.

** When I say "sexually weird," I don't mean kinky. I am robustly pro-kink. I'm referring to the tangled web of politicized, racialized, and hierarchical meaning that fascists attach to sex, and their utter inability to live up to even the most basic standards of consent and decency.

Examples include:

Bates, Laura *Men Who Hate Women*

Du Mez, Kristen Kobes *Jesus and John Wayne*

hooks, bell *The Will to Change*

Serano, Julia *Whipping Girl*

*** Cowen writes for *The Free Press*, a publication whose headline as I write these words today is "Inside Harmeet Dhillon's Civil Rights Revolution: From fighting DEI to suing blue states, Harmeet Dhillon is remaking civil-rights law in the age of MAGA." Another hard-hitting article? "Will Trump End the War in Ukraine Next?"

† I warned you. I will take every single opportunity in these pages for Juggin'.

1 Spindler, Emily (November 24, 2023). "Cannibalism Is Somehow Only The Second Worst Thing You Can Do In The Coffin Of Andy And Leyley". *Kotaku Australia*.

2 Godwin, Joscelyn (1996). *Arktos: The Polar Myth in Science, Symbolism, and Nazi Survival*. (Adventures Unlimited Press, Kempton). Chs 5- 6,

10.

3 Crawford, Blyth (2022). “Sleeping with the Enemy: Sex, Sexuality and Antisemitism in the Extreme Right”. *International Centre for the Study of Radicalization and Political Violence.*

4 Terrell, Laura (2/16/2025). “GRAPHIC: University student credited for exposing neo-Nazi child pornography ring, officials say”. *WDBJ7.*

5 Gedeon, Joseph (9/17/2025). “US justice department removes study finding far-right extremists commit ‘far more’ violence: Report finding rightwing extremists have killed more Americans than other domestic terrorist groups vanished from DoJ website”. *The Guardian.*

6 Snyder, Timothy (4/20/2017). “Don't underestimate the harm 'brittle masculinity' can do to the world”. *The Guardian.*

Tebaldi, Catherine & Burnett, Scott (1/18/2025). “The Science of Desire Beauty, Masculinity, and Ideology on the Far Right”. *Journal of Right-Wing Studies.* (2) 2.

7 Butler, Judith (10/23/2021). “Why is the idea of ‘gender’ provoking backlash the world over?” *The Guardian*:

> For instance, they object to “gender” because it putatively denies biological sex or because it undermines the natural or divine character of the heteronormative family.

8 Posey, Brianne M. (2023). “Reproductive

slavery: Historical and present-day discussions of the Black female body as a condition of confinement". *Women's Studies International Forum.* (98) May/Juune.

9 Baer, Judith A. & Goldstein, Leslie Friedman (2006). *The Constitutional and Legal Rights of Women: Cases in Law and Social Change* (3rd ed.). (Oxford University Press, Oxford). P264.

10 Farrell, Noreen (7/16/2025). "How Trump Gave America License to Roll Back Women's Equality – And How We Take It Back". *Ms. Magazine*.

Brechenmacher, Saskia (6/5/2025). "The New Global Struggle Over Gender, Rights, and Family Values". *Carnegie Endowment for International Peace*.

11 McIntire, Lynnette (2025). "Messages of Misogyny on the Rise–and Boys are Listening". *Global Rights for Women.*

Blake, Suzanne (6/12/2025). "Is Feminism Losing With Young Men? Large Majority Say Men Should Be on Top". *Newsweek.*

Silverman, Rosa (2/1/2024). "The Gen Z gender gap: why young men are turning their backs on feminism". *The Telegraph.*

12 Roberts, Steven (6/30/2025). "The crisis that always is, but never was: A brief reflection on 150 years of panic about men, masculinity and social change". *Monash Lens*. Monash University.

Gasda, Matthew (2025). "Masculinity at the

End of History". *American Affairs*. (9) 3.

> "The cliché of American masculinity, widely disseminated in the academy, is that masculinity is in a crisis. This is the exact inverse of the truth. Masculinity is desperate for a crisis."

13 Alptraum, Lux (6/3/2025). "Was the #MeToo Backlash Inevitable?" *DAME Magazine*.

Grady, Constance (2/3/2022). "The mounting, undeniable Me Too backlash: How Susan Faludi's feminist classic predicted this moment." *Vox*.

14 Sigilliato Serena (1/27/2019). "Rejecting Toxic Masculinity Isn't an Attack on Men". *Public Discourse*.

Ferguson, Christopher J. (2023). "The American Psychological Association's practice guidelines for men and boys: Are they hurting rather than helping male mental wellness?". *New Ideas in Psychology*. Vol. 68.

15 Botto, M., & Gottzén, L. (2023). "Swallowing and spitting out the red pill: young men, vulnerability, and radicalization pathways in the manosphere". *Journal of Gender Studies*. 33 (5).

16 Wang, Francis Kai-Hwa (12/27/2021). 'You don't teach prejudice by discussing its existence.' How to talk to children about race and discrimination." *PBS News*.

16 Polos JA, et. al. (2022) "Structural racism in school contexts and adolescent depression: Development of new indices for the National

Longitudinal Study of Adolescent to Adult Health and beyond". *Social Sciences and Medicine Population Health*. Vol. 19, September.

Weir, Kirsten (2016). "Inequality at school: What's behind the racial disparity in our education system?" *Monitor of Psychology*. (47) 10. P42.

Garvey, Laquan (4/11/2019). "'I Hate Myself': A Look Into Internalized Racism Among Black College Students". *Binghamton University Undergraduate Journal*. (5) 1.

17 Totenberg, Nina (10/7/2025). "Supreme Court seems highly doubtful of limits on conversion therapy for minors". *NPR*.

Staff. (2020). "It's Torture Not Therapy: A Global Overview of Conversion Therapy, Practices, Perpetrators, and the Role of States". *International Rehabilitation Council for Torture Victims: Thematic Report*.

18 Tolentino, Jia (11/14/2024). "A New Rallying Cry For the Irony-Poisoned Right: It took less than twenty-four hours after Trump's reelection for young men to take up a slogan that could define the coming era of gendered regression: 'Your body, my choice.'" *The New Yorker*.

Duffy, Claire (11/13/2024). "'Your body, my choice': Attacks on women surge on social media following election". *CNN*.

McCord, Kate (11/22/2024). "'Your Body, My Choice' and the Danger of a Growing Manosphere". *Virginia Sexual and Domestic Violence Action Alliance*.

19 Roberts, Steven et. al. (2025). "Beyond the Clickbait: Analysing the Masculinist Ideology in Andrew Tate's Online Written Discourses". *Cultural Sociology*. 0 (0).

Roberts, Steven et. a. (2025). "'Adolescence', manufactured outrage and instructed victimhood: How the discourse on boys' alienation is fuelled by anti-feminist agendas". *European Journal of Cultural Studies*. September 2025.

20 Lewison-Waldman, Rachel et. al. (1/7/2022). "Social Media Surveillance by the U.S. Government". *Brennan Center for Justice*.

Hsu, Jeremy (5/5/2025). "US government is using AI for unprecedented social media surveillance: Under the Trump administration, multiple US government agencies are using AI and other tools to broadly track the social media of tourists and immigrants – and potentially to watch US citizens as well". *New Scientist*.

21 Greyson (2/22/2022). "Let's Talk About Bæddels: A comperehensive retrospective on Tumblr's movement to make gender essentialism 'trans-friendly.'" *Medium*.

Penner, James (2011). *Pinks, Pansies, and Punks: The Rhetoric of Masculinity in American Literary Culture*. (Indiana University Press, Bloomington). P232.

22 Survey Center Staff (10/31/2024). "Why Young People Feel Misunderstood By the Opposite Sex". *Survey Center on American Life*.

Our most recent survey revealed that only

> 42 percent of young men believe young women understand the problems men face in American society. Similarly, a majority (72 percent) of young women feel young men don't understand their struggles.

23 Trepany, Charles (7/17/2025). "Gen Z men, women have a deep political divide. It's made dating a nightmare". *USA Today*.

Moore, Elena (5/22/2025). "Majority of Gen Z swipe left on dating people with opposite political views". *NPR*.

24 Vakil, Caroline (9/21/2025). "Gen Z voter data shows warning signs for Democrats". *The Hill*.

25 Peterson, Loney (2025). "Loneliness is positively associated with populist radical right support". *Social Science & Medicine*. (360) February.

26 Monacelli, Steven (6/9/2021). "The Christofascism of QAnon: Steven Monacelli, who attended the 'Qonference' of the paranoid conspiracy theory in Dallas earlier this month, fears the quasi-religious movement might not die out without a fight". *Byline Times*.

Conner, Christopher (2023). "QAnon, authoritarianism, and conspiracy within American alternative spiritual spaces." *Frontiers in Sociology*. (June 2023)

27 Sleven, Colleen (8/26/2022). "Colorado mom guilty of Qanon kidnapping conspiracy". *Associated Press*.

Staff. (5/10/2019). "QAnon conspiracy theory

on James Comey shuts school festival". *BBC News*.

Staff (4/2/2021). "How a Custody Fight Plus QAnon Turned Deadly". *Wall Street Journal*.

Pierce, Scott D. (10/6/2020). "Utah woman who fled state with her 6-year-old son is facing felony charge". *The Salt Lake Tribune*.

Hinnant, John (10/5/2021). "French child kidnap plot shows global sway of QAnon style". *AP News*.

28 Gabbatt, Adam (6/27/2022). "QAnon's 'Q' re-emerges on far-right message board after two years of silence: Cryptic posts on 8kun ask 'Shall we play a game once more?' and 'Are you ready to serve your country again?'." *The Guardian*.

Francescani, Chris (9/22/2020). "The men behind Qanon: Experts and researchers said the key to 'Q' is hiding in plain sight." *ABC News*.

29 Robertson, Adi (8/5/2019). "8chan goes dark after hardware provider discontinues service". *The Verge*.

Gallagher, Sean (11/5/2019). "Breaking the law: How 8chan (or '8kun') got (briefly) back online". *Ars Technica*.

Brennan, David (March 19, 2019). "4chan, 8chan, LiveLeak and Others Blocked by Australian Internet Companies over Mosque Massacre Video". *Newsweek*.

30 Dewey, Caitlin (1/13/2015). "This is what happens when you create an online community without any rules". *The Washington Post*.

O'Neill, Patrick Howell (11/17/2014). "8chan, the central hive of Gamergate, is also an active pedophile network". *The Daily Dot*.

31 Rogovin, Vadim Z. (1998). *1937: Stalin's Year of Terror*. (Mehring Books, Oak park). P17, 23,

Deutscher, Isaac (5 January 2015). *The Prophet: The Life of Leon Trotsky*. Verso Books, London). P1370.

Findlay, Mark (1989). "Show Trials in China: After Tiananmen Square". *Journal of Law and Society*. 16 (3): P352–359.

Staff. (12/25/2009). "Chinese dissident Liu Xiaobo jailed for subversion". *BBC News*.

Crampton, R. J. (1997), *Eastern Europe in the twentieth century and after*, (Routledge, Abingdon-on-Thames). P262.

32 Kennedy, Lesley "Inside Jonestown: How Jim Jones Trapped Followers and Forced 'Suicides': The over 900 deaths in Guyana under cult leader Jim Jones were more mass murder than suicide." *History.com*.

Reiterman, Tom; Jacobs, John (1982). *Raven: The Untold Story of Rev. Jim Jones and His People*. (E.P. Dutton, Boston). P167.

33 Lamoureux, Mack (7/20/2023). "Why Do Neo-Nazis Keep Getting Arrested For Child Sexual Abuse Material?" *Vice*.

34 Bernard, Charles R. (2024). *Black Sunrise on Piss Earth: Nihilism, Fascism, and the 21st Century Occult*. (Gutter Mystic Press, Austin). Ch. 7.

35 Harte, Julia & Ulmer, Alexander (5/6/2022). "U.S. police trainers with far-right ties are teaching hundreds of cops". *Reuters*.

German, Mike (9/1/2020). "White Supremacist Links to Law Enforcement Are an Urgent Concern". *Brennan Center for Justice*.

Davies, David Martin (1/6/2025). "White supremacists with a badge". *Texas Public Radio*.

Levin, Sam (1/16/2021). "US Capitol riot: police have long history of aiding neo-Nazis and extremists". *The Guardian*.

36 McCrummen, Stephanie et. al. (11/9/2017). "Woman says Roy Moore initiated sexual encounter when she was 14, he was 32". *The Washington Post*.

Tillett, Emily (11/13/2017). "New accuser steps forward in Roy Moore case". *CBS News*.

37 Chandler, Kim (12/8/2017). "Expert confirms Roy Moore's signature in accuser's 1977 yearbook". *KTVU Fox 2*.

Staff. (12/8/2017). "Expert concludes Roy Moore wrote disputed entry in accuser's yearbook, lawyer says". *WESH 2*.

38 Taylor, Jeff (11/23/2017). "While defending Roy Moore, preacher Flip Benham invites speculation about his own past". *QNotesCarolinas*.

39 Elizalde, Elizabeth (11/21/2017). "We were also told to make sure he didn't hang around the cheerleaders'". *The Seattle Times*.

40 Richardson, Jon (2023). "Meta-analytical

evidence that males prefer virgin females". *Ecology Letters*. 27(1).

Nikirashidi, Fatemeh et. al. (2019). "A study on association of premarital attitude toward intact hymen in new grooms: A cross-sectional study". *Journal of Education and Health Promotion*. (March 2019)

41 Kohler, Pamela et. al. (2008). "Abstinence-Only and Comprehensive Sex Education and the Initiation of Sexual Activity and Teen Pregnancy". *Journal of Adolescent Health*. (42) 4. P344-351.

Staff. (8/22/2017). "Abstinence-Only Education Is a Failure: Two new papers highlight the scientific and ethical shortcomings of the abstinence-only-until-marriage approach." *Mailman School of Public Health*. Columbia University.

42 Ro, Christine (1/19/2021). "Why do we still distrust women leaders?" *BBC*.

L'Erving, Christy et. al. (2022). "An Intersectional Analysis of Women's Social Role Engagement and Mental Health". *Journal of Marriage and Family*. 84 (5). P1387-1407.

43 Weiss, Phelia et. al. (2024). "A narrow gateway from misogyny to the far right: empirical evidence for social media exposure effects". *Information, Communication, and Society*. P1-19.

Evreeva, Maria et. al. (2024). "Internalized Misogyny: The Patriarchy Inside Our Minds". *Journal of Integrated Social Scientists*. 14 (1). P82-108.

44 Graff, E.J. (1/4/2013). "Purity Culture Is Rape

Culture". *The American Prospect*.

Owens, Bretlyn C. et. al. (2020). "The Relationship between Purity Culture and Rape Myth Acceptance". *Journal of Psychology and Theology*. 49 (4). P405-418.

45 Shahid, Rudabeh et. al. (1/26/2021). "Understanding 'rape culture' in Bangladesh, India, & Pakistan". *SouthAsiaSource*.

John, Tara (3/6/2019). "Denmark has a 'pervasive rape culture,' says Amnesty International". *CNN*.

Hill, Mathew et. al. (2/2/2021). "'Their goal is to destroy everyone': Uighur camp detainees allege systematic rape". *CNN*.

Luo, Tsun-Yin (2000). "'Marrying my rapist?!' The cultural trauma among Chinese rape survivors". *Gender & Society*. 14 (4). P581-597.

Kol'tsova, Maria (9/15/2022). "Has Russia's Toxic Masculinity Fuelled War Crimes?" *Global Campus on Human Rights*.

46 Philosophy Bear (10/12/2024). "(Extremely NSFW) The movement to annul the marriage of Riley Reid". *Substack*.

47 Darby, Seward (2020). *Sisters in Hate: American Women on the Front Lines of White Nationalism*. (Little, Brown and Company, New York City). Extensive sections.

CHAPTER FIVE

FIELD NOTES ON THE MATING HABITS OF THE MASTER RACE: I THINK WE'RE ALONE NOW

I hope I left you hanging (or well-hung) at the close of last chapter! In it, we reviewed one Nazi's plan to purify the family genes through "fucking [his] smoking hot sister" and gelding the undesirable offspring, discussed the fictional and real masculinity crises besetting men in broad outlines, discussed the way the Manosphere is isolating young men (although I'll go into more depth on that here), and went over the connections between fascism, purity culture, rape culture, and pedophilia.

Rough ride, huh? Well I hope you saved the good drugs, because while we won't be discussing harm to children in this chapter, we *will* be discussing some weird, distasteful topics (to some), so be advised that we'll be dealing with sexual assault, misogyny, pornography, masturbation, "masculinism," and the solitude and personal dysfunctions which drive some men to do unconscionable things or die deaths of despair. We'll also talk about the women who love these men, participate in anti-feminist and anti-woman spaces, and seem more than happy to live in a gilded cage of sorts, provided they get access, clout, and underlings.

Full disclosure of my own biases and who I am in the midst of this dissection of right-wing men and women. I'm an anti-natalist, which means that I don't want kids and that I consider human reproduction broadly undesirable. I don't believe in inflicting my opinion on others, let alone using the force of law or violence to enshrine my views, however. I've never married, although I was engaged once (well twice, but only once in what I'd call a serious way). Instead of children, I helped pay for a former partner's abortion while we were still together. We're still friends, and I consider her proof positive that abortion is a net good for society. Whereas she would have had to drop out of our freshman year of college to have the kid (her statement, not mine), instead she graduated, went on to grad school, and because a psychologist and therapist specializing in substance abuse and PTSD among veterans. I do not hold Christianity in contempt, but I don't think Christians have the right to inflict their religion on others. I'm bisexual, I'm pro-LGBTQIA+ inclusion, and I think that while pornography can be problematic, it can also be unproblematic and that attempts to limit porn are often aimed primarily at silencing queer voices. Overall, I'd call myself robustly pro-porn and pro-masturbation. Those opinions are not contingent on me being single or coupled up. I genuinely enjoy dating both men and women (and enbies and genderfluid people), as in "going out on the town and being seen in public, because I have no 'secret shame' sexuality."

It turns out I'm a fucking freak these days, especially compared to Gen Z!

Solitude Ain't Just A Ski Resort In Utah

Any social process involving men and women is a situation involving patriarchy. (6) It's inevitable. Both men and women are raised within a patriarchal system. Even in unusually progressive households like the one that I grew up in, and which seek to level the playing field, male supremacy manages to creep into a surprising number of nooks and crannies of a developing human's mind; education, (7) civic life, (8) religion (if it's part of one's upbringing), (9) business, (10) etc. It's in the air we breathe, the articles we read, and the video content we watch. Any issue that involves an imbalance between men and women thus becomes political, especially when a society is sinking into an increasingly fascist quagmire.

What it "means to be a man" has changed radically since I was a young person, but not in the way that far right pundits believe and bemoan. Gender roles were stricter when I was young, sure, but many people flaunted them. I am a cisgendered guy who's a he/him and presents as masculine, but when I attended the University of Utah starting in 2002, I'd often wear an army-green, thigh-length cargo skirt to class. I don't consider myself a non-gender-conforming person, but I find the obsession modern men and boys seem to have with masculine presentation risible. When I was a child in grade school in the 80s, our school janitor—Lyle—would occasionally show up as "Lyla," his "sister," much to the delight of the kids. This was in a screamingly conservative community, and Lyle/Lyla received zero shit from the principal over the many years I went there, which implies to me that no devoutly Mormon parent in the deep red beating heart of Ronald Regan's America saw fit to make a fuss in those days. Am I saying that mainstream conservatives are more far right and sex-obsessed now? Yes, I am. And it's having consequences.

Polls indicate that young men are exceptionally lonely. It's not *just* young men, but men lack the deep social networks that women tend to develop, according to researchers. (11) More broadly, men can also have a sense of self that's "fragile" (12) and thus easily manipulated by fascist rhetoric regarding performative gender roles and individual worth. To men insecure about, say, their body image, fascism offers a framework for friendship and masculinity, albeit a deeply toxic one. (13) Young men in 2025 have a harder time talking to—and are less appealing to—members of the opposite sex than any generation in recent history. (14) Whatever the cause (COVID lockdowns, social media saturation, misogyny—all of the reasons I can think of seem threaded together in an overdetermined knot of doom), this isn't a great place for anyone in the US to find themselves. I don't cite these facts to dunk on young people. I'm pointing out a positive feedback loop between sexual cognitive dissonance and vulnerability to right-wing ideas.

It's wild what you can find out when you dive into the data. In a moment we'll be looking at a 2025 study from DatePsychology which found, among other remarkable things, that 45% of men 18-25 had never asked a woman out face-to-face in person. (15) Now, as I mentioned, there are certainly some explanations for this that aren't as sinister as a generation of redpilled frat boys with atrophying emotional intelligence. One is online love, of course, and that includes long-distance love. That's a perfectly valid means of finding romance, and one that's on the rise at an astonishing rate. (16) The COVID pandemic also had a cataclysmic impact, both socially (17) and politically (18): it made young adults more anxious, depressed, and isolated, while exposing them to an increased risk of online radicalization. It's not all bad news, however—those same studies have found resilience and flexibility to be outcomes of the same milieu, and thus higher in younger generations.

Back to that DatePsychology survey I cited regarding young men and romance. Young men (and women, but especially men) haven't gone through many of what previous generations considered crucial rites of passage like having a boyfriend/girlfriend, partaking of drugs or alcohol, or spending much time in person with friends. This isn't some win for the Moral Majority or Reaganite conservatives, however: Gen Z also has the lowest church attendance of any generation yet surveyed, and they are also less likely to have worked a summer job while in school. Hardly the stuff paleoconservatives used to value in the young. Something in perception of what's important and unimportant has changed; many things, in fact.

Please don't think I'm "kids these days"-ing. I don't believe that *any* group is a monolith, especially a generational cohort. I only find generational analysis useful in certain contexts. The most important context is each generation's unique material conditions, which contribute to each generation's worldview with that worldview's attendant strengths and weaknesses. My own generation, along with Gen X, is responsible for the "wild west internet" which in no small part produced our present political moment. We drafted the blueprints for mass radicalization through irony, memes, and shitposting. (19) I was a very active member of the Awful Forums back in the 2000s (my account names variously were The Meat Handler, Mad Mangosteen, and a few other variations) I'm not proud of how I acted on those forums in my twenties, though the worst I got up to was mocking furries. That was childish, shitty bigotry on my part and I've gotten past it. I love and cherish furries, and count myself lucky enough to be friends with many of them these days.

In that spirit, I don't think it's fair to judge a generation based on averages regarding sexual "milestones." That's weird and small-minded. What *is* concerning, looking over the data, is the growing divide in worldviews between young men and young women. What is also concerning is that same divide growing *among older generations*, (20) which points to a society where men and women are having trouble communicating across nearly a century of generational socialization. People these days are married at a rate that reactionary heteronormative society deems undesirable. My proof? The ongoing campaign to end no-fault divorce, (21) which could effectively trap progressive, liberal, or leftist women with MAGA men in an environment of increasing patriarchy and violence.

I fiercely support the right to no-fault divorce, but

full disclosure: I don't personally give a shit about the "institution of marriage." It's yet another area where I wonder what the fuck reactionary men are thinking in trying to make marriage escape-proof and herd everyone into unhappy, inescapable relationships. I consider marriage an outdated institution, and scuffles over it confuse me. Heteronormative society can keep or discard it as they see fit. Likewise, were a reactionary person to read this book (hello if you're out there, congratulations on making it this far!) they'd be as confused as I am, since they'd be me reflected in a funhouse mirror. They'd point to the increasingly everyday misogyny-to-fascism pipeline I find so distressing (22) and call it "a recovery from feminism and a welcome revival of long-weakened American masculinity." That same person might refer to efforts to curtail interracial relationships as "the preservation of human biodiversity." *

What isn't a matter of dispute or clever rhetorical games is this. Men, as an answer to these trends, are turning to some very crazy shit to cope with, obfuscate, or attempt to subvert reality. Examples of this really got their start with "Gamergate," a right-wing temper tantrum in a teapot about female video game reviewers that grew like an obscene fungus into a netroots movement of right-wing video game louts. Many of the young, lonely, reactionary men swept into the masculinist movement by Many former Gamergaters (and gamer culture more generally) (23) now spend their days whining about how "women are ruining video games" and "DEI is ruining video games" and "woke is ruining video games," despite the very games they pillory as "woke" often breaking sales records.

While some gamers, especially the young and male, feel alienated by games with trans representation and people of color in them, sales figures suggest that they're an extremely loud, very online minority. (24) Demographically and socially, life is passing these angry white boys by.

All part of the gynocracy's conspiracy to keep men down! I'm not sure about that, but what I *am* sure about is the fact that it doesn't speak well of men that we have enough spare time to review-bomb movies we perceive as too feminist or "woke," (25) review-bomb games of the same variety, or send death and rape threats to female game journalists, creators, and social media personalities. (26) That's not "guys with stuff going on in their lives" activity. Nearly all online harassment is men directing vile, thuggish rhetoric at women in response to the gentlest criticism imaginable. "Entitled" doesn't begin to describe these assholes. Do any of these review-bombing, game-obsessed misogynists have girlfriends? That's a valid question, and the answer is yes, *some* do. The female partners in those hetero relationships aren't necessarily doing great, though. (27) Other men in this contingent, however, don't have intimate partners. (28)

Some puritanical (and single) young men dismiss their horny, lonely brethren as "gooners," a term that's the modern American equivalent of "wanker." The term has connotations of looking at the world through a lust-sodden, mouth-breathing, and onanistic fog. On the one hand, there *are* a lot of men like that out there. On the other, the amount of condemnation masturbation receives these days would be disturbing if it weren't so hilariously childish. In particular, the far right spends an extraordinary amount of time thinking and bloviating about masturbation: especially for people who allegedly don't engage in the Sin of Onan.

So, keeping in mind that both the 2020s "male loneliness epidemic" and the idea of a glut of single (not just unmarried) younger men both have scientific validity, let's look at the perfectly normal, perfectly healthy way the hetero far right mainstream is dealing with it.

Cockblocking Rosy Palm and Her Five Sisters

Time-as-context is a thing which never ceases to amaze me. What I'm about to say wouldn't have been controversial in enlightened society since the 1940s or 1950s, or even in mainstream society between about 1969 and 2010. Since 2015 and before the 1940s, this was and is about to be a controversial statement. Yet what I'm about to say is irrefutably, scientifically, and societally true. It's irrational to argue against this assertion, and not just that, it's inhuman. It's a powerfully liberating phrase to embrace, even taken to its ad absurdum lengths. That statement is this: There is absolutely nothing wrong with masturbation. (29)

Who exactly is trying to take this Nature-given gift away from our opposable thumbs and soft, fleshy digits? Usually throughout history the answer to that has been some version of "the Church," AKA the fuck police. They'll tell you whom you can fuck, and when, and how, and that includes yourself. It's funny, but it's less funny that it that has been one of the primary provinces of religious moralism since the dawn of the priestly caste. (30) For a group with such disproportionate power to focus so obsessively on something so clearly and inarguably not their business is concerning.

It still is their obsession, to some extent, albeit beneath a slightly different rubric that intentionally conflates several different individual issues. I admit, my personal perspective colored my initial reaction to this phenomenon, but my instincts were in this case correct. When I first heard the phrase "porn addiction," it struck me as off. Then I tried to rationalize it. Sure, I figured. I mean, I *love* porn, and I *am* a recovering addict (the bottle in my case). I can see how *anything* that makes you feel good can be mistaken for addiction, or, in the right circumstances, legitimately become addiction.

Do I think "porn addiction" is real? I think it's a dishonest question and that the term these people are looking for is "masturbation addiction." So, is *that* real? Allow me to give you my "yes, but" answer in the form of a parallel. I know that eating disorders are real. I know they can and do kill people. I know that there's an appallingly dystopian community of pro-eating-disorder people on social media, and that the beauty standards of patriarchy as vomited forth then filtered through capitalism pour fuel on this fire—for women, men, and nonbinary or genderfluid people alike. I don't, however, think there is such a thing as a fucking "chocoholic" in the sense that they wake up shaking until they eat a Hershey's kiss. As a recovering/former alcoholic, I *did* need a few slugs from my nightstand pint of Barton vodka (yes, I was a class act) before I could so much as shower, brush my teeth, or eat something, let alone get to my job. Without those system rewetting morning slugs of booze, I'd have the shakes and soul-deep nausea all morning.

Sex addiction is quite real, and I believe that a problem with self-perceived excessive or compulsive masturbation falls nicely under that umbrella. Some people don't think that's enough, though. Aren't sex addicts, like, whores or players? Sluts or total studs? Or just plain faggots, if they swing that way? Why include these fetid, sallow-skinned, hairy-palmed creeps in the "sex freak" tent? This is where the bizarre and meaningless societal distinction between sexual excitement with one's self and with another (or many other) consenting parties comes in. Sure, adding other people *complicates* sex and, hormonal chemistry suggests, enhances the experience.

The stimuli in the brain are nearly identical in both types of sex addict, though, as is the "excessive" action being pilloried. Except with the caveat that the virtuous masturbator can claim absolute harmlessness, while even the most well-intentioned otherfucker is likely to get their signals crossed now and then, causing emotional distress if nothing else. Honestly, the worst the onanist must deal with is shame, and, get this—*shame only exists in one's brain.* If *you* know you aren't doing anything wrong, and nobody complains because nobody else is impacted or involved, what the fuck do you have to be ashamed about?

Quite a bit, according to society in general—but particularly the far-right.

When I heard the phrase "porn addiction" being bandied about, as I said, it felt off. I suspected what the *real* agenda was. Don't give me too much credit for my powers of prophecy. I currently live in (and grew up in) Utah, a state that pushed and continues to push the boundaries of how radically anti-porn a state in a country with the First Amendment can be. Utah is a state which, in fact, pushed the legal boundary of how clean we can make *normal* movies for Our Precious Children, and got our collective dicks caught in a bear trap for our trouble. It turns out artists don't like third parties making edits of their films. Surely not if it's just to take out all the *nasty* stuff they obviously didn't mean to put into them in the first place, right? Wrong, as it turns out. (31)

We were one of the first states to institute legislation that led sites like PornHub to IP-block us out of fear of legal retaliation. (32) We also banned VPNs in 2026. We have the dubious distinction of being the only state in this fair union to ever appoint a "Porn Czar." That was a now-thankfully-defunct cabinet level executive position below the Governor dedicated to regulating (and hopefully eliminating) pornography in the State of Utah. (33) The woman appointed to this position was an unmarried middle-aged woman who was also a devout Mormon. (34) Doing the theological-social arithmetic, this means that for a time pornography in Utah was being overseen by a middle-aged religious fundamentalist virgin who had likely never had a glimpse at the devil's dirty picture books before she got the job.

Being a hellspawn long marooned in one of America's many religious microstates, I have a pretty good instinct when it comes to people trying to roll the clock back to the 1950s using manipulative language. "Porn addiction" is a way to finally attach harm to porn in a way that Evangelicals (and Mormons, and fascists, and other reactionaries) can sell to normies. The first attempt to do this, and in my opinion the most justified and convincing one, was made by feminists. Many national and local feminist anti-porn groups were formed in the 1970s through now, but the best-known was called Women Against Pornography. (35) Unfortunately, the feminist anti-porn movement abandoned the pro-sex-worker stance that would have led them to adopt legalization and community safety measures to improve compensation and safety for sex workers. (36) Instead, prominent second-wave feminists like Andrea Dworkin combined forces with and even *marched alongside* the Religious Right of the 1980s, losing both their credibility as feminists and their credibility (along with the Religious Right of the time's) as anti-porn crusaders in the bargain. Much of this can be chalked up to a single feminist thinker I already mentioned named Andrea Dworkin. Dworkin is now mercifully dead, but her legacy of hate lives on, carried by the lesser light of the 1980s "feminist sex wars," Catharine MacKinnon. (37)

The exploited porn star didn't and doesn't make a convincing enough player on the political stage for these people. They do for me, which is why my personal consumption habits are ethical (go to the asterisks if you want to know more about it than that, or want to think about making your own consumption habits ethical). ** Other types of sex workers, like strippers, also rarely make convincing political victims. Instead, the far-right's take on "vice reform" tends to be on banning and attempting to abolish practices as old as humanity. That's the exact opposite of the correct approach, which is to center workers and their safety, autonomy, comfort, and compensation. (38)

Much like the federal government's approach to the War on Drugs, the tactic that the modern porn prohibitionists have landed on is twofold: strike at the supply while trying to tamp down on demand. I don't think I need to remind anyone how the War on Drugs went or is going, *** but let's investigate a familiar tactic that dates back to *Reefer Madness*, the 1936 anti-cannabis film. I don't think the word "impressed" matches how I feel about the disinformation and propaganda approaches to the War on Porn already adopted by reactionaries and how the effort has been handled. The Big Lie is one thing when it's directed at something not many in the mainstream know much about, like cannabis in 1936. I was startled the first time I encountered what the new right, from alt-lite to National Socialist diehards, are claiming (and think) porn actually is, does, and is for.

Since fascists and reactionaries view pornography as a problem, it was no surprise to discover that they blame Jews for its existence and dissemination in the West. (39) This is an old conspiracy theory, and one that has weird, tentacle-like roots in American politics, all of which have culminated in the treelike trunk of its current unified position. Its American roots are in early crackpots like Louis Beam; an incredibly influential mid-20th-century American white supremacist affiliated with the Ku Klux Klan who was a theorist of terrorist tactics and structure. Beam, like many of his peers, thought that pornography was introduced by Jewish communists to weaken Western white, Christian values and induce societal collapse. (40) The theory predates Beam, though, having been bandied about in in the 1950s and 1960s in a more euphemistic form ("moral degeneracy") by groups like the racist, anti-communist conspiracists of the John Birch Society. (41) The Christian Right's self-taught origin story is that it began as a grassroots fight against abortion, but in reality, the nascent political arm of Evangelical Christianity became united in the mid-20th century by their support for segregation. (42) Perhaps unsurprisingly, those racist fucks were also vehemently opposed to the sexual freedom represented by the nascent porn culture of the 1970s, which they saw as nothing less than a sign of the impending apocalypse. (43) These attacks on porn have a few things in common.

First, they are pseudomedical. They make claims that were unsupported initially and are long disproven now. These pseudomedical attacks on pornography continue to this day, but the form they've taken has varied over the years. First, they argued that pornography can directly harm the viewer by stunting mental development, causing physical maladies, etc. None of that is true. (44) Then, during the 1970s and (especially) 1980s, they argued that pornography can act on the male brain in such a way that it causes men to rape and murder women. This, too, has been called into question stridently. (45) The most vocal proponent of this theory, by the way? *Ted fucking Bundy*, who used a "too much porn defense" the same way that Harvey Milk's assassin used the famous "Twinkie defense." (46)

The second track these attacks take is conspiratorial. It can never be that people are just horny, and want to watch people fuck and/or be watched while they fuck. It always has to be the Jews. No wait, according to other Christians, it's Satan. No, according to feminists, it's the patriarchy (and they have a very strong case for this, which I'll address in a moment). No, it's the gynocracy seeking to ensnare young men and render them beta simps so that swarthy swordsman can cuckold and Great Replace them. The feminism argument regarding patriarchy is absolutely true to an extent, but it also presupposes in the case of porn that the patriarchy is *one* entity with *one* interest which speaks with *one* mouth. The patriarchy is both *for* porn (because the objectification of women and the exploitation of their sexual labor is profitable) and stridently *against* it (because it allows women to act publicly in a role it considers shameful, exciting, enticing, and repulsive in equal measures—dangerous, in short).

Finally, these attacks are moralistic. The superficial form of that moralism has shifted over the years, even while reactionary opposition to porn hasn't. Need I add that hypocrisy is a huge part of this conversation? The Nazi Party kept Germany's 1871 law prohibiting pornography in Germany and cracked down on it—except when they didn't. Prominent Nazi Party officials *loved* porn, particularly Hitler protégé and anti-Jewish "journalist" Julius Streicher. After the war, Streicher was found to have one of the largest private porn collections in modern human history (up to that time). (47) That didn't stop Streicher from labeling Jews sexual predators and perverts, however. The Marquis de Sade's works were banned in pre-Revolutionary, Revolutionary, *and* Napoleonic France, and some were only made available in the 20th century, more than a century after they were penned. Yet, since then, France has come to see de Sade as a national treasure. (48) The former is hypocrisy; the latter is societal growth.

People having sex on film seems to scare every sort of State. Pornography was banned in the Soviet Union, that bastion of free expression and sexual liberation. Not only was it banned until the USSR dissolved in 1991, the first Soviet film *of any kind* to feature an explicit sex scene was 1988's *Little Vera*, a whopping three years before the empire collapsed. (49) In the United States, porn became legal the same year that abortion did: 1973. Before that, it was heavily regulated to the point of illegality. That was especially true during the time of the infamous Comstock Act, one of the most bizarre and far-reaching uses of the power of the US Mail ever perpetrated. (50) Porn is banned across the Arab world. India and Singapore have convoluted laws whereby viewing pornography is legal, but creating, distributing, selling, or possessing it is illegal.

What of North America? Mexico, our freewheeling southern sibling, has a very United States approach to porn; it's legal to make, consume, possess, etc., with the obvious exception of child sexual abuse material (which *isn't* pornography and is illegal everywhere). Canada, our stuffy northern sibling with the taste for cans of Molson consumed with Timmy's donuts, takes a dimmer view of explicit material. While porn is technically legal there, the types of content one can consume are highly restricted compared to other nations. This is, in part, due to a successful push by feminists for stronger legislation there. (50)

You might ask, "Why conflate pornography and masturbation?"

That's a good, intelligent question! I'm not attempting to conflate them, but I view them as part and parcel of the same basic human value. It's one that's central to my moral-ethical core: bodily autonomy. Fucking where other people can watch and fidget with themselves is a time-honored kink, be it a cuckold doing the watching or a voyeur (see the glossary where necessary). Some people enjoy showing off (see **Appendix B: Glossary; exhibitionism**). Some enjoy watching people show off (see **Appendix B: Glossary; voyeurism**). Ideally, the two interests can intersect—should other parties *not* get involved with things like statutes, cops, and fines.

This brings us to the subject of modern anti-onanism, which consists of a precise strategy. At a time when fewer young men go out with or even talk to women than in previous generations, how do the sexual busybodies of the far right intend to keep men from even looking at sexy videos of their supposed gender enemies? How, in 2025, do you clamp down on pornography that involves nobody but consenting adults? I've studied the plan, so let me give you the quick tour.

First, you must problematize porn. This means casting it as a social evil, but a big part of this is also an effort to convince men (porn's primary consumers) that if they watch it, then *they* have a problem, thereby personalizing the problem. Now it's time to sell those men a solution to their "problem." That's a key part of this strategy, and a once-in-a-generation chance to inject emotionally open victims with your ideology's larvae while they're vulnerable, paralyzed by your shame-venom. Finally, once the opprobrium around porn becomes widespread enough, push for bans. First piecemeal bans, even soft bans that are more or less for show. Later will come more serious efforts.

A cottage industry of self-help groups, books, podcasts, Christian ministries, and more have sprung up to help men with the scourge of "porn addiction" (and masturbation). Very few of these manfluencers are professionally trained or certified in psychology, therapy, couples therapy, or anything but how to flaunt fake wealth and look like Lotharios on camera. That's why when a female, credentialed (eh, kinda) "therapist" stepped into the lives of Utahns recently, it drew flocks of followers. This charismatic leader's name was Jodi Hildebrandt, and she and her disciple Ruby Franke brought the only kind of attention Utah gets (the "what the fuck is wrong with Utah" kind) to southern Utah in 2023, when Hildebrandt and Franke were arrested for a cornucopia of child abuse and neglect charges.

Hildebrandt got her start in marriage counseling with a failed marriage. As the HBO docu-series *Ruby*

& Jodi: A Cult of Sin and Influence notes, for a devout Mormon seeking to practice family therapy in Mormon circles, a divorce is an odd way to start. The Mormon Church technically allows but very much frowns on divorce. Hildebrandt built her brand around a scaffolding of faith-based, code word laden therapy that the Mormon church could endorse however, and she soon became a therapist that Mormon bishops (lay ministers, a little like pastors) could refer congregants with troubled marriages to. Hildebrandt's predatory technique, as documented by *Ruby & Jodi* when she carried it out on the Franke family, included the following steps, usually carried out at one of Hildebrandt's ConneXions seminars: 1) separate husbands and wives into gender-segregated cohorts, 2) encourage deep, soul-bearing confession of sexual sin among the men, 3) encourage the women to remove sex from the marriage until the husband can be "fixed," 4) suggest the husband move out of the house until they can improve themselves, and thus 5) gain power over the household. Hildebrandt also preached abuse as good for children and eventually descended into the type of "prophecy" and conspiracy-laden "visions" that seem to be the final stop on any Mormon journey to oblivion.

Hildebrandt, like a weird, anti-feminist, Mormon version of Andrea Dworkin, thought that sex was inevitably and inescapably predatory and destructive between men and women. Once the father in one of her Mormon client families moved out, Franke encouraged women to sue for divorce while holding future paternal child custody hostage by threatening to claim abuse that hadn't happened. This worked for an astonishing length of time, even after Hildebrandt's therapy license was revoked when the Utah Psychological Association got wind of her antics. The LDS Church discontinued their formal relationship with her as well, although bishops continued to refer clients to her until her eventual arrest. (51) And what did it all start with? "Porn addiction."

The sales pitch for men to avoid pornography and the sin of self-abuse isn't usually, strangely, an outside-in phenomenon these days. Men seem to be leading the charge for other men to stop tickling their pickles. One example of this is the policy of "No Wanks" † (52) in aging street gang the Proud Boys (see **Chapter Nine—Proud Boys, Femboys, and Towel Boys**). According to the brain trust who sculpted Trump's private army of street brawlers, foregoing masturbation was a part of being a real man. Why? The logic, which is recurring in these newer anti-masturbation campaigns, is that masturbation reduces a man's virility, decreases his testosterone, and renders him passive and unlikely to actively seek a girlfriend whom he can then wife up and impregnate to save the West from foreign invasion. (53) In other words, it's natalism.

Giving up masturbation is also something required of many religious believers, but when religion is only tangentially involved in the reasoning (as is the case with the Proud Boys and some openly National Socialist groups), I find the taboo more interesting. For example: for men who aspire to chaste perfection but fall victim to the weakness of the flesh all too often, there's a vacation month that they can test drive—sort of like giving up jerking it for Lent, but with much more ridiculous rules and a fair degree of discussion about the topic happening on porn site comment sections (which indicates, to me at least, that such a vacation might not be such an outrageous idea for some—those, for example, who create accounts on porn sites to comment on the videos with other eager masturbators). Lent for masturbators has a catchy name, at least: No Nut November.

I guess "Jerktoberfest" sounded too pro-masturbation? Yes, "No Nut November" is the monthlong meme-turned-far-right-celebration (53) that men in the more mildewed sectors of the internet participate in. As though the public promotion of taking a month off from cranking it weren't embarrassing enough, No Nut November has rules! It turns out that you can, in fact, masturbate *a little*—you just can't ejaculate or climax. This preserves their male essence, I guess, thus increasing their testosterone, producing clouds of pheromones, and granting them temporary superpowers. This strange belief has historic roots in pseudomedicine and religion going back to ancient days, and has traditionally been tied to both virtue and virility. (54) However, this cultish masturbate-but-don't-cum technique seems about as effective at "making you more attractive to women" as asking the gods to send you a girlfriend. Which is to say: not *100%* ineffective! The problem is the magic was inside *you* all along.

The upshot of my research into the men most susceptible to radicalization—young, single, lonely, clueless about sex and women, bad at communicating—was this. There are skills that need to be, and can be, taught. Saying that young men have had a raw deal coming up is not unfair to young women or young genderfluid or genderqueer people. Framed properly, this recognition broadens the tent. It affords men an opportunity to realize that the real villain, when you pull off the Scooby Doo rubber monster mask, is patriarchy. Well, that and purity culture, rape culture, and an increasingly fascist State that's driving cultural brutalization and deliberately making people confused about what is and isn't "degenerate," permissible, legal, or acceptable. The point of having plentiful draconian rules that are only sporadically enforced is fear and leverage. Anyone can be busted—or forgiven—for anything at any moment. Adolf Hitler knew how to play this game, with sex scandals as well as political dirt. That, and more thuggish tricks.

Forcing people to grow up with their naturally occurring sexuality pushed into a box labeled "degeneracy" alongside *genuinely* harmful things like violence, political extremism, self-harm content, CSAM and pedophilic abuse can only have bad outcomes. Tying masculinity and gender to fascist myths while promoting transgression and selectively *rah-rah*-ing certain token queer people has predictable outcomes. Those outcomes are a byproduct of what the authoritarian culture of the West has done to concepts like purity, masculinity, femininity, transgression, and dominance. These seemingly-strange outcomes and their repercussions constitute the rest of this book. To get there, we had to build a foundation of understanding regarding the real history of queerness and fascism, and the modern crises of masculinity, loneliness, identity, and social connection, along with bodily autonomy and freedom.

You don't have to be pro-pornography to be a good person or to fight fascism. There are plentiful reasons to hate the industry as a whole and wish to reform it from the roots up. You don't have to be pro-porn, but you *do* have to be pro-sex worker. To that end, and to hear a voice not heard often enough before we move on, I'll let Elle have the last word (from our interview) about the anti-porn crusade the right is engaged in: "Overly restricting porn is a long-standing so-called canary in the coal mine for the much wider restriction of all speech, at least among sex workers. But I think it's clear these are the first steps in a much wider crackdown on speech."

*"Human biodiversity" is pseudoscience and thinly veiled race science. It's scientifically invalid:

> "Genetic data refute the notion of racial substructure for human populations and address naive interpretations of race across the biological sciences, including those related to ancestry, health, and intelligence, that help to perpetuate racist ideas... Scholars interested in race and ethnicity concur that human races are social constructs, and that there are no meaningful genetic differences between socially defined races. However, this belief is not held by the general public. Despite decades of public education, surveys show that people still regard race as a biological concept, a belief linked to

racist attitudes." [a]

[a] Lala, Kevin N. & Feldman, Marcus W. (2024). "Genes, culture, and scientific racism." *Proceedings of the National Academy of the Sciences of the United States of America.* 121(48).

** Whether I'm watching single people, couples, or polycules, the trick is to watch porn *made by the creators*, and for which they are fairly compensated. It helps if exhibitionism is a turn-on for them, rather than just a job, and usually couples/polycules for whom that is true make it clear in both their statements and peformances. The "fairly compensated" part Is still difficult, as sites like OnlyFans, PornHub, Fansly, and others aren't as creator-focused or driven as would be ideal.

*** Drugs continue to win. Which means all of us are winners, really!

† Again, consult the glossary, but "wank" (or "fap"), "wanking" (or "fapping"), and "to wanks" (or "no faps") are all onomatopoeic references to male masturbation. As in, the sound of one man masturbating, i.e. *fap-fap-fap*. Hey, *you're* the one reading this book, you sicko.

1 Maloney, Marcus etl. al. (6/13/2022). "'How do I become blue pilled?': Masculine ontological insecurity on 4chan's advice board". *New Media & Society*. 26 (6). P3307-3326.

Stanaland, Adam et. al. ((1/3/2023). "When Is Masculinity 'Fragile'? An Expectancy-Discrepancy-Threat Model of Masculine Identity". *Personality and Social Psychology Review*. 27 (4). P359-377.

2 Alexander (7/14/2023). “Risk Aversion and Dating”. *DatePsychology*.

3 Vogels, Emily & McClain, Colleen (2/2/2023). “Key findings about online dating in the U.S.”. *Pew Research Center*.

4 Cox, Daniel A. etl. al. (11/9/2023). “Generation Z and the Transformation of American Adolescence: How Gen Z’s Formative Experiences Shape Its Politics, Priorities, and Future”. *Survey Center on American Life*.

5 Beran, Dale (2019). *It Came From Something Awful: How a Toxic Troll Army Accidentally Memed Donald Trump into Office*. (All Points Books, New York). Ch. 4.

6 Van Roosmalen, E. (2000). “Forces of Patriarchy: Adolescent Experiences of Sexuality and Conceptions of Relationships: Adolescent Experiences of Sexuality and Conceptions of Relationships.” *Youth & Society*, *32* (2). P202-227.

7 Miller, A. L. (2023). “Intersectionality in US educational research: visibilizing the historically excluded and under-recognized experiences of disabled girls of color.” *Educational Review*, *76* (1). P166–180.

Ngo, B., Abdi, N., & Chandara, D. (10/272020). “Gender, Education, and Immigrant Children in the United States.” *Oxford Research Encyclopedia of Education.*

8 de Benedicts-Kessner, Justin “Women are still underrepresented in local government, despite a woman running for president: Research shows that in

cities and counties, women remain underrepresented among local officeholders in nearly every political office.” *Ash Center for Governance and Innovation*. Harvard Kennedy School.

9 Stopler, Gila “’A Rank Usurpation of Power’ – The Role of Patriarchal Religion and Culture in the Subordination of Women”. *Duke Journal of Gender Law & Society*. Vol. 15. P365-397.

10 Foggin, Sophie & Chen, Connie (3/7/2025). “Why work is (still) not working for women”. *CNN*.

Fry, Richard & Aragão, Carolina (3/4/2025). “Gender pay gap in U.S. has narrowed slightly over 2 decades”. *Pew Research Center*:

> In 2024, women earned an average of 85% of what men earned, according to a Pew Research Center analysis of median hourly earnings of both full- and part-time workers. In 2003, women earned 81% as much as men.

11 Vigers, Benedict (5/20/2025). “Younger Men in the U.S. Among the Loneliest in West: One in four U.S. men under age 35 report feeling lonely”. *Gallup*.

Goddard, Isabel & Parker, Kim (1/16/2025). “Men, Women and Social Connections: Roughly equal shares of U.S. men and women say they’re often lonely; women are more likely to reach out to a wider network for emotional support”. *Pew Research Center*.

12 Swami, Viren (3/21/2022). “Body image issues affect close to 40% of men – but many don’t get the support they need”. *The Conversation*.

Barnes, Matthew et. al. (2/25/2020). "Associations between body dissatisfaction and self-reported anxiety and depression in otherwise healthy men: A systematic review and meta-analysis". *PLoS ONE*. 15 (2).

13 Marcotte, Amanda (8/23/2022). "Andrew Tate shows how fascists recruit online: Men fall victim to the insecurity-to-fascism pipeline: Young men's dating woes attract them to online misogynists, who then convert them to authoritarianism". *Salon*.

Bratich, Jack (2024). "Patriarchal pacts in the neo-archaic manosphere: warband brotherhoods as fascist masculinity". *Journal of Gender Studies*. 34 (1). P1-15.

14 Otte, Jedidajah (9/27/2025). "'Men seem to make life for women worse': single US women share the woes of dating in 2025". *The Guardian*.

Cox, Daniel (10/17/2024). "' "We Don't Feel Safe, Heard, or Understood.'" *The Survey Center on American Life*.

15 Alexander (7/14/2023). "Risk Aversion and Dating". *Date Psychology*.

16 Vogels, Emily A. & McClain, Colleen (2/2/2023). "Key findings about online dating in the U.S.". *Pew Research Center*.

17 Wiedemann, Anna et. al. (10/5/2022) "The impact of the initial COVID-19 outbreak on young adults' mental health: a longitudinal study of risk and resilience factors" *Scientific Reports*.

Cerutti, Jamine et. al. (2024) "Declines in

social–emotional skills in college students during the COVID-19 pandemic". *Frontiers in Psychology*. Vol. 15.

18 Wilf, Sara et. al. (2023). "Youth civic development amid the pandemic". *Current Opinion in Psychology*. Vol. 52.

Levinsson, A. et. al. (2021). "Conspiracy Theories, Psychological Distress, and Sympathy for Violent Radicalization in Young Adults during the COVID-19 Pandemic: A Cross-Sectional Study." *International Journal of Environmental Research and Public Health.* 18 (15).

19 (5) ibid.

20 Koul, Sarah (3/4/2025). "The Women Who Wanted to Leave Their Husbands Over Politics". *Slate*.

21 Berger, Eric (6/25/2024). "Conservative US lawmakers are pushing for an end to no-fault divorce: Republicans in Louisiana, Oklahoma, Nebraska and Texas have discussed eliminating or restricting such cases". *The Guardian.*

Kruesi, Kimberlee (11/26/2024). "Repealing no-fault divorce has so far stalled across the US. Some worry that'll change under Trump". *AP*.

22 Miller-Idriss, Cynthia (7/15/2025). "Misogyny incubators: how gaming helps channel everyday sexism into violent extremism". *Frontiers in Psychology.*

23 Heath, Nicola (7/14/2022). "Alt-right groups are targeting young video gamers — and finding a

culture where extremist views can flourish". *ABC Radio National.*

D'Anastasio, Cecilia (6/10/2021). "How *Roblox* Became a Playground for Virtual Fascists: Thousands of players flocked to a digital world filled with draconian rules, slavery, and anti-Semitism—and tested how far "just a game" can go." *Wired.*

24 Tassi, Paul (8/28/2024). "The Woke War: Why The Right Believes It's Dominated Gaming And TV In 2024". *Forbes.*

Lang, Wong Kit (2/26/2025). "15 million copies sold: Baldur's Gate 3 and the power of knowledge reuse". *Real KM.*

Admin. (8/29/2025). CD PROJEKT earned over $120 million in six months, with 60% coming from Cyberpunk 2077". *Game World Observer.*

25 Gibbons, Ben (4/5/2025). 10 Movies That Were Unfairly Review Bombed". *ScreenRant.*

Cantone, G.G., et. al. (2025). "Review bombing: ideology-driven polarisation in online ratings: The case study of The Last of Us (part II)." *Quality & Quantity.* 59 (Suppl 1). P315–341.

26 Cornish, Aude (8/30/2019). "How Gamergate Became A Template For Malicious Action Online". *NPR.*

27 Taylor, Samuel (8/2/2017). "Gamer Bros Have a 'Gamer Girlfriend' Problem". *Vice.*

28 Jacobs, Harrison (5/15/2016). "Pro gamer making 6 figures explains why many players don't

have girlfriends". *Business Insider*.

29 Kaestle CE & Allen KR (2011). "The role of masturbation in healthy sexual development: perceptions of young adults". *Archives of Sexual Behavior*.40 (5). P983-94.

Fuss, Johannes et. al. (2017). "Masturbation to Orgasm Stimulates the Release of the Endocannabinoid 2-Arachidonoylglycerol in Humans". *The Journal of Sexual Medicine*. 14 (11). P1317-1379.

Dubinskaya, A. et. al. (2024). "Masturbation: An Underutilized Treatment?" *The Journal of Sexual Medicine*. Vol 21, Suppl 5.

Coleman, Eli (2002). "Masturbation as a Means of Achieving Sexual Health". *Journal of Psychology & Human Sexuality*. 14 (2-3). P5-15.

30 Murdock, George (1945). "On the universals of culture". In: Linton (ed), *The Science of Man in the World Crisis*. (Columbia University Press, New York)

Campbell, Marianne et. al. (2019). "A systematic review of the relationship between religion and attitudes toward transgender and gender-variant people". *International Journal of Transgenderism*. 20 (1).

Geissinger, Aisha (2012). "Islam and Discourses on Same-Sex Desire". In Boisvert, Donald L. & Johnson, Jay E. (eds.). *Queer Religion: Homosexuality in Modern Religious History, Volume 1*. (Praeger Publishers, Santa Barbara). P80–90.

31 Horiuchi, Vince (7/8/2006). "Utah film sanitizers ordered to cut it: Court ruling: Deleting objectionable language, sex and violence injures artistic expression". *Salt Lake Tribune*.

32 Rascoe, Ayeesha & Miller, Saige (5/7/2023). "A new Utah law led PornHub to ban access to its site for everyone in the state". *NPR*.

33 Janofsky, Michael (3/16/2000). "Utah Law Creates First 'Pornography Czar'". *New York Times*.

34 Janofsky, Michael (3/24/2001). "PUBLIC LIVES; First State Porn Czar, in Utah, Is Set to Draw a Fine Line". *New York Times*.

35 Goode, Erich & Ben-Yehuda, Nachman (2009). *Moral Panics: The Social Construction of Deviance, Second Edition*. (Wiley-Blackwell, Hoboken). P218-244.

36 Hammes, Aaron (2023). "SWERF Necropolitics: Three Sites of Feminist Mistranslation and the Politics of Feminist Exclusion". *Journal of Feminist Scholarship*. 23 (23). P52-69.

37 Brooks, Ellis (9/14/2021). "The Pernicious Bigotry of SWERFs: Catharine MacKinnon continues to work tirelessly to ensure you don't mistake sex workers for actual human beings." *An Injustice!*.

38 Sanchez, Naiymah (12/17/2023). "It's time to end violence against sex workers. That means decriminalizing the industry." *ACLU Pennsylvania*.

Marshall, Rachel (2016). "Sex Workers and Human Rights: A Critical Analysis of Laws Regarding Sex Work". *William & Mary Journal of*

Race, Gender, and Social Justice. 23 (1).

39 Black, Bill (6/6/2021). "Why the Alt-Right Thinks Porn is a Jewish Conspiracy: It's safe to say your favorite OnlyFans is not a sinister plot to neuter and desexualize white men and ultimately doom the white race. Still, this bizarre Nazi myth persists — here's why". *MEL*.

Fox, Mira (9/23/2021). "The antisemitic conspiracy behind the anti-porn movement". *Forward*.

JNS. (3/18/2024). "Trump campaign deflects ads on Rumble appearing before Nazi videos: The streaming platform featured messages promoting the former U.S. president ahead of a video by a pro-Hitler conspiracy theorist." *JNS.org*.

> One video with [neo-Nazi Stew] Peters narrating describes Nazi Germany as needing to storm "perverted libraries" and "perverted bookstores," featuring black-and-white antisemitic political cartoons while asking, "Why do Jews push pornography & degeneracy on our children?"

40 Lewis, Jon & Ingram, Haroro J. (2023) "Founding Fathers of the Modern American Neo-Nazi Movement: The Impacts and Legacies of Louis Beam, William Luther Pierce, and James Mason". *George Washi9ngton University: National Counterterrorism, Information, Technology, and Education Center*. P25-26.

41 Stewart, Charles J. (2002). "The Master

Conspiracy of the John Birch Society: From Communism to the New World Order". *Western Journal of Communication*. 66 (4). P423-447.

42 Balmer, Randall (5/10/2022). "The Religious Right and the Abortion Myth: White evangelicals in the 1970s didn't initially care about abortion. They organized to defend racial segregation in evangelical institutions — and only seized on banning abortion because it was more palatable than their real goal.". *Politico*.

43 McGrady, Michael Jr. (10/6/2025). "A History of Gendered Censorship and the Costs of Faith-Based 'Porn' Panics". *The Humanist*.

44 Drevitch, Gary (4/4/2025). "Science Stopped Believing in Porn Addiction. You Should, Too: What does it mean that religion, not porn use, predicts porn-related problems?" *Psychology Today*.

NOTE: Psychology may have decided this, but Jesus Christ, is it hard to find that out. Using Google is especially unhelpful here, as, having abandoned their laughable "Don't Be Evil" motto, they are now flooded by paid misinformation, which, for example, use journal articles about a tiny alteration in the visual center of the brain observed in long-time heavy porn users to claim that "porn actually *does* make you blind":

Leffer, Lauren (12/20/2023). "How Search Engines Boost Misinformation: Data voids in search results can lead down rabbit holes that bolster belief in fake news". *Scientific American*.

"Unfortunately, this time science seems to be on

the conspiracy theorists' side. Encouraging Internet users to rely on search engines to verify questionable online articles can make them more prone to believing false or misleading information, according to a study published today in *Nature*."

45 Grossman, Alice (1/13/2024). "Porn Does Not Incite Violence". *Woodhull Freedom Foundation.*

Ludden, David (7/17/2022). "Who Likes Violent Porn? New Research Upends Expectations: New research challenges the received wisdom of viewer preferences." *Psychology Today*.

46 Staff. (1/24/1989). "BUNDY BLAMES PORNOGRAPHY". *New York Times*.

Bullough, Dean (April 1989). "On Ted Bundy, Pornography, and Capital Punishment". *Free Inquiry*.

Fagg, Ellen & Gates, Chuck (1/28/1989). "BUNDY MESSAGE DIVIDES PSYCHIATRIC COMMUNITY". *Deseret News*.

47 Barrett, Claire (12/4/2023). "Inside the Infamous Porn Obsession of Adolf Hitler's Nazi Protégé". *Military Times*.

48 Agence France-Presse in Paris (3/18/2017). "France saves Marquis de Sade's 120 Days of Sodom from auction: Manuscript of 18th-century erotic masterpiece given treasured status and withdrawn from auction in Paris". *The Guardian*.

49 Lawton, Anna (1992). *Kinoglasnost: Soviet Cinema in Our Time*. (Cambridge University Press, Cambridge). P97.

50 McCormick, Thelma (1993). "Censorship in

Canada". *New York Law School Law Review*. 38 (1).

51 Neumann, Susan (7/28/2025). "How Jodi Hildebrandt's Arrival Led Ruby Franke to Go 'Off the Rails': 'Wolf in Sheep's Clothing'". *People*.

Grant, Olivia Crist dir. (9/1/2025). "Ruby & Jodi: A Cult of Sin and Influence". *Investigation Discovery*.

52 Ramirez, Nikki McCann (7/23/2023). "The Proud Boys Have Really Strict Rules About Jerking Off". *Rolling Stone*.

Davis, Charles R. & Italiano, Laura (7/23/2023). "The Proud Boys' initiation manual has a detailed 'No Wanks' policy". *Business Insider*.

53 Dickinson, E.J. (11/8/2019). "How A New Meme Exposes the Far-Right Roots of #NoNutNovember: A month-long masturbation-abstinence challenge has a new 'coomer' meme, mocking men who masturbate". *Rolling Stone*.

Sarah Manavis (11/13/2018). "No Nut November: the insidious internet challenge encouraging men not to masturbate". *New Statesman*.

Samantha Cole (11/30/2018). "Let This Be the Last No Nut November". *Vice*.

54 Levin, Roy J. (2018) "Male Sexual Arousal and Orgasms—New Enigmas of Their Activation". *Current Sexual Health Reports*. 10 (3). P76-78.

Gardella, Peter (1985). *Innocent Ecstasy: How Christianity Gave America an Ethic of Sexual Pleasure*. (Oxford University Press, New York and Oxford). P14–16.

CHAPTER SIX

FUR, FASCISM, AND THE FRINGE

While many of my readers know this, it's never best to just *assume* widespread knowledge of relatively esoteric things; even ones which have increasingly become at least vaguely known of by mainstream people. Thus, it's fair to start this chapter with a question and a quick and dirty summary. "What, Charles," you might ask, "is a 'furry?'"

That's a question with both a simple and a complex answer, so let's start simple. A "furry" is slang for a member of the fandom surrounding anthropomorphic animal characters, particularly in cartoons like *Helluva Boss* or *Zootopia*. In many cases, this includes the desire to role-play and often dress up like these anthropomorphic animals. I say "often" because so-called fursuiters—those who don full-body anthropomorphic animal suits, many with heads not unlike something a very cuddly mascot might wear—are a *subset* but not the *entirety* of furry fandom, though they certainly draw the most media attention. People debate when the culture or fandom started, but it's generally agreed upon that the phenomenon was a going concern by the 70s and a nascent identity by the mid-1990s. (1) Some furries date the anthropomorphic fandom earlier than that, and I have no problem with scholars who trace the bones and development of the culture back further than the 70s. (2)

The fandom includes an enormous community of artists and people who devote an impressive amount of time to creating, drawing, and worldbuilding while interacting with each other online and in person. Furries are distinct from cosplayers who dress up as characters from established media properties or their own human or anime-human original characters (OCs). The adult scene's culture has a sexual side ("furry porn" being most definitely A Thing), and sex between partners in which both (or one) partner wears a fursuit has been known to happen. (3) If the sexy side of dressing up like an anthropomorphic animal seems mysterious to you, remember that even mainstream, non-furry streamers, sex workers, and VTubers now regularly incorporate a cute pair of cat or fox ears into their presentation. Furry fandom also has a massive *non*-sexual side: some people's interest in furry fandom is quite chaste. Many trace their feeling of identification to very innocent properties like Disney's *Robin Hood* or *The Secret of NIMH*.

What "furry" is, beyond a fandom, is an identity. (4) A sexual identity? Yes, sometimes. But more importantly, an identity as in "I identify as (or with) an anthropomorphic animal representation of my human self." If that sounds outlandish, be aware that at many points in human history, kinship (spiritual or otherwise) between humans and animals was quite common, (5) and that "a lady kissing a lady" was an outlandish concept not 1.5 centuries ago. We're all adults here, and I think it's time we get over our pearl-clutching, blushing, and giggling and let each other live our lives in peace.

I've mentioned a few times that in my early days on what I now think of as a particularly mean and toxic section of the internet—the Something Awful Forums—I made great sport of furries. This usually consisted of dunking on photos of people in mascot-looking costumes from conventions having fun doing something that, to me and at the time, looked silly. I'm now older, very slightly wiser, and have learned enough that I'd like nothing better than to slap the shit out of my former self. I've grown and changed, and have come to appreciate the fandom for what it is: a mostly positive, supportive community that trends heavily queer and extremely bright and optimistic, for the most part. I've turned my attitude around enough that I'm now lucky enough to count many furries among my friends. Still: I am sorry for the way I acted. All I was doing, I now realize, was mocking people for having harmless fun in a way that I didn't understand. That's an asinine, childish thing to mock someone for.

The Venn diagram overlap between the furry community and the LGBTQIA+ community isn't a perfect circle, nor are furries directly a subset of queer identity, but the furry community is *very* queer. How queer, you ask? Well, I could reel off anecdotes, but thankfully the fine people at FurScience (an outlet of the International Anthropomorphic Research Fund) conducted multiple surveys with excellent methodology to get the following results:

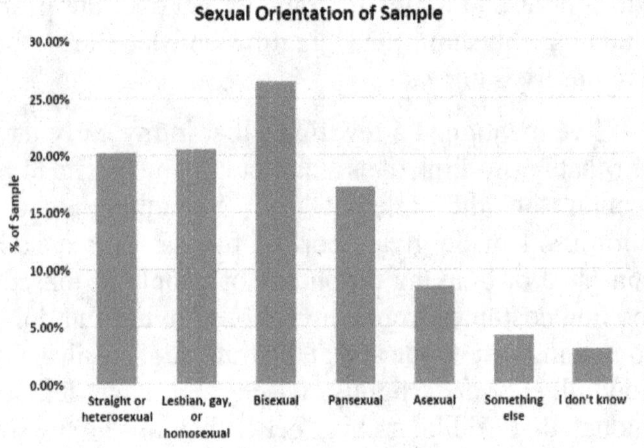

(6) Courtesy of FurScience ("Research Findings: 5.1 Orientation")

20% of furries identify as heterosexual. The most common identity is bisexual. This might explain why I get along with furries so well—they're my people! I consider myself bisexual *or* pansexual, because while I recognize the distinction between attraction to only two genders and attraction to people regardless of gender, and am more a case of the latter, I've found it easier for people to understand "bi" than "pan." That's why FurScience included not only a Kinsey Scale-based methodology, but a variety of ways for participants to describe themselves. As I said, FurScience has excellent methodology.

The furry community is predominantly made up of sexual minorities, but being a furry isn't a sexual identity in and of itself. They've built up enough of a distinct, unique "scene" that they're a heavily queer subculture. They are an example of what I'd tentatively call a neosexuality * scene which was infiltrated more than a decade ago by fascists; particularly neo-Nazis. It was after I grew out of my furry hate that an extraordinary event came to my attention—one that planted at least one of the seeds that grew into the tangled mass that is this book.

Sing, muse, of the time that a neo-Nazi furry derailed one of America's biggest furry conventions.

You Owe Me One Hundred Nazi Pelts

The furry scene isn't particularly new, as new identity-related categories go. It *is* new compared to the gay leather scene, or biker dyke scene, but it has been around for at least a quarter-century. Even Nazi furries can trace their lineage to 2005, which is long enough ago that someone who posted on MySpace about their fursona being a German Shephard named Himmler might feasibly have a kid in college now, if they either hid their hideous dark side from or found another Nazi mate with whom to raise a mewling cub.

Let's turn the clock back to 2005, that year of filth and squalor. I was working in a record store (still the best "job" job I've ever had). George W. Bush had just been elected to a second term, and the Iraq war was a fucking shambles with a climbing death toll. JibJab was a thing. And so was LiveJournal (I had one)! On LiveJournal, a community emerged calling themselves "Nazi Furs—Pelz der Schutzstaffel" (Furs of the SS).

They adopted as their symbol something they called the pawstika (how very cute): (7)

This group claimed to be furry uniform fetishists. Yes, uniform fetishes are a well-established part of the kink community—especially among hard bondage enthusiasts. (8) They were ostensibly against hate. A still-archived community FAQ states:

> This community is in no way related to—nor will tolerate— racial hatred,

> genocide, anti-Semitism, or any political ideology relating to the former. We are simply a group of furries who enjoy either learning the history of World War Two or have a fetish pertaining to Nazis and Nazi uniforms, or both.

Now, anonymous furry authors of the page intro, let me stop you right there. Being sexually excited by the NSDAP and their crimes against humanity is *not* a politically neutral trait—it's an incredibly shitty and damning thing to have turn you on.

"Politically Neutral" Nazi Furry Art

Uniform fetishism has contributed to the normalization, appeal, and revival of fascism across the West. (9) Yes, gasp in shock, because I'm about to yuck somebody else's yum: Nazi play is not okay.

Reenacting Nazi-concentration-camp-victim or nazi-subordinate fetish relationships is fucking hateful shit, and if one is turned on by crimes against humanity, I'd recommend one treat it like a fetish for murdering live animals or making children cry: get therapy. Not all fetishes are harmless.

With that said, Nazi fetishists are not all necessarily committed National Socialists in their politics, so there seems to be some plausible deniability for Furs of the SS. At least, at first blush. Their act is loathsome and gross, yes, but at first glance it could just be in bad taste. This isn't the case with an even more clear-cut case like Marilyn Manson, who not only has a Nazi rape kink, but Nazi ink! (10) Manson is a fascist, plain and simple. Nazi Furs, by all accounts, primarily tried to represent themselves as an apolitical fetish community. They even attempted to stick to the "no racial hatred" policy—except what's this? They had an exemption for "satire and humor?"

> Any posts pertaining to anti-Semitism, racial hatred, ethnic cleansing, and the like (*unless they are obviously sarcastic or humurous [ed.: emphasis mine]*) will be deleted, and the posting user will be banned.

Oh, well shit! Why didn't you lead with the fact that being a Nazi Fur who is *actually* a Nazi furry is fine as long as the joke lands! It's not like the alt-right and our current far-right nightmare moment grew out of the fascist sense of irony or "ironic fascism" online! (11)

The long and short of it is this: if "just kidding" racism, anti-Semitism, etc., had a moment, it has passed. We're hip deep in shit and it's only getting deeper. The time for laughter is always, but laughing *with* fascism is no longer anything but complicity. Honestly, this has always been the case. The envelope-pushing "edgy humor" that was so in vogue around the turn of the millennium was predicated on something most dumbasses trying to keep the dream alive forget. To some degree those eras in humor happened because outlets from *The Onion* to the New York Times thought the presidency of Barack Obama signaled a major shift in American politics; some even referred to this false honeymoon as "post-racial America." (12) It was this assumption (even while fascists of various stripes were still recruiting and trying to take over punk and metal shows worldwide throughout the 70s, 80s, 90s, and 2000s) that helped to shelter the nascent alt-right from too much harsh scrutiny and allow for the ideology's new, mutated form.

Nazi Furs—Pelz der Schutzstaffel was a niche LiveJournal community that never had a large audience or saw much traffic. It appears to be defunct now. Even so, both their original semi-ironic *cri de coeur* and their pawstika flag were picked up by a few different neo-Nazi furry communities on Second Life, a sort of VR online chatroom (yes, there are enough Nazi furries there that there are *a few* groups of them). These included, and still include, the so-called Furzi (a German group) and another community called Furry Raiders.

And that brings us to...

Überfuchs

The modern era of the furry Nazi provocateur in the United States started with a semi-professional pain in the ass and internet troll named Lee Allen Miller who lived in and around Fort Collins, CO (a lovely town with a top-notch veterinary hospital). Miller's fursona** name is variously Foxler Nightfire or starfoxACEFOX, but he's best known by the mononym Foxler (yes, as in "fox Hitler" because Miller's fursona is a fox). Back in the practically neolithic days of the late 2000s, Foxler started causing serious shit within the furry scene by showing up to conventions in an elaborate fursuit that included a Nazi officer's uniform and pawstika armband. Furries are persecuted enough already, and given the preponderance of queer folk and the presence of people of color in the community, this caused exactly the series of firestorms that Foxler was hoping for.

Things came to a head in 2017. Miller, often politely asked to leave conventions for upsetting other patrons, decided to start a group of "alt-furries" (Nazi furries) called the Furry Raiders. A tiny dab of backstory; before branching out to trying to shock people in real life, Miller was an active Second Life user, where he trolled people with Nazi imagery in virtual life. That's where the Furry Raiders were born and was the digital milieu that forged their sense of identity. Eventually, they decided to escape the confines of the internet and try their luck in person.

Furry Raiders threatened to attend Rocky

Mountain Fur Con in 2017, promoting their attendance online by using all the requisite "edgy" alt-right imagery. In essence, they tried to stage a fascist takeover of a public safe space for furries before the doors had even opened (a "safe space" meaning one where people wouldn't feel threatened, be harassed by assholes, and could meet each other, dance, drink, party, and occasionally hook up). To their credit, AnthroCon did not let this happen. To their discredit, and speaking to the nonconfrontational nature of most furry conventions, the eventual and disappointing result was that Denver Fur Con was canceled that year. (13) Nazi furries essentially shut down a popular regional convention without even setting foot inside of it.

This is typical of the fascist public engagement style. While the MAGA movement might like to pretend that the late, quite hilariously lamented Charlie Kirk and his peanut gallery are lovable, peaceful angels engaged in a philosophical exchange of ideas, the real agenda of fascism is to *shut down* debate, *exclude* people, *take over* spaces and venues so they can exclude others, and in the end, to *destroy community.* (14) It's the "just want to buy a drink" theory of community space management. I call it that because of the oft-shared parable it comes from. I'll paraphrase.

A guy is having a beer after work at a dive bar that caters to a punk and metal clientele. A skinhead walks in—no big deal so far, not all skinheads are racist. *** The bartender gets one look at him and pulls a baseball bat from underneath the counter, slams it on the bar, and barks "*No. Nope. Out. Now. Fucking now.*" The skinhead, whom the after-work beer guy can now see is wearing neo-Nazi patches and pins on his battle jacket, holds his hands up to show how harmless he is and starts mewling about "just wanting to buy one drink and leave" and "my money is as good as anyone's." The bartender starts to come out from behind the bar, clearly prepared to use his swatter to empty the skinhead's brainpan. He's done talking. The bonehead backpedals, whining about how he "thought it was a free country," and scuttles away like the crawling thing he is.

"Wow," the off-work guy says to the bartender when he returns to his station. "That was intense. What was *that* about? Why not just give that asshole a beer and send him on his way?"

"Because," the bartender says, "that's how you get a Nazi bar."

He elaborates.

"First, they send one or two guys in to 'just get a beer.' They act polite, they don't cause trouble, and they even tip well. But if you let them in, they'll start to bring their friends. Before you know it, there are *lots* of them, and not all of them are well-behaved. Once they've driven off your normal clientele, they drop the mask completely. They stop tipping well. They start chasing your oldest regulars away, old barflies just minding their own business. They act like they're bouncers who control the door. Then you've got a Nazi bar. It's why you've got to get rid of the first motherfucker who comes in, and keep him out. You can't let that shit take root."

Foxler's 2017 attempted takeover—hell, him

starting the Furry Raiders in the first place—was him asking for a beer. “I won’t cause trouble,” is even something he assured Dever Fur Con organizers. Motherfucker, *you’re dressing up as a Nazi*. You’ve already moved the goalposts to the point where you claim that dressing in full Nazi uniform “isn’t causing trouble’—*and it is*. Anyone who has read my previous nonfiction book knows that I’ve been a regular at no less than two metaphorical bars where I was one of the regular patrons. In both cases, the metaphorical bartenders didn’t kick the first Nazi out and I wound up getting the boot instead. I didn’t want to share space with fascists. This happened with a large, now-expunged Chaos Magick community on Facebook, and later with The Satanic Temple (although in the latter case, it was more crypto-fascism and religious authoritarianism that got let in than neo-Nazi style fascism). I know what it’s like to have a gatekeeper who refuses to gatekeep. So, when I heard about a few furry conventions’ further exploits (and Foxler’s), I wasn’t entirely surprised. Let’s start with Foxler, then move on to community vetting and its importance in any subculture—especially a heavily queer one.

The furry community loudly praises itself for its inclusivity, and it should. It’s inclusive in that it welcomes anyone who wants to be a part of it. However, it also loudly praises itself for its ability to self-regulate problematic members and “keep its scene clean.” (15) That boast is, regrettably, bullshit. Thanks in part to Foxler and the Furry Raiders, but also to groups like Furzi and Nazi Furs on Second Life and LiveJournal (respectively), this shit should have been stomped out by now. How can you say that, Charles?

You've been part of *two* communities that didn't push out Nazis or authoritarian elements!

True! But I left them or was excommunicated for complaining insistently and "fermenting" rebellion (in the words of one of the people involved in my expulsion). I didn't keep on moderating *CMG* after the group founder let fascists stay, and I didn't stay on Core Council at our local TST Congregation without calling our unaccountable, unelected chapter head an authoritarian prick until I was formally expelled from the religion. Furthermore, the groups I *have* stayed active in for the longest time (including the punk scene, the Juggalo scene, and others) are the ones who *have* gatekept. Not for coolness, not for beauty, but for whether someone is a fucking Nazi. That's a pretty low bar to clear, but the persistent failure of groups to clear it is an indication that the best organizations to join – whether they are concerned with fursuiting or gardening – are explicitly antifascist.

So, has Foxler had much success in infiltrating conventions? He didn't at first. In 2016, Foxler and a group of Furry Raiders were asked not to wear Nazi regalia at a furry-friendly series of dance nights called Foxtrot Club. He decided rules were for losers and was kicked out of the venue and, after an altercation with the bouncers, a patron, or both, he was banned for life from further FoxTrot events. In 2018 he was banned from DenFur. 2017 saw Foxler and a group of Furry Raiders attend Biggest Little Fur Con in Reno, NV (much to the dismay of other con-goers, as Foxler himself documented delightedly). (16)

As if that year weren't rough enough for furry con-goers, there was the peculiar case of Rocky Mountain Fur Con 2017. The event already had a checkered history. A Twitter user called Deo TasDevil posted about links between the con and Furry Raiders, and the response from the con was both swift and revealing. RMFCon sent a legally dubious cease-and-desist letter to Deo (over tweets!) and threatened to put a lien on her wages. (17) This is a tactic beloved of right-wing assholes (just look up "sovereign citizens and nuisance liens"), but backfired. For one thing, it brought more attention to the fact that head threat-writer and RMFCon CEO Kahuki Lairu, real name Kendal Emery, has a previous conviction for sexual contact with a minor. (18) This led Dogpatch News, a site dedicated to furry news run by Patch O'Furr (a primary participant in *The Furry Detectives*, an excellent HBO docu-series) to write up the controversy with the memorable headline "Rocky Mountain Fur Con backs neo-Nazis, sex offender to intimidate critic for reporting threat." (19) Do I need to point out that this is yet another example of neo-Nazis cozying up with pedophiles?

Well, unfortunately it gets worse.

Animal Skeletons (and Worse) in the Closet

First off, I need to emphasize this yet again as loudly as I can: MOST FURRIES ARE PERFECTLY LOVELY PEOPLE. The vast majority care deeply about animals, and in a vegan way (not a creepy way). They are generally whimsical, loyal, compassionate, and a little freaky. I'm quite fond of them. *However...*

Every scene and subculture has horrors lurking in the shadows, and some are more horrifying than others. In the case of the furry scene, neo-Nazi regalia is—as it is in the rest of life—an indicator that someone is probably harboring secrets even darker than a sympathy for Adolf Hitler's war of ultimate extermination. Let's look at Foxler, for example. While his political beliefs are infamous and have even garnered him a little mainstream press attention, other facts about him are less well-known outside of niche sites dedicated to keeping track of furry lore.

Foxler, as it turns out, is a zoophile and a pedophile. That isn't simply me calling him names. He admitted, in his own posts, to having fetishized his dog and to having had sexual contact with a dog while he was a teenager. He's also admitted, in his own posts, to grooming underage people for sex and having sexual contact with underage people as well. (20) Why isn't this fucker in prison? Because, as it turns out, it practically takes an Act of Congress and a god damned miracle to get cops to do hard work. And as it turns out, solving and prosecuting crimes involving the internet often constitutes hard work. Cops are also still averse to listening to the queer community. (21) Not quite as averse as when their queerphobia led directly to the torture and murder of 14-year-old Konerak Sinthasomphone, (22) but almost that queerphobic.

I knew this about cops already before I watched the HBO docu-series I mentioned called *The Furry Detectives*. The series, which features many positive examples of furries for every bad egg, *did* reveal to me the extent of certain problems within the furry community that I didn't even know existed. For example, and content warning for cruelty to animals: it turns out that there's a going trade on Discord, encrypted messenger apps, and the dark web for zoosadism videos: videos meant to sexually arouse people (mainly men) by featuring the torture and murder of animals.

The Furry Detectives traced how a massive leak of chatlogs revealed that some very prominent and well-loved members of the furry community were zoosadists. Let's pause here to note that zoosadism is eternally a huge indicator that bad shit is going on inside a human brain. (23) AGAIN: most furries are extremely kind to animals, and most are highly intolerant of zoophilia, as they should be. Animals cannot consent, so every act of zoophilia is an act of rape and abuse. Anyone who actually cares about animals wishes nothing but a painful comeuppance for zoophiles and zoosadists.

That brings us to the nature of the source of the zoosadism leak that rocked so many people's worlds. Who were the people behind these screen names, and who had leaked the information? Obviously, someone who had been in the chats for *some* reason, since what was leaked was screenshots. A team of internet sleuths and a furry journalist (the aforementioned Patch O'Furr) began working together to uncover the identities of and report people involved in the uncovered zoosadism ring. (24) This prevented several difficulties. One was the relative anonymity of the internet, which afforded people in the chats some plausible deniability and a thin layer of anti-doxx armor with regards to who they really were. Another difficulty is the way the law treats animals, which speaks to how deeply sick our society is. Depending on the jurisdiction in which a crime takes place, animal cruelty can be treated as a minor offense—barely worse than, say, speeding—or as a more serious crime. (25) Nowhere in the United States does the law provide anything like justice for non-human animals, but that does not surprise me. The law, after all, exists solely to serve elites and allow for the smooth functioning of our social hierarchy.

As I mentioned, a mystery also posed by the zoosadism leaks was the leaker's identity. As the masks of people in the chats began to come off one by one, the leaker's name emerging was inevitable: as I said, whoever they were, *they had been in the chats*. After some investigation, the "Furry Detectives" (who chose the adorable name the Furvengers, which I imagine HBO didn't pick for a title for copyright reasons) solved the mystery. The chat screenshots had been leaked by a then-23-year-old man named Hakan Yote. Yote is known by many fursona aliases; Radiance Wolf, Radiance, Yokai of Lunari, etc. He's best known by the name that brought him fame and a wide following on YouTube: Kero the Wolf. Kero is—or was, at any rate—beloved of the furry community. I can see why! Looking over his past videos, he radiates positivity. The fursona he presents is animated, charming, and funny. He has a great-looking fursuit. He is—or was, at any rate—also a frequent attendee of cons and known for interacting with his fans in a way that left them feeling happy.

There's only one problem. Why was Kero in those chats to start with? Because, as it turns out, Kero is a zoophile. (ibid.)

Zoophilia is a paraphilia, but not a valid sexuality (any more than pedophilia or necrophilia are valid sexualities). To be legitimately a sexuality or even acceptable sex act, a preference has to hinge on *consent*. Animals *cannot consent*. Remember: every sex act that takes place between a human and a nonhuman animal is rape. This logic isn't particularly hard for most to understand, as it's the same logic behind child sex abuse not being "consensual," whatever a pedophile might claim or even believe. It is some creeps' loose gasp on consent that leads to so many zoophiles also being busted with CSAM, in my opinion. Yote—who I will refer to as Kero from this point on—has a particular fetish for dogs, which he isn't alone in within the zoophile "community." At this point, I should point out that furries do not, as a group, condone zoophilia and indeed frown on it as much as anyone on Earth. Some furry conventions frown on it, too: but not as much as they frown on bad press. But we'll get to that in a moment.

Kero's plan, as explained in *The Furry Detectives* in his own words in an interview, was to publish the zoosadism leaks to draw a line in the sand. His leak was an attempt to differentiate between "good" zoophiles (like him) and "bad" zoophiles (the ones who engage in or enjoy watching zoosadism). Are torture-freak animal rapists worse than animal rapists? I'll grant Kero that. But that doesn't justify or normalize zoophilia. The distinction Kero seeks to make—between "good" and "bad" animal rapists—doesn't exist. Torture and murder of animals should be additional charges, I agree, but raping animals is bad in and of itself. Attempting to make a "worse" group an out-group to gain acceptance for your own inexcusable behavior is not a winning strategy.

Do the broad outlines of this strategy sound familiar? They should. What Kero engaged in with the zoosadism leaks was an attempt at zoophile respectability politics. The problem is this: unlike LGB without the T, the LGB Alliance, or similar groups, zoophilia is not a valid sexuality to begin with. They'll never be part of the LGBTQIA+ coalition, any more than pedophiles will. For a sexuality to be valid, the participants in a sex act *must always all consent*. It's honestly just that simple. The dark web sadists behind much of the material circulated in the zoosadism chats can't grasp this. Many videos were shared by a user named Snake Thing, and another user/producer went by Monster. The Furvengers' doxxing skills are not to be fucked with, and ultimately, they led police right to Monster's door. Monster's real identity? British-born, Australia-dwelling celebrity zoologist Adam Britton. In an outcome surprising nobody (except for the police and his vast Australian television audience), Monster was also involved in the production and distribution of CSAM. (ibid.) At this point, I feel like we're detecting several running themes.

The zoosadism leaks (which happened in 2018) provided ample evidence of a phenomenon in the furry community that is concerning for its implications in the Nazi / furry community controversy. There were a lot of names in those leaks. Not a sizable minority of furries, but evidently enough influential con-goers that conventions like AnthroCon declined to investigate the leaks and ban users who could be identified participating in the chats (but not sharing videos). This wasn't because of some Eyes Wide Shut-style conspiracy of high-ranking zoosadist freaks. It was simpler than that. They didn't want the bad press to lead people to associate an already-persecuted group with bestiality and zoosadism.

A 2021 article by Kameron Dunn (26) documented efforts underway in the furry fandom to deradicalize right-wing members and diffuse the "Nazi furry problem." However, Dunn concedes that:

> It's been a few years since the big stuff around "Nazi furries" happened, and it's with a heavy heart that I report the right-wing members of the fandom are still around. They are diffuse and varied in their ideologies, and they continue to recruit members to their ranks...
>
> For Nazi furries, the "outcast" component is crucial. As Deo [TasDevil] told me, a lot of furries find their way into these hate groups when they're young and still figuring themselves out. Many are closeted and hold inward resentment to their queerness. Nazi furries use "degeneracy"—a word deployed in the Third Reich to describe a stain on society that needed to be purged to secure a white homeland—to draw a dividing line between themselves and other furries. These young, could-be-Nazi furries see

> openly queer people who share their same weird interest in cartoon animals. Because they have not accepted their own identity and are psychologically pliable, older Nazi furries can steer their inward resentment outward. They can take a stance: “Being furry is fine, sure, but we shouldn’t be *degenerates*.” The process that follows is a cultlike descent into brotherhood, blood and soil, and (what’s most feared) possibly acts of violence.

The first sentence of that second paragraph I cited should be engraved in the flesh of every 21st century extremism researcher: the outcast component is crucial. Yes, neo-Nazis still recruit among both veterans and active-duty Army and other armed forces service members. (27) Yes, rurality is still a big predicter of extremism. (28) However, the single thing one should look for above all else when spotting potential school shooters or neo-Nazis (and boy, those two categories overlap often) is outcast status. It’s especially important these days to look for the communities where this dynamic is happening that are too often overlooked. People even worse and equipped with more desperate tactics than the fucking *US military’s recruiters* are on the prowl out there, reaping souls for Adolf’s rotting empire of lies.

Hell, take it from a Satanist; when you’re already on the margins and hear that there might be an extremism problem in the community you’ve managed to scrape together outside the warmth of the firelight, it's a very human thing to want to put your backs together and play defense instead of doing difficult soul-searching about what you might have overlooked. It's hard enough to believe, or be interested in, or identify as something not considered "normal" by society. Who wants that society to also give your group the label "and also probably a Nazi" based on a few stories mixed with stereotypes and preconceptions?

And I don't intend to do that to furries here. As the *Slate* article I cited documents, the furry community has done a brave (but possibly naively optimistic) thing. Rather than deciding to simply exclude (or beat the shit out of) Nazi furries who try to attend cons, infiltrate the community, etc., they've decided to opt for deradicalization. Now, deradicalization *is* possible. (29) That's absolutely true. I know enough ex-Nazis (including Scott Kelley, whom you've already met) to know that it's rare, but real. Deradicalization is a tactic that's been around for a long time. It's an established psycho-social process of getting someone out of what early researcher and pioneer Robert Jay Lifton called "a totalist ideology." (30) While Lifton's original work was on re-education camps in China in the 1950s, his findings have been applied to cults both religious and political. In the 1970s and even to this day, those applications included well-intentioned but extremely damaging attempts at "de-programming." Most of these attempts were made by families who became distraught when their loved ones joined the Unification Church (AKA the Moonies), or Scientology, or any number of extremely closed-off new religious movements. Deradicalization is not "deprogramming." Deradicalization is a voluntary, therapeutic practice; deprogramming has often amounted to pointless physical and emotional abuse. (31)

Legitimate deradicalization has a success rate that's higher than zero. (32) As is the case with people doing something statistically improbable like kicking a heroin habit, putting down the bottle, or any other major behavioral alteration, I wish them nothing but the best of luck. Honestly. And fortunately, there are people who specialize in de-radicalization, like that ex-Stormfront friend I mentioned earlier.

I caught up with Scott to ask him about furry fandom and deradicalization (if you'll recall, he's the extremism and deradicalization expert I interviewed earlier). Here's what he had to say from that conversation when I brought this subject up.

> With Nazi furries in particular, there's been a concerted effort (according to one Slate article) to deradicalize community members rather than ostracize or expel them. What are the potential benefits and potential risks of such a strategy?
>
> SK: People can't deradicalize Nazis. Only Nazis can deradicalize themselves. Do I think it is a waste of time to reach out in such a way? No. People just need to be aware that those people will only deradicalize if they want to deradicalize. And if someone says they do, then by all

> means. But my organization Center for Extremism Prevention and Intervention does not actively pull people out. They come to us.
>
> The furry fandom is majority-queer (heterosexuals make up 20%). Do you think that may have something to do with this approach as opposed to the one embraced by, say, the punk music or metal communities, which tend to violently expel fascists?
>
> SK: I don't particularly oppose either method since deradicalization is a process the extremist has to go through. So there is nothing wrong with expelling them. Also, it really shouldn't be up to the furry community to deradicalize anybody anyway. (33)

Regardless of the efficacy of deradicalizing a community the way that furry fandom is attempting to, it shows that their hearts are in the right place. If large conventions are willing to tackle and confront the seedier sides of the community by barring bad actors and holding attendees with problematic behavior and views accountable, I'm cautiously optimistic.

* Neosexuality is not a term which should

frighten anyone. A sexuality – or, rather, the *expression* of a sexuality – that's native to industrial or post-industrial modernity is no less valid than, say, modernity largely rejecting rape as legally permissible. As the hyperreality of 21st century mediated life sinks deeper into our collective psyches, even "traditional" sexual positioning like the tradwife can be considered a neosexuality. Nobody in history actually lived like these neo-traditional "trad" wives do.

** Fursona is a portmanteau of "furry" and "persona." Remember the original characters (OCs) I mentioned earlier? Furry fandom is a tremendously creative enterprise, and it's typical for a furry to construct an elaborate fursona involving a name, physical appearance, attitude, etc. It's a fairly advanced combination of worldbuilding, improv acting, kayfabe, and pageantry that puts one of my own passions – professional wrestling – to shame.

*** The 80s were actually something of a civil war between skinheads that continues to this day. There are SHARPs, or Skinheads Against Racial Prejudice, and "boneheads," "knuckleheads," or "Hammerskins," all slang for neo-Nazi skinheads with the Hammerskins being a particularly murderous neo-Nazi skinhead gang. The skinhead lifestyle originally started as a working-class movement in Great Britain, where white blue-collar workers and Black immigrant workers would dance together at Jamaican-style dancehalls. Many music styles emerged from this syncretic union, and many of them are among my favorites. Then, the National Front came long, started recruiting working class Brits, and a wedge was driven within the skinhead scene between the racist and anti-racist skins.[a]

[a]Brown, Timothy S. (2004). "Subcultures, Pop Music and Politics: Skinheads and 'Nazi Rock' in England and Germany". *Journal of Social History*. 38 (1). P170.

1 Kurutz, Daveen Rae (6/17/2006). "It's a furry weekend in Pittsburgh". *Pittsburgh Tribune-Review*.

Patten, Fred. (1995). "The Yarf! reviews". *ANTHRO*.

2 Patten, Fred (7/15/2012). "Retrospective: An Illustrated Chronology of Furry Fandom, 1966–1996". *Flayrah*.

3 May, Mark (3/2/2023). "How Being A Furry Helped Me Explore My Sexuality". *Vice*.

4 Wall, Kim (2/4/2016). "t's not about sex, it's about identity: why furries are unique among fan cultures: Furries tend to get a bad rap as perverse fetishists when in reality, the subculture is about playful escapism and a fascination with what links humans to animals". *The Guardian*.

Amarta, Rifiqi Zuhdi & Kartika, Dilah Ratna (2024). *Jurnal Media dan Komunikasi Indonesia*. 5 (2). P170-186.

5 Teeter, Emily et al. (2000). *A History of the Animal World in the Ancient Near East*, Vol. 64, ed. Collins, Billie Jean. (Brill, Boston). P355.

Kadgaonkar, Shivendra B. (2008). "The Role of Animals and Birds in Ancient Indian Art and Culture." *Bulletin of the Deccan College Research*

Institute. 68 (69). P163–65.

6 https://furscience.com/research-findings/sex-relationships-pornography/5-1-orientation/

7 https://en.wikifur.com/wiki/Nazi_Furs

8 Lopez, David A. et. al. (2013). "Nazi Uniform Fetish and Role Playing: A Subculture of Erotic Evil". *Popular Culture Review*. 24 (1). P69-78.

9 Burton, Tara Isabella (8/19/2017). "'Sexualized fascism': how the taboo nature of Nazi imagery made the alt-right more powerful". *Vox*.

Cheves, Alexander (3/24/2025). "Does the leather community have a Nazi problem?" *Out*.

10 Andelane, Lana (2/6/2021). " Marilyn Manson abuse allegations: Evan Rachel Wood claims rocker threatened her with anti-Semitic abuse, has Nazi tattoos". *Stuff.co.nz*.

Harrison, Ellie (1/25/2022). "Marilyn Manson allegations under spotlight following Evan Rachel Wood documentary: disgraced singer has been accused of abuse by numerous people, including actors Evan Rachel Wood and Esmé Bianco". *Independent*.

Grow, Kory & Newman, Jason (11/14/2021). "Marilyn Manson: 10 Key Takeaways From Our Nine-Month Investigation". *Rolling Stone*.

11 Pinto, Ana Teixeira (2017). "Irony and the Alt-right: The transgressive masks of reactionary techno-futurism". *springerin*. Issue 4.

12 Cantor, Matthew (11/1/2022). "Behind the

scenes at the Onion: 'Trump is the emperor who admits he's naked'". *The Guardian.*

Hannah-Jones, Nikole (11/15/2015). "The End of the Postracial Myth: Pundits are quick to say that it couldn't be about prejudice in states like Iowa, where Obama voters went for Trump. But racial anxiety is always close to the surface — and can easily be stoked." *New York Times Magazine*.

13 Staff. (4/15/2017) "Rocky Mountain Fur Convention canned over furry fascists". *News.com.au.*

14 Stanley, Jason (9/12/2018). "When Fascists Weaponize Free Speech Absolutism: How Donald Trump's Rise Has Been One Long Attack On 'Political Correctness'". *Literary Hub.*

Dash, Serena (10/17/2025). "Censorship in the Age of American Fascism". *Fordham Political Review*.

15 Dickson, EJ (9/16/2019). "Furries Got An Alt-Right Troll Banned From Their Convention". *Rolling Stone*.

Evans, Robert et. al. (1/14/2020). "How the Furries Fought The Nazis And Won". *Worst Year Ever*. IHeartRadio.

16 https://furryraiders.org/pages/2017-blfc-raider-monsters

17 https://x.com/DeoTasDevil/status/851462631026196484

18 New Mexico Courts Case Number D-1215-

CR-92000256.

19 https://dogpatch.press/2017/04/10/rocky-mountain-fur-con-threat/

20 https://en.wikifur.com/wiki/Foxler_Nightfire

21 Girardi, R. (2021). "It's easy to mistrust police when they keep on killing us': A queer exploration of police violence and LGBTQ+ Victimization". *Journal of Gender Studies*. 31 (7). P852–862.

22 The Associated Press (8/20/1991). "Officer Defends Giving Boy Back to Dahmer". *The New York Times*.

23 Vaughn MG, Fu Q[a], DeLisi M, Beaver KM, Perron BE, Terrell K, Howard MO. (2009). "Correlates of cruelty to animals in the United States: results from the National Epidemiologic Survey on Alcohol and Related Conditions". *Journal of Psychiatric Research*. 43 (15). P1213-8.

[a]Ordinarily, I would have used et. al. in this citation, as is my eccentric wont. However, "Fu Q" is my all-time favorite citation throughout untold years of college papers, blog posts, personal research, and published work. Please pause a moment to appreciate it.

24 Love, Theo (2025). "The Furry Detectives". *HBO Max*.

25 Wood, Kathleen et. al. (2025). "Animal Protection: US State Animal Protection Laws Ranking Report". *Animal Legal Defense Fund*.

26 Dunn, Kameron (11/18/2021). "What's Going

On With Those Nazi Furries?" *Slate*.

27 Makurch, Ben (4/14/2025). "Fears over extremism in US military as soldier revealed as neo-Nazi TikTok follower: US army investigates after young private follows the Base, which has vowed to recruit soldiers for so-called race war". *The Guardian*.

28 Berlet, Chip & Sunshine, Spencer (2019). "Rural rage: the roots of right-wing populism in the United States". *The Journal of Peasant Studies*. 46 (3).

29 Dechesne, Mark. (2011). "Deradicalization: not soft, but strategic." *Crime, Law and Social Change*. (Kluwer Academic Publishers, Dordrecht). P287-292.

30 Lifton, Robert Jay (1961). *Thought Reform and the Psychology of Totalism: A Study of "Brainwashing" in China*. (Norton, New York).

31 Ikemoto, Keiko & Nakamura, Masakazu (2004). "Forced deprogramming from a religion and mental health: A case report of PTSD". *International Journal of Law and Psychiatry*. 27 (2). P147–155.

32 Staff. (9/8/2021). "Violent Extremism in America: Pathways to Deradicalization". *The RAND Corporation*.

33 **Appendix A**, Interview Five

CHAPTER SEVEN

RAPEHONS AND ROY MILTON BLANCHARD THE THIRD

In Chapter Three, I touched on sexuality in Nazi Germany; specifically on the fact that, for a time, a relatively small, well-insulated group of ranking Nazi gay men were tolerated if not fully accepted. Ernst Röhm was an openly gay man with an exemplary military record who was personally close to Adolf Hitler (until Hitler had him murdered). Despite the ending of the story, Röhm can provide an example of sorts to modern gay neo-Nazis who can project themselves into his boots in power fantasies. Röhm and other SA men allow a historical self-insertion for a certain type of person.

There is absolutely no corollary to Röhm for trans or gender-nonconforming fascists. Not a single case that they can point to. No exceptions made for the trans lovers of high-ranking Party officials. No free passes given to an embarrassing practice that nonetheless was temporarily tolerated and didn't embarrass Hitler *too* much, as was the case with the tiny cabal of occultists present in the inner circle of Himmler's SS. (1) There's just literally *no* blueprint for acceptance as a trans or gender nonconforming Nazi. Or, at least, there wasn't until the brave new world of 21st century imageboards, those ever-bubbling pits of corrosive disinformation and boiling reactionary discourse.

Our story starts before that point; long before that point, so let's back up a bit.

To understand a phenomenon as strange, complicated, and alarming as trans fascists, you have to understand that it only seems to exist (based on my research) in younger trans and gender nonconforming people. Specifically, the very youngest cohort of Millennials, Gen Z, and even a few members of the oldest cohort of Gen Alpha. (2) Both generations are online in incredibly toxic spaces to an extent that *really ought to scare the absolute shit out of parents*. My younger self is shrieking at me as I type those words, calling me a withered old man, but the data doesn't lie. Hell, in my interviews with trans National Socialists (see **Appendix A: Interviews**), one woman stated that she first started reading and posting on 4Chan *at age 11*.

"Get off my lawn, old man!" No, I get it. When I was 11, before the Internet existed in a way that anyone today would recognize, I got into petty theft with a friend from grade school. That was the same friend who introduced me to Pink Floyd's *The Wall,* * so overall he was a pretty cool fucking dude in my opinion. What this friend did *not* try to get me into was neo-Nazi propaganda, child pornography, or mass shootings as hilarious spectacle. Those are all things you'll find on 4Chan. (3) Other friends throughout my adolescence introduced me to fairly vanilla "hardcore" pornography, *very* gory horror movies, gangsta rap, and other things considered forbidden fruit at the time. *None* of that pornography was CSAM. Those horror movies weren't *actual* beheading videos, which young people have been able to stumble upon since the Forever Wars began, and which are measurably damaging to one's psyche. (4) Not one of my friends tried to get me into the neo-Nazi punk band Skrewdriver. Believe me, there *were* neo-Nazi-curious kids at my school—hell, on my street. I didn't fucking want to know them.

Why does anybody want to know the fascists of 4Chan, let alone young, queer people?

First, a bit about a dark web site that plays a big part in this chapter. 4Chan is an imageboard founded in 2003. It's a place where people anonymously post images and text and reply to each other. This faceless culture is why 4chan users call each other "anon"—short for anonymous. "4Chan," the board's name, is a play on 2Chan, which is a popular Japanese imageboard. The hideous American version was created by Chritopher "moot" Poole. Its history is intertwined with another site that I know well—the Something Awful forums. (5) After SA shuttered a few legally questionable and quite objectionable subforums to avoid a lawsuit (and because the site owner didn't like them), ** moot's nascent 4Chan became a place for "refugees" to post anime porn and racist rants.

4Chan has about 41 million monthly site visitors. (6) That is, in layman's terms, a shit ton. It's exponentially higher than even a large business; it's the equivalent of a large news site or social media platform's audience. It's not a top 10 (or even top 25) trafficked site these days, but its popularity waxes and wanes based on the month and year. The site has a checkered past I don't need to document here, although I can suggest books on the topic. ***

What is important for our purposes is one of 4Chan's boards (the imageboard equivalent of a subforum). That board isn't /pol/ (or "politically incorrect,"), which is without a doubt one of the most infamous, toxic, and persistently fucking awful places on the internet. /Pol/ is also the most newsworthy. But no, we're going to discuss a board called /lgbt/. Users don't call it that, however. It's known by all and sundry as /tttt/, or sometimes just 4Trans. The joke is that the board is so dominated by trans people, especially trans women, that instead of being "lesbian, gay, bisexual, and transgender," it's just "transgender, transgender, transgender, and transgender." As I see it, /tttt/ is a case study in how community can be both liberatory and oppressive at the same time, and how that combination of cure and poison can mix up one's thinking and personality.

Growing Up In Homeland America

In the portion of the political spectrum I occupy (anarchist, which is generally but not always seen as a species of leftist) there is a persistent debate. I call it the "nothing ever happens" debate. On one side are people who trace the history of the United States from its blood-soaked, genocidal roots to the present and see an unbroken line of atrocity. "Donald Trump is a fascist," one might say to them. "Welcome to the party, pal," they would sneer in reply. "America has *always* been a fascist country."

They have a point. It's easy for people to forget how awful this country's history really is. As (especially nonwhite) scholars continue to plumb the depths of American atrocity, it feels like we learn something new and damning every year. For people at the bottom of the US hierarchy—trans women of color, for example—not much has ever been great in terms of what the State has to offer them. What it has had to offer them has mostly been brutality. At the same time, I lean more toward the other school of thought—the "things happen" crowd. While history is rife with inhumanity, simply claiming that things never change lacks nuance and borders on reality-agnosticism.

Within my lifetime, I've observed an enormous rightward shift in the United States. That's damning, because I was born when the infamously right-wing Ronald Reagan ruled this cursed land with an iron fist and a sandblasted white smile. I have clear memories of George H.W. Bush's first Gulf War being on the news and showing all of us at home what America's arsenal looked like tested out on a more or less helpless nation (it was a deliberate move on the part of the first Bush administration to allow camera crews from CNN to take spectacular photos and live footage of the bombing of Iraq, footage that was unlike anything seen on TV up to that point.) (7) Bill Clinton slithered into office while I was running out the last of my K-12 education, and for the last third of that education I'd say I was politically aware. I say all this to explain my own perspective: I call the era that began in my childhood "Homeland America." I think it started with Reagan, was made palatable to (and weakened) the mainstream left under Bill Clinton, was first imagineered in its full flowering by George W. Bush, continued under Obama and Biden, but found its truest realization in Donald Trump.

The oldest cohort of Gen Z was five years old when the PATRIOT Act was passed in 2003, the same year we invaded Iraq, the year I turned 21, and a year after the Forever Wars began. It's weird to say, but I remember a time when America was not *quite* actively "at war." Sure, there were "police actions" and bombings aplenty, and America ruthlessly took lives abroad. But that foreign policy was substantially different from the maniacal, omnidirectional war started by George W. Bush.

Before 9/11 and the flurry of police state bills passed immediately afterward in a frenzy of fear and jingoism, (8) there was no TSA at the airport. (9) ICE didn't exist (although INS and Customs did, and served much the same function, albeit with a fraction of the budget, rate of deportation, and arrests. (10) Warrantless surveillance was quite thinkable, but people had reason to believe that some of it wouldn't stand up in a court of law. Torture was something we outsourced and kept off the books and out of the press, rather than trumpeting it on social media like an edgy 4Chan /pol/ poster desperately trolling for sempai's attention (11) (sempai, in this case, being the insatiable white nationalist base). Before 9/11, there were roughly 80 million fewer security cameras monitoring our every move, (12) and smartphones didn't exist. Tracking someone's location by their cell phone was a primitive technology admissible in court, but highly questionable in quality. People also didn't make it a routine part of their life to share every detail of their whereabouts, activities, and opinions all day every day. Culturally speaking, 9/11 pulled the US hard to the far-right. (13) That was predictable. Populations tend to turn to strongman leaders and those leaders' totalitarian tactics in a time of war or crisis, (14) despite that strategy having mixed results at best. (15) +

Now imagine this. Hell, maybe you don't have to.

In the information environment that soon emerged after 9/11, imagine you're a kid just figuring out that you might be queer. You grow up steeped not in ABC, NBC, or CNN, but in Fox News, Jack Bauer, and, if your grim god was kind, the maniacally beneficent presence of Spongebob Squarepants. Your school curriculum, if public, has been touched by the fell hand of George W. Bush's No Child Left Behind policies (16) followed by the rotting touch of Common Core. (17) If you're rich, you're likely a private school pupil. Your grades are probably marginally better than those of your public-school contemporaries, but that comes with a heavy dose of Jesus, white supremacy, and exurb cultural isolation and homogeneity. (18) You might attend a megachurch. And throughout your milieu, amidst the cultural backdrop that every American adolescent since Holden Caufield has accurately flagged as phony, the idea of queerness is *deeply transgressive.* (19) It's frightening, in terms of realizing who you are, but a little bit exhilarating, too. Despite the reactionary backlash of the US in recent decades, you've got two major legs up on queer youth coming of age throughout countless prior generations. You have two magic windows that let you look out of the life you've been locked inside. One window is your smartphone, particularly text chat apps and social media. The other is the wider, searchable internet.

You *could* spend time watching ESPN, and maybe you do. You probably watch some porn, and some of it is fairly extreme; and that increased exposure in youth is having a wide variety of depressing effects. (20) Statistically speaking, you become interested in anime—a form of art in which the Isekai, or a fantasy world to which one is transported from the mundane, is a common trope. You have, as one of my interview participants put it, "heard all the fuss about 4Chan." So, having explored other transgressive or strange online environments, you head there and check things out. Hey, you don't even need to register a username or profile picture! You can be completely invisible—or anyone you want. The world is a confusing, oppressive place, and 4Chan seems like your Isekai. All of the things adults in your life seem angry or worked up about are lampooned there: just like on South Park! Irreverence is prized, as is bigotry. Sacred cows are ground into hamburger daily (the fact that 4Chan always punches down and never up most likely doesn't register for you). It's exciting. What's more, you're *learning*.

You're definitely not learning things the they

teach in school. Some of what you learn—the vast majority, in fact—is a pack of poison-laced lies. (21) But you've been driven to the margins and 4Chan, one of the most seemingly freewheeling places in the world, is like a wonderland. You're allegedly anonymous, (22) and you can post about your anxieties, sexual and otherwise. Anons are uncaring, brutal, callous, and emotionally damaged people by and large, but they won't turn anyone away directly. That's entirely because they can't.

Meanwhile, while accessing 4Chan is as easy as reaching for your phone, books about growing up queer have disappeared from your local library. (23) That sucks, because you have questions you can't go to your megachurch-attending, homophobic parents with. 4Chan is happy to answer them! And also happy to assure you that those banned books are for degenerates, anyway. The memes and wojacks (a subspecies of meme featuring very crude and sneering caricatures) that cruelly mock trans people seem funny, but they hurt your feelings, too, though you play it cool and even try to outdo the haters.

Where are young trans women—one of the most hated groups on 4Chan—supposed to go?

/Tttt/. Welcome to hell, anon.

Cesspool Oasis

It's hard to convey to newcomers how toxic the culture of 4Chan's trans board is.

Every trans National Socialist I interviewed denied that /tttt/ was part of their "political awakening" as fascists. They say that was /pol/, or other 4Chan boards entirely. For the most part, I believe them. /Tttt/ is an obsessive, psychologically corrosive cesspool, but its fixations are rarely *directly* political. Indirectly, however, the seeds planted in /tttt/ bear nothing but reactionary fruit. In real terms the primary obsessions of /tttt/, namely beauty, desirability, sex, othering, and cruelty, are all load-bearing struts within fascism's psychosocial makeup. How influential is this niche community? Influential enough to have impacted slang across the trans community, with terms and concepts grown in the poisonous hothouse of /tttt/ infiltrating even the lexicons of people who've never heard of the imageboard.

Almost all the slang cooked up in /tttt/, despite having been created by trans people (trans women in particular), is hateful and transphobic. (24) I'll run through a few examples for the uninitiated, but be warned that /tttt/ terminology is... pungent. The peculiar self-hating ideology that saturates the board has warped the ways its posters talk about and perceive themselves—and all the poison comes from a single, discredited source. 4Chan's trans board has adopted "AGP" (short for autogynophiliac— more on that in a few paragraphs) and "homosexual transsexuals" from the same source, with the latter shortened into "husstussies" (HSTS). All of this is toxic, transphobic, debunked psychology from another one of the University of Toronto's finest, and we'll meet him soon.

Taxonomy is almost as big as a crude, "who can

look like a woman and who can't" species of phrenology on /tttt/, so many slang terms have to do with one's appearance and "passing" (the ability of an AMAB woman to avoid being "clocked" as trans, with women who don't look feminine enough classified as "clocky" or as "bricks"). On /tttt/, clocky transfems who dress poorly are referred to as "AGPs" and "hons," and a hon suspected of only wanting to gain access to women's locker rooms and other spaces for sexual reasons is referred to as a "rapehon." (25)

Again—these are 4Chan's trans women talking *amongst themselves*, not some obsessive Nazi fetishist-cum-hatemonger (although, believe me, there is overlap between the two categories). Some of /tttt/'s slang, especially the kind that's fairly funny and less filled with self-hatred, has caught on more widely. For example, "boymoder" has its origins in /tttt/. Boymoder is a term used to refer to closeted trans women still in the process of publicly coming to grips with their identity, and who can still pass as cisgendered men and thus dress accordingly to pass undercover. According to /tttt/, the process of moving from boymoder to girlmoder (a publicly trans-identifying woman) is called "boy removal," and consists of, well, let's let /tttt/ speak for itself: "The boy is kept in the prostate and the only way to remove it is with a dick." (26) The darker version of boymoder hasn't escaped containment quite so much. That term is manmoder, and refers to trans women with "irredeemably masculine features" doomed to forever be AGP hons.

As you can see, it's some hateful shit; the type of slang you'd expect to emerge from a board buried in the middle of a deeply fascist, eliminationist, queerphobic snake-pit full of mass shooters with lit and slowly burning fuses. The type of thing you'd expect to find on 4Chan, in other words. I find two things remarkable about /tttt/. First, that it exists at all. 4Chan is scorched earth. Razed clean, salted, and irradiated so severely that it is incapable of sustaining an even minimally healthy simulacrum of human interaction. There is no saving it. Its culture has its roots, quite literally, in a now-long-expunged Awful Forums subforum called Anime Death Tentacle Rape Whorehouse. Despite this, after the imageboard's collective membership was launched out of Something Awful like a terminally damaged rogue moon, a small group of queer people decided to plant a pride flag on it. That was one microscopic and poorly-thought-out step for a tiny group of (mostly trans) queer individuals, and one giant leap backwards for queer progress overall.

The second strangest thing about /tttt/ is that the board wholeheartedly embraces—indeed, helped revive—the same outdated psychological theory of trans identity, Blanchardism, that the TERFs I wrote about in Chapter Two cling to. Let me repeat that: trans women in /tttt/ have latched onto *the same exact niche, outdated psychological theory* as the cis women who think trans women aren't valid or don't exist. That's remarkable. It would be like finding a board dedicated to Jewish identity on 4Chan † that wouldn't shut the fuck up about Oswald Spengler or Heinrich Himmler and criticized the least anti-Semitic and nationalistic among their number as "rootless cosmopolitans." †† That goes beyond respectability politics; indeed, it's hardly self-gentrifying. It's getting down on all fours and rolling around in shit in the hopes that such an act of self-abasement might endear one to neo-Nazis. Considering that this American fascist regime gives zero fucks how slavishly one worships it if one is not of the proper ethnicity and sexuality, that strikes me as dangerous naivete at best and as a form of deliberate self-harm at worst.

The outdated psychologist both TERFs and /tttt/ love is a fellow named Ray Milton Blanchard the Third. Blanchard is a Baby Boomer who racked up his PhD and postdoctoral work in the 1970s. He got his PhD only four years after Stonewall, when sodomy was still illegal in all 50 states. In the early 70s homosexuality was still listed in the DSM as a mental illness. That changed in 1974 with the DSM-II, but that was after a year of fierce debate and internal politicking within the American Psychiatric Association. Blanchard did not meet the qualifications to participate in the debate in 1973, so it's hard to know what his thoughts on the removal of homosexuality from the canon of mental illness was. But whatever the case, from the get-go, Blanchard's training and education were steeped in queerphobia.

Ray the Third's late education and mentorship are incredibly concerning. In 1973, while practicing at the Ontario Correctional Institute, he met a fellow named Kurt Freund (more on him in a second.) Freund became Blanchard's mentor. What was Kurt Freund doing at OCI at the time? Why, conducting research on chemical castration, naturally. (27) Blanchard's areas of specialty are unusual for a supposed "expert" on trans issues. He's done work on paraphilias, for example. Please note that there are countless harmless, even fun, paraphilias, but some of the most harmful types of sexuality (like pedophilia and zoophilia) are paraphilias. Credit where credit is due: Blanchard was instrumental in the DSM-IV distinguishing between "paraphilias" like foot fetishism and "paraphiliac disorders" like pedophilia. (28) To conduct his legitimately important research on paraphilias, however, Blanchard did two questionable things. First, his entire scheme was predicated on conducting experiments on prisoners. Second, to get the job done Blanchard rolled up both sleeves and took a tight grip on the most fraught "medical instruments" devised since the magic metal sticks (Elisha Perkins' "tractors") George Washington used to try to treat his gout. (29)

I'm talking, of course, about the penile plethysmograph (PPG).

The penile plethysmograph is a mercifully obscure piece of equipment used to measure involuntary penis responses to stimuli like slide shows of child pornography or naked, sexy men. Its history is checkered enough that Jello Biafra of Dead Kennedys fame and toweringly influential metal/punk band Melvins combined forces on an album to write a song about it during the Bush years (speaking of Homeland America). (30) The PPG was invented in 1957 in then-Czechoslovakia by the aforementioned Dr. Kurt Fruend, then a physician and sexologist still trapped in the Soviet satellite state. Perhaps I'm allowing my own political beliefs to color my thinking a little here, but in my opinion the Soviet sphere in the 1950s is one of the few space-time coordinates that could have produced a gizmo like the PPG.

You see, the PPG was developed as *literal* gaydar.

A thumbnail sketch of postwar Soviet action in Czechoslovakia goes a little like this: from 1945-1948, the country a democracy with the Communist Party gaining popular support. In 1948, a coup consolidated one-party rule under the Communists, ushering in a period of Stalinist purges and life as a satellite state in the 1950s USSR. This was followed by national liberalization in the 60s, with a brutal direct invasion launched by the USSR in 1968 as a result. Before they were properly conquered in 1968, Czechoslovakia didn't necessarily want to give up her blood for Mother USSR, as it turned out. (31) Military conscripts in the 1950s, much like those in the United States in the 1960s, would sometimes try to avoid the draft by claiming that they were gay. Remember, in those days, homosexuality meant that you obviously couldn't shoot for shit, would quail when confronted by the enemy, and likely would molest the other troops in the showers. I exaggerate, but only slightly. Stalin-aligned Czechoslovakia was having none of *that* shit, thank you very much: they needed troops! They tapped a team of scientists and when the dust cleared, in the words of one scholar, "Freund (1957) [had] developed the first device... to distinguish heterosexual and homosexual males for the Czechoslovak army." (32) HAIL SCIENCE!

I want to make one thing clear about Kurt Freund. He worked with dangerous sexual offenders and not sexual minorities for the majority of his career. (Does that excuse the practice of experimenting on prisoners?

No.) During the Stalinization of Czechoslovakia, Freund was tapped to "cure" homosexuals. He very quickly realized that most of what psychology had to say about gay men was bullshit. He became an early medical advocate for the decriminalization of homosexuality by 1957, and his work was some of the first clinical evidence that so-called conversion therapy has no scientific validity. Looking back on his career in 1991, Freund wrote:

> In the early fifties homosexual interaction was still an indictable offense in Czechoslovakia. I was of course opposed to this measure, but I still thought, as did my colleagues at the psychiatric university hospital in Prague where I was working, that homosexuality was an experientially acquired neurosis. (33)

That hardly makes him a hero of queer liberation, but he and his worst disciple, Ray Blanchard the Third, are both mixed bags. Regrettably, some of the work that Freund did with Blanchard became foundational to the later development of Blanchardism. (34) Unlike Freund, Blanchard also seems in no way eager to evolve with scientific evidence; nor to recognize that time is passing and societal mores are not what they once were (nor is the psychiatric consensus). Blanchard, incredibly, *is in dialogue with /tttt/,* (36) as if he's pleased that his outdated, bigoted work has collected a coterie of new fans. I can only imagine that the discredited race scientist Charles Murray of *The*

Bell Curve fame probably feels much the same. Plenty of 21st century racists find Murray's debunked work on "race and IQ" *quite* persuasive!

Ray Blanchard the Third has some very strange thoughts about homosexuality and other queer sexualities in general. Instead of believing that being gay is an "acquired neurosis," ala Comrade Freund did at one point, Blanchard has posited that gay men happen when a woman's womb is poisoned by having too many sons. I'm not making this shit up, although I'll admit to caricaturing his beliefs a bit. Blanchard and another researcher named Jacques Balthazart conducted four studies which suggest a higher rate of homosexuality in families for the youngest brother as compared to older brothers. (37) Now, admittedly, those studies might pose interesting questions about same-sex family dynamics, heteronormativity, and male socialization. For example: are youngest brothers allowed more emotional vulnerability with other men than their older brothers were, being raised in part by brothers? If that's true, then in a study with three brothers Blanchard might be tracking two closeted and one out gay brother, with only the youngest, most emotionally grounded brother reporting on the massive piece of the iceberg which isn't observable.

Instead, Blanchard came up with a novel explanation for the (still-unproven) hypothesis that men with older brothers have a higher probability of being gay. This is whimsically called fraternal birth order effect theory, or just older brother effect for short, by the way. Blanchard's proposal is that women's uteri interact with male fetuses in a unique way that produces "H-y antigens." Since male fetuses react this way with a pregnant person's womb, in the rather euphemistic way that chickenshit fringe science likes to use, each male pregnancy "is more likely to produce *a reaction* [emphasis mine] with each successive exposure to a male fetus." (38) An innocent (I might say naïve) reading of Blanchard's work on homosexuality might lead one to think that, as was the case with the quest for the so-called gay gene, the goal is to once and for all prove that homosexuality is not a lifestyle choice. Call me cynical, but given Blanchard's overall career, I think that it's more likely he sees queerness as a birth defect. My opinion on the matter isn't as important as this simple fact, however: Blanchard's view, and fraternal birth order theory in general, is more "controversial as hell" than "proven." (39)

Blanchard's work on trans people is entirely troubling and has managed to raise eyebrows in professional circles, though that hasn't slowed him down. That seems to be the case with alumni of the University of Toronto, which turns out right-wing activists dressed in the priestly mantle of psychiatry or psychology at an alarming rate—and their work is often more influential in the US than in Canada (see also, for example, pop-fascist self-help guru Jordan Peterson). In conducting studies of what we would call "trans women" these days, Blanchard coined the term "autogynophiliac," which is enough to damn him in my eyes. It refers to a man who is sexually aroused by the thought of himself as a woman.

Blanchard studied trans women he considered AGPs, but filed other trans women into another category (yes, there are only two). This group supposedly consists of good, valid trans women, who Blanchard called "homosexual transsexuals." These are always, he maintained, *effeminate* and *feminine-looking* gay men. Those are the broad, Blanchardist categories of trans women, cut and dried. Blanchard framed all of this as observation and early work; the true, hateful fruit of his work wouldn't emerge for some years. Perhaps because much of Blanchard's work wasn't popularly known and remained relatively niche while he rubbed elbows on committees, he stayed in good odor until 2003, and continued to be taken seriously until 2008.

2003 was a rougher year than most for Blanchard in terms of credibility. That year, a Blanchardist disciple named J. Michael Bailey penned *The Man Who Would Be Queen*. Both Blanchard's initial work and Bailey's further work based on Blanchard's premises constitute the one degree of separation between J.K. Rowling and 4Chan's /tttt/ community. In fact, the book was released the year that 4Chan was founded and /tttt/ opened its hellmouth to visitors. Coincidence? Zeitgeist? Conspiracy? I don't know. What I *do* know is that *The Man Who Would Be Queen*, which heavily cited Blanchard's work, led to Blanchard voluntarily leaving the Harry Benjamin International Gender Dysphoria Association (now called the World Professional Association for Transgender Health †††). (40). That same year, Blanchard came out of the fascist closet: he and Bailey were outed by the Southern Poverty Law Center as having joined Steven Sailer's Human Biodiversity Project. (41)

Steven Sailer used to be a writer for white

supremacist publication VDARE, and is a white nationalist extremist. (42) The Human Biodiversity Project, which he founded, is an explicitly racist, eugenicist organization. "Human biodiversity" is a term used by white supremacists to make arguments against interracial relationships and in favor of "racial purity." HBP, which Ray Blanchard the Third (along with his protégé J. Michael Baily) is a proud member of, is a think tank dedicated to providing a veneer of legitimacy to the modern iteration of long-debunked race science. (43) Remember Charles Murray, author of *The Bell Curve*, the "race and IQ" book I mentioned earlier (and which holds that some races are "genetically more intelligent" than others, a National Socialist belief)? *Also* a member of HBP!

The Man Who Would Be Queen was simply Bailey's reworking of Blanchard's typology, penned to take a variety of wild, offensive swings at the queer community. Since Bailey and Blanchard are practically inseparable, aren't you glad the American Psychiatric Association put Blanchard on the Gender Identity panel for the DSM-V? For those not in the know, that's the Diagnostic and Statistical Manual version 5, which, in short, categorizes what is diagnosable as a mental illness and what is not. Great job, mental health professionals!

Blanchard's disciple Bailey was more explicit than Blanchard was willing to be. His book claims that gay stereotypes are based in fact, and that gender nonconforming children are actually homosexual, not potentially trans, due to the aforementioned fraternal birth order theory. Summarizing Blanchard, Bailey took his biggest and most hateful swing at trans women yet, formally introducing something known to this day as "the Blanchard typology of trans women." This bullshit typology shored up Blanchard's attempt to categorize the entirety of trans women into two types. On the one hand, you have "homosexual transexuals." On the other, AGPs. None of this was new, but Blanchard's ideas from 1989 hit different in 2003. (44)

/Tttt/—an image board predominantly populated by young trans women—is *awash* in Blanchardism. There is a thin veneer of irony in most posts on any board on 4Chan, but most in /tttt/ don't pass even cursory scrutiny. Like any online space, particularly far-right online spaces, /tttt/ is saturated by a slangy, ironic, and highly idiomatic communication style generously peppered with slurs, nihilistic self-hatred, and a narcissistic hyper-fixation on beauty. The Western beauty standard, to be specific, and even more specifically a fascist performance of it. Concepts from Blachard's typology have been converted into memes and filtered through modern trans slang. We'll get to all that in a second, but first I want you to consider this.

Blanchard is a guy who, in a 2017 interview with *Vice*, had the following to say about trans issues and his "autogynophilia" theory:

> I think that a transsexual should be considered as whatever their biological sex is plus the fact that they are transsexuals. … The point that sticks in the craw of a lot of activists is that in order to get sex reassignment surgery

> paid for by a third party, it has to be deemed a disorder. The transgender community has tried to get around this in a way that they seem to think is very creative.

Other gems from the same interview:

> I always say "normal" is the other n-word. You just aren't allowed to say it. I would say I have almost never written the word normal because for decades now, since I was a graduate student, and I'm an old man, normal has been a dirty word. (45)

No wonder Blanchard spends so much time with people who are infatuated with *both* n-words! As I said, Blanchardism infests /tttt/, and we'll spend more time with it in the next section of this chapter.

Consider this, before we move on. For some people just getting online (and perhaps getting online at all against their parents' wishes, unsupervised, and on an unlocked device), it's hard to know where to turn to for advice on coming out in Homeland America. You might not have anyone in your family or friend group with whom you can discuss what your feelings might mean, or what potential identities are available for you to try on.

Recent years have seen the broad rollback of sex

education throughout the United States, and sex ed was pretty shit here to begin with. (46) At the age where one starts getting curious about sex, one would probably also be interested in the most offensive or edgy humor you weren't supposed to have access to. Also in pornography (due to hormones and curiosity), in extreme forms of rebellion, and in flexing one's fledgling social tools for bullying and othering (yes, I remember adolescence), (47) both assertions of dominance which can feel powerful to largely powerless kids. To many young people, 4Chan and places like it seem to offer exactly what they're looking for. In a Homeland American desert devoid of resources on non-heteronormative sexuality, some young people turn to the shiny, exciting, very cutting-edge oasis of unregulated content that is 4Chan.

And the oasis—where some young trans folks go to find identity and solidarity—is a cesspool.

Fuck Ray Blanchard III. And fuck J. Michael Bailey, too. I'm not the only one who feels this way! Blanchardism has been utterly eviscerated by the academy—and I do mean eviscerated. (48) Despite this, somehow in the decades since Blanchard and Bailey were last relevant to mainstream psychiatry and psychology regarding trans issues, Blanchardism and Bailey's execrable book have come roaring back. They've found new life in TERF circles and on /tttt/. Those are the type of allies a douchebag who's a member of the Human Biodiversity Project *would* cultivate. So, keeping in mind where the terms "autogynophilia" and "transsexual homosexual" come from and how heavily they've been strafed by people who *aren't* obviously hateful dipshits like Blanchard, let's take a look at /tttt/'s unspeakable syncretic communion with these concepts, and where it might intersect with radicalization.

Phrenology and Rapehons

At times, the /tttt/ community makes the incel worldview look positively charming.

Remember, to Blanchardists, there are only two types of trans women. There are AGPs ("hons" in /tttt/ slang) and homosexual transexuals ("husstussies", or HSTS, in /tttt/ lingo). Like Blanchard, /tttt/ is fixated on superficial gender presentation. While Blanchard uses the language of pseudo-psychology to mask that "presentation" is, to him, indistinguishable from "appearance," /tttt/ doesn't bother to maintain the lie. The board obsessively picks apart photos of random trans women who don't meet their beauty standards. To /tttt/, you can spot an AGP just by the look of her. The terminology anons use to describe the physical features of their crude archetypes are straight out of National Socialist body imagery:

Der Untermensch, 1942 SS Pamphlet on how to spot subhumans by their physical appearance

This is also something that trans-exclusionary radical feminists practice. The version of this practice TERFs engage in is referred to as "transvestigation," a term for investigating photos of women they suspect (almost always incorrectly) of being trans for allegedly male facial or skull features. Transvestigation has a false positive rate of about 99.9%, and the phrase "they can always tell" is used as a catchphrase online to reflect and mock the fact that these appearance-obsessed TERFs have recently claimed that Michelle Obama, Brigitte Macron (wife of French President Emmanuel Macron), Taylor Swift, Lady Gaga, Margot Robbie, and two different Olympic athletes (Lin Yu-ting and Ilona Mahar) are trans (49). None of them are. This is precisely why feminists reject to the F in TERF, by the way.

Other talking points are freely shared between TERFs and /tttt/, too. Take the term "rapehons." Allegedly, these physically less "feminine" women only want access to changing rooms and restrooms to sexually assault AFAB women. This is a common transphobic lie used by hate groups to push their agenda. "Rapehons" is an exact, crude, mirror image replica of how TERFs talk about the same exact topic (a nonissue in real life, by the way). (50)

Let's take the following screencap from /tttt/ as a case study. Compare its fixation on certain facial features to the Nazi SS pamphlet above. I've reprinted the /tttt/ post here, but I've also partially transcribed it due to the tiny print:

[Return] [Catalog] [Bottom] [Update] [Auto]

File: D8d9Tb4XkAEz3IE.jpg (46 KB, 686x477)

HSTS vs AGP body language Anonymous 07/15/19(Mon)06:54:04 No.12902259 ▶

Anonymous 07/15/19(Mon)12:31:00 No.12903662 ▶

>>12902259 (OP)
this is honestly the funniest picture i've ever seen on the internet
his vaguely threatening gesture and stance, the woman meekly clasping her hands together in fear, the difference in size between his massive skull and hers, his caveman-tier slouch making him look like a hunchback versus her standing up straight, the remnants of what appear to be sideburns on the side of his face versus the woman's clear cheeks, the intense expression on his face versus the bewildered expression on hers, the sheer difference in size between their torsos - his is probably double the size of hers, his masculine profile with his chin jutting out and his longer face versus her wider face. i could go on, but you get the idea
all of this contrasted with the constant assertion that these people are identical to women and there is no meaningful difference between them makes for the most exquisite form of irony when their differences are juxtaposed so vividly. the contrast is almost divine - on the left is man's hubris, his desire to capture the beauty of nature and make it his own, his cerebral and conscious understanding of what it means to be what he thinks he is, his intentional "becoming", while on the right is nature, effortless being, no doctors appointments or hormones or surgery, just an "is" that needs nothing added to it in order to be complete. he tries so hard and yet, the harder he tries to "become", the further he takes himself away from the effortless "is" that is the thing he wants to be. it's comedy on a cosmic scale, a joke only god himself could come up with

"this is honestly the funniest picture I've ever seen on the internet his vaguely threatening gesture and stance, the woman meekly clasping her hands together in fear. The difference in size between his massive skull and hers, his caveman-tier slouch making him look like a hunchback versus her standing up straight, the remnants of what appear to be sideburns on the side of his face versus the woman's clear cheeks, the intense expression on his face versus the bewildered expression on hen hers, the

> sheer difference in size between their torsos—his is probably double the size of hers, his masculine profile with his chin jutting out and his longer face versus her wider face, I could on but you get the idea all of this contrasted with the constant assertion that these people are identical to women and there is no meaningful difference between them makes for the most exquisite form of irony when their differences are juxtaposed so vividly. … [*blah blah blah, etc. etc. etc.—Ed.*]

I quote this not because I think the "AGP" vs. "HSTS" typology has any validity—it doesn't. I wanted to illustrate that posters in /tttt/ tend to be intensely shallow, glibly arrogant, risibly narcissistic, and childishly hateful. That has something to do with the youth of the posters there, sure, but *damn* that's a stupid, shallow, meanspirited group.

The idioms of 4Trans (another portmanteau slang term for /tttt/) have escaped the imageboard to other fascist-friendly platforms like Twitter—just coincidentally, I'm sure. From there, I predict they may eventually find their way into wider discourse. An example I spotted recently may as well be written in Etruscan as far as most normies are concerned. To someone who has spent as much time spelunking in the right-wing sewers of the internet as I have, it's legible:

dysmorphic fishoids who relentlessly diet and gua sha their faces back into brickdom

2:04 PM · Nov 28, 2025 · **34K** Views

29 7 485 21

Okay, get out your decoder rings! “Dysmorphic” is a valid term from psychology, but the rest is Chanspeak. “Fishoids” refers to “fishy” trans women (or women who can easily “pass” for AFAB women). -oid is what qualifies as a classic 4Chan suffix. Its original use was in the incel slang term “foid” (for “female humanoid”). “Gua sha” is a Chinese face-revitalization technique that is popular with some trans women. “Brickdom” is the state of being a “brick,” or a “clockable” trans women (one able to be clocked as visibly trans). It’s all a bunch of very shallow, shitty self- and other-hate.

Not every topic explored in /tttt/ is as shallow as discussing “the AGP smirk” (allegedly a particular way that some trans women smile). An example of less hateful content is /tttt/’s take on “brainworms,” a novel description of intrusive thoughts related to gender and body dysmorphia. Or take the concept of “meta-attraction” (known in different spaces as “comphet,” a shortening of “compulsory heterosexuality”). This occurs when a so-called baby trans, newly transitioned, feels the need to date members of the opposite gender, even if they aren’t attracted to them. So, for example, a freshly transitioning woman might date men, though her primary attraction is to women, because dating men is “what women do” (in actuality, gender identity and sexual orientation have nothing to do with one another). Note that this goes completely against Blanchardism, which views all trans women as, essentially, homosexual men. Shades of Nazi Germany's gender ideology, Blanchard. No wonder you were such a get for the Human Biodiversity Project! The cognitive dissonance of a community of trans women associating with the debunked ideas of a disgraced fascist psychologist is never acknowledged or addressed on /tttt/. This lack of critical thinking skills among 4Chan alumni will become even more relevant when we get to the subject of the sex lives of National Socialist trans women and femboys, who wish to fit into a "tradwife" role that couldn't be more comphet if it had been designed in a lab at Patriarchy Industries. Except for one defect in the fantasy, but we'll get there next chapter.

It's incredibly frustrating to look at /tttt/, a supposed oasis in the wasteland of fascism, and find a cesspool. Technically, there is water in a cesspool, although it's not mixed with anything you'd like to drink. 4Trans is the same. For every valid exchange that leads to someone realizing that they're actually t4t (trans for trans, or transbian—a woman primarily or only attracted to other women who've transitioned), there are ten Blanchardist rants about AGP and the "degeneracy" of "troons." If "troon" is a new word to you, you're lucky! It's a very stupid neologism; a hateful slur for trans people that sounds like something Dr. Seuss might cook up if he'd been a J.K. Rowling-style asshole.

An eerie parallel between the girls of /tttt/ and the boys of incel culture is a fixation on one's physical appearance and the belief that it's an insurmountable obstacle to acceptance and happiness. (51) Likewise, neither community seems in any hurry to snap out of these spirals of self-and-other-hating rhetoric. A constant feature of /tttt/ culture is trans women posting either a) photos (allegedly of themselves, though I suppose it could be random strangers), seeking negative attention which other anons readily supply, and b) lengthy diatribes about how everything they've done to transition has been too late, far too late, and that if one doesn't start puberty blockers early, one will never be beautiful. (52) That's simply not true, by the way. I know older trans people—including the creator of one of my favorite webcomics, Haus of Decline—who didn't transition until they were middle-aged. Madame Haus is gorgeous, and happier than her grumpy, frumpy former self. To take a page from the film *I Saw The TV Glow*'s book, there is still time. As long as you draw breath, there still is time.

How much of /tttt/'s culture is due to its demographics? I don't mean in terms of orientation or identity, but rather in terms of age, affluence, and country of origin. 4Chan, while popular worldwide, is still primarily a Western phenomenon, and especially popular in the United States. US users account for about half of 4Chan's traffic. (53) While little data on its anonymous audience is readily available, it started out—and has stayed—young. Perhaps *very* young, if a few of the interviews I did are any example. Young folks tend to be angsty, and for damn good reason. One of those is purely hormonal and has to do with brain wiring (and is only the smallest part of why relationships between adults and teens are always abusive, inappropriate, and gross) but other aspects of it have to do with the process of figuring out one's identity amidst sexual frustration, a vicious pecking order, and isolation much more extreme than what I had to deal with when I was growing up.

Why does this matter? Well, for one thing, 4Chan is very good at incubating one thing and one thing only, and its fuel for what is turning politics into Nazi Germany by way of Florida Man crossed with Liberace right now: hate. But don't take my word for it. Steeped in Blanchardism and 4Chan lingo, here's the result of time in /tttt/:

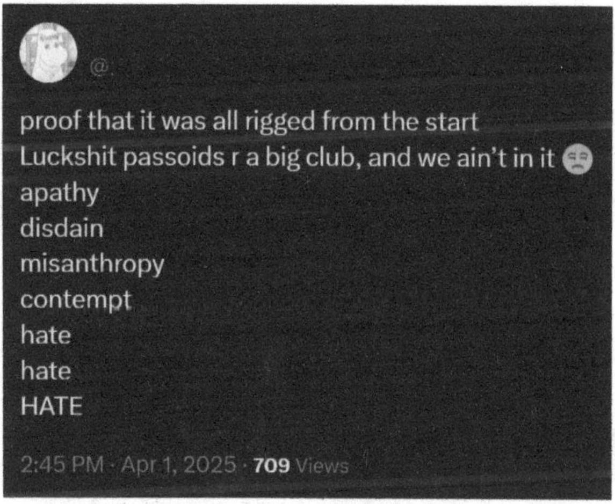

It's helpful to remember that 4Chan is a board designed to offend, trigger, outrage, disgust, and horrify normies. However, it's very easy to tell how much of the content there (and downstream of it) is bullshit and posturing and how much is honest hate hiding beneath irony. As Chapter Three and Chapter Four demonstrated, neo-Nazi "jokes" about incest and pedophilia become successively less funny each time a group of them gets busted for a CSAM manufacturing ring or unironically advocates for incest as a path to racial purity. There's something else worth noting here. The "black market theory" of drugs applies to information about sex and sexual politics, too. If *all* drugs are illegal, from the harmless joint to the fearsome baggie of fentanyl, it logically follows that those who go to a dealer for a bag of cannabis might decide to dabble in other illicit substances available from the same source. This is a long-established argument for the decriminalization of drugs. (54)

In a similar way, Homeland America has forced young people into some very dark online alleyways to learn about non-heteronormative sex—hell, to learn about sex in general. In the case of sexual minorities (particularly trans women), one of those alleyways is 4Chan. Sure, plenty of young people are initially drawn to 4Chan for its hateful content and chaotic environment, but those who hang around in /tttt/ obviously found something there that spoke to them about their own identity and perhaps even provided a toxicity-laced form of community. Example: 4Chan, like much of Western culture, has been thoroughly overtaken by anime. People in my generational cohort (Millennials) and younger are generally familiar with and conversant in the genre of Japanese animation, but Gen Z? They watch the genre more than sports. (55) I'm picky about anime myself and absolutely detest otaku culture, but virtually everyone I know is obsessed with anime, and regrettably Nazis are, too. One reason for this attraction might be that anime has a sizable, rarely-spoken-of, extremely troubling fascism problem. (56)

Not just the fandom; there are bigots in almost any fandom. The material itself. Several highly popular anime titles either normalize or glamorize fascist regimes, with politics that Hitler or Hideki Tojo would have drooled over and uniform aesthetics straight from Hugo Boss. These include shows like *Attack on Titan* and *ACCA: 13-Territory Inspection Dept*, just to name two shows from very opposite poles of the art form. Part of this is cultural. Japan never fought the Nazis, nor fought against fascism anywhere else or at any other time. After the war, we subjected Germany to a very half-assed but at least cursory de-Nazification process, and regulated speech and the display of political messaging after that for decades. (57) The U.S. overhauled Japan politically and economically—but less so culturally. (58) Sure, Japan doesn't have the Nazi problem of, say, India, but you'll find more fascist sympathy in anime than most genres of entertainment outside of early Homeland America classics like the execrable *24*.

Many—not all, but many—young trans women are *very* into anime. One reason for this is very simple; compared to Western fare, anime and manga (the Japanese graphic novel form from which anime is often adapted) are artforms that have rich, complex representation of trans, queer, and gender nonconforming characters. (59) Sometimes, I wonder if the infiltration of /tttt/ by fascist ideas happened at first through pure aesthetics. You'll find this in some of my interviews; one femboy, for example, talks about how his interest in dressing up in sexy Nazi uniform drag is (almost) entirely out of a sense of fashion. Nazi chic has certainly been a thing throughout modern fashion history in various times and places up to this day. (60)

I'm extremely skeptical of claims that the influence of the swastika in fashion and fetish communities runs only clothing deep. I think it might *start* that way with some people. However, there's more to the Nazi trans phenomenon than just fashion, kink, or anime. It's more than self- or other-hatred, too. In fact, I think that growing up in Homeland America, coupled with the miasmic right-wing political culture of the last few decades, has combined with all these things to create a unique and niche radicalization funnel—and one worth paying attention to.

If you read my previous nonfiction book, the first portion of the next chapter will be familiar ground. For those of you who are new to the topic of Esoteric Hitlerism and/or postmodern fascist irony, well, flex those brain muscles and get ready to absorb some very, very strange shit.

*If I remember correctly, this would have been 1992. That means that this friend could have introduced me to petty theft and Insane Clown Posse's masterful *Carnival of Carnage* instead, an album which dropped that year. No hate against *The Wall*, but I think it's a little overhyped, whereas *Carnival of Carnage* remains an underappreciated gem.

**I have no affection for the late Richard "Lowtax" Kyanka, Something Awful's founder and unquestioned tyrant. He took his own life in 2021, and had a history of domestic violence[a] and extreme cliquishness and fits of pique when it came to what was and wasn't allowed on SA and where.

[a] Gault, Matthew (11/11/2021). "Richard 'Lowtax' Kyanka, Founder of Something Awful, Is Dead at 45". *Vice*.

*** Such as:

Lavin, Talia (2020). Culture Warlords: My Journey Into the Dark Web of White Supremacy. (Legacy Lit, New York).

Nagle, Angela Kill (2017.) Kill All Normies: Online Culture Wars from 4Chan and Tumblr to Trump and the Alt-Right. (Collective Ink, London.)

Wendling, Mike (2018.) Alt-Right - From 4chan to the White House. (Burning Books, Oakland.)

† This is something that will never happen, however. The red thread running through the entirety of 4Chan, like the one Hitler described running through his ideology in Mein Kampf, is white-hot, genocidal hatred of all things Jewish.

†† For those who haven't read my previous book, "rootless cosmopolitan" was a term coined by Joseph Stalin, but the concept was taken from proto-fascist German nationalist Oswald Spengler, who in his 1918 two-volume screed The Decline of the West made the (incoherent) case that Jews have no true allegiance to any nation or *ethnos* other than their own, and thus can't be trusted in *any* community to which their

diaspora was driven after the Romans scattered them in 70 CE. While Spengler was unwilling to take his premises to their logical conclusions, this really leaves only one solution (a "final" solution, if you will) available to German nationalists worried about the decline of the West.

††† Harry Benjamin, the psychologist after whom the Center was originally named, is another dinosaur when it comes to the psychology of trans sexuality. If you see someone online with anything in their information that says, for example, "HBS Type IV," they are referring to Harry Benjamin Syndrome, a now-debunked framework and approach to the classification of gender dysphoria. Like Blanchardists, "Harry Benjamin Syndrome" trans femmes are engaged in a form of pseudomedical psychological self-harm.

1 Staudenmaier, Peter (1/9/2017). "The Nazis as occult masters? It's a good story but not history". *Aeon*.

2 https://meta.wikimedia.org/wiki/Research:Online_Community_Conduct_Policies/4Chan

3 O'Sullivan, Donie (5/16/2022). "Buffalo massacre puts spotlight on hate-filled website". *CNN*.

https://irc.rice.edu/?movies=4chan-archives – "Legal and Ethical Considerations"

Thorleifsson, C. (2022). "From cyberfascism to terrorism: On 4chan/pol/ culture and the transnational production of memetic violence". *Nations and*

Nationalism. 28 (1). P286–301.

4 Redmond, S. et. al. (2019). "Who watches an ISIS beheading—And why". *American Psychologist*. 74 (5). P555–568.

5 Beren, Dale (2019). It Came From Something Awful. (All Points Books, New York). P65-68.

6
https://www.semrush.com/website/4chan.org/overview/

7 Smith, Perry M. (1991). How CNN Fought the War. (Birch Lane Press, New York). Extensive sections.

8 Staff. (2/2/2025). "Surveillance Oversight: PATRIOT Act". *Electronic Privacy Information Center*.

Staff. (5/30/2006). "Librarians Speak Out for First Time After Being Gagged by Patriot Act". *ACLU*.

Khan, Sahar & Ramachandran, Vignesh (9/16/2021). "Post-9/11 surveillance has left a generation of Muslim Americans in a shadow of distrust and fear". *PBS News*.

Eddington, Patrick (10/21/2021). "The PATRIOT Act Has Threatened Freedom for 20 Years". *CATO Institute*.

9 Staff. (2003) "U.S. Immigration and Customs Enforcement." *Federal Register: The Daily Journal of United States Government*.

10 O'Herron, Margy (8/13/2025). "Big Budget

Act Creates a 'Deportation-Industrial Complex': The result will be a lopsided, enforcement-only machine that will be hard to dismantle." *Brennan Center For Justice*.

11 Demopoulos, Alaina (7/23/2025). "The nefarious message behind the DHS 'manifest destiny' painting: 'four pillars of propaganda'". *The Guardian*.

Merlan, Anna (8/15/2025). "The Official Voice of the US Government Is Cruel, Gross, and Weird. What Is That Doing to Us? Joking memes about imprisonment, deportation, and death by alligator are designed to radicalize and desensitize." *Mother Jones*.

12 Rosenbaum, Eric (10/16/2025). "Amazon Ring security cameras moving deeper into law enforcement with Flock Safety, Axon deals". *CNBC*.

Moore, Meg (6/26/2023). "Surveillance Cameras Provide Vital Evidence for Law Enforcement". *LiveView Technologies*.

13 Schüller, Simone (2015). "The 9/11 conservative shift". *Economic Letters*. Vol 135. P80-84.

Hartig, Hannah & Doherty, Caroline (9/2/2021). "Two Decades Later, the Enduring Legacy of 9/11". *Pew Research Center*.

14 Travers, Mark (1/19/2023). "Why Are We Attracted to Strongman Leaders? A professor deconstructs our age-old attraction to tyrants." *Psychology Today*.

15 Downing, Jared (5/20/2025). "The 'strongmen' who are breaking democracies: Autocratic leaders are more likely to score highly on dark personality traits and perform poorly. Why do people vote them into office?" *The University of British Columbia Magazine*.

16 Darling-Hammond, Linda "Evaluating 'No Child Left Behind'". *Stanford Center for Opportunity Policy in Education.*

Ward, Steven C. "No Child Behind Goes To College". *Academe Magazine*.

17 Loveless, Tom (3/18/2021). "Why Common Core failed". *The Brookings Institution.*

Arnold, Benjamin W. & Shakeel, M. Danish (2021). "The Unintended Effects of the Common Core State Standards on Non-Targeted Subjects". *Annenberg Exchange: Ed Working Papers*.

18 Flanagan, Caitlyn (2021). "Private Schools Have Become Truly Obscene: Elite schools breed entitlement, entrench inequality—and then pretend to be engines of social change." *The Atlantic.*

19 Staff. (6/12/2025). "Discrimination and Barriers to Well-Being: The State of the LGBTQI+ Community in 2022". *Center For American Progress*.

Sullivan, Andrew[a] (6/26/2025). "How the Gay Rights Movement Radicalized and Lost Its Way". *The New York Times*.

[a]: Andrew Sullivan has been milking this same outrage for over twenty years. The fact that he's still

a gay "I'm just concerned about" troll after this many decades simply speaks to my point.

20 Paulus, Frank W. et. al. (December 2024). "The impact of Internet pornography on children and adolescents: A systematic review". *L'Encéphale*. 59 (6).

21 Broderick, Ryan (4/22/2025). "4chan Is Dead[a]. Its Toxic Legacy Is Everywhere: It's likely that there will never be a site like 4chan again. But everything now—from X and YouTube to global politics—seems to carry its toxic legacy." Wired.

[a]With all respect to former anon Ryan Broderick, this is about the fifth time I've heard 4Chan declared "dead." Each and every time, site traffic has come roaring back.

22 Arriens, Jaap (4/15/2025). "Suspected 4chan Hack Could Expose Longtime, Anonymous Admins: Though the exact details of the situation have not been confirmed, community infighting seems to have spilled out in a breach of the notorious image board." *Wired.*

23 Yurcaba, Jo (2/27/2025). "More than half of books banned last year featured LGBTQ characters or people of color, report finds: Of history and biography books that were banned last year, 26% featured Black people, and 25% featured LGBTQ people." *NBC News*.

24 https://www.reddit.com/r/CuratedTumblr/comments/1kmbobi/imagine_a_prison_where_everyone_stews_in/

https://www.reddit.com/r/CuratedTumblr/comments/1c75z58/r4tran_and_tttt_users_really_invented_an_entire/

https://x.com/Ranting_Trans/status/1926423574266446184

25 https://knowyourmeme.com/memes/subcultures/tttt

26 https://archived.moe/lgbt/thread/29762121/#29762508

27 Freund, Kurt (1980). "Therapeutic Sex Drive Reduction". *Acta Psychiatrica Scandinavica*. Vol 62. P5–38.

28 Moran, Mark (2013). "*DSM* to Distinguish Paraphilias From Paraphilic Disorders". Psychiatric News. 48 (9).

29 Quen, Jacques M. (1963). "Elisha Perkins, Physician, Nostrum-Vendor, or Charlatan?" *Bulletin of the History of Medicine*. Vol 37. P159-166.

30 "Plethysmograph" (2004). Track 1. *Never Breathe What You Can't See*. Jello Biafra With the Melvins. (Alternative Tentacles).

31 "Document No. 50: Memorandum of the Academic Staff of the Czechoslovak Military Academies on Czechoslovakia's Defense Policy". P271. *Geroge Washington University: National Security Archive.*

Wilson, R. J., & Mathon, H. F. (2006, fall). "Remembering Kurt Freund (1914-1996)". *Association for the Treatment of Sexual*

Abusers Forum.

32 O'Donohue, W. & Letourneau, H. (1992). "The psychometric properties of the penile tumescence assessment of child molesters". *Journal of Psychopathology and Behavioral Assessment.* Vol 14. P123-174.

33 Ha, Nathan (2015). "Detecting and Teaching Desire: Phallometry, Freund, and Behaviorist Sexology". *Osiris*. 30 (1). P205–227.

34 Freund, K., & Blanchard, R. (1983). "Is the distant relationship of fathers and homosexual sons related to the sons' erotic preference for male partners, or to the sons' atypical gender identity, or to both?" *Journal of Homosexuality.* Vol 9. P7-25.

35 Freund, Kurt (1991). "Reflections on the development of the phallometric method of assessing sexual preference". *Annals of Sex Research.* 4 (3–4): P221–228.

36 https://x.com/BlanchardPhD/status/1578081778706808843

37 Balthazart, Jacques (2017). "Fraternal birth order effect on sexual orientation explained". *Proceedings of the National Academy of Sciences*. 115 (2). P234–236, for example.

38 Blanchard R, Bogaert AF (January 1996). "Homosexuality in men and number of older brothers". *American Journal of Psychiatry*. 153 (1). P27–31.

39 Bailey JM et. al. (2016). "Sexual Orientation,

Controversy, and Science". *Psychological Science in the Public Interest*. 17 (2). P45–101.

Bogaert AF; Skorska M (2011). "Sexual orientation, fraternal birth order, and the maternal immune hypothesis: a review". *Frontiers in Neuroendocrinology*. 32 (2). P247–54.

40 Dreger, Alice D. (2008). "The Controversy Surrounding *The Man Who Would Be Queen*: A Case History of the Politics of Science, Identity, and Sex in the Internet Age". *Archives of Sexual Behavior*. 37 (3). P366–421.

41 Beirich, Heidi; Moser, Bob (12/31/2003). "Northwestern University Psychology Professor J. Michael Bailey Looks into Queer Science". *Southern Poverty Law Center*.

42 Hermansson, Patrik et. al. (2020). "For Whom the Bell Curves: The alt-right and pseudoscientific racism," *The International Alt-Right: Fascism for the 21st Century?* (Routledge, Milton Park).

43 Feldman, Ari (8/g/2016). "Human Biodiversity: The Pseudoscientific Racism of the Alt-Right". *Forward*.

Panofsky, Aaron et. al. (2021). "How White nationalists mobilize genetics: From genetic ancestry and human biodiversity to counterscience and metapolitics". *American Journal of Physical Anthropology*. 175 (2). P387–398.

44 Blanchard, R. (1989). "The classification and labelling of nonhomosexual gender dysphorias". *Archives of Sexual Behavior*. **18** (4). P315–334, for example.

45 Cameron, Laura (4/11/2013). "How the Psychiatrist Who Co-Wrote the Manual on Sex Talks About Sex". *Vice*.

46 duRivage-Jacobs, Sarah (1/23/2024). "How did Sex Ed in the U.S. Become Such a Disaster?" *Origin.*

Finkel, Ed (10/1/2025). "A growing number of state bills target sex education, report says: Of more than 650 state-level bills on the topic, nearly a quarter sought to pare back or remove access, a SIECUS report found." *K-12 Dive*.

47 Lo Cricchio, M. G. et. al. (2023). "Adolescents' ethnic hate speech exposure and ethnic bullying perpetration: The moderating role of tolerance towards diversity and gender". *Cyberpsychology: Journal of Psychosocial Research on Cyberspace*. 17 (5). Article 4.

Kansock-Dusche, Julia (2023). "A Systematic Review on Hate Speech among Children and Adolescents: Definitions, Prevalence, and Overlap with Related Phenomenon." *Trauma, Violence, & Abuse*. 24 (4).

48 Serano, Julia (2020). "Autogynephilia: A scientific review, feminist analysis, and alternative 'embodiment fantasies' model". *The Sociological Review*. 68 (4). P763–778.

Serano, Julia (2007). *Whipping girl: a transsexual woman on sexism and the scapegoating of femininity*. (Seal Press, New York). P178.

Serano, Julia (2010). "The Case Against Autogynephilia" *International Journal of*

Transgenderism. 12 (3). P176–187.

Bettcher, TM (2014). "When selves have sex: what the phenomenology of trans sexuality can teach about sexual orientation". *Journal of Homosexuality*. 61 (5). P605–620.

Ashley, Florence (2020). "A critical commentary on 'rapid-onset gender dysphoria'". *The Sociological Review*. 68 (4). P779–799.

Nuttbrock, Larry; et al. (2011). "A Further Assessment of Blanchard's Typology of Homosexual Versus Non-Homosexual or Autogynephilic Gender Dysphoria". *Archives of Sexual Behavior*. 40 (2). P247–257.

Moser C (2010). "Blanchard's Autogynephilia Theory: a critique". *Journal of Homosexuality*. 57 (6) P790–809.

49 Lopez, Quispe (8/14/2024). "How "Transvestigation" Crawled Out of the Worst Corners of the Internet Into the Mainstream: The most committed transvestigators believe a cabal of secretly trans celebrities controls the world." *Them*.

Smith, Ian (4/2/2025). "Why are false rumours about Brigitte Macron being transgender resurfacing?" *euronews*.

50 Serano, Julia (6/7/2021). "Transgender People, Bathrooms, and Sexual Predators: What the Data Say". *Medium*.

51 Conti, Allie (6/20/2018). "Inside the Disturbing Forum Incels Use to Brutally Criticize Each Other's Faces". *Vice*.

Aiolfi, I. et al. (2024). “The incel phenomenon: A systematic scoping review.” *Current Psychology*. Vol 43. P26264–26278.

52 https://archived.moe/lgbt/thread/26919230/#26920758

> “Ossification happens as late as 20. That’s the latest. If you haven’t trooned out at like, 14 or 16 you are a lateshit by these standards.”

53 lley, Ben (3/9/2021). "’The rebirth of the West begins with you!’—Self-improvement as radicalisation on 4chan". *Humanities and Social Sciences Communications*. 8 (1) 67. P1–10.

54 Patrick Fouch (2023). “Decriminalization: A Way Out of the Unwinnable War on Drugs”. *Appalachian Journal of Law*. 22 (2).

55 Patches, Matt (1/23/2024). “For Gen Z, anime is bigger than the NFL”. *Polygon*.

Gassert, Laura (11/16/2024). “Anime Is Now More Popular Than Major Sports in the US”. *GameRant*.

56 Villanueva, Michelle (10/8/2018). “The troubling relationship between anime and fascism”. *Authorly*, archived from *SyFy Wire*.

57 German Constitution: Article 5, Paragraph 2.

58 Dobbins, James (2008). *After the War: Nation-Building from FDR to George W. Bush*. (RAND Corporation, Santa Monica). P11-36.

59 Staff. (4/12/2023). “A Deep Dive Into Queer

Genders and Gender Non-Conformity in Anime and Manga". *Sabukaru Magazine*.

60 Manning, Charles (2/13/2015). "Trendy Teens in Asia Are Dressing Up Like Nazis". *Cosmopolitan*.

Duane, Daniel (9/28/2019). "The Long, Strange Tale of California's Surf Nazis". *New York Times*.

Mozgovia, Natasha (6/12/2006). "Auschwitz t-shirts for sale?". *Ynetnews*.

CHAPTER EIGHT

SCHWARZE SONNE DOLLS

In Chapter Four, I introduced you to Andy and Leyley, the murdering, incestuous brother-sister couple beloved of fascist meme magicians. Let me refresh your memory with another slap in the chops with this unforgettable banger:

While I focused on the "fuck your sibling" plan for

genetic purification in that chapter (and for good reason), I glossed over that background sigil a bit while focusing on the peccadillos of Nazi sex. The sigil is an instant identifier for a person who is under the spell of an obscure Nazi ideology, and in some ways it's how I spotted my very first trans Nazi. (1) That wheel-looking device behind Andy and Leyley is called the Schwarze Sonne, (2) or Black Sun. It's the most widely used symbol of a syncretic, mystical neo-Nazi belief system called Esoteric Hitlerism. What's that, you justifiably ask? During World War Two, Savitri Devi, a French-born Greek woman and Adolf Hitler's biggest fan, moved to India. This was ostensibly to work for the Reich's efforts there. After Adolf ventilated his musty skull, Devi whipped up a combination of obscure Nazi source material, misread Hinduism, and worship of Adolf Hitler as a literal avatar of Vishnu the Sustainer that became known as Esoteric Hitlerism. It spread like a particularly unpleasant rash. (3)

Here's a better look at the Schwarze Sonne, not obscured by the happy couple above:

We don't need to go into the various meanings and interpretations of the symbol. It suffices to say that it's a sunwheel (a sigil-form common in many religious traditions) composed of twelve radial *sig* runes, (4) the same rune which, when twinned like lightning bolts, made up the sigil of the SS. In fact, a Schwarze Sonne—while never deployed widely in the NSDAP or Nazi Germany—appeared in a mosaic on the tile floor of Wewelsburg Castle, where Himmler intended to locate the headquarters of the SS. (ibid.) The sig rune is not a real rune. Real runes are letters in an ancient set of related alphabets of the ancient Germanic Peoples.

That's peoples, plural. And don't let "Germanic" fool you; modern Germans have as much to do with these peoples as present-day citizens of Rome do with the Roman Empire's outer reaches. The use of these alphabets stretched from Scandinavia and parts of Switzerland to Poland. These sets of runes form different alphabets throughout different eras, and were replaced by Latin script. Ancient letters from these alphabets are all what I'd call *real* runes: real letters from real extinct alphabets. Oh, and despite the Nazi fixation on "Ancient Germans," that term is an entire backhoe full of bullshit. (5) Runes have been found in Iceland, on the Isle of Man, in Greece, on the Black Sea, in Maine, Scotland, Minnesota, Denmark, and Türkiye. Not all of those are places the various peoples crudely described by Roman historians as "Germanic" lived, but all of them were visited by them. "Ancient German letters" these were fucking *not,* just because the Romans decided to slap the label "Germania" on the region occupied by present-day Czech Republic, Austria, Slovakia, Hungary, Switzerland, France, Belgium, and the Netherlands. (6) Now let's talk about the magic set of bullshit runes that the so-called *sig* rune comes from.

The sig rune is from the "Armanen runes," which were received in a vision by an Austrian mountaineer named Guido von Lizst. Von Lizst saw these runes while he was temporarily blinded while, one would assume, mountaineering in the early 1900s. (7) Von Lizst had some very peculiar ideas regarding German racial mysticism; ideas which, while never widely adopted by Hitler, which influenced the specific brand of (in the words of one scholar) "bio-mystic racialism" the Nazis were peddling. (8)

Every day it seems that I discover how naïve I've been up to that point. Example: the last fucking place on Lucifer's black beach that I expected to see the Black Sun used as part of an aesthetic was among trans women (and younger trans girls.). Yet, in the mid-2020s, that's exactly what has happened. Make no mistake, I'm not saying this is a *widespread* problem—just *too* widespread. Many of the examples I noticed and collected were from Twitter * for a few reasons. First, it's a very Nazi-friendly platform. (9) Second, unlike 4Chan, it's not anonymous and allows users to create relatively intricate profiles for themselves and to receive private messages. Lastly, it's an easily searchable platform and the freewheeling environment lends itself to both conflict and communication (for example, see my interviews).

The first profile that got my attention was this one. She followed a trans friend of mine out of nowhere. This isn't an infrequent occurrence with trans folks on Twitter—fascists, after all, never stop recruiting and/or trolling.

Yes, that is the Schwarze Sonne crossed with the trans pride flag. Note the slogan "trans rights are white rights," a variation on the slogan "trans rights are human rights." Leveraging one's race to gain acceptance in far-right spaces is nothing new: framing trans rights as "white rights" is. Generally, the line from both original-recipe Nazis and neo-Nazis has been that trans identity is the type of moral degeneracy that ought to be stamped out completely through a national policy of "racial hygiene." Trans literature was burned as "filth" by the NSDAP and an incredible wave of destruction of trans communities and infrastructure followed Hitler's seizure of power. (10) Despite this, the trans Nazis I interviewed seemed utterly certain that *their whiteness overrode their queerness.* A few claimed that they'd found more acceptance on the right than they had in leftist spaces. When people say this, they are invariably talking about the perceived scolds of "wokeness" versus the seemingly welcoming far-right's recruitment efforts. That's a sentiment that deserves to be broken down step by step.

The idea that whiteness ever will—or could—overcome *any* other identity is incoherent because it presupposes the idea of a "white" race, which does not exist. (11) Any extremism researcher, or anyone else who has had reason to spend more than a few moments around a group of Nazis online or elsewhere, will tell you that racial paranoia, infighting, and ethnic nitpicking have been a central characteristic of fascism from its roots to its current incarnation. (12) A trans person's whiteness can never override other identities because *one's white identity is literally never above question or beyond reproach.* One of the great 21st century neo-Nazi pastimes is calling each other "brown" and "Jew"—and that's not new.

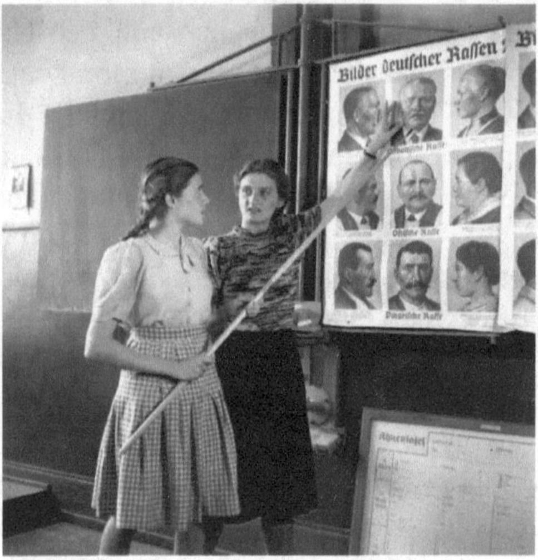

A German student learning the difference between Jews and "Aryans," 1943 (Deutsches Historisches Museum, Berlin)

Second, the queer fascist conception of *ethnos* is not shared by other fascists, who see *ethnos* as inseparable from *eros*. Sex can never, in the world of fascism, be separated from procreation and the perpetuation of the *volk.* (13) Sex serves only to strengthen and perpetuate the race. Thus, the sex lives of straight couples where the wife or husband happen to be trans, or the sex lives of all queer folks, are invalid in the eyes of any fascist social scheme.

Lastly, while I don't doubt that there are *some* deeply bigoted trans people who are naturally amenable to fascism, I think that the wave of trans fascists now present in the 2020s on boards like /tttt/ and apps like Twitter are more indicative of a temporary pseudo-identity than they are an enduring wave of politically radicalized queer neo-Nazis. Strip away the layers of irony, self-reference, self-hatred, otaku posturing, shitposting, meme culture, and a shallow understanding of ideas concealed by volume and vehemence. I think that a large percentage of the current wave of Schwarze Sonne dolls will find their way out of the fascist sinkhole, given time. What's worrying is that this happened at all, and it's also concerning to think what the long-term effects will be. While, as I've mentioned, deradicalization is possible, fascism's claws leave their marks. Those marks take the form of habits of thought, lingering prejudices, and the social opprobrium every ex-Nazi will have to deal with for the rest of their life. At least, if they are honest about their past with loved ones throughout the coming years.

The situation is, in short, a mess. Not only for the victims of the rhetoric and hate spewed by these women, but for them as well. They aren't just perpetuating an inhuman social-political order: *they're victims of it, too.*

Skin Deep?

One way to resolve the cognitive dissonance of an identity like "trans National Socialist" is to simply deny that any dissonance exists. I can't think of a better example than this one, spotted in the wild:

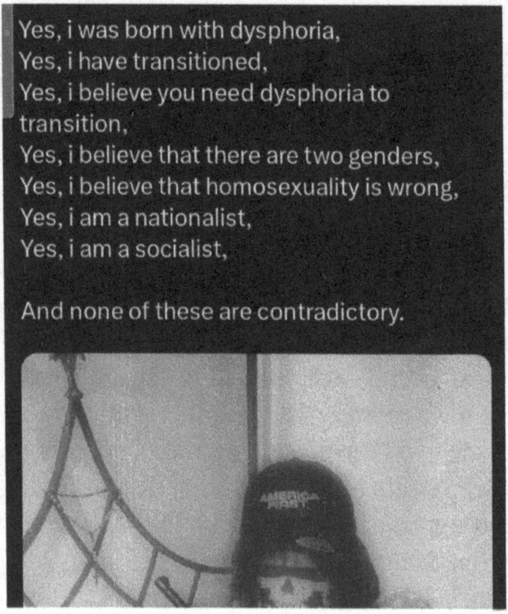

To hell with the Nazis looting of the Berlin Institute of Sexology and the burning of their books and manuscripts (which set trans rights and the ability for people to transition back by decades)! (14) To hell with the Nazi regime classifying trans women as male homosexuals and sending them to death camps! (15) Never mind the so-called Röhm Putsch and the executions of Röhm and his gay SA inner circle (see Chapter Three)! Being a trans Nazi *just isn't contradictory*, got it?

The consistency and density of this denial is impressive. In Interview 1 in **Appendix A: Interviews**, I speak with a trans woman who wanted to be identified as Jade Augustus. I asked her if she thought identifying as a trans woman and identifying as a National Socialist were contradictory. Here's her response:

> Not really. I'm more so a National Socialist that just so happens to be a tranny, too. I don't really think the two are implicitly compatible, but they can be made to co-exist in a "stop indoctrinating kids and you get to live" kinda thing. I say if you want to advance the regime, you should be able to do so even if you're a tranny. i really do think Whiteness should be prioritized. Besides there are so many gorgeous White trans girls that i don't think they should be executed solely for being trannies. Once you get rid of interlopers, fetishists, and predators, there really is not a whole lot to complain about regarding the trans community. (1)

Referring to herself as a "tranny" is very /tttt/, where semi-sarcastic self-hatred and the use of slurs to describe oneself are very much in fashion. Still: "I really do think Whiteness should be prioritized" speaks volumes. These aren't the words of someone who knows her history, nor one who has had serious contact with the fascist movement, nor even observed its close workings and then processed that reality.

It's interesting to note the subtle Blanchardist eliminationism here as well. Jade distinguishes between "gorgeous White trans girls" and "*fetishists* [emphasis mine], and interlopers." Jade is talking about virtuous, beautiful husstussies being acceptable to the coming Reich, while AGPs and brickhons will be dealt with. The crude taxonomy developed by Ray Blanchard, the still-respected, fascist, eugenicist mind behind the DSM-V, would in Jade's mind one day undergird atrocities even greater than those he's already culpable for**! Getting "blackpilled" (turned to nihilistic despair and hopelessness at the state of one's appearance, future, prospects, racial status, etc.) on 4Chan seems to be part of the reason why people go there. That probably explains the site's longstanding connection to mass public shootings. (16)

As for whiteness overcoming or at least coming to an accommodation with queerphobia, there's no evidence that such an exchange is currently possible. Gays For Trump might talk a good game, but the Supreme Court that Trump mostly appointed still nearly overturned gay marriage in the United States (17) and Trump has dismantled vital, life-saving resources for queer youth in what I honestly believe is a very lazy, passive attempt at a cull. (18) For its part, the Nazi regime was thoroughly and murderously transphobic, full stop. (19) Modern neo-Nazis (except for the trans variety) are equally virulent in their hatred for trans people, and are actively engaged in a wave of anti-trans hate crimes. (20) It isn't Black trans, or Latina trans, or Jewish trans people these neo-Nazis are menacing: its trans people *including* "gorgeous White trans girls." So much for that theory, Jade Augustus.

Even *if* white supremacist and neo-Nazi

organizations made exceptions for white trans people, "white" is a moving target for these numbskulls. White is a definition of exclusion, not a race. (21) White supremacists aren't just traditionally "white" (see the fact that prolific federal snitch Enrique Tarrio was leader of the "Western Chauvinist" Proud Boys for a while, for example). "European" is not a race or ethnicity. (22) None of the taxonomies these dipshit Nazis and white nationalists have invented have any scientific or social validity. One's "whiteness" is determined entirely by the racist, judgmental eyeballs of one's peers. In this case, these eyes belong to 4Chan, Twitter, and other heavily white supremacist online spaces. This means that they mainly deal in a) presentation, and b) an extreme version of the Western beauty standard. That's all well and good for "hot or not," I guess, but when it comes to determining race? Much like transvestigation, calling someone's race by eye and gut leads to some hilariously stupid judgment calls by the Vanguard of the White Race.

I wanted to find an example of this dynamic happening with a trans person, and I didn't even have to search past the day I wrote these words. As the metadata indicates, this exchange took place *one hour before* I tried to find an example. These exchanges happen literally constantly, every single day, between National Socialists, ultranationalists, etc. Let the race science begin:

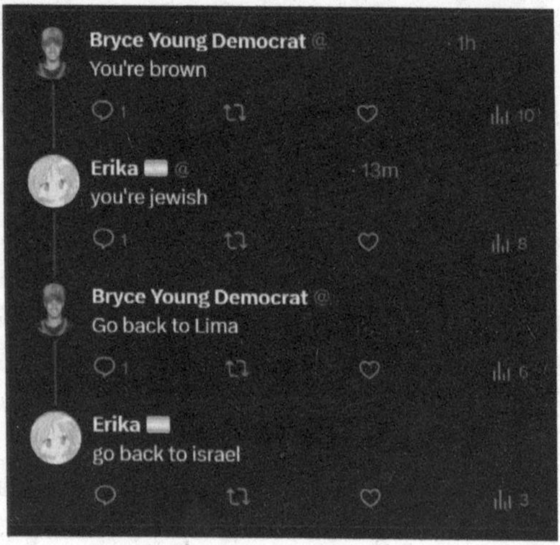

Is Bryan Jewish? No. Is Erika a person of color? No. Does that matter? *Fuck* no. Whiteness isn't going to save any of these angry, confused people, because—and gather round to hear this so I don't have to scream it at the top of my lungs—*whiteness doesn't exist.* "White" is not a race. Most Americans are mutts. Whiteness was constructed by exclusion of certain groups—and not always just based on appearance, either. And even if "whiteness" did exist in quantifiable form? It wouldn't matter. In-group persecution of an out-group is the foundation upon which fascism is built. (23) You know what? I think Violent J of Insane Clown Posse may have said it best in "Everybody Rize:"

> Fuck skin color, everybody's blue
> Then what would all these bigots do?
> Instead of your tone, they'd hate your size

> That's why I must pluck out all of their
> eyes

Whoop whoop. I also think that's a rock-solid anti-racist strategy on Violent J's part.

Let's leave "beautiful White trans girls" to one side for a moment. As the supposed embodiment of the *ethnos*, a *Völkisch* State concerns itself, first and foremost, with the perpetuation, bodily integrity, and "moral health" of its people. This is, in short, bad news for trans Nazis.

Trans-Exclusionary Compulsory Heterosexuality

To understand how misguided the trans Nazi's drive for acceptance is, you must comprehend the worldview (or *Weltanschauung* in the devil's tongue) of the Nazis. The NSDAP was more than a political movement. It was more than just weaponized Jew-hatred, and more than a style or aesthetic. Germany's brand of fascism was described by one scholar whom I've already mentioned as "bio-mystic racialism." The "mystic" part of that is fascinating, but we don't have room to get into it in depth here. However, that description is enough to tell you that a specific, pseudoscientific conception of biology—especially human biology—was and is a tentpole in Nazi ideology. Their definition of "human" includes only fit bodies, as was proven by the Nazi's choice of their first victims of mass extermination—the disabled. A primary obsession of Nazism was the subject body; or, more accurately, the *perfected Aryan subject body.* (24)

This included both killing the disabled and the promotion of eugenics, including a fixation on natalism. Natalism was a huge part of National Socialism's domestic agenda—but natalism of a very specific type. The first step was to eliminate undesirable bodies from the larger German body politic. This was done through sterilization and extermination, both of which were carried out on people with physical and mental disabilities, including homosexuals and "the insane." (25)

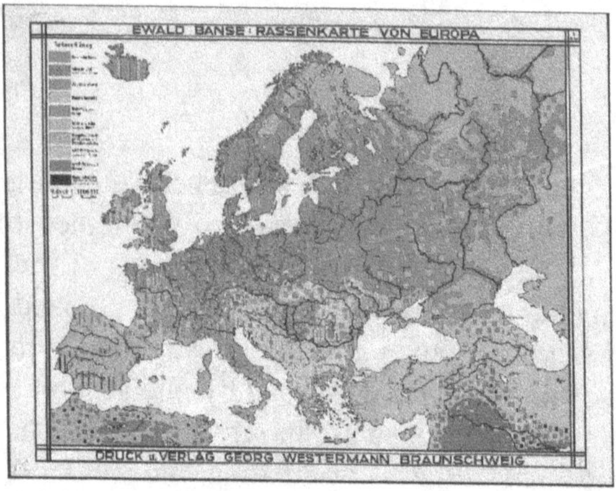

A map of the different races of Europe, according to National Socialism circa 1934. They would not have accepted "of European descent" as a definition of white, let alone Aryan. (Rassenkarte von Europa by Ewald Banse)

While the primary victims of the Holocaust were Jews, they weren't the only ones—and race/ethnicity was not the sole criteria for extermination. Indeed, designs for the use of gas at Auschwitz and other camps was tested via the use of "gas vans" that were deployed in a mobile fashion to exterminate the mentally and physically disabled throughout Germany. (25) These disabled bodies—unfit for reproduction and even for feeding—were categorized as "useless eaters." (26) This wasn't just because their bodies weren't fit to fuel the German war machine. It was because their bodies weren't fit for reproduction, and thus for projection into the genetic future of the "Thousand-Year Reich" Hitler imagined he was building. ***

National Socialism—both past and present—is a deeply natalist ideology. That means that they promote high childbirth rates as a good in and of itself (provided they're the right kind of children). Like most natalist regimes, Nazi Germany used the State to recognize especially fecund women, awarding them medals. (27) From the debunked white supremacist "Great Replacement" conspiracy theory (28) to Elon Musk's fixation on "Western birth rates" (read: white birth rates), (29) one of the largest sources of fuel for right-wing paranoia and radicalization in 2025 is the fictitious idea that "the white race" (no such thing, remember?) is going extinct. Thus, it's every good neo-Nazi's duty to find a white partner, marry her, and breed, breed, breed. (30)

Fascists aren't alone in this fixation. In Thomas Ligotti's philosophical work of genius *The Conspiracy Against the Human Race*, Ligotti (along with an earlier author whose work he draws on, Peter Wessel Zapffe) argues that one of the primary ways humans blank out our fear of death is through the lie of "genetic immortality"—having kids to "carry our legacy" and provide us with the illusion of our own permanence in some sense. Zapffe via Ligotti is correct. From the Catholic Church to the Mormon Church to the likes of Elon Musk (an evidently godless materialist), the fear of death has led institutions and individuals to wax natalist throughout human history, albeit at different volumes and heights of pitch.

This natalist fixation excludes trans women and trans men from full humanity in the eyes of National Socialism and white nationalism more broadly. An "Aryan" who can't reproduce and thus perpetuate and train up the race is no Aryan at all, according to these bio-reductionist fucks. Does that mean that infertile men and women aren't human either? Not as long as they're cisgendered and heterosexual. To paraphrase one fascist I observed making this transphobic argument, "at least they have the right equipment and potential, even if it's not working." This goes hand in hand with the irrationality of some trans Nazis' desire to be a "tradwife" or "waifu" for a big, strong, Nazi man. The same is true of reactionary Catholics, a group that heavily overlaps with neo-Nazis. And speaking of the Catholic Church:

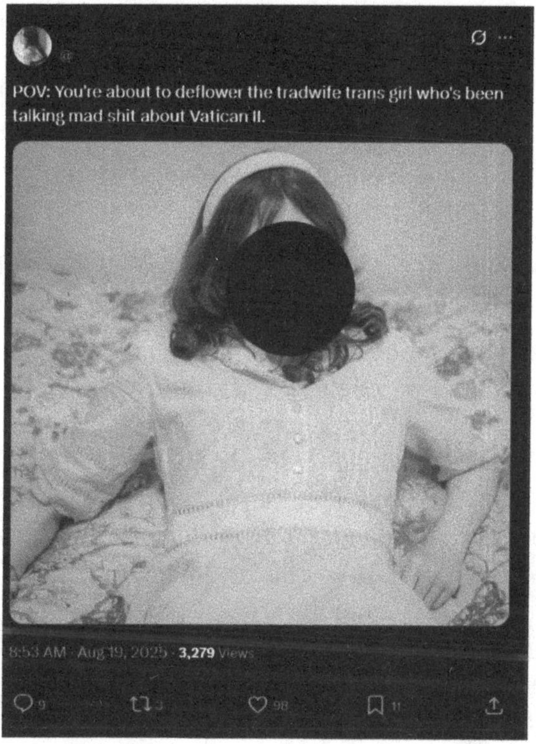

For those of you unacquainted with Catholicism's inner workings, Vatican II (formally the Second Vatican Council) was the gathering of Papal higher-ups from 1962 to 1965 that has managed to keep the most right-wing and Jew-hating Catholics on the planet constantly pissed off for about 60 years now. (31) Why? One document in particular: namely, *Nostra aetate*, or the Declaration on the Relation of the Church with Non-Christian Religions. One of *Nostra aetate*'s major declarations was that Catholics should stop persecuting Jews for their alleged role in the death of Jesus. (32) This was the first time—*in 1965!*—that the crude "de-Judaization" embarked on by Church Fathers in the early centuries of Christianity was addressed by the Roman Catholic Church. Many people haven't forgiven Pope Paul VI for it, including the above trans woman, Catholic fascists, and, (need I say it?) Mel Gibson. (33)

In short, this would-be trans tradwife is bragging about how much she hates Jews.

Now, the above example is not explicitly National Socialist. It's a heretical (34) right-wing version of Catholicism, and represents a different faction within the Fascist Internationale. Even so, "traditionalist Catholicism" has an ideological overlap with National Socialism that I'd call *trans-exclusionary compulsory heterosexuality*, or TECH. Whether one is a "traditionalist Catholic," a Russian Orthodox hardliner, a neo-Nazi, or an Evangelical MAGA diehard, TECH is part of modern reactionary ideology's DNA (with a few exceptions, one of which we'll meet in the next chapter). Does this mean that there are no gay or trans Nazis? Of course not, or this book wouldn't exist. Not only are there openly queer fascists, you can bet that for every one of them that's out and proud, there are five who are quite open about their fascism but deeply closeted about their sexuality.

‡

Zooming back a bit from the specifically fascist section of the right, one can see this warped version of trans respectability politics in a variety of places. On the MAGA right:

... and on what passes for the mainstream left, responding to what passes for the mainstream right:

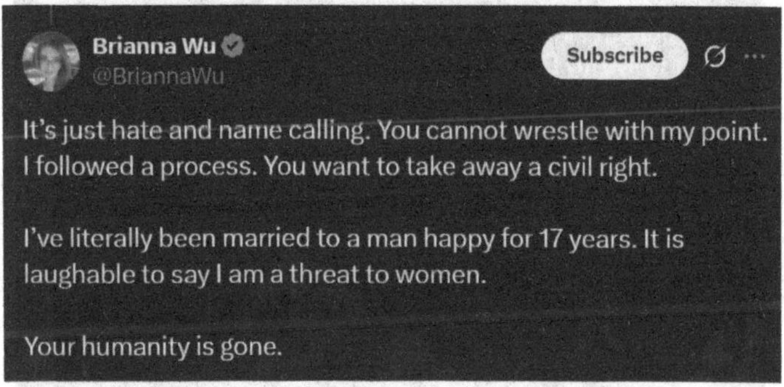

Regarding why I didn't redact Brianna's name in the second screenshot, a little background here is due. First, Brianna Wu is a streamer, commentator, video game industry veteran, and would-be politician. She's a public figure if ever there was one. Second, Wu used to be something of a right-wing Democratic quisling on trans issues, but recently apologized to "her trans sisters" for stances which haven't been paying dividends. It seems Wu has realized—at this late date, in November 2025—that things weren't going well:

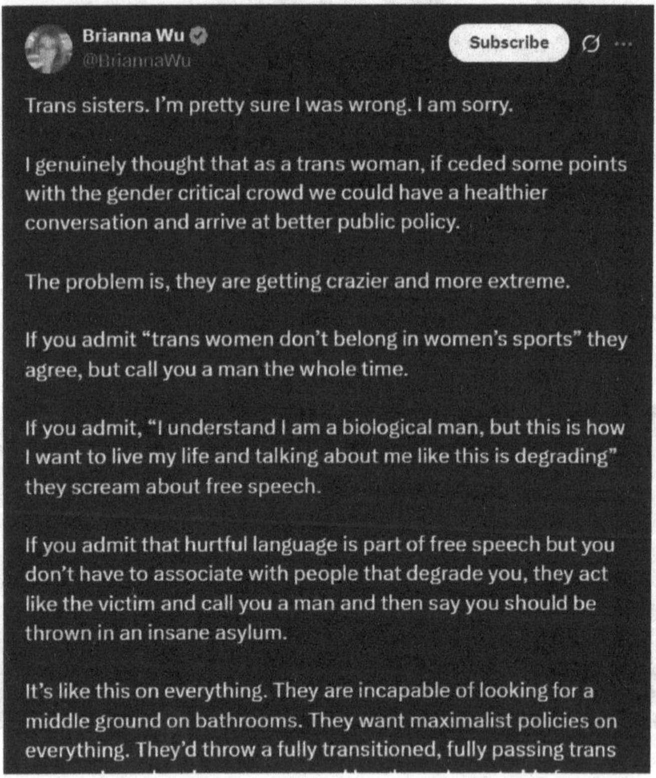

Brianna Wu
@BriannaWu
Subscribe

Trans sisters. I'm pretty sure I was wrong. I am sorry.

I genuinely thought that as a trans woman, if ceded some points with the gender critical crowd we could have a healthier conversation and arrive at better public policy.

The problem is, they are getting crazier and more extreme.

If you admit "trans women don't belong in women's sports" they agree, but call you a man the whole time.

If you admit, "I understand I am a biological man, but this is how I want to live my life and talking about me like this is degrading" they scream about free speech.

If you admit that hurtful language is part of free speech but you don't have to associate with people that degrade you, they act like the victim and call you a man and then say you should be thrown in an insane asylum.

It's like this on everything. They are incapable of looking for a middle ground on bathrooms. They want maximalist policies on everything. They'd throw a fully transitioned, fully passing trans

It goes on from there, but if Wu wants me to reprint her tweets beyond 258 characters, she'll have to pay me $8 per month.

Wu's brand of respectability politics isn't TECH but TICH, if you will: trans-*inclusive* compulsory heterosexuality. Brianna Wu is vocal and highly judgmental about the fact that she is married to a cisgendered heterosexual man and the less "respectable" trans women should follow her example. Wu has, as she says above, made a big deal on Elon Musk's platform for the last several years of "reaching out" to TERFs, right wing politicians, and other transphobes. She did this in an evident peace mission no one ever asked her to embark upon. Wu's views are not mainstream among trans women. She's a transmedicalist for one, (35) meaning that she thinks the only valid form of transitioning is gender reassignment surgery. Transmedicalists are sometimes called "truscum," a shortening of "true transsexual scum," a phrase with its origins on the weird radical feminist hothouse environment that used to exist on Tumblr.

The surgeries truscum think are necessary to be "truly trans" are incredibly expensive, not covered by many insurance providers, painful, and frankly just not what everybody *wants.* (36) If they do and have access to the means, I wish those people nothing but the best: but it's not the *only* way to transition. Wu seeks to limit "legitimate" trans self-expression and police identity in other ways, too. You might note she mentioned her husband above. *She never shuts the fuck up about her 17-year marriage go a cisgendered man.* She constantly brags about being married, which, congratulations, I guess?

On that note, I would say one thing here in conclusion regarding tradwives and trans women.

Women are allowed to be tradwives. I'm not the Grand Vizier of Gender Roles or whoever the fuck decides those things, nor do I think I or anyone *should* or *could* take on such a role. Everyone is allowed to make their own happiness however they see fit, in my book, so long as they don't violate anyone else's ability to do so for themselves. Whether anyone *can* successfully pursue their joy is another matter, and I'm allowed to express my skepticism at the rationality of an identity like "transgender National Socialist" or "transgender TradCath" (a portmanteau of traditional/conservative Catholic). Do I have the same skepticism of trans tradwives? No, I don't. Hell, I've met at least one in person, and she was a delight. If some trans person can be made happy and make someone else happy in return by performing a (to me) strange modern version of a mythic past through homemaking, I say that they should go for it. The dark gods only know there's little enough joy to go around these days.

So why should I judge Nazi dolls at all? Well, for one thing, Nazis aren't well known for leaving other people the fuck alone to find their own joy. For another, and importantly, Nazism doesn't seem to be making these dolls happy *in the least*. If anything, it's a severe warning sign of how bad things are getting for them—especially those trapped physically, financially, or practically in non-accepting cisnormative, heteronormative milieus.

A Liquor So Toxic It Corrodes Any Bottle

The ideologies driving the phenomenon of National Socialism among trans women, including the ideologies promulgated on boards like /tttt/, are a liquor so toxic it corrodes any bottle that tries to hold it, and which will murder anyone who drinks it. The twentieth and twenty-first centuries alike are littered with the fruits of these beliefs: tens of millions of corpses, (37) burned cities, shattered families, raped and tortured men, women, and children, (38) and scientific sadism in the name of nonsense theories and provably bullshit claims—including a little-known Nazi attempt to find a "cure" for homosexuality. (39)

Fascism isn't and wasn't stylish. It isn't and wasn't tough. None of what these (primarily) young and distressed people are seeking out is worthwhile. None of it can or will help them; not with their dysphoria, not with their loneliness, not with their depression, and not in their search for an authentic self. Nor does fascism *want* to. People are just grist for it, and the most soul-sick fascists will even brag about this fact and their own disposability. Fascism doesn't want trans people's bodies for its ranks, however: it simply wants them dead, and a stubborn, tiny minority of the community refuse to accept or acknowledge that fact. (40) Let me emphasize this one more time: *most trans people are extremely great and have nothing but scorn (and possibly lead) for fascism.*

The fact that Hitler's Mouseketeers (National Socialists) have made a roaring comeback in the 2020s is, I'm sad to say, depressingly predictable. Consensus among the "great nations" of the world never seems to last for long, and enough people have forgotten enough history (with help from a variety of carefully constructed pseudo-historical groups) (41) that everything that once was commonplace knowledge now seems like forgotten lore. The war's cost to the capitalist economies and nation-states of the world? Seemingly forgotten. The cost of fascism's quest for world domination to the Christian populace of the world, and to the churches of Nazi Germany under fascist rule? I must have dreamed about all that. The Catholic Church *itself* went from Vatican II (speaking of that old wives' tale) to making a fucking *former member of the Hitlerjungen Pope* in 2005. Benedict XVI (AKA Joseph Ratzinger) and his supporters tried to claim that his attendance was compulsory, and in 2005 I guess nobody bothered to check his assertion, because it turns out that he lied about that. We had a Pope *who voluntarily joined the Hitler Youth.* (42)

How we got here is the subject of many books, journal articles, and works of art, many of them wildly divergent in their explanation or accusatory finger-pointing. Some of these accusations have more merit in my eyes than others, but just to be up front, opinions differ. There is, nonetheless, some consensus on *some* of the forces which have contributed to the rise of online far right radicalization. Some of these are, in turn, applicable to the niche community of trans women † who spend a lot of time online.

First, those who become radicalized tend to have been exposed to a great deal of hateful content online, often at a relatively young age. No platform even attempted to correct the far-right radicalization funnel created by the supposedly neutral algorithm until shockingly late in the game. (43) Sure, Millennials *and* Gen Z (*and* Gen Alpha) all spend a worrying amount of time online, but Gen Z and Gen Alpha both were young on the internet at a time when the unchecked indoctrination of children by Nazis and other far-right weirdos was at an all-time high. Remember, none of this algorithmic radicalization was addressed until *2020* at the earliest. It might have been causal, it might have been (and be) correlative: people simply seeking out content that corresponds with their burgeoning beliefs. Either way, it appears that what's being sought in many cases isn't simple indoctrination or propaganda. People are legitimately skeptical of traditional sources of news, and this has never been truer than during the Gaza genocide perpetrated by the State of Israel. These abyssal, terrifying years have been a time in which the US (and much of the West's) media was so saturated with transparently bullshit anti-Palestinian bias (44) that the "red pill" of neo-Nazi fantasies and lies may have briefly seemed like something other than undiluted human waste. Especially to young, newly politically aware people watching Israeli soldiers commit war crimes on TikTok for clicks and lols.

Israel as a state would not exist with US military support††. Since Israel's founding—or, in a more material sense, since the Six Days' War—Israel has served as an imperial outpost of US power in the MENA region. (45) While Israel is a white- and Jewish-supremacist ethnostate, especially under the reign of Benjamin Netanyahu and the Likudnik regime, (46) Israel's primary role on the geopolitical stage is as what is called a "proxy state." The US is what is called Israel's "client state." (47) This means that when Israel acts, they do so with the blessing of the U.S., and, indeed, often using our guns and bombs. The US news media, with few exceptions, toe the line of the Israeli foreign ministry. Again—this is not because some shadowy cabal of Jews runs U.S. politics. It's because *it is in the imperial interests of the United States* for the news media to run cover for Israel, a friendly (read: pliable) outpost in a tumultuous region.

Gone are the days of a handful of homogenous State-approved line of news and information in the United States. Long gone. During the Gaza genocide, Palestinians have documented every atrocity committed by the State of Israel. Hell, *Israeli soldiers* have documented their *own* war crimes, (48) taking great pleasure in posting themselves wreaking havoc and humiliation on Palestinians in retaliation for the October 7th attacks by Hamas. From the events of October 7th to this day, the Palestinian cause has had a better media strategy than the State of Israel. The Palestinian cause is on the right side of history, but also largely because it has been decentralized, citizen-led, and mostly composed of the truth as opposed to the Israeli State's hilariously transparent dishonesty in their assertions.

Israel has defined itself from the beginning as a Jewish ethno-state. As recent flagrant violations of human decency have been broadcast daily by cell phone video on TikTok, Twitter, Instagram, and other sites, and as Israel's ridiculous, lie-driven, fascist propaganda machine (which often invokes the Holocaust to justify its crimes) has kicked into high gear, younger people have fallen into an easy mental trap: associating Jewishness with Israel. Hell, that's exactly the worldview that *Israel itself* promotes.

So, with all of that in mind, put yourself in the mental shoes of a young person. You grew up entertained by Nazis like PewDiePie while watching a Nazi radicalization accelerator (YouTube) unsupervised. Now, years later, you're experiencing the war in Gaza firsthand through incredibly heartrending, bloody videos of atrocities carried out in the name of a Jewish ethno-state against children, hospital patients, innocent families, and pretty much every other Gazan the Israeli military can get their bloody hands on. Imagine that you hear about Israel's network of rape and torture camps, (49) or the riots that took place in Israeli regions to support the Israeli military's "right to rape," or members of the Knesset trumpeting the rapists' defense. (50) While all of this very real news is flashing across your phone screen as you doomscroll, online packs of National Socialists, white nationalists, and other assorted fascists have toned their rhetoric down for a moment. They're reposting Palestinian accounts and criticizing "Zionists" (a valid criticism)—although when they say "Zionist," they mean Jew (*not* a valid critique—the majority of Zionists, numerically speaking, are American Evangelical Christians). (51)

Many of these seemingly innocuous "anti-Zionist" accounts have anime profile pictures of cute anime girls in stylish Nazi Totenkopf caps or with armbands that aren't quite swastikas. (52). Their slang is vicious, often funny to someone your age, and their online aesthetics and chilly pseudo-nihilism seem cool and cutting edge. The atrocities committed by Israel are far fresher in your mind than the older, vaster atrocities committed by Nazi Germany. Gaza is happening right now, live, on your phone. That World War II shit you learned in school was probably anti-Socialist propaganda from Cold War-era lies, right? And some of these online edgelords are talking about a dude named Strasser ††† whose ideas sound like Bernie crossed with Nick Fuentes—stuff that, to you, sounds like it's for the common working person. You're not rich. You might be middle class, but you're not *rich*, and Strasserism is *exactly* the type of niche ideology popular with the sectors of Twitter and other apps where people who participate in "what is my 19th century political belief" hyper-fixation games tend to be awarded for the ability to cite something obscure like Strasserism or Posadism instead of boring old liberalism or communism.

Is it any wonder that digital natives, from my generation down, seem uniquely vulnerable to this rotting-out? The internet in 2025 is owned and ruled by Nazis to a distressing extent. Elon Musk owns Twitter (along with a bunch of other slowly dying companies). I'm not one to mince words: Musk is a fascist and a white supremacist, and has made those views abundantly apparent in both his rhetoric and his actions as 21st century media mogul. (53) He might not be an outright National Socialist, (I'll let the reader decide about his famous "peculiar gesture" at Trump's second inauguration rally for themselves) but he checks the broader fascist boxes. Rabid natalist?

Check. Concerned with the nonexistent Great Replacement conspiracy theory (and therefor a white supremacist)? Check. A contributor to far-right, ultranationalist parties in *multiple countries*? Big checks for large amounts.

Elon Musk is the Henry Ford of our era. Not because he builds great cars (he builds shit cars), and not because of his extreme wealth (although they *do* have that in common). Like Ford, Musk has dedicated no small part of his fortune and reputation to the promulgation of white supremacy. Like Ford, Musk has done this in every medium he can. In the 21st century, those media aren't newspapers, radio, or pamphlets like they were in Ford's day. Instead, Musk sows his hate in apps and "new media." In AI. By directly funding a trans-national form of nationalism (the phenomenon I call "the Fascist Internationale"). It's not just Musk's shitty app, either. Sites like YouTube only *very recently* un-fucked their *own* algorithms which, up until that point, were radicalizing more young white folks than The Turner Diaries in that poorly written racist jerkoff fantasy's heyday.

Tech fascism is the air we breathe without seeing. An increasing amount of life takes place in spaces mediated by corporate overlords who play footsie with fascists, if they aren't outright Nazis themselves. Shit, I was reviewing this very chapter today when I caught a news story about how Apple Wallet and Google Pay will soon be accepted by TSA at airports as valid ID—even as it becomes increasingly difficult for trans Americans to leave this country safely. (54) Even my own, beloved Boomer parents (hi, mom and dad! Proud of you for making it this far!) have been known to doomscroll, although they consume much tamer fare than that these at-risk younger folks prefer.

What I'm saying is this: the 21st century is, for many people, a greased neon-lit funnel leading them to far-right extremist ideas. The chute is lubricated with memes subtly promoting Nazi ideas and with lengthy video essays about Esoteric Hitlerism or by prominent spots in new media by influencers advocating white supremacy. Most folks have no real handholds on this rapid, terrifying downward spiral: no real understanding of the actual horrors of World War II and the Nazis, or the violent, hateful doings of modern right-wing assholes (thanks to history and social science erasure by the Trump Justice Department. (54) People might not *want* off the slide. They might be insulated by so many layers of detached irony that it makes feeling anything about war crimes of which there isn't TikTok footage *deeply* uncool. This last is not necessarily a new thing. Based on decades of pitch-black, exquisite fiction, Bret Easton-Ellis would certainly recognize this pose, and he graduated from high school in 1981: a full year before my birth.

Speaking of Bret, let's leave the world of trans National Socialism for now and journey to the figurative Isle of Man. That is to say, the variety of femboys, proud boys, and other boys involved in (or peripheral to) the "homofascist" right.

* Until Elon Musk allows me to take a free field goal kick at his nutsack, I will never call the website I was on before he was even there, let alone owned it, by its new name.

** I'm mainly thinking of the Minneapolis shooting in August 2025 here, where the trans-identifying shooter decorated her weaponry with a variety of 4Chan memes. Being trans and being on that imageboard, there's absolutely no question in my mind that Robin Westman spent time on /tttt/.

*** Adolf Hitler didn't build jack shit in the grand scheme of things. Sure, the autobahn, but counterpoint: Despite Savitri Devi's assertion that he was "the lightning and the sun," that motherfucker was just the lightning. He destroyed not only his own nation but much of Europe, decimating historic sites, holy sites, and cultural treasures, killing millions, and destroying many nations' industrial capacity. He set Europe back at least three decades in terms of its economic and social wellbeing, and the ripples of the postwar period across nations not involved heavily in the war were mixed in their effects.

† Fascism and far-right radicalization among trans men is a curiously less severe phenomenon; at least, in my research and experience. The reasons for that are complex, a matter of speculation at the moment, and I wish I had two volumes of this book so that I could go into detail on my theories on why this might be (I suspect fascist trans men of being DEEPLY closeted as trans and trying to pass as AMAB, but that's just a guess) – but alas, I have but one book here, and it's already pretty long.

†† This is actually an understatement on the level of "Violent J enjoys Faygo":

††† Speaking of Ernst Röhm, one of the victims of the so-called Röhm -putsch (AKA the Night of the

Long Knives) was Gregor Strasser. Strasser was an avid advocate of the "socialism of fools" (the banks and capital rip you off because THEY'RE ALL JEWISH, in short) and cultivated a more working-class base interested in National Socialism's *material* benefits for workers than Hitler cared for. Adolf, never one to allow a competing cult of personality with its own troops to exist, had Strasser murdered along with Röhm and others.

‡ See my interview with Scott Kelley (**Appendix A:** "Interview 5 (Scott Kelley, Former Stormfront Moderator)"

1 **Appendix A**: "Interview 1 (Jade Augusta AKA Sweetypuss, Trans Nazi)"

2 Goodrick-Clarke, Nicholas (2002). *Black Sun: Aryan Cults, Esoteric Nazism and the Politics of Identity*. (New York University Press, New York). P125.

3 Kaplan, Jeffrey, ed. (2000). *Encyclopedia of White Power: A Sourcebook on the Radical Racist Right*. (Alta Mira Press, Lanham). P92.

4 Goodrick-Clarke, Nicholas (2002). *Black Sun: Aryan Cults, Esoteric Nazism and the Politics of Identity*. (New York University Press, New York). P148.

5 Green, Dennis H. (1998). *Language and History in the Early Germanic World* (2001 ed.). (Cambridge University Press, Cambridge). P8.

6 Wolfram, Herwig (1999). "Germanic Tribes".

In Bowersock, G. W.; Brown, Peter; Grabar, Oleg (eds.). *Late Antiquity: A Guide to the Postclassical World*. (Belknap Press, Cambridge). P466.

7 Von Lizst, Guido (Flowers, Stephen [aka Edred Thorsson]), transl. (1988, or. 1908). *The Secret of the Runes*. (Destiny Books, Rochester).

8 Gardell, Mattias (2003). *Gods of the Blood: The Pagan Revival and White Separatism*. (Duke University Press, Durham). Extensive sections.

9 Morrow, Allison (12/5/2022). "Welcome to the 'free-for-all hellscape' that is Twitter". *CNN* Business.

10 Marhoefer, Laurie (2015). *Sex and the Weimar Republic: German Homosexual Emancipation and the Rise of the Nazis*. (University of Toronto Press, Toronto). P174.

Bauer, Heike (2017). *The Hirschfeld Archives: Violence, Death, and Modern Queer Culture*. (Temple University Press, Philadelphia). P92.

Fitzsimons, Tim (7/5/2019). "Historian unearths evidence of one of America's earliest gay rights activists". *NBC News*.

11 Davenport, Lauren (2020). "The Fluidity of Racial Classifications". *Annual Review of Political Science*. 23 (1).

Obasogie, Osagie (7/1/2009). "Return of the race myth?". *New Scientist*. 203 (2715). P22–23.

12 Starkey, Brando Simeo (2/20/2017). "White immigrants weren't always considered white — and

acceptable: Italians, Greeks, Poles, Hungarians, Slavs and other European groups had to overcome prejudice over many years". *Andscape*.

Ignatiev, Noel (2008, or. 1995). *How the Irish Became White*. (Routledge, Milton Park). Extensive sections.

13 Sophia Quine, M. (2012). "Racial 'Sterility' and 'Hyperfecundity' in Fascist Italy: Biological Politics of Sex and Reproduction". *Fascism*. 1 (2). P92-144.

14 Connelly, Irene Katz (6/7/2023). "It was a pioneering trans library — until the Nazis burned it". *The Forward*.

Bartrop, Paul R.& Dickerman, Michael (2017). *The Holocaust: An Encyclopedia and Document Collection* [4 volumes]. (ABC-CLIO, Santa Barbara). P457–458.

15 "Transgender Experiences in Weimar and Nazi Germany". *Museum of Jewish Heritage*.

Document: Heinrich Himmler's 1936 order establishing the Reich General Office for the Combating of Homosexuality and Abortion: https://upload.wikimedia.org/wikipedia/commons/7/7c/Reichszentrale-Erlass-1936.jpg

16 Ling, Justin (5/18/2022). "How 4chan's toxic culture helped radicalize Buffalo shooting suspect". *The Guardian*.

Ling, Justin (5/15/2023). "A New Lawsuit Puts the Online White Supremacy Pipeline on Trial". *Wired*.

Staff. (10/2/2015). "Oregon shooting and the anonymous '4chan' message board". *BBC News*.

17 Marinow, Anne E. (11/7/2025). "A Decade Later, Supreme Court Is Asked to Revisit Same-Sex Marriage Decision". *The New York Times*.

18 Staff. (9/8/2025). "We Aren't Going Anywhere: Our Response to Cuts to 988's LGBTQ+ Youth Service". *Trans Lifeline*.

Ryan, Benjamin & Bendix, Aria (4/3/2025). "Trump administration axes more than $125M in LGBTQ health funding, upending research field". *ABC News*.

19 Marhoefer L. (2023). "Transgender Life and Persecution under the Nazi State: Gutachten on the Vollbrecht Case." *Central European History*. 56 (4). P595-601.

Marhoefer, Laurie (6/6/2023). "Historians are learning more about how the Nazis targeted trans people". *The Conversation*.

20 Greensmith, Helen (10/18/2022). "Violence Against Transgender People is on the Rise, Stopping it Requires a Holistic Solution". *Just Security*.

Murray, Ashley (6/5/2024). "White nationalist, anti-LGBTQ activity on the rise, annual hate report shows". *Missouri Independent*.

Stiverson, Hanah et. al. (6/30/2023). "Anti-Trans Extremism: The Far Right's New Strategy to Spread Hate". *Human Rights First*.

21 Cole, Nicki Lisa (5/15/2025). "The Definition of Whiteness in American Society: How white skin

color determines social attitudes and constructs". *ThoughtCo*.

Asare, Janice (2/22/2022). "The Evolution of Whiteness In the United States". *Forbes*.

Tehranian, John (2000). "Performing Whiteness: Naturalization Litigation and the Construction of Racial Identity in America". *The Yale Law Journal*. 109 (4). P817–848.

22 Nirenberg, David (2009). "Was there race before modernity? The example of 'Jewish' blood in late medieval Spain" In Eliav-Feldon, Miriam et. al. (eds.). The Origins of Racism in the West.(Cambridge University Press, Cambridge). P232–264.

Vaulin, Andrey et. al. (2024). "Europeans and Americans of European origin show differences between their biological pathways related to the major histocompatibility complex". *Scientific Reports*. Vol. 14, 21816.

Günther, Torsten; et al. (2015). "Ancient genomes link early farmers from Atapuerca in Spain to modern-day Basques". *Proceedings of the National Academy of Sciences*. 112 (38). P11917–11922.

23 Mahlkuch, Jacob R. (2024). "Angst Uber Alles: The Role of Fear in Nazi German Governance". *Armstrong Undergraduate Journal of History*. 14 (1).

Yousef, Odette (1/19/2023). "'Active club' hate groups are growing in the U.S. — and making themselves seen". *NPR News*:

> A viral video taken near the Oregon City Pride event last month showed Proud Boys, a violent neo-fascist group, beating members of an active club on a sidewalk. In the video, Proud Boys are heard calling the active club members "racists" and Nazis.

24 "Hitler Youth Training Film." (RG-60.1381) *Public Health Under the Third Reich*. United States Holocaust Memorial Museum Archives, Washington, DC.

25 Longerich, Peter (2010). *Holocaust: The Nazi Persecution and Murder of the Jews*. (Oxford University Press, Oxford). P30.

Robert Proctor (1988). *Racial Hygiene: Medicine Under the Nazis* (Harvard University Press, Cambridge). P108.

25 Gellately, Robert. (2007). *Lenin, Stalin, and Hitler: The Age of Social Catastrophe*. (Knopf, New York). P460.

26 "September 1, 1939: Backdated Order Authorizes 'Euthanasia' Program". *Holocaust Encyclopedia*.

27 "Gold Mother's Cross". *National Holocaust Museum*.

US Holocaust Museum. (1/16/2020). "Selling Motherhood: The Nazi Attempt to Increase the Master Race". *Medium*.

28 Buncombe, Andrew (5/17/2022). "Inside the data that debunks the 'Great Replacement' theory". *The Independent*.

Ekman, Mattias (5/6/2022). "The great replacement: Strategic mainstreaming of far-right conspiracy claims". *Convergence: The International Journal of Research into New Media Technologies*. 28 (4). P1127–1143.

Bauder, David (5/16/2022). "What is 'great replacement theory' and how does it fuel racist violence?" *PBS News*.

29 Christensen, Jen (8/30/2022). "Elon Musk thinks the population will collapse. Demographers say it's not happening". *CNN Health*.

Bove, Tristan (2/25/2025). "Elon Musk, father of 13, thinks the world is facing an 'underpopulation crisis'; the UN says the population will continue growing until 2100". *Fortune*.

https://x.com/elonmusk/status/1821408782712291808?lang=en

Shaw, Jonathan (8/22/2025). "Harvard Panel Debunks the Population Implosion Myth". *Harvard Magazine*.

30 Del Valle, Gaby (4/28/2024). "The Far Right's Campaign to Explode the Population". *Politico Magazine*.

Sherman, Carter (3/11/2025). "The rise of pronatalism: why Musk, Vance and the right want women to have more babies". *The Guardian*.

Bruening, Elizabeth (3/12/2025). "The Pro-Baby Coalition of the Far Right". *The Atlantic*.

31 Faggioli, Massimo (4/4/2022). "Opposition to

Pope Francis is rooted in a rejection of Vatican II". *National Catholic Reporter*.

Madrid, Patrick & Vere, Peter (2004). *More Catholic Than the Pope: An Inside Look at Extreme Traditionalism*. (Our Sunday Visitor, Huntington). P169.

Jarvis, Edward (2018). *Sede Vacante: The Life and Legacy of Archbishop Thục*. (Apocryphile Press, Berkeley). P8-10.

32 Editors. (11/30/1963). "The Jews and Vatican II". *America: The Jesuit Review*.

Markoe, Lauren (12/10/2015). "The 'Splainer: What is 'Nostra Aetate,' and what does it have to do with Catholic-Jewish relations?". *Religious News Service*.

33 Heschmeyer, Joe (1/14/2025). "The Hidden Danger of Mel Gibson on Joe Rogan". *Catholic Answers*.

Lewis, Mike (7/8/2024). "Mel Gibson praises Vigano, invites him to California". *Where Peter is*.

34 Madrid, Patrick & Vere, Peter (2004). *More Catholic Than the Pope: An Inside Look at Extreme Traditionalism*. (Our Sunday Visitor, Huntington). P169.

35 https://x.com/BriannaWu/status/198689007786025001 8

https://x.com/BriannaWu/status/198673223400360801 0

36 Baril, Alexandre (November 2015). "Transness as Debility: Rethinking Intersections between Trans and Disabled Embodiments". *Feminist Review*. 111 (1). P59–74.

Wijnants, Alexander (Spring 2013). "Identity of Neurology Social Media and the Politicization versus Medicalization of Trans People". *Synaesthesia*.

37 "World War Two". *Defense Casualty Analysis System*. https://dcas.dmdc.osd.mil/dcas/app/conflictCasualties/ww2

38 Fox-Bevilacqua, Marisa (6/16/2014). "Silence Surrounding Sexual Violence During Holocaust". *Haaretz*.

Ravitz, Jessica (6/24/2011). "Silence lifted: The untold stories of rape during the Holocaust". *CNN*.

Havryshko, Marta (5/18/2020). "Sexual Violence in the Holocaust: Perspectives from Ghettos and Camps in Ukraine". *Heinrich-Böll-Stiftung*.

39 Kondziella D, Hansen K, Zeidman L (2013). "Scandinavian Neuroscience during the Nazi Era". *Canadian Journal of Neurological Sciences*. 40 (4). P493–502.

40 Comeriato, H.L. (12/22/2023). "'There Will Be Blood': How neo-Nazis and white supremacists are fueling Ohio's anti-LGBTQ+ movement". *The Buckeye Flame*.

Gill, Gerard (7/21/2023). "Extremist Violence Against the Trans and LGBTQI+ Community in Australia: A Review of Recent Events". *Global*

Network on Extremism & Technology.

Staff. (6/5/2025). "Offline events, online threats: Analyzing online extremist targeting of LGBTQ+ communities". *Institute for Strategic Dialogue*.

Lagerman, Julia (10/12/2023). "Neo-Nazi Heteroactivism and the Swedish Nationalist Contradiction". *ACME*. 22 (3).

41 Popper, Nathaniel (1/15/2009). "Revisionist: It's Time To Quit Shoah Fight". *The Jewish Daily Forward*.

McGraw, Meridith (11/25/2022). "Donald Trump dined with white nationalist, Holocaust denier Nick Fuentes". *Politico*.

Roose, Kevin (6/8/2019). "The Making of a YouTube Radical". *The New York Times*.

Basu, Tanya (1/29/2020). "YouTube's algorithm seems to be funneling people to alt-right videos". *MIT Technology Review*.

42 Schurenberg, Barbara (1/3/2023). "Joseph Ratzinger's choice to join the Hitler Youth". *The Guardian*.

43 Stewart, Emily (6/5/2019). "YouTube finally banned content from neo-Nazis, Holocaust deniers, and Sandy Hook skeptics: Plenty of dodgy content is still allowed." *Vox*.

O'Brien, Matt (10/2/2020). "Facebook bans Holocaust denial, distortion posts". *PBS News*.

44 McGreal, Chris (2/4/2024). "CNN staff say

network's pro-Israel slant amounts to 'journalistic malpractice'". *The Guardian.*

Staff. "Failing Gaza: Pro-Israel bias uncovered behind the lens of Western media". *Aj-Jazeera News.*

Al-Najjar, Abeer, & Zaid, Bouzjane. (10/22/2024). "Western media's ethical collapse: silencing Gaza's voice". *Third World Quarterly.* P1–20.

45 Staff. (2/26/2018). "Israel's Intelligence Contribution to US Security: The Cold War Years". *Begin-Sadat Center for Strategic Studies.*

George Lenczowski (1990). *American Presidents and the Middle East.* (Duke University Press, Durham). P105–115.

Staff. (2/26/2018). "Israel's Intelligence Contribution to US Security: The Cold War Years". *Begin-Sadat Center for Strategic Studies.*

46 Menchik, Jeremy (August 2024). "Introduction: Symposium on the Jewish Left". *Critical Research on Religion.* 12 (2). P210–214.

Saïd, Ibrahim L. (10/1/2020). "Some are more equal than others: Palestinian citizens in the settler colonial Jewish State". *Settler Colonial Studies.* 10 (4). P481–507.

Mekelberg, Yossi (5/25/2015). "The plight of Ethiopian Jews in Israel". *BBC News.*

47 Bar-Simon-Tov, Yaacov (1998). "The United States and Israel since 1948: A 'Special Relationship'?" *Diplomatic History.* 22 (2). P231-

262.

Benn, Aluf (6/5/2025). “America and Israel Follow the Same Old Script: Trump Restrains Netanyahu’s Regional Ambitions—but Gives Him a Free Hand With the Palestinians”. *Foreign Affairs*.

48 Thomas, Merlyn et. al. (5/16/2024). “Israel troops continue posting abuse footage despite pledge to act”. *BBC*.

49 Robertson, Nick (2/19/2024). "UN experts condemn 'credible' reports of executions, sexual assault by Israeli soldiers". *The Hill*.

Mraffko, Clothilde (7/12/2024). "Beatings, deprivation, torture, rape: Palestinians speak of the 'hell' of Israeli prisons". *Le Monde*.

McKernan, Bethan et al. (8/5/2024). "Palestinian prisoners describe systemic abuse in Israel's jails". *The Guardian*.

50 Goodman, Amy (8/1/2024). “Israel’s Torture & Rape of Palestinian Prisoners Defended by Knesset Members, Far-Right Mobs”. *Democracy Now!*.

Kingsley, Patrick (7/31/2024). “Unrest at Army Bases Highlights a Long Battle for Israel’s Soul”. *The New York Times*.

51 Lipka, Michael (10/3/2013). “More white evangelicals than American Jews say God gave Israel to the Jewish people”. *Pew Research Center*.

52 Bowes, Joshua (12/19/2024). “Anime and the Extreme-Right: Otaku Culture and Aesthetics in Extremist Digital Propaganda”. *Global Network on Extremism and Technology*.

53 Montgomery, Blake (11/6/2023). "Elon Musk agrees with tweet accusing Jewish people of 'hatred against whites'". *The Guardian.*

Ingram, David (4/16/2024). "Verified pro-Nazi X accounts flourish under Elon Musk". *NBC News.*

Hagan, Lisa et. al. (7/9/2025). "Elon Musk's AI chatbot, Grok, started calling itself 'MechaHitler'". *NPR.*

Alper, Amanda & Satter, Raphael (2/7/2025). "Staffer with Elon Musk's DOGE amplified white supremacists online". *Reuters.*

54 Wells, Ava (10/3/2025). "Page Not Found: The Politics of Deletion in the Trump Era". *Princeton University Journal of Public & International Affairs: Annotations Blog.*

CHAPTER NINE

PROUD BOYS, FEMBOYS, AND TOWEL BOYS

In Chapter Three, I briefly went over the career of Ernst Röhm and his subsequent betrayal and murder during the Night of the Long Knives. That event was orchestrated in no small part by Henrich Himmler, the architect of the Holocaust and one of history's foremost proponents of the industrial slaughter of human beings. In February of 1937, three years after Röhm's death, Himmler gave a speech to SS Gruppenfuehrers (essentially SS cadres). In it he addressed the then-ongoing policy of mass extermination of gay men. Himmler explained his reasoning:

> ... With a static number of women, we have two million men too few on account of those who fell in the war, then you can well imagine how this imbalance of two million homosexuals and two million war dead, or in other words a lack of about four million men capable of having sex,

> has upset the sexual balance sheet of Germany, and will result in a catastrophe.
>
> I would like to develop a couple of ideas for you on the question of homosexuality. There are those homosexuals who take the view: what I do is my business, a purely private matter. However, all things which take place in the sexual sphere are not the private affair of the individual, but signify the life and death of the nation, signify world power or 'swissification'. The people which has many children has the candidature for world power and world domination. A people of good race which has too few children has a one-way ticket to the grave, for insignificance in fifty or a hundred years, for burial in two hundred and fifty years...

This is as clear an articulation of trans-exclusionary compulsory heterosexuality as I can imagine. Himmler was as into TECH as Elon Musk! Himmler then went on to make the extraordinary claim that recently discovered peat bog mummies in Germany were ancient queers drowned for their sodomite ways:

> The professorial gentlemen who find these corpses in the peat-bogs are certainly unaware that in ninety out of a hundred cases, they have a homosexual before them, who was drowned in a swamp, clothes and all. That wasn't a

> punishment, but simply the extinguishment of abnormal life. It had to be got rid of, just as we pull out weeds, throw them on a heap, and burn them. (1)

I don't really feel like I need to add this, but just to be sure: the idea that "in 90 cases out of 100" peat bog mummies were homosexuals who were drowned, clothes and all, for their anti-natalist sex practices is batshit, wild-eyed nonsense. Of all the scientific theories regarding bog people, "they were fags" is not one of them. (2) Was Himmler "joking?" Who cares? Despite the backdrop of Nazi homophobia (of which this is but a mosaic tile), the curious case of Milo Yiannopoulos proves that even in the 21st century some gay men seem drawn to National Socialism and fascism. I can only liken this to a moth who is drawn to a nocturnal oil well fire. Whatever happens, it won't end well.

Example: in 1977, perhaps inspired by Sid Vicious, * a gay man named Michael Kühnen founded a West German neo-Nazi organization called the Action Front of National Socialists. The ANS (later called the ANS/NA) has a decades-long history we don't need to get into here. For our purposes, I want to draw attention to the fate of Herr Johannes Bügner. Bügner was a member of ANS who was murdered in 1981 for attempting to leave the group—and also for being gay. (3) This happened while Michael Kühnen, the group's openly gay founder, was already in prison for inciting racial hatred and founding a terrorist organization. He spent his time there writing *The*

Second Revolution, a plan for the ANS. The title quite literally comes from statements made by Ernst Röhm. (4) As I stated earlier, Ernst's life continues to resonate with some gay men who can project themselves into his place in their power fantasies. (5) History repeats itself, however, often to a maddening extent. When I think of Johannes Bügner, I think of the fate of some of the gay men who joined the SA while Röhm it was in Hitler's good graces. At least some of them were thinking of their own skins: namely, that beating the shit out of Jews and communists would keep them safe. As it turns out, some of the same men who did this thinking it would keep them safe wound up in the concentration camps. (6)

Queerness and National Socialism are incompatible, as are queerness and fascism more generally. Nazis—from Hitler after 1934, to Himmler (pretty much constantly), to American Nazi Party founder and general shit-starter George Lincoln Rockwell—have made this quite clear. Fascism in general views homosexuality as being at its core a Jewish conspiracy designed to undermine and eventually destroy the West. (7) Despite this, syncretism tries to find a way. Over the years, "homofascism" as a term has mainly been used by hatemongers to describe queer drives for equal legal rights and acceptance. (5) This is homofascism as in, "I can't call my employee faggots anymore! That's HOMOFASCISM!" Other than that usage, at least a handful of groups tried to make queer fascism an actual ideology, and I'll touch on their history momentarily.

The omnidirectional mindfuck of the early 21st

century has made for some (excuse the pun) strange bedfellows and some *very* strange trends within American and Western fascism. For example: a funny thing happened on the way from grizzled 20th century Western masculinity to its slicker, more slippery 21st century incarnation; it took a dip into pederasty, and decided it quite liked it there. We've covered Nazi CSAM, but in this chapter, we'll touch on another, stranger phenomenon.

Closeted homophobes are as old as homophobia itself, but the pressure cooker of melt-brained modern fascism has led some ostensibly, proudly heterosexual men to admit some very unwholesome things about themselves. I'm not talking about simply being gay or bi on the downlow—whether someone remains closeted is, as far as I'm concerned, their business. However, the type of heteroflexibility these men perform has a distinctly rapey edge that is both grotesque and chilling.

Meanwhile, a queer contingent of the new far right is drawing the fascist male gaze in interesting ways. This phenomenon has become so widespread that this specific subtype of gender nonconforming men—popularly called "femboys"—have nearly become synonymous with modern online neo-Nazism. How did this happen? That's a good question. To answer it, we must address both the supply and demand in these subcurrents of the libidinal economy of the non-heteronormative far-right.

In modern America, that means we start with the National-Socialist League (NSL).

Politics As Fetish, Fetish As Politics

The future did not, in fact, belong to the NSL

The National Socialist League was founded in 1974 in Los Angeles. It was founded by a man named Jim Cherry, but the real leader soon arrived courtesy of Ohio in the form of a man named Russell Veh. Like many in this great nation, Veh failed his way to California. He was a high school dropout who founded a nationalist party in Ohio in 1970, renamed it a *white* nationalist party in 1971, and then bailed on Ohio completely to find his racist fortune in the Golden State in 1974. Veh was a prolific neo-Nazi writer and printer who specialized in creating and distributing racist propaganda. He was involved in this brisk, pre-4Chan trade to the extent that in 1990 an article about him in the *San Diego Union* called Veh "one of the largest purveyors of white supremacist information in the country." (8)

Starting in the mid-1970s, Veh worked in print and sometimes video and used the proceeds to fund the National Socialist League. Early on, the League claimed as many as 400 members in San Francisco. (9) In addition to the trade in racist publications, Veh's video work included distributing Nazi films like Leni Riefenstahl's *Triumph of the Will.* (ibid.) The NSL was an organization that restricted membership to gay men only. It's twelve-point credo stated that gay men were vital to the survival of the "Aryan race." Given Himmler's lengthy disquisition on natalism and National Socialism, how did Veh square this circle? The same way that Ernst Röhm did. Both Röhm and Veh maintained that gay men made better fighters, (10) and Veh further maintained that gay men represented a military and cultural vanguard. (11) Weirdly, that was half-true of the SA in the earliest days of the Nazi Party (although, unlike the NSL, the SA was not exclusively made up of gay men.) The SA stormtroopers *were* the military vanguard of the Nazi Party, if street brawlers and bullies can be considered a military.

Given the persecution of homosexual men and trans women by the Nazis, the murder of Ernst Röhm and other gay members of the SA during the Night of Long Knives, and the promulgation of the theory that homosexuality is a Jewish conspiracy to weaken the "Aryan race," how in the sainted name of Judy Garland did the NSL ever recruit more than a handful of deeply troubled members? Maybe a profiteer like Veh could swallow that lie (or pretend to), but 400 members in San Francisco *alone*? The answer is regrettable, but let's not flinch from the truth: the gay community of

California bears much of the responsibility for the NSL's existence and growth.

The NSL advertised in gay publications—and gay publications *let them advertise*. Two publications (popular San Francisco gay publication *The Bay Area Reporter* and leather fetish magazine *Drummer*, were more than happy to take money from a group like the National Socialist League. (12) Hell, *Drummer* took the money even though its editor—Jack Fritscher—detested Nazism. Even the NSL's advertisements were an incoherent, self-contradictory mess. Some of them featured sexy, nearly nude SA men with their dangly bits concealed by swastikas, a provocative and "sex sells" form of propaganda that's straightforward in its methods. They also adopted the slogan "Tomorrow belongs to you," an apparently ironic (and sardonic) comment on the song "Tomorrow Belongs to Me" from *Cabaret*, a musical popular with the LGBTQIA+ community that *documents the rise of fascism and its disastrous consequences*. Truly, the NSL were the meme warriors of their day.

The gay fetish scene of the time bears much of the responsibility for this incoherent mess making sense to anyone. Specifically leather culture, which is why Russell Veh targeted *Drummer*'s audience. As early as the 1950s, gay masculinity began to transform. Some men became sick of "traditionally queer" cultural products like musical theatre and camp style, and began to lean into outlaw motorcycle culture. With major influences like popular artist Tom of Finland emphasizing the biker look with well-hung men in skin-tight leather, a new, more aggressively masculine American gay culture began to emerge. (13) This is probably (albeit not provably) why Veh chose his grotesque "tomorrow belongs to you" tagline—to shit on *Cabaret* fans as effeminate sissies and drum up a few members with a calculated bit of masculinist queer trolling.

Up until remarkably recently, any expression of gay male fascism had to be intensely masculine. This started with Ernst Röhm himself, whose version of National Socialism was shaped by his experiences in World War I in which he said, "only the real, the true, the masculine held its value." (14) The National Socialist League helped shape this vision of a tough, American, but *very* gay National Socialism. It published a journal called *NS Kampfruf* ("National Socialist battle cry") that blended Nazi rhetoric with erotic illustrations of young SS troops letting it all hang out. NSL materials promised recruits a "sexual kick" and their propaganda magazine was the teaser for that reward. (15) It's interesting that *NS Kampfruf* sexualized the SS, the organization headed by Heinrich Himmler, rather than the much gayer SA. Remember, Himmler was a virulent homophobe responsible in large part for the persecution of gay men within the NSDAP. Veh's photo spreads were either another piece of "fuck you" irony or a result of his innate ideological perversity.

I said that California's gay community helped the NSL emerge, and that's true. But the California gay community also played an important role in marginalizing and ultimately forcing the NSL to go extinct. In 1977, the National Socialist League applied for a table at the Los Angeles Gay Pride Parade and was told to go eat a fucking bullet. (16) This was the first time in LAGPP history that they deviated from their "no exclusion" policy, and it underlines a vital point for anyone studying fascism: "free speech" and acceptance do not fucking apply to Nazis, whether the American Civil Liberties Union thinks they do or not. I feel like the Onion's headline poking at the ACLU on this subject was, as always, devastatingly accurate: "ACLU Defends Nazis' Right to Burn Down ACLU." (17) After their encounter with the NSL, the LAGPP revised their stance to allow for exclusion based on community values—as it should be.

By the 1980s, the NSL only had one trick left in their arsenal. They managed to pirate a copy of an infamous anti-Semitic 1930s film called *Jud Süß* (*Suss Out the Jew*) and tried to sell it. This brought unwelcome attention to their doings in California's Jewish press, including an article in *Heritage and SW Jewish Press*. This article named Russell Veh and the NSL in the piracy. (18) Perhaps something happened behind the scenes besides the bad press—I don't know. Personally, I like to imagine Veh having a run-in with some very, very scary antifascist Jews, *Inglorious Basterds* style. Whatever it was, the NSL evaporated by 1984. Literally. The organization ceased to exist completely, along with their publications. Veh continued to publish one magazine called *Race & Nation*—which made no mention whatsoever of homosexuality. Ever again.

What lessons can we learn from the National Socialist League? First, that all politics really is libidinal. In this case, it appears that a masculinist expression of gay male culture in the US cross-pollinated with outlaw motorcycle club culture, which by the 1970s was chockablock with Nazi symbolism and heavily populated by white supremacists. (19) This syncretism only worked because of leather fetish culture in the gay BDSM scene, with artists like Tom of Finland depicting hyper-sexualized bikers. This evidence is reinforced by the presence of "Nazi play" in the hetero *and* gay BDSM scenes. (20) Are these people committed National Socialists? Some of them are. Most of them just seem vaguely horned up by notions of Nazi "strictness," "discipline," and "harsh punishment."

Second, while gay Nazis certainly exist, they aren't accepted by "mainstream" Nazi organizations. The NSL was ignored by the much larger and better-funded groups throughout their less than a decade of existence. All except for the National Socialist Liberation Front, which privately tolerated them while publicly denouncing gay men as degenerates and perpetrators of an anti-white Jewish conspiracy. (21) Does that seem like some sad shit to you; hanging out with people who volubly hate you in public, but *tolerate* you in private? It's a running theme with token minorities of all kinds within the right, let alone the far-right. In the NSL's decline, starved of wider support beyond a tiny circle of kink-drunk racist gay men, Veh slunk back into the closet and commenced toiling on *Race & Nation*, an acceptably heteronormative Nazi publication.

Lastly (and this is distinct from the point "politics is libidinal"), there exists a small group of aggressively masculinist gay men who are very susceptible to the power fantasy of fascism. In the wild and swingin' 70s, many of these men—or at least the ones living in big cities in California—were out of the closet. Now, however, there's some evidence that many gay or bisexual men who've grown up in Homeland America are deeply closeted. What's my evidence of this? You might be sorry that you asked!

Some fascist men are so closeted that even *they* may not be aware of what's coming out of them when they let their horned-up Nazi side do the typing online.

When PTA Dads Talk About "Towel Boys"

A funny thing happened on the way to the Roman revival modern fascists engage in rhetorically, aesthetically, and now, it seems, sexually. They took the MAGA masculinist's logic of "Alpha better than Beta" and transformed it into "Alpha rapes Beta, no homo." I wish I were exaggerating, but I had a front-row seat to some truly unhinged male behavior that amply demonstrates this fact—and not from National Socialist League throwbacks. From ostensibly heterosexual MAGA men.

It all started on November 2, 2024. Election hijinks were in full swing. A friendly-looking young man named Harry Sisson and his friends went to vote for Kamala Harris and afterwards took a celebratory photo. This has become a tradition among American voters, but Harry's rather mild contribution to this oeuvre was met with a tidal wave of jaw-dropping MAGA responses like this:

Liberals and leftists were quick to ask if Mr. O'Neill (and fuck no I'm not editing his information out of that tweet) if he knew what "concubines" meant. He made it very clear that he did:

For future reference? In a world that is familiar with Jeffrey Dahmer, "you'll be used for sex and food" doesn't make that statement more heterosexual.

This was another response to Sisson's tweet:

But hey! Just an isolated incident, right? Sadly, no. The "towel boys" in the title of this chapter and section is a reference to a specific tweet, but first I need to provide a little real-life historical background about Rome. Pre-Christian Rome was largely a homophobic culture—but not as homophobic as it would later become. Several Emperors were queer, including, yes,

Caligula and the (in my opinion) misunderstood Nero, but also heavy hitters like Hadrian, Tiberius, and even Julius Caesar. (Note: queer includes bisexual.) All of the men I listed had relationships or encounters with men and boys, but many of them also had public marriages to women. Of them, Nero is the exception. Late in life, he married a slave boy he had castrated. It's a ghastly story that involves, among other things, Nero believing that the slave (named Sporus) was inhabited by the ghost of his previous wife Poppaea Sabina. Despite this, there's ample evidence that Nero was affectionate, if not genuinely loving, to Sporus, and, more remarkably, that Sporus may have returned the sentiment (albeit not in a way that resembles anything like consent).

Sexual relationships between older men and young men or boys were normalized to an extent in Roman life, especially in the military. (22) Adolf Hitler, remember, embraced the so-called "Roman salute" and was almost as obsessed with ancient Rome as Mussolini. (23) Given fascism's emphasis on masculinity and violence (referred to by fascism scholar Robert O. Paxton in a memorable turn of phrase as "the cult of manly action,") (23) perhaps this shouldn't be surprising.

Neither should this, then:

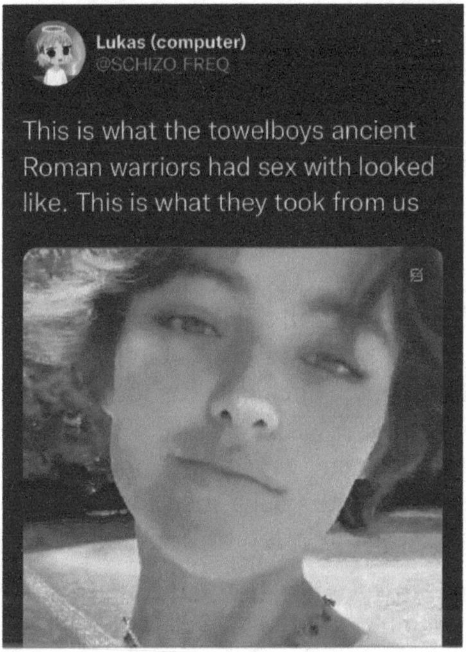

That image is from a TikTok reel publicly posted by a cisgendered woman. She was transvestigated, and no, I don't know why. Honestly, I have no idea what drives these people to scream "MAN!" at women, whether cis or trans. Whatever the reason, Lukas (along with many other far right weirdos) seized on this young woman's post, decided she was trans, and then weirdly fetishized her as a "Roman towel boy."

"This is what they took from us" is a semi-ironic (but not really ironic) catchphrase that originated on the far-right internet in traditionalist "RETVRN" circles. (24) It usually accompanies something aesthetically pleasing to a young, white Western male: blonde women with large breasts, AI-generated ranches bathed in golden sunlight and populated by smiling "Aryan" children, or a manly man in the mode of Sean Connery's James Bond enjoying some now-outlawed-by-the-gynocracy pleasure like, oh, a glass of Scotch. In this case, "what they took from us" is also aesthetically pleasing. Lukas just thinks those beautiful "Roman towel boys" have transitioned to become trans girls. Oh, the "they" in "they took this from us" is always the Jews, by the way. (25) It's funny how that works in fascist circles, isn't it? When "Aryan family men" get caught with pornography, it's because porn is a Jewish conspiracy. When those same "Aryan family men" get boners looking at what they think are effeminate young men turned into "troons," that's also somehow a Jewish conspiracy.

There's a neosexuality self-identification on the rise I think will make big inroads in fascist circles. I'm not disputing its validity—I haven't studied it enough to know if it's a fetish, an orientation, or something else. I certainly don't have a problem with it, per se. That term is "gynesexuality," (26) or the attraction to femme-presenting or effeminate appearing people, regardless of gender. From twinks to "towel boys," this orientation would let non-heteronormative fascists off the hook in one sense. However, as I established in the last chapter, trans-exclusionary compulsory heterosexuality (TECH) dictates that these attractions will be considered invalid by the larger movement for the simple reason that they can't result in teeming broods of nation-saving Aryan children.

Because it's new(ish) and fascinating, though, let's look at fascist gynesexuality.

Femboys In Uniform

So, just to kick things off, what is a "femboy?"

The term is a neologism dated to the 1990s, (27) and refers to any man or nonbinary person who adopts a feminine aesthetic such as traditionally female clothing, wigs, or other accessories to embrace a femme aesthetic in defiance of gender conformity. (28) This counts as gender *expression*, not gender *identity*. Femboys are still male-identifying (even if they look cute in skirts)—they're gender nonconforming men, who often dress up for sexual or fetishistic reasons. (29) Femboys are generally (although not always) young and cisgendered.

Starting in the early 21st century, "femboy" started making its way into the most unfortunate place possible. You guessed it—4Chan. In fact, by 2018, the term femboy could almost exclusively be found on 4Chan's /lgbt/ (AKA /tttt/) board. Later, it spread to Reddit and TikTok. (30) TikTok, which I haven't talked about much in this text as it's a video platform, currently has a terrifying right-wing extremism problem. (31) Thus, it's unfortunately safe to say that the Gen Z femboy's identity was born online in a milieu alongside a strong current of fascism, racism, misogyny, and hate.

Femboy culture has a certain style that's distinct from more campy gender nonconforming fare like drag performances. For one, it's a mixed performance that incorporates elements of youthful masculinity as well as femininity. (31) Standard accessories that make up the femboy look include thigh-high stockings, jewelry, hair dye, and the like. Cosplay (dressing up in costume as a character from comics, games, film, or, especially, anime) is a big part of photoshoots and selfies. (32) The extent to which femboy cosplay reflects their interests and fandoms can be fun and harmless—and often, it is. (33) The impact of anime on femboy culture is another malign influence when it comes to fascism. Anime and otaku culture are huge in femboy spaces, and anime is, unfortunately, also the base note upon which a lot of online fascist aesthetics are constructed. (34)

Anime-influenced fascist femininity performed by femboys is present to a startling degree in places like 4Chan, TikTok, and Twitter. A few examples of the aesthetic I'm talking about will speak more loudly than a description:

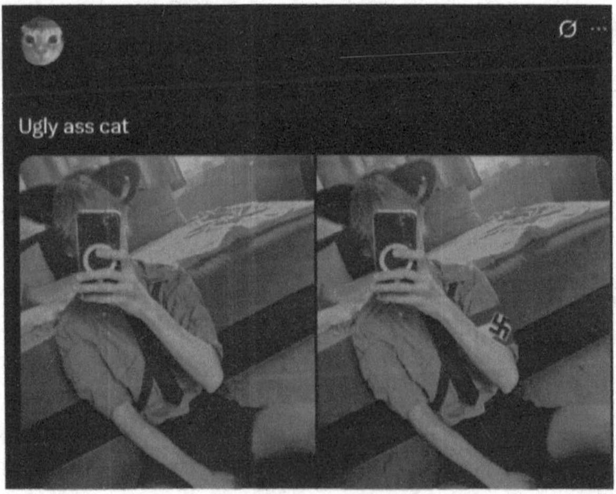

There's even more going on in this photo than it seems. ** The person in these photos is one of the interviews you'll find in **Appendix A**. I won't say which one, even though they're pseudonymous. Why am I so concerned with not doxxing fascists when that's something of a pastime of mine? Because it was a condition of people speaking to me, and because I don't want to put sexual minorities—even hateful ones—at increased risk, even if the risk is mostly likely to come from their fellow fascists. I think this means I have an ethical code, but I'd have to ask an ethicist to be sure.

Because the 21st century femboy aesthetic and framework for identity was born online, memes are a big part of it. Memes like this one circulate on fascist femboy Twitter, for example:

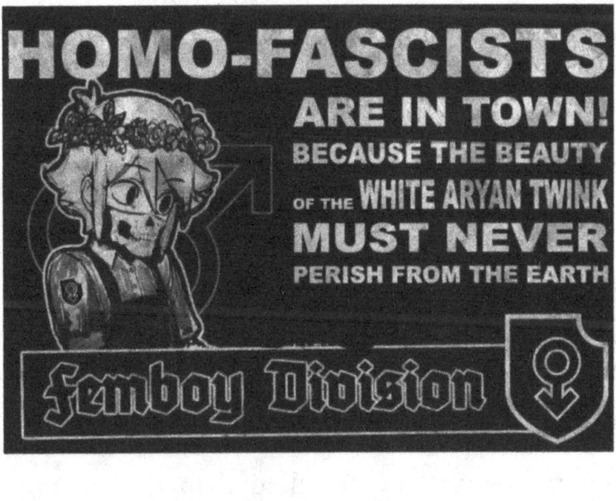

The phrase "because the beauty of the white 'Aryan' twink must never perish from the blah blah" is a reworking of a frequently used neo-Nazi phrase about "Aryan" women. It is, in fact, basically the response in the call-and-response of the "14 words" that form the liturgy of American violent white supremacy. (35)

This piece of online propaganda aspires to a silliness and playfulness that is intentionally utterly at odds with fascism's reality. The reference to a non-existent "Femboy Division" of "homo-fascism" is a reference to the Atomwaffen Division, an American-based terrorist organization (36) founded in 2015. Some of its members (and cells) were heavily influenced by the Order of Nine Angles, (37) a theistic Satanist neo-Nazi group I wrote about in *Black Sunrise on Piss Earth*. They are an incredibly dangerous cult, and Atomwaffen's aspirations to mass casualty attacks reflects the small-n nihilistic and violent influence of O9A. (38) Atomwaffen (Atomic Weapons) Division targeted college campuses and the military looking for young recruits, and the above flyer is, essentially, a femboy riff on the original. (39)

Pretty funny, I guess! Just one thing, "twink division."

In 2018 Blaze Bernstein, a young, femboy-adjacent gay man (a "twink," in gay terminology) was murdered by Atomwaffen Division member Samuel Woodward. It was a savage attack motivated by both violent homophobia and anti-Semitism (40)—more proof that homophobia and anti-Semitism are all too often inseparable. That cutesy flyer is 100% more likely to get a femboy killed than drawn into the welcoming arms of National Socialism. By now, I'm sure astute readers have detected a pattern among queer folk who gravitate to far-right spaces online (and off). It might be motivated by self-hatred (I favor this hypothesis based on my interviews). It might be motivated by pure masochism or Stockholm syndrome. The last chapters in this book explores the braid of phenomena I think are causing queer Nazis to strut onto the stage of 21st century far-right politics.

But before we get there, we should address some other gender nonconforming men: the proto-SA of Trump's fascist America. I'm talking about the Proud Boys.

No Homo, Bro

First, a quick thumbnail history of the Proud Boys. In 1994, a Gen X piece of shit named Gavin McInnes helped found *Vice* magazine, which would go on to become (in my opinion) one of the leading publications documenting far-right activity in the 21st century. In 2008, *Vice* shitcanned McInnes and he began gravitating to far right circles. (41) McInnes is the type of loud jackass edgelord who peaked in the 1980s and 90s in "Morning Zoo" radio, so naturally he transitioned into podcasting. McInnes is an interesting figure for the founder of a US American fascist paramilitary. Born in Scotland, he emigrated to Canada as a kid and then to the United States in 2001 at age 31. That was probably a bright move. The Proud Boys (which we'll get to in a moment) has been declared a terrorist organization by multiple Commonwealth countries. (42) so America was probably a good choice compared to Scotland or

Canada.

The Proud Boys have their roots in 2016 in *Taki's Magazine*, a white supremacist and Nazi-adjacent Greek publication that's a favorite of the Fascist Internationale, (43) including Americans. The Proud Boys' name itself, of course, is taken from a musical. (44) They are, in a variety of ways, like the dog who caught the car she'd been chasing. I'm not sure McInnes knew what he was getting into when he founded the group and fanned its flames. The Proud Boys rapidly became a violent, neofascist, criminal organization. (45) That's more than our Scotch-Canadian friend bargained for. This is evidenced by McInnes' frankly chickenshit approach to leading the group. First, he leaned away from their quite apparent racism, using the code phrase "Western chauvinist" to describe the group. (46) Then, he called them "alt-lite" instead of "alt-right," again hoping to distance himself from the kind of neo-Nazis he'd previously courted the support of. (47) Finally, he up and quit the group. (48) What followed was one of the funniest fucking stories to emerge from 21st century fascism (so far).

McInnes made a pretty penny peddling hate (no, that's not the funny part). He's worth an estimated $10 million. (49) As such, he doesn't live in some commoner's pigsty in the Bronx or, god forbid, a rural property in flyover country. No, he and his wife live in Larchmont, a luxe village in New York. Unsurprisingly, the milieu of Larchmont politics is not exactly MAGA. Affluent New Yorkers have different politics than, say, affluent Texans. *** Upon learning that the McInnes family of Larchmont Village was the same McInnes family of MAGA stormtrooper fame, the neighbors did not respond well. I'll let the *Huffington Post* recap the story from here:

> For months, Proud Boys founder Gavin McInnes and his wife, Emily, have been fighting to win back their neighbors in the upscale village of Larchmont, just north of New York City.
>
> Though some townspeople have posted "Hate has no home here" signs for months — some of them in reaction to domestic acts of terrorism, like the shooting at a synagogue in Pittsburgh last October — others, having realized that their neighbor Gavin was the leader of an assault-prone street gang, added signs to their front yards, too.
>
> In response, the McInneses lashed out. Gavin sent letters to those neighbors who displayed anti-hate signs in their front yards, lamenting that they represented an act of aggression against his family. Out of the other side of his mouth, he mocked them and called them "retards" on his podcast. Emily, meanwhile, publicly defended her husband and claimed that the neighbors' messaging had put their children in danger, while privately she intimidated and threatened legal action against them. (50)

Aww! Poor widdle crybully Gavin didn't like that his rich neighbors didn't like him! How sad! Maybe he shouldn't have started a violent, right-wing street gang that routinely engages in targeted harassment and acts of criminal conspiracy and violence if he wanted to live in a lovely neighborhood in New York? Nah, that's just my anarchist brainrot talking. Clearly the neighbors (or "r*tards," as Gavin calls them) are in the wrong. Gavin's Larchmont behavior is everything loathsome about the far-right captured in a nutshell: hate, hypocrisy, bluster, threats, playing the victim while victimizing others, cowardice, and a refusal to take responsibility for the consequences of his actions.

Gavin McInnes, staunch heterosexual, is not why the Proud Boys get a mention in this section. Much of the most important action that the Proud Boys got into (including the criminal conspiracy that led to four Proud Boy convictions following January 6th) happened after Gavin left. Most took place under the leadership of a white Hispanic man named Enrique Tarrio. Tarrio, if he's remembered by history at all, will be remembered as one of the most easily flipped snitches in US law enforcement history. (51) Some of the *thirteen* (!) dudes Tarrio turned State's Evidence on are still doing federal time while he struts around with his chest puffed out making hollow threats on Twitter. There *is* honor among thieves, but not among fascists.

Tarrio isn't the reason I bring the Proud Boys up, either. In fact, while Enrique Tarrio was briefly imprisoned and under the leadership of a decentralized network of regional cadres, the Proud Boys turned directly against the LGBTQIA+ community and added them to the top of the target list. (52) The Proud Boys *as an organization* are straight, white men who embrace a very performative version of masculinity: muscles, beards, guns, trucks, the whole nine yards. (53) Well, that's *one* aspect of their performance, anyway, and the one that's meant to be most widely seen and associated with them. It's the one that plays well on Fox News, OANN, and interviews with influencers.

When you look more deeply into the Proud Boys, though, the *form* of masculinity promoted by the organization is *very weird* compared to what the men they try to emulate—whether John Wayne or Adolf Hitler—would recognize as masculine. That's what can happen when your right-wing street gang is started by someone like Gavin McIniss, who founded the group at least in part as a gag or bit. (54) In fact, the goofiness of the Proud Boys is one factor in their current obsolescence. (ibid.) A form of deeply immature dudebro culture was baked into the Proud Boys from day one. Sure, they eventually reached the dizzy heights of being imprisoned for their participation in a failed coup d'etat, but along the way they got up to shit that didn't exactly scream "masculine gender conformity."

Proud Boys often attempted to ape rituals of masculinity from other, *actually* dangerous subcultures to unintentionally hilarious effect. For example: gangs like MS-13 have, since time out of mind, engaged in a practice known as getting "jumped in" (sometimes "squared in," "a street baptism," etc.) This means that a prospect (potential member) must survive a beating by a certain number of other members of the gang and/or for a specific time to prove how tough they are and, therefore, how worthy of membership. In real street gangs that aren't a fascist joke, People die during these initiations. (54)

The Proud Boys membership structure is a weird, Scientologyesque stepped pyramid of dumbassery. Their version of a street baptism (required to become a "second degree" Proud Boy) is so watered down that it's the equivalent of proving how much you can drink in one sitting by drinking a single 4-point beer instead of a jar of moonshine. A Proud Boy prospect is required to let other members punch him. How hard or even, get this, whether being punched in the face is allowed, varies by chapter and location. As their friends gently pat them, they're required to name five breakfast cereals. Third degree members get a Proud Boy tattoo and promise not to masturbate (don't worry, we'll get to that). Only fourth degree Proud Boys are expected to get into a fight—and even that is unlikely to be one on one, as Proud Boys tend to travel in packs. (55)

To paraphrase "Lola" by the Kinks, I'm not the world's most masculine man but I know what's silly bullshit and what at least proves that you can take a beating. These dumbasses are not the SA Stormtroopers they try to emulate, many of whom were World War I veterans and some of whom were gay. The Proud Boys are completely fucking ridiculous compared to a real American gang like the Crips. A single, late-1970s, PCP-factory-running LA Crip could kill every Proud Boy in the world with very little effort. Yes, some individual Proud Boys—and one quartet of them, including snitch Enrique Torrio—

have committed acts of violence. Even so, the organization as a whole is a laughingstock, even when compared to less masculinity-forward groups like Satan-worshiping, murderous pedophiles the Order of Nine Angles.

Take the Proud Boys' anti-onanism pledge: or the "no wanks" promise, thanks to Gavin McInnes' fucked up Scotland-via-Canada Commonwealth diction. That alone is enough to render them unserious to me. It's a little like when I got super into Arthurian legend and read all of the oldest collections of legends. Imagine my surprise to learn that two of the prerequisites to seek the Holy Grail were virginity and chastity. Galahad was on solid ground there; Lancelot not quite so much, but that's a different book. It took the bloom off the rose a little bit for me regarding those sword-swinging legendary badasses. Not because asexual, celibate, or virgin people are ridiculous. It's because making such a *public show* of being very fussy about sex and pleasure strikes me as goofy.

One final story about the Proud Boys, who until recently were at the forefront of MAGA's self-image as a cult of manly action. That story involves Roger Stone, the Nixon creature who was inescapable for a time during Trump's first run for President. Roger Stone, like Nixon lawyer Roy Cohn, is gay. Unlike Cohn, Stone has been openly gay for quite some time. In a very Ernst Röhm or National Socialist League twist, dirty old man Roger hired the Proud Boys to be his personal bodyguards during his moment of relevance. He quite enjoyed being photographed with the tough, bearded young men and loved their stormtrooper aesthetic. Stone even became a "first degree" Proud Boy by saying some words, and no, not *those* fourteen words. He stopped at first degree, however. Roger didn't seem to want to play tickle fight with his tough boy soldiers. (56)

Even when it tries to perform straight-as-an-arrow, heteronormative masculinity, something in American fascism seems to twist things slightly out of joint. When fascism encounters sexual minorities (masculine or otherwise), things get *profoundly* warped. That's became fascism is not a clarifying or useful, but rather a muddying and paralytic, form of ideology. Fascism is bad for the development or maintenance of even a ruthlessly conformist personality on a long-term basis. In the minds of children of the 21st century, things have veered off course.

We've reached the point where it's time to ask the question.

What the fuck is going on?

* A few notes about the Sex Pistols: 1) they sucked shit, 2) they weren't punk, and 3) they were, in many ways, a boy band 4) I would have paid good money to watch Steve Ignorant from Crass (an *actual* punk band started in 1977) beat Sid Vicious to death with a hammer.

** The cat ears and profile picture tell me that this person is a furry. On top of that, there's a debate about whether femboys might be "eggs" (trans slang for trans people who haven't realized they're trans yet), or a boymoding (closeted) trans women playing with gender fluidity. Is someone an egg, or a hetero cisgendered man experimenting with his gender presentation? Identity is complex. This book is a relentless onslaught of (for normies) seemingly strange identities, but parsing the finer points of this kind of thing is a good way to understand aspects of fascism you won't find in a single *Vice* writeup or an explainer.

*** This is part of why Elon Musk and Joe Rogan moved to Texas. Affluent Californians *also* have different politics from affluent Texans, and many people, especially the affluent, like living amongst their own political kind.

1 Vashem, Yad et. al. (1991). *The Racial State: Germany 1933-1945*. (Cambridge University Press, Cambridge). P136-138.

2 Randsborg, Klavs (2015). *Roman Reflections: Iron Age to Viking Age in Northern Europe*. (Bloomsbury Publishing, London). P7-8.

3 Sin, Desirae (4/4/2024). "Undergraduate students present research on Black liberation and homofascism". *The Daily Campus*.

4 Staff. "Such Elements" (trans. from German). (12/8/1985). *Der Spiegel*.

5 https://en.wiktionary.org/wiki/homofascism

6 Schwartz, Michael (2021). "Homosexuelle im modernen Deutschland: Eine Langzeitperspektive auf historische Transformationen" [Homosexuals in Modern Germany: A Long-Term Perspective on Historical Transformations]. *Vierteljahrshefte für*

Zeitgeschichte (in German). 69 (3) P386.

7 Kerl, Kristoff et. al. (2022). "The 'Conspiracy of Homosexualisation': Homosexuality and Anti-Semitism in the United States, 1970s–1990s". *Journal of Modern European History*. 20 (3).

8 Himmelspach, Darlene (4/23/1990). "Book, Video Salesman Has Hot Product – Racism." *San Diego Union*.

9 *ONE National Gay & Lesbian Archives*. "National Socialist League Collection". Folder 6.

10 Crouthamel, Jason (9/19/2018). "Homosexuality and Comradeship: Destabilizing the Hegemonic Masculine Ideal in Nazi Germany". *Central European History*. 51 (3). P419-439.

11 Newton, Michael (2014) [2007]. *The Ku Klux Klan: History, Organization, Language, Influence and Activities of America's Most Notorious Secret Society*. (McFarland & Company, Jefferson). P182.

12 Fritscher, Jack (2017). Hemry, Mark (ed.). *Gay Pioneers: How Drummer Shaped Gay Popular Culture 1965-1999*. (Palm Drive Publishing, San Francisco). P128.

13 Snaith, Guy (2003). "Tom's Men: The Masculinization of Homosexuality and the Homosexualization of Masculinity at the end of the Twentieth Century". *Paragraph*. 26 (1/2). P77–88.

14 Penny, Daniel (1/24/2017). "#Milosexual and the Aesthetics of Fascism: Milo Yiannopoulos was the paradoxical poster boy for the alt-right—until he wasn't." *Boston Review*.

15 Kaplan, Jeffrey. "Russell Veh." (2000) *Encyclopedia of White Power: a Sourcebook on the Radical Racist Right*. (Altamira Press, Lanham). P317.

16 *ONE National Gay & Lesbian Archives*. "National Socialist League Collection", Folder 1.

17 Staff. (10/14/2003). "ACLU Defends Nazis' Right To Burn Down ACLU Headquarters". *The Onion*.

18 Staff. (9/16/1983). "Gay Nazis Peddling Vile 'Jud Suss' Film". *Heritage and S.W. Jewish Press*. [a]

[a] While it is accurate, I don't love this specific source. Why, you ask? Because Scott Lively leans very heavily on this incident in *The Pink Swastika*, a worthless fucking excuse for a book. I, however, am not Scott Lively. One of the central points of this text is that National Socialism is incompatible with homosexuality, not fueled by it. Lively is a conspiracy cultist, but in the interests of full disclosure I felt the need to point out that we share this citation.

19 Matthews, Dylan (5/19/2015). "A beginner's guide to biker gangs". *Vox*.

Piano, Ennio E. (2017). "Outlaw and economics: Biker gangs and club goods". *Rationality and Society*. 30 (3). P350-376.

Barker, Tom (2005), "One Percent Biker Clubs – A Description". *Trends in Organized Crime*. 9 (1). P111.

20 Lopez, David et. al. (2013). "Nazi Uniform

Fetish and Role Playing: A Subculture of Erotic Evil". *Popular Culture Review*. 24 (1). P69-78.

21 Sunshine, Spencer (2024). *Neo-Nazi Terrorism and Countercultural Fascism: The Origins and Afterlife of James Mason's Siege*. (Routledge, New York). P383-384.

22 Ross, Jenna (5/23/2020). "Pedophilia in Ancient Greece and Rome". *The Collector*.

Danna, Francesco (7/21/2022). "A Brief History of Homosexuality in Italy from Ancient Rome to Today". *Italy Secreta*.

23 Martin, Paula Maher (4/12/2018). "Nazi Germany, Ancient Rome: The appropriation of classical culture for the formulation of national identity". *The Gale Review*.

Chapoutot, Johann (2016) "Origin Myths: Ex septentrione lux" in Richard R. Nybakken (ed.), *Greeks, Romans, Germans: How the Nazis Usurped Europe's Classical Past*. (California Scholarship Online, Oakland).

24 https://knowyourmeme.com/memes/this-is-what-they-took-from-us-and-unbelievable-honkers-right-wing-nostalgia

25 Wilson, Andrew Fergus (2018). "#whitegenocide, the alt-right and conspiracy theory: How secrecy and suspicion contributed to the mainstreaming of hate". *Secrecy and Society*. 1 (2).

Winston, Andrew S. (April 2021). "'Jews will not replace us!': Antisemitism, Interbreeding and Immigration in Historical Context". *American Jewish*

History. 105 (1). P1–24.

26 Weiss, Suzannah (3/14/2025). "Are You Gynosexual? Here's What It Means, According to Experts." *Men's Health*.

Staff (12/6/2024). "Understanding gynesexuality: Attraction to femininity". *FEELD*.

Engle, Gigi (3/24/2023). "What Does It Mean to Be Gynesexual? Attraction to 'femininity' that isn't rooted in BS cishet gender norms? We're listening." *Cosmopolitan*.

27 Staff. (1/26/2021). "What is a 'femboy?'". *Dictionary.com*.

Staff. "Femboy". *Gender Wiki*.

Staff. "What are femboys?" *FEELD*.

28 Cristalli, Beatrice (01/01/2021). "Talking About Gender Fluidity: Inside Generation Z". *Enciclopedia Treccani*.

29 Vaught, Emerald (7/6/2023). "Saturated femininities: trans women in porn beyond the shemale". *Porn Studies*. 11 (4).

30 Gleeson, Jules Joannne (2/3/2018). "An Anatomy of the Soy Boy". *New Socialist*.

Patston, Manning (7/29/2022). "Femboy is the TikTok trend shaking up gender norms". *Happy Mag*.

31 O'Connor, Ciarán (2021). "Hatescape: An In-Depth Analysis of Extremism and Hate Speech on TikTok". *Institute for Strategic Dialogue*.

Ozduzen, Ozge et. al. (2023) "'Let us teach our children': Online racism and everyday far-right ideologies on TikTok". *Visual Studies*. 38 (5). P834-850.

32 Staff. (9/15/2020). "Femboys: The Movement That Goes From Fashion Week To TikTok". *FFW*.

33 Foster, Jordan & Baker, Jayne (2022). "Muscles, Makeup, and Femboys: Analyzing TikTok's 'Radical' Masculinities". *Social Media + Society*. 8 (3).

34 Bowes, Joshua (12/19/2024). "Anime and the Extreme-Right: Otaku Culture and Aesthetics in Extremist Digital Propaganda". *Global Network on Extremism and Technology*.

Fairbrother, Zachary (1/30/2024). "Fascist Femininity in Japanese Pop-Culture". *History Workshop*.

35 Potok, Mark (2/14/2023). "Secrets of the Sisterhood". *Southern Poverty Law Center*.

36 Upchurch, H. E. (12/22/2021). "The Iron March Forum and the Evolution of the 'Skull Mask' Neo-Fascist Network". *CTC Sentinel*. 14 (10).

37 Weill, Kelly (3/22/2018). "Satanism Drama Is Tearing Apart the [sic] Murderous Neo-Nazi Group". *The Daily Beast*.

Lamoureux, Mack (3/6/2023). "US Soldier Jailed for Satanic Neo-Nazi Plot to Kill Troops in Al Qaeda Attack". *Vice*.

38 Wending, Mark (2/6/2023). "Brandon Russell: Leader of neo-Nazi Atomwaffen group charged with Baltimore power grid plot". *BBC*.

Spinoza, Lauren (2/6/2023). "Suspects planned to attack Baltimore power grid, authorities say". *thehill.com*:

> Two Atomwaffen members expressed a desire to “completely destroy this whole city” of Baltimore.

39 Lowe, Derek (11/17/2015). "UCFPD Investigating Multiple Nazi Symbols, Fliers at UCF". *KnightNews.com*.

Crews, Julian (12/6/2016). "Neo-Nazi group claims responsibility for Hitler poster on U of C campus". *WGN-TV*.

Staff. (3/28/2016). "ODU police investigating Nazi fliers posted on campus". *WTKR*.

40 Thompson, A.C. et. al. (2/25/2018). “Inside Atomwaffen As It Celebrates a Member for Allegedly Killing a Gay Jewish College Student”. *ProPublica*.

41 Houpt, Simon (8/18/2017). "Vice co-founder Gavin McInnes's path to the far-right frontier". *The Globe and Mail*.

42 West, Leah (2/9/2021). "The Complicated Consequences of Canada's Proud Boys Terrorist Listing". *Lawfare*.

Staff. (6/27/2022) “Designation of Two Terrorist Entities". *New Zealand Government*.

43 Kriner, Matthew; Lewis, Jon (2021). "Pride & Prejudice: The Violent Evolution of the Proud Boys". *CTC Sentinel*. 14 (6).

44 Coaston, Jane (10/15/2018). "The Proud Boys, the bizarre far-right street fighters behind violence in New York, explained". *Vox*.

45 Ward, Ian (9/23/2022). "Jan. 6 Was Just the Beginning for the Proud Boys". *Politico*.

Reilly, Ryan J. (5/4/2023). "Four Proud Boys members found guilty of seditious conspiracy in Jan. 6 trial". *NBC News*.

46 Kutner, Samantha (2020). "The Allure of Hyper Masculinity and Cryptofascism for Men Who Join the Proud Boys" in *Swiping Right: The Allure of Hyper Masculinity and Cryptofascism for Men Who Join the Proud Boys*. P1.

47 Marantz, Andrew (7/6/2017). "The Alt-Right Branding War Has Torn the Movement in Two". *The New Yorker*.

48 Wilson, Jason (11/22/2018). "Proud Boys founder Gavin McInnes quits 'extremist' far-right group: Move comes after the Guardian exclusively revealed that the FBI had categorized group 'with ties to white nationalism'". *The Guardian*.

49 Staff. (11/14/2025). "Gavin McInnes Net Worth: $10 Million". *Celebrity Net Worth*.

50 Campbell, Andy (1/15/2019). "Gavin McInnes Is Losing The Battle To Win Over His Neighbors". *Huffington Post*.

51 Reuters. (1/27/2021). "Proud Boys leader 'prolific' snitch for law enforcement: Court transcript shows FBI agent and prosecutor saying Proud Boys leader Henry Tarrio helped convict 13 people." *Al-*

Jazeera.

52 Farivar, Masood (5/11/2023). “With Leaders Locked Up, Proud Boys Embrace New Cause: Anti-LGBTQ Activism”. *VOA*.

53 Travis, Candice K. (2023). “Nostalgia, Hypermasculinity, and the American Far Right: What Ever Happened to Being Proud of Your Boy?” *New Political Science*. 45 (4). P591-612.

54 Staff. (4/19/2017). “MS-13 gang: The story behind one of the world's most brutal street gangs”. *BBC*.

Vigil, J. D. (1996). “Street Baptism: Chicano gang initiation”. *Human Organization*. 55 (2). P149–153.

55 Ellis, Emma Grey (5/22/2017). "Your Handy Field Guide to the Many Factions of the Far Right, from the Proud Boys to Identity Evropa". *Wired*.

Gilmour, David (9/7/2017). "Meet the Proud Boys, the pro-men, anti-masturbation enemy of 'antifa'". *The Daily Dot*.

Hall, Alexandra (11/26/2017). "Controversial Proud Boys Embrace 'Western Values,' Reject Feminism And Political Correctness". *Wisconsin Public Radio*.

56 Sommer, Will (7/5/2019). "Proud Boys Rally Rocked by Sex, Cocaine Allegations". *The Daily Beast*.

Herron, Elise (3/7/2018). "Right-Wing Provocateur Roger Stone Asked Proud Boys For Protection at Dorchester Conference Last

Weekend". *Willamette Week*.

Weill, Kelly et. al. (1/29/2019). "How the Proud Boys Became Roger Stone's Personal Army". *The Daily Beast*.

Chapter Ten

EVERYTHING NOW

Every song that I've ever heard
Is playing at the same time, it's absurd
And it reminds me, we've got everything now

We turn the speakers up 'til they break
'Cause every time you smile it's a fake
Stop pretending, you've got

Everything now

Arcade Fire, "Everything Now"

In my first nonfiction book about fascism, one chapter is called "Gates." The name is a bit of a pun, but the main thrust of it has to do with cultural gates and gatekeeping. I claimed (and demonstrated) the following (1): conventional wisdom has it that the internet has removed cultural gatekeepers, but that's not true. In fact, we have more gateways than ever, and almost all of them are guarded by self-appointed gatekeepers of some kind. In some ways this has been a tremendous blessing. For example, voices marginalized by the "big media" era of mass communication can now be heard (although I'm not sure that they are to the extent they should be). These days, a few coastal newspapers owned by wealthy elites don't necessarily dictate the national political conversation to the extent they once did.

On the other hand, these new gatekeepers are often, arguably, worse than the previous batch. Instead of ABC, NBC, and a handful of other stations dominating the news, the loudest voice is Fox News, with a growing flotilla of remora-like right-wing social and media networks clinging to the Fox viewership. The far right dominates and has dominated terrestrial radio virtually since radio was born—now they dominate satellite radio, too. The world of podcasts, once a primarily liberal space in the early days, is now dominated by extremists of varying stripes (only a few of which match my own anarchist brand of extremism). Where a few large gatekeepers once stood, vested with (largely imaginary) wisdom and (often very real) elite education to judge what should be heard and what should not, we now live in a neon hellscape Thunderdome where what gets clicks gets seen.

Our modern gatekeepers and cultural icons are, arguably, the worst that any culture has ever had. I'm not talking about popular scapegoats like Ben Shapiro (although that twerp *does* suck). I'm talking about the plague blighting humanity known as influencers. I'd like to have this on record, in writing: *fuck influencers*, every single one of them, from sea to shining sea and from right wing to left. Influencer could only be a "job" in the type of hypercapitalist, narcissistic, underread, video-saturated, hallucinating America that we now inhabit. Influencers are the worst cultural gatekeepers we've had since the era of the courtiers of the Sun King Louis XIV. Concerned to a truly absurd degree with physical appearance, convinced that cultivating insecurity and parasocial (emotionally damaging) relationships is key to their profit margins, these shit merchants have crept into almost every aspect of how people shape their identities in the early 21st century.

"But Charles," I hear you say. (Hi, by the way.)

"But Charles, surely there can be influencers for *good* if there are influencers for *evil*! Every tool is use-neutral!" Well-said, reader! I used to believe that, too, and still do, to some extent. The medium of at-home (or on-the-go) video streaming to others Is not inherently bad. "Influencer culture," as it has developed and exists, is rotten to its fetid core and I will have none of it. Literally any time a person turns to streaming to "get the message out" I refer to it as stooping, because it is. The format of TikTok is especially bad here, but longform content on (pre-2020) YouTube has done the most damage by the numbers (though Twitch is close).

They aren't the only ones to blame, but they're a good place to start. So get ready to hear noise, noise, noise: everything from startlingly well-stated arguments for drinking poison to the most baldfaced lies you've ever seen. Because we've got everything now. And we're paying the price for it.

The Theater of the Self and Its Double

How does one define an "influencer?" Well, you can define "influencer" a few ways, since the term is related to social media clout. The simplest is by number of followers on a platform. Someone with 1,000—10,000 followers is known as a nano-influencer. 10-100,000 followers? Congratulations, you're a micro-influencer. Between 100,000 and 1,000,000 is generally considered standard "influencer" territory, with over 1 million followers making one a "mega-influencer." (2) Another way to define influencer is by, well, their influence. Good, old-fashioned pull, sometimes in an economic sense (selling a product or "lifestyle brand" to the public, which is how the term and concept "influencer" started), but increasingly often, in a socio-political sense (3)

Before I continue, I need to make one thing clear: this isn't a "kids these days" rant I'm about to go on. I don't blame anyone for what has been done *to* them, nor for the choices they made under tremendous commercial and algorithmic pressure. Especially since increasing numbers of people raise themselves on screens while their parents work four jobs between them (or just can't be bothered to involve themselves in what their kids consume). Yes, I believe people are responsible for the choices they make, and plenty of people subjected to the same pressures haven't fallen into the fascist funnel: but I feel tremendous sympathy for young people growing up under the conditions of 21st century capitalism, omnipresent social media, and influencer saturation.

Every time I hear “I grew up watching Mr. Beast” or “I grew up watching PewDiePie” or “I grew up going down YouTube conspiracy rabbit holes” it hits me like slap. I grew up watching and listening to plenty of offensive and controversial shit, but the differences are quantitative and qualitative. Social media and influencers are doing a variety of measurable harms to children. (4) Many popular influencers and streamers are bigots – and my Juggalo homies know the only thing bigots are good for (the hatchet). (5) There has been a concerted rightward shift in the media Overton window over the last few decades. I trace it to the election of Barack Obama, which seemed to deeply break something within the white American psyche. (6)

I remember Obama’s election as the day that Free Republic, a popular forum for right wing posters, “broker the ni***r barrier,” as some Awful Forums wits later put it. Up to that point, Freepers (as Free Republic posters are called) were allowed to tiptoe up to the line of openly using racial slurs, but not across it. They could freely discuss “welfare queens,” “affirmative action hires,” “crime rates by race,” and so forth. Likely the euphemisms didn’t make a difference in the end. Still, when the US got our first Black President, Free Republic’s longstanding ban on the use of racial slurs was temporarily lifted and those pent-up white boys yearning to breathe racial slurs (or type them, anyway) were free at last—to be the racist assholes everybody already knew they were. (7)

Free Republic isn’t a forum for kids, though. It’s a forum for political obsessives, and back in its heyday (in the 2000s and very early 2010s) politics were still boring stuff for children overall. Content aimed at young people has been a concern to dipshit puritans before, but mostly in terms of things like sex, foul language, or violence. Seldom do you hear concerns expressed about overt fascist brainwashing. That's weird, because you should. Not long ago a streamer named Felix Kjellberg (AKA PewDiePie), whose audience contained millions of adolescents, turned "Kill the Jews" into a running joke. (8) That's not something that would have fucking flown in anybody's youth in this country in recent memory. PewDiePIe is such a piece of shit that after he got his wings clipped for the "kill the Jews" thing, he pledged half a million dollars to the Anti-Defamation League—then canceled the donation after his legion of Nazi fans wouldn't stop howling about it. (9) Again: this guy was hugely popular with, primarily, adolescents, teens, and young adults. (10) This Swedish meatball made his name in video game streaming, by the way—an incredibly toxic, misogynistic, racist, and anti-Semitic space where young people spend a lot of time, (11) just coincidentally.

Influencers are a new twist on an old trend that has, over the years, included radio personalities, TV talk show hosts, celebrity spokespeople, and the like. Influencers, however, have gained a strange new edge in this strange new age. Influencers and their audience tend to develop what psychologists and sociologists call a "parasocial" relationship. That means that the relationship between the content creator and content consumer is intimate, in an illusory way. It can even *feel* intensely intimate for fans, at times. The relationship is almost totally one-way, however. A fan might think they know practically every detail about a streamer. The streamer might even respond to the fan's messages in a stream, or take selfies with them at a convention. Despite this, all the fan knows about the influencer is their persona: the artificial (though three-dimensional) personality they've constructed to create content. Fans usually don't acknowledge this reality: it would shatter the illusion. (12) And influencers, for their part? They neither know nor give a single fuck about their fans.

Influencers are people who largely become famous because their performances are a substitute for human companionship for their increasingly-isolated viewers. This dynamic became especially pronounced during the early days of the COVID-19 pandemic, when lockdown orders led young people (and others) to seek sociality where they could find it. (13) In the end, however, these quasi-real characters don't know or care about much other than what gets clicks, as their behavior all too often shows. The behavior of their fans also all too often indicates that the parasocial dynamic can attract unstable personalities and can also destabilize personalities. (14) Another reason people get sucked into influencers' sphere of orbit is that influencers, like all of us in the age of social media, carefully curate their image; it's arguably the only thing at which they excel. They *seem to be* a certain superlative archetype, and always an aspirational one.

Maybe they're supposed to be the epitome of masculinity, like alleged rapist and human trafficker Andrew Tate. Maybe they're supposed to be a cryptocurrency kingpin with brilliant inside knowledge of how finance works. Maybe they're supposed to be the most motivated salesman on the planet, ready to kick your grindset into gear so you can get rich smart. Whatever they're selling, a hyper-realistic vision of life is part of it; "virtual" not only in the sense of it being online, but in its original modern sense. "Virtual reality" (*la réalité virtuelle*), which gives us both modern meanings of virtual in a certain sense, was coined by a French playwright named Antonin Artaud to describe characters and objects in theater. The sense in which Artaud meant this can be detected in the title of the essay collection containing the description: *The Theater and Its Double.* (15) As I see it, a good description of life in the age of social media might be "the theater of the self and its double."

Whatever an influencer's niche might be, they have one central message in common. It's not one that they bluntly say out loud, but it's one that they promote using camera filters, Air BnB sets, special lighting, outright lies or trickery, and similar tactics—*lies*, in plain parlance. (16) They lie to send the following message.

"All of this," they say, referring to your life, your material conditions, your real-life feelings about your gender, your nascent sexuality, your old beliefs, "is bullshit. Come to me. Come into the hyper-real* world. In the screen you can have, and be, and say, and do, anything. *Everything*."

When I hear some of the verbal avalanches that pass for "serious discussions of political theory" on YouTube or go to Twitch and see the polygon animal avatars VTubers wear over their real selves while using voice modulators** to spew homophobic hate or sling slurs, I'm reminded of a song by Arcade Fire. In particular, I think of the lines: "Every song that I've ever heard / Is playing at the same time, it's absurd / And it reminds me, we've got everything now." Our boneless reality, where we don't even own the things we own, feels like that: a cacophony of the semi-familiar. And it feels like someone is turning the speakers up 'til they break.

I've even got to hand it to one of my least favorite philosophers, Mr. Karl Marx, who (along with Friedrich Engels) said the following in *The Communist Manifesto*, shooting his anxiety load a bit early in my opinion (this was published in 1848):

> All that is solid melts into air, all that is holy is profaned, and man is at last compelled to face with sober senses, his real conditions of life, and his relations with his kind. (17)

That last bit hasn't come to pass, in part because I think Marx vastly underestimated the guile, cruelty, and creativity of capitalism's and hierarchy's deceptive masks. All that is solid has melted into air. In the flux and chaos that has ensued, life—from the online, to the political, to the social and sexual—feels like every song that we've ever heard is playing at the same time. And it *is* absurd.

Influencers have contributed—might, in fact, be the primary agents of—a great detachment from reality that kicked into high gear in the age of Donald Trump. There are people out there in the year of their foul and rotting lord 2025 who are still convinced that the infamously batshit PizzaGate conspiracy theory had some validity:

One young, recent convert to this conspiracy- and politics-based new religious movement (QAnon) whom I encountered recently was sure that the Comet Ping Pong gunman hadn't checked the place thoroughly enough for a basement. Or was an FBI plant. He switched seamlessly between these explanations, with no apparent awareness of, nor distress at, the incompatibility of these beliefs. He has become the perfect fascist subject.

Am I blaming that person's confused media illiteracy on influencers? You're goddamned right I am. Kids who've grown up on PewDiePie can post about him like this and experience no cognitive dissonance:

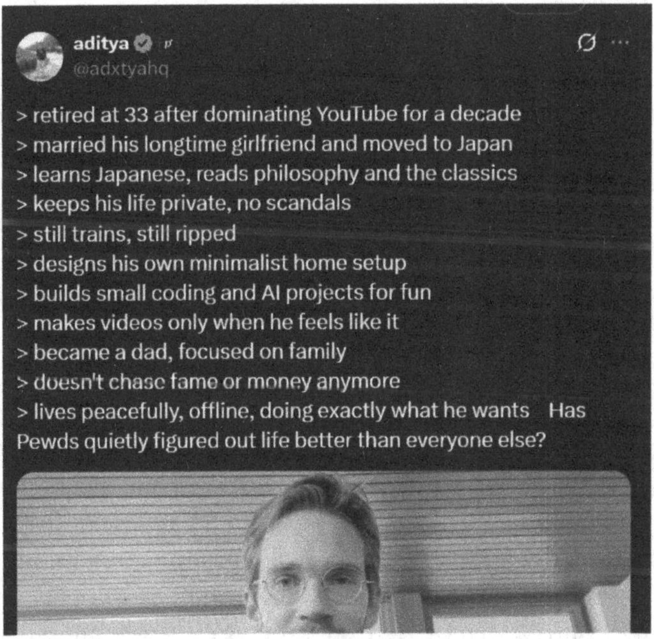

"No scandals." Yeah. The guy who was deplatformed for Nazi shit multiple times, including just last year, (18) and whose rabid fanbase are responsible for a range of hijinks including home camera hacks and death threats sent to critics. (19) To people raised in hyperreality, reality *just isn't flexible enough.* The real world—with its stubborn insistence on relating to real, imperfect people living real, unglamorous lives, and its equally stubborn insistence on real, uncomfortable facts—is a hard pill for some to swallow in the 2020s.

A guy on his fifteen-minute smoke break from an unbearable, soul-crushing job might stare down at his smartphone, *** watch Mr. Beast peel out in a Lamborghini for some epic prank, and simply see it as escape. It never occurs to him that the very systems propping up the bullshit illusion of influencer-as-"job" are mashing him into his own fate in the cruel gears of living-nightmare-as- "job." Mr. Beast and the soul-crushing job are part of a single, unbroken skein of hyperrealistic downward grind; either the death throes of capitalism or its rebirth into something newer, stranger, and possibly even worse.

Anti-LGBTQIA+ influencers are a persistent and vile presence on platforms from Twitter to TikTok to YouTube. A few are household names: J.K. Rowling and Jake and Logan Paul, for instance. Both Rowling and the brothers Paul are best known for projects aimed at young adults, and all of them have used their social media presences to vilify and harass queer folks. Other hatemongers transitioned from more traditional media jobs into the role of queerphobic influencers, like Matt Walsh or Ben Shapiro. But there's an entire crop of people who made their name initially by being professional homophobes. These people are the lowest scum in media, in my opinion: people who make a comfortable living by ruining innocent lives. One example is a woman named Chaya Raichik who runs a

Twitter account called "Libs of TikTok." Raichik once agreed to an interview with a gay influencer in which It quickly became apparent why Chaya Is an influencer instead of, say, a debate bro like Ben Shapiro or Charlie Kirk. Chaya is not particularly good at thinking or expressing herself, as it turns out. (20) (21)

And yes, there *are* LGBTQIA+ influencers—lots of them! They create great content, much of which is appropriate for and accessible to young people trying to figure out their identity. And the majority of queer youth *don't* wind up fascists, so the overall trend is not as terrible as the outliers can make it seem. Does this go against my previous statement regarding influencer being a job that must go extinct? No. As well-intentioned as these queer influencers are, the "relationships" they cultivate with viewers pose the same parasocial dangers and contribute to the larger trends of social alienation and isolation, even with the good they do. Do I have an easy answer? No. Might these positive queer influencers be the best place closeted youth with homophobic parents can go for advice right now? Likely so. The situation is deeply troubling. Even with those positive, friendly influencers, it's easy to see how the edgier, thornier, or more oppositional queer folks growing up can get sucked into the radicalization funnel. This is where I get to tee off on Trey Parker and Matt Stone briefly, two fucking meatheads who I don't think get enough credit for completely fucking up society. I'm an OG South Park hater, and have never found the show's "Oh my! So controversial!" humor amusing.

Part of Parker and Stone's schtick—hell, 99% of it—is to try to make caring about anything, anything at all, seem deeply fucking cringeworthy. † I mean, all the stuff people care about is stupid and so fucking gay, right dudes? Kids who grow up watching "edgy," queerphobic, disability-mocking shit like South Park will, I think, obviously be more predisposed to develop parasocial relationships with "edgy" streamers like Mr. Beast or PewDiePie. That's while hearing slurs nonstop in the multiplayer lobbies of their favorite games. Is it any wonder that later, if they develop questions about their sexual or gender identity, they log on to fucking *4Chan* for answers? Once they've stepped into that candy-colored Nazi hell, there's rarely any coming back. In a virtual, hyperreal world where nobody cares about anything, who's to say you can't be a queer fascist? Two songs playing at the same time, it's absurd. We have everything now.

As should prove surprising to literally none of my readers given my philosophical outlook, I don't have children and never will. Most of my friends and family have kids, and I've been around them a fair piece in my life. I can't claim to know what it's like to be a parent. I don't know what the pressures are like when one or more parents are bringing up a kid or kids while working, especially as the final crushing phases of capitalism in the imperial core collapse. I've heard stories from my friends and family, but that's not the same thing as experiencing the lived reality for myself. With *that* said.

Things aren't okay for queer youth out there. The kids will be all right, I hope. But while I haven't been a parent, what I *have* been is a freelance suicide helpline for queer youth, usually between the ages of 17 and 22. Those are hard years. They were for me, and I didn't even know that I was bi at the time (although I had my suspicions). I feel like the least that I can do is keep tabs on people via Twitter and Discord and make sure that they're all right. It's remarkable how "why don't we talk about it" as a reply to a post about self-harm can make a difference. And I can hear some of my readers thinking "that's great or whatever, middle-aged Juggalo author guy, but where are these kids' fucking *parents*?"

The parents *are the problem* in nine cases out of ten. I know multiple people, personally and online, who've been disowned and thrown out of their home by their birth family for being queer. In the tenth case out of ten, when parents aren't the problem, the young person is worried that if they *do* go a parent—even a supportive one—they might wind up medically incarcerated in a locked psychiatric ward:

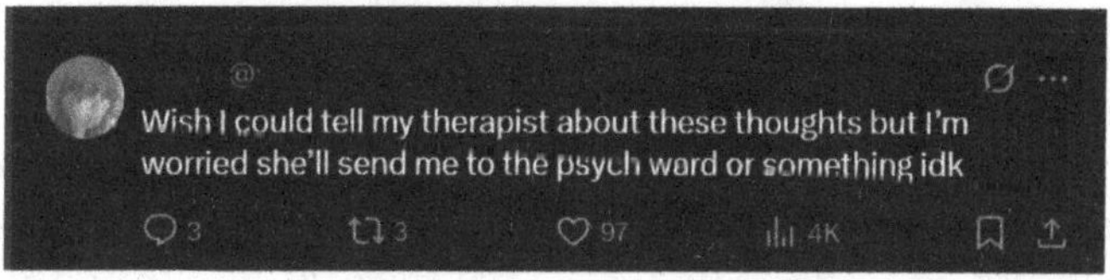

This is also a concern that adult queers have. Psychiatric and psychological discrimination and bias against queer people is endemic, (22) and medicine and psychology have both historically labeled queer people deviants and monsters. Even when therapists have a positive view of queer clients, often they lack the cultural knowledge and sensitivity to get therapy for LGBTQIA+ people right. (23) Besides, that's talking about reputable therapists, not the growing ranks of crackpots who use Jesus to appoint themselves "trusted religious advisors" or even "Christian counselors" with quite literally no training whatsoever. (24)

Why bring up "faith therapy" specifically? Our new fascist regime is much more Christian than its figurehead. I'll give it to Christian Nationalists: they've learned to fight even dirtier than they already did back in my day. They've always thought that prayer in schools is great for indoctrination, but they've also found a *literally* captive population that's possibly even more vulnerable than average schoolkids.

Get Clean And Shiny

People take drugs. That includes me—I'm a people, and I *love* drugs! Sometimes, however, even the best of us take drugs too much or often or in harmful ways. This is especially the case when one is coping with anxiety and depression, (25) not to mention dysphoria (which also causes depression and anxiety on top of other symptoms). Oh, and screen time worsens all these pre-existing issues, (27) although it might be more accurate to say that sometimes all of them are correlated with and worsen each other in a tangled knot of dysfunction. (26) In the absence of reliable psychiatry (or any therapy at all in many cases), people self-medicate. Especially poor people and people of color. (28) Those people also happen to be the ones most likely to get into trouble with addiction and, subsequently, our thoroughly nightmarish and inhuman law enforcement and carceral systems. (29)

In other words: if someone is a lower-SES / working person, queer, and experiencing anxiety and depression from dealing with societal homophobia, they're not alone. They undoubtedly feel that way, but they aren't. It's a not-uncommon plight in this homophobic country. Dealing with that anxiety through drug or alcohol abuse makes it more likely they will run afoul of the police, and thus they will likely face a choice at some point. Either before or during incarceration (while talking about early release), you're probably going to rehab—whether it's been proven to be effective or not. (30) If one is "lucky" enough to get drug court instead of original recipe court for nonviolent drug crimes, you're absolutely, without question going to rehab. That's what drug court is for.

Rehab in America is a private industry. At some point I plan to write about it at length. Rehab in America is—and I say this from a combination of from my own experience, the experience of friends and family, research, and every other way it's possible to know something except divine revelation—a fatally flawed, crooked, ideologically-driven trainwreck. It might help some people, but it's far from a cure-all. There are a few inpatient treatment centers that strive to do things the "right" way, but rehabilitation was born in infamy, educated at the altar of lies, and now is almost completely in the clutches of a cabal of Christian Nationalists. Whether for adolescents or adults, American rehab is Jesus Camp with locked doors, guards, and the legal power to send your ass to prison if you talk back to a counselor. (31)

Court-ordered Jesus Rehab is a side effect of the same problem afflicting rehabilitation and recovery in the US overall: it's ideological, not evidence-based. Some decades ago, state-by-state, the United States decided that for-profit rehabilitation centers could cut deals with the government to scarf up inmates. As a result, some legendarily shitty rehab experiences were born: the result of maximizing profit over maximizing care. (32) Why do I bring this up? Because the type of Christianity bandied about in addiction recovery spaces isn't always queer-friendly. Christianity itself is not particularly queer-friendly, as it's one of the primary motors driving the persecution of LGBTQIA+ people in the West.

If one self-medicates and is lucky enough to avoid the prison-to-Jesus-Camp pipeline, things still aren't exactly great out there. Everything from yoga to self-help has become part of the vast, dazzling, neon funnel leading to neofascism. The wellness industry (which includes many self-directed rehab efforts) is especially vile in this regard. (33) In my last nonfiction book, I touched briefly on "Granola Q," the portion of the QAnon new religious movement who came to it from the world of crystal healing, "natural remedies," and holistic healing. Since then, the pressure in the wellness-to-fascism pipeline has only intensified. (34)

My readers might remember shambling, worm-brained health minister Robert F. Kennedy Jr.'s "concentration camps for mental illness" plan (which has mercifully not come to pass as of this writing), but if not, allow me to refresh your memory. *Teen Vogue*, a deceptively brainy and political publication, has an excellent summary:

> In a clip from a July 2024 virtual town hall that recirculated online earlier this year, now Health and Human Services Secretary Robert F. Kennedy Jr. argues that the US should combat addiction by opening "wellness farms" to help people get off opioids, antidepressants, and stimulants. Kennedy says people taking medications for conditions like depression and attention-deficit/hyperactivity disorder (ADHD), along with those living with addiction, could spend three or four years growing organic produce on these farms to be "re-parented" and "reconnect with communities."

That article goes on to talk about how this isn't even a novel idea (honestly, I'd be surprised if Health Secretary Herman Munster were capable of a novel idea):

> In short: America has already tried wellness farms. Beginning in the 1890s and continuing through the first few decades of the 20th century, epileptic and "feebleminded" colonies sprung up around the US. The initial purpose of

> these colonies was to remove patients from overcrowded, badly run asylums and poorhouses in favor of farm life where they would have access to the outdoors.
>
> ...
>
> It didn't work. (34)

It didn't work because epilepsy—like depression, ADHD, autism, anxiety, and a variety of other conditions—*isn't just an attitude problem.* In the rogue's gallery of villains menacing young queer people, I'd put "bullshit health culture" near the top of the list. That content isn't just present in far-right online spaces; it's present in nearly *every* online space. When I say bullshit health culture, I'm not talking about gender-affirming care, which is evidence-based. (35) I'm talking about the sort of attitude which has become more and more prevalent since the 1990s; one which says evidence-based treatments for depression, anxiety, ADHD, and the like amount to "overmedication." That sort of parental attitude is an example of the overapplication of a specific case (such as the American opioid epidemic) to the general ("all medication is bad").

I say this as a disabled person with diagnosed and complex mental health issues myself: medication isn't a cure-all when it comes to mental health. But, in my case, it saved my life. In many cases, it saves lives. Provably. The introduction of SSRIs to psychiatric medicine is strongly correlated with a worldwide reduction in suicide rates. (36) SSRIs also, in a minority of cases, increase suicidality, but this statistically uncommon side effect (37) has, in the popular imagination, led to a generally oppositional stance toward them in many people. I repeat: medication isn't a cure-all. But therapy isn't a cure-all, either. In combination, they can and do prevent many people from finding themselves in a place where self-hatred spirals into self-harm and, eventually, annihilation.

The problem is that under the current regime, mental health resources in the United States are being phased out, particularly for those most vulnerable. (38) Access to evidence-based mental health care is becoming more difficult, and poor, young people (which is an increasing number of young people every year) (39) have to seek alternatives. Those might include self-medication which, as we've discussed, can lead to incarceration and a forced introduction to Jesus the alleged Christ. Another option is to just take the black pill (online slang for embracing nihilistic despair). That's where 4Chan comes in. Even if a labyrinth of screens has convinced Americans that we've got everything now, many of us feel emptier than we ever have. (40)

Those of us who have (or have had) substance abuse problems are all too often herded into the Christian cult masquerading as recovery that calls itself Alcoholics Anonymous (or it's cousin NA). Evidence-based recovery has been shown to be more effective than twelve-step programs. (41) In that case, why are AA and NA still around? Because evidence-based modalities require professionals (and, therefore, a budget). No professional is needed for a faith-based shame circle in a church basement, complete with group prayer and a passing of the collection plate. Those tend to be cheaper than actual solutions, and not just cheaper: the church-basement, faith-based milieu of AA follows a Christonormative script that Americans have had pounded into their brains since childhood. Therapy, on the other hand? That's for crazy people!

If AA or NA works for you or someone you know, great. Forgive my saltiness—I stopped drinking without AA and am a thoroughgoing AA hater, although my hatred is neither irrational nor strictly ideological: one of AA's oft-repeated claims is that nobody can truly get sober without them. That offends the lover of truth in me. But I wouldn't try to mess with what's working for you or anyone. As a one-size-fits-all solution, however, twelve step programs can't be justified.

Ultimately, if a proposed solution to people being in distress is "Who cares? Let them figure it out," it's fair to call that a policy of malignant neglect. The disparity in outcomes for the disabled (42) and/or people of color (43) during the COVID pandemics are proof of America's commitment to culling those it finds undesirable through systematic neglect. The same is true of the MAGA regime's deliberate removal of lifesaving resources from those same communities *and* queer people, especially queer youth. Let's say that someone is drowning right in front of you, and you have a life preserver or raft. Instead of deploying it, you holler "THOUGHTS AND PRAYERS! STAY POSITIVE AND PRAY!" with a shit-eating grin on your face. You can't claim you aren't responsible for that person's death when they drown in front of you. Inaction amounts to action in those circumstances. When "those circumstances" result in someone's death, you've committed passive murder.

And all of this is chillingly familiar. My grandparents on my mother's side were involved in AIDS education, prevention, and counseling during the HIV/AIDS crisis of the 1980s and 1990s. I remember hearing stories around the dinner table (from the time I was too young to truly understand up until their final years) about the lives lost through the inaction of the Reagan and George HW Bush administrations. Turns out: those weren't just stories! (44) Both Reagan and Bush have the blood of AIDS victims on their hands, a phrasing I'm sure would have freaked the living fuck out of them. That era was another example of a policy of passive murder (see also: people who die of chronic illness while incarcerated.) Nobody pulled a trigger. There are no mass graves. Yet these policies still serve to end the lives of "undesirable" populations.

Turn the Speakers Up 'Til They Break

At the heart of what's going on with sexual minorities in far-right online spaces seems to me to be a confusing, SS-lightning-bolt streaked pixelstorm. The soundtrack is the amplification and admixture of the "everything now" that we've been given. Messages—all messages—are *loud* these days. They're loud tonally, in their frequency, in how they dumb down and oversimplify issues, and in how they tend to break down along too-easy-to-be-true lines of ideology or political party. Modern reality is more of a choose your own adventure game than it ever has been, with "consensus reality" having been fractured by an onslaught of information freely remixed with mis- or disinformation, with the whole mass easily sculpted and pruned into whatever shape an influencer, party cadre, MAGA loudmouth, or elected official wishes. That doesn't make what they say true; it's quite easy to debunk a startling amount of what passes for political discourse these days. The thing is, *the facts don't matter* on a practical level. Perhaps they do in some metaphysical sense, as the writing of Russian expatriate and journalist Masha Gessen seems to imply.

And yet, a (small) crop of queer youth consistently embracing fascism, despite history, logic, and ideological incoherence tells me that something in the way our society teaches people to process information is deeply broken—likely by design. I don't have a magic cure-all. I *do* have a few thoughts on how the specific issues I've highlighted in this book might be applied in certain circumstances.

* Hyperreality is another concept useful in discussing influencers. The term was coined by poststructuralist thinkers to refer to the modern breaking down of the distinguishment between signifiers and the signified (a symbol of something and the thing itself), culminating in the dissolution of consensus reality. The ultimate effect of hyperreality is that fiction and reality become so seamlessly

blended and intertwined that it becomes impossible to differentiate between them. Sound familiar? It's just my opinion, but poststructuralism has a better track record of prophetic mutterings than any other philosophical discipline I've studied. [a]

[a] Lawson, Tony & Garrod, Joan (2001). *Dictionary of Sociology*. (Fitzroy, Dearborn). P114.

** A phenomenon called "VTubing." The V, of course, stands for virtual.

*** Smartphones, servers, and everything else composing the real-world infrastructure that makes the hyperreality of "Web 2.0" possible is made possible by rare earth elements, especially neodymium (chemical element symbol Nb). Neodymium is a fucking nightmare to extract from the Earth, environmentally speaking. Also speaking in terms of human rights, as it is largely a product of child slave labor. [a]

[a] Harvey, Fiona (4/26/2024). "UN-led panel aims to tackle abuses linked to mining for 'critical minerals'". *The Guardian*.

† I am not the only one who feels this way.[a]

[a] Donovan, Derek (2/25/2025). "Opinion: 'South Park' slams Trump. Great, but the show helped make him president".

1 Bernard, Charles R. (2024). "Chapter Six: Gates" in *Black Sunrise On Piss Earth: Nihilism, Fascism, and the 21st Century Occult*. (Gutter Mystic Press, Austin).

2 Bousquet, Kristen (8/6/2024). “What's An Influencer And How Can I Make Money As One?” *Forbes*.

3 Lai, Stephanie (11/2/2022). "Campaigns Pay Influencers to Carry Their Messages, Skirting Political Ad Rules". *The New York Times*.

4 Vasconcellos, Roberta Pires et. al. (2025). “Electronic Screen Use and Children’s Socioemotional Problems: A Systematic Review and Meta-Analysis of Longitudinal Studies”. *American Psychological Association*. 151 (5). P513-543.

Vidal, Carol et. al. (2023). “Social Media and Mental Health in Children and Teens”. *Johns Hopkins Medicine*.

Tolbert, Amanda N. & Drogos, Kristin L. (2019). “Tweens’ Wishful Identification and Parasocial Relationships With YouTubers”. *Frontiers in Psychology*. Vol. 10.

5 Dodgson, Lindsay (8/24/2020). “Stories of racist jokes, microaggressions, and tokenism from YouTubers highlight a widespread problem within the influencer industry”.

Staff. (1/5/2022). “Influencer Elle Darby apologises over racist tweets”. *BBC*.

Hokka, Jenni (2021). “PewDiePie, racism and YouTube’s neoliberalist interpretation of freedom of speech”. *Convergence: The International Journal of Research into New Media Technologies*. 27 (1). P142-160.

Burkett, Eric (5/4/2023). “YouTube urges judge

to dump race discrimination case by Black content creators". *Courthouse News Service*.

6 Headlee, Celeste (1/15/2013). "Shifts In Race Relations Since Obama's Election". *NPR: Talk of the Nation*:

> "I just know that I spent 20 years in the Air Force, and there are people that are there that are retired now, too, that openly make racial comments, you know, towards black people or people on welfare that you never heard before [the election of Barack Obama]."

Xavier, Jonathan (7/15/2016). "How Racial Threat Has Galvanized the Tea Party". *Stanford Business*.

Martin, Michel (4/16/2010). "The Tea Party And Race". *NPR: Tell Me More*.

7 Martin, Michel (7/28/2009). "Online Racism: Who's to Blame?" *NPR: Tell Me More*:

> The conservative Free Republic blog has been criticized, including by other conservatives, for allowing readers to post racist remarks about one of the president's young daughters, after she wore a T-shirt featuring a peace sign, while on an overseas trip.

The blog owner first took the comments down and then restored them, citing free speech rights.

8 Staff. "Disney drops YouTuber PewDiePie over anti-Semitism claims". *BBC News*.

Domonoske, Camila (2/14/2017). "Disney

Company Drops YouTube Star PewDiePie Over Anti-Semitic Jokes". *NPR: The Two Way*.

9 Paul, Kari (9/12/2019). "YouTuber PewDiePie scraps $50,000 pledge to anti-hate group after fan backlash: Vlogger embraced by far right apologizes for planned donation to Anti-Defamation League, after fans claim conspiracy". *The Guardian*.

Andrew, Scottie (9/13/2019). "YouTube star PewDiePie cancels a $50,000 donation to an anti-hate charity". *CNN*.

10 O'Connell, Jennifer (2/18/2017). "What children learn from PewDiePie, Stampy and DanTDM: Anti-Semitic messages have been found in the videos of one of YouTube's 'Let's Play' stars. So how child-friendly are the hugely popular vloggers?" *The Irish Times*.

Moran, Robert (8/17/2019). "Who is PewDiePie, YouTube's record-setting personality? PewDiePie's subscription count has surpassed 100 million. Who is the world's most famous YouTuber and who are his fans?" *The Sydney Morning Herald*.

11 Ramirez, Marc (9/3/2023). "Racism in online gaming is rampant. The toll on youth mental health is adding up". *USA Today*.

Gray, Kishonna L. (4/1/2012). "Intersecting Oppressions and Online Communities". *Information, Communication & Society*. 15 (3). P411–428.

Staff. (2/1/2023). "How Racist Groups Use Online Video Games To Spread Hate". *Bloomberg: Big Take Daily*.

12 Hoffner, Cynthia & Bond, Bradley (2022). “Parasocial relationships, social media, & well-being”. *Current Opinion in Psychology*. Vol. 45.

Chung, S. & Cho, H. (2017). "Fostering Parasocial Relationships with Celebrities on Social Media: Implications for Celebrity Endorsement". *Psychology & Marketing*. 34 (4). P481–495.

13 Bond, Bradley J. (2022). “Parasocial relationships as functional social alternatives during pandemic-induced social distancing”. *Psychology of Popular Media.* 11 (3). P250–257.

14 Romano, Aja (8/29/2025). “The one-sided intimacy of being a fan”. *Vox*.

Selo, Monica (11/22/2024). “15 Toxic and entitled influencers on the internet and my piece of advice to them- part 1.” *Medium*.

Manavis, Sarah (2/27/2024). “Why angry ‘anti-fans’ turn on the influencers they once loved”. *The Guardian*.

15 Artaud, Antonin (1938) [1958]. *The Theatre and its Double* trans. Mary Caroline Richards. (Grove Weidenfeld, New York)

16 Boozel, Jessica (6/23/2024). “Hear Me Out: The Influencers You Love Are Lying to You”. *Stella Social Media*.

Huddleston, Tom Jr. (2/2/2021). “How Instagram influencers can fake their way to online fame”. *CNBC*.

Fry, Naomi (2/20/2021). “‘Fake Famous’ and

the Tedium of Influencer Culture". *The New Yorker*.

Royle, Orianna Rosa (1/21/2025). "TikTokers confessed the lies they used to get millions of followers before the U.S. blackout: Now they're backtracking as angry fans blast their fake videos". *Fortune*.

Lorenz, Taylor (2023). *Extremely Online: The Untold Story of Fame, Influence, and Power on the Internet*. (Simon & Schuster, New York). P224-225.

17 Marx, Karl & Engels, Friedrich (1848). *The Communist Manifesto*. (Kommunistischer Arbeiterbildungsverein, London).

18 Choksi, Miraj (2/14/2017). "Disney Drops PewDiePie and YouTube Distances Itself After Reports of Anti-Semitic Videos". *New York Times*.

Gach, Ethan (2/13/2019). "PewDiePie Clashes With Roblox, Which Appears To Have Banned His Name". *Kotaku*.

Flint, Emma (10/4/2024). "PewDiePie quietly and suddenly banned from Twitch". *Gaming Bible*.

19 Staff. (7/18/2018). "The 10 Most Difficult-to-Defend Online Fandoms". *Wired*.

Staff (7/23/2019). "Nest Cams Hijacked in the Name of PewDiePie and North Korea Pranks". *Wired*.

20 Wiggins, Christopher (11/11/2025). "12 far-right influencers targeting the LGBTQ+ community". *Advocate*.

21 https://www.youtube.com/watch?v=XL-

40gDBRx0

22 Kalinoski, Mara (4/22/2024). "New Study Shows LGBT Adults Face More Discrimination in Health Care". University of Colorado *Anschutz School of Medicine*.

Casey, Logan et. al. (2019). "Discrimination in the United States: Experiences of lesbian, gay, bisexual, transgender, and queer Americans". *Health Services Research*. Vol. 54. P1454-1466.

23 Cruciani, Gianluca et. al. (2024). "Attitudes and knowledge of mental health practitioners towards LGBTQ+ patients: A mixed-method systematic review". *Clinical Psychology Review*. Vol. 113.

24 Owens, Whitney (11/17/2025). "What Is Required To Call Myself a Christian Counselor?" *Practice of the Practice*:

> There is no specific required training to be a Christian counselor. However, it is advised that you receive some type of ethics training on how to appropriately integrate your faith in your clinical work.

Guest. (7/23/2018). "Testing [Mormon] Bishops for Skills, Aptitude, and Narcissism". *By Common Consent*:

> Last week a report issued that "Anglican leaders are considering expanding its assessments of clergy candidates to include more rigorous psychological testing." The LDS Church does none of this. I think we should.

25 Esmaeelzadeh, Sarvenaz et. al. (2018). "The association between depression, anxiety and substance use among Canadian post-secondary students". *Neuropsychiatric Disease and Treatment*. 23 (14). P3241-3251.

26 Cioffredi, Leigh-Anne et. al. (2021). "Effects of depression, anxiety and screen use on adolescent substance use". Vol. 22.

27 Li, Liqing (2022). "Screen time and depression risk: A meta-analysis of cohort studies". *Frontiers in Psychiatry*. 22 (13).

28 Nguyen, Cuong Tat et. al. (2023). "Prevalence and impacts of self-medication in a disadvantaged setting: the importance of multi-dimensional health interventions". *Frontiers in Public Health*. 27 (11).

29 Zore, Hossein et. al. (2025). "Exploring the association between income inequality, racial composition, and fatal police shootings in U.S. counties (2015–2022)". *Journal of Criminal Justice*. Vol. 96.

30 Riddle, Katia (5/13/2024). "Is it right to force someone into rehab? The man whose life inspired a landmark law". *The Guardian*.

Werb, D. et. al. (2015). "The Effectiveness of Compulsory Drug Treatment: A Systematic Review". *International Journal of Drug Policy*. 18 (28). P1-9.

31 Harris, Amy Julia & Walter, Shoshana (10/17/2017). "Why courts' use of religious work camps could be 'patently illegal'". *Reveal News*.

Barrow, Bill & The Associated Press (10/25/2022). "Herschel Walker's Christian Alcoholics & Addicts in Recovery 'work camp' uses unpaid labor from drug offenders, critics say". *Fortune*.

Urquhart, Jim (5/7/2024). "Nearly half of Utah's wilderness programs for 'troubled teens' closed in the last year. Here's what's happening." *Salt Lake Tribune*.

32 Rayasam, Renuka & Farmer, Blake (1/30/2023). "Some addiction treatment centers turn big profits by scaling back care". *CBS News*.

Farmer, Blake (1/25/2023). "Private equity investment is flooding into addiction treatment. Is that a good thing?" *Marketplace*.

Mann, Brian (2/15/2021). "As Addiction Deaths Surge, Profit-Driven Rehab Industry Faces 'Severe Ethical Crisis'". *NPR*.

33 Ball, James (8/2/2023). "'Everything you've been told is a lie!' Inside the wellncss-to-fascism pipeline". *The Guardian*.

34 Waring, Kathryn (4/17/2025). "RFK Wants to Send People to 'Wellness Farms.' The US Already Tried That." *Teen Vogue*.

35 Boerner, Heather (5/12/2022). "What the Science on Gender-Affirming Care for Transgender Kids Really Shows: Laws that ban gender-affirming treatment ignore the wealth of research demonstrating its benefits for trans people's health". *Scientific American*.

Budge, Stephanie L. et. al. (2024). “Gender Affirming Care Is Evidence Based for Transgender and Gender-Diverse Youth”. *Journal of Adolescent Health.* 75 (6). P851-853.

36 Isaacson, Goran (2010). “The increased use of antidepressants has contributed to the worldwide reduction in suicide rates”. *British Journal of Psychiatry*. 96 (6). P429-433.

37 McCain, Jack Allan (2009). “Antidepressants and Suicide in Adolescents and Adults”. *P.T.* 34 (7). P3355-378.

38 Counts, Nathan (8/15/2025). “Proposed Federal Budget Cuts Could Exacerbate the Behavioral Health Crisis”. *The Commonwealth Fund.*

Staff. (6/9/2025). “America’s mental health crisis would worsen if the budget bill becomes law”. *ASCFME.*

Staff. (7/16/2025). “Update on Cuts to Medicaid Funding and Restrictions to Medicaid Access”. *APA/APASI.*

Faguy, Ana (11/12/2025). “Trump signs spending bill to end longest shutdown in US history”. *BBC.*

39 Levitz, Eric (11/18/2025). “Is Gen Z ‘utterly screwed’?” *Vox.*

Tur, Katy (9/19/2025). “Gen Z faces growing economic struggles amid higher inflation and cost of living”. *MS NOW.*

40 Witters, Dan (9/9/2025). “U.S. Depression Rate Remains Historically High”. *Gallup.*

41 Mendola, Annette & Gibson, Richard L. (2016). "Addiction, 12-Step Programs, and Evidentiary Standards for Ethically and Clinically Sound Treatment Recommendations: What Should Clinicians Do?". *AMA Journal of Ethics*. 18 (6).

42 Goyal, Divya et. al. (2023). "Impact of the COVID-19 pandemic on people with disabilities and implications for health services research". *Journal of Health Services Research and Policy*. 28 (2). P77-79.

43 Hill, Latoya & Artiga, Samantha (8/22/2022). "COVID-19 Cases and Deaths by Race/Ethnicity: Current Data and Changes Over Time". *KFF*.

44 Petro, Anthony Michael (2015). *After the Wrath of God: AIDS, Sexuality, and American Religion*. (Oxford University Press, Oxford). P67.

Brier, Jennifer (2009). *Infectious Ideas: U.S. Political Responses to the AIDS Crisis*. (University of North Carolina Press, Chapel Hill). P83.

Gessen, Masha (12/7/2018). "George H.W. Bush's Presidency Erased People With AIDS. So Did the Tributes to Him". *The New Yorker*.

CHAPTER ELEVEN

UNDERSTANDING SEXUAL MINORITIES IN FAR-RIGHT ONLINE SPACES

Sexual minorities exist in far-right spaces: of course they do. Queer folks exist in *every* community, as is made apparent by every scandal involving a member of a supposedly queer-exclusionary group who can't help wanting what their heart wants. The examples are too numerous to list, from every Mormon missionary who "experimented" with a fellow missionary on their mission, to right-wing politicians who are closeted queers, to the ranks of the actual Nazi Party, from ancient history right until today. Queers like American football, too. There are queer Trekkies, queer NASCAR fans, and queer Warhammer 40K enthusiasts.

Even so, it isn't an incorrect reaction to say "what the *fuck*" when one sees a trans Nazi or a fascist femboy urging anons to have a happy No Nut November. Part of healthy identity formation is the drive to avoid as many instances of cognitive dissonance as possible. Such instances cause psychological distress. Social media hasn't helped in this regard. (1) As humans, we strive to live in harmony with our self and our identity and to be devoid of obvious logical short-circuits. Whether one lives a life or faith or a life or reason, it causes psychological distress to feel that one is an imposter, or otherwise inauthentic in who one is.

We all contain contradictions. When we are aware of and work with them, we can carry these contradictions as tensions rather than inconsistencies. For example, I'm a communitarian (neighborhood- and consensus-minded) at heart, but I'm also a radical individualist. That's a tension, not a contradiction: I believe that individualism flourishes within the supportive structures of a community of some kind, and that our perspectives and strengths as individualists strengthen communities. It leads to interesting discussions with others and internal debates about things I might otherwise glibly gloss over with an easy answer, not giving them the due thought that they deserve. It allows me to be aware of multiple sides of an issue, and to lean to one side or the other as the situation warrants. It makes me aware of my own shortcomings, and aware that I need to be *more* aware of them. As I grow older and wiser (not to mention crankier), I'm increasingly drawn to the idea that through this process human beings can resolve these seeming contradictions. That, and we can square our competing perspectives with one another into one that sees through multiple lenses to perceive reality *more or less* correctly. For example, I think studying politics is useless without studying psychology and vice-versa.

I think sociology should be informed by medicine and vice-versa. That's one reason I'm glad to be a gutter academic: we specialize in whatever interests us and is interrelated.

Hundreds of books have been published in the last decade which contain the phrase "America is at a crossroads." Counting magazine articles, it's probably something more like thousands of uses of that phrase. And do you know what? *Every single one of them* has been right. Fascism in the 21st century in America is both a rapid and a creeping phenomenon—which is par for the fascist course. Having studied the rise of the Third Reich, I don't think most people realize how long those fuckers were on their grind before they hit it big. Right now, however, America really is at—let's not call it a crossroads. Let's call it a *Turning Point*, in honor of that dead flaccid bigot Charlie Kirk. * Because of the time in which we live, a variety of things are happening simultaneously and it's important not to get so locked into only one that we lose sight of the others. Before I launch into what I have to say next, it's important to remind my gentle readers of a few things.

I have zero sympathy for fascism, and very, very little sympathy for fascists. What sympathy I *do* have is for the fascist who is on the cusp of becoming one of the only two good types of Nazi: an *ex*-Nazi. While I advise extreme caution, ex-fascists aren't necessarily intrinsically untrustworthy. I've known people who were raised in white supremacist cults literally from birth in isolated Idaho compounds, and who, even after escaping that nightmare, still bore the claw-marks of bigotry. It's eminently doable to keep our communities and persons safe with ruthless and uncompromising force while also attempting to reach the wavering fascist who might be safely reached. With that in mind, we must never stoop to the level of our enemies while interacting with them. We can walk and chew gum and listen to music at the same time. I promise.

Sure, some “dark woke” assholes think rules don’t apply anymore. Most of them are Democrats who have decided saying slurs is easier than tacking left to win a fucking election. (2) That’s not the case. In theory, “dark woke” is meant to emulate the disruptive power of Donald Trump’s discursive style (I wish that I were kidding, but I’m not). As far as I can tell, in practice “dark woke” means calling Donald Trump a fag who sucks Bill Clinton’s cock. (3) Many Democrats (including relatively prominent ones) did this a matter of months after losing an election in which Kamala Harris threw trans people under the bus. (4) After Kamala took that courageous stand, her party *blamed trans people’s existence* for her loss. (5) In electoral terms, this is what’s called “punching left to tack right:” In other words, it means attacking Americans more liberal than the Democratic Party’s leadership as communists and terrorists to increase the party’s supposed appeal to conservatives. The Democrats really are just playing desperate right-wing catch-up at this point.

Say what you want about the tenets of the Republican Party, dude, at least it’s an ethos. The Republicans did a Party postmortem after they got their asses severely kicked in an election: namely, the 2012 election in which my former Twitter mutual Barack Obama handed Lord Mittens of Romneyshire his ass on an exquisite silver plate. (6) In those days, the Republicans had the courage to look at a thorough, remorseless post-election analysis. *Then* they said, "fuck it, we'd rather go hard on bigotry and blatant corruption." (7) It's adorable when organizations like political parties pretend that they can think or learn.

Ah, "dark woke." It's good to see the Democrats have learned so much that they're still trotting out Blowjob Bill Clinton to own the MAGAs, neatly disregarding Clinton's record of homophobia (8) and his record of sexual assault (9) alike. That's the party to get me back in the ballot box, yes sir! With "dark woke" riding high in the mid-2020s, it's easier than ever for supposed progressives—even supposed leftists—to think that they can get away with bullshit like using the word "r*tard" against opponents. Or engaging in queerphobic rhetoric. Or helping warm Gaza's children not with blankets, but with bombs.

My guess is that a certain amount of this is a desperate bid for Democratic Party preservation. There may be an attempt under way to throw one segment of their coalition—the T part of the LGBTQIA+ community—overboard to keep the raft afloat. Not surprisingly, and judging by the turnout at *direct action* anti-ICE events, (10) Americans (including young people) aren't interested. They've started to explore other options than the Democratic Party. Or protest marches more generally when it comes to engaging with politics. Some of these choices are great, and options I would recommend myself: exploring anarchism through mutual aid with a local distro like Food Not Bombs, for example. Others are much less desirable, like the unfortunate return of various constantly infighting Marxist-Leninist (or Maoist) cliques and at least one syncretic fascist-State Socialist group, the American Communist Party (ACP). (11) They call themselves "MAGA Communists," and are queerphobic, anti-feminist, and generally reactionary assholes who use very silly misinterpretations of Marx and Lenin to flog Trump's and other fascists' policies. (12) Not great.

As destabilization increases within the imperial core in the coming months and years, watch for strange alliances and realignments. At least one (I'm rooting for both) of our major political parties is likely to die within my lifetime, and I suspect that politics will soon become much more kinetic and much less representational, if you catch my drift. Until then, it's best to be aware that it's an especially shitty time for sexual minorities of all political persuasions. Don't do "dark woke." In fact, if all you feel like you can do is "dark woke," it's better to do nothing at this point.

Certain guidelines apply when interacting with sexual minorities who are members of far-right groups—most likely online, where these people are most visible and have the most clout (which is still next to none). Based on my research, my interactions, my observations, and my overall thinking, what follows are the best ways to interact with far-right sexual minorities online in a productive way. If one is not going to engage them productively (or if one lacks patience or a masochistic streak), they might be best avoided. Even if you do decide that, however, please at least think about my advice.

Don't Perpetuate What We Fight Against

This should go without saying, and for the most part leftists understand what I'm about to reiterate. Still, I feel like I must repeat it. Just because a gay, lesbian, transgender, or other queer person is a fascist asshole, ***you do not have license to treat them with queerphobic vitriol***. In fact, if one does that, if *that's* one's go-to response to fascists, one is the same type of asshole one thinks one is roasting. This leads me to something I have noticed and which I believe bears remark.

You don't "reclaim" a slur by using it as a slur. I love that "fag" and "faggot" have become playful terms of flirty, queer endearment. It's an example of *actual* slur reclamation. For instance:

That is reclamation. Using words like "faggot" as slurs against right wing sexual minorities is not reclamation. The same is true of the word "r*tard," which 1) one does not reclaim by using as a slur (and I've never seen it used any other way), and 2) this "reclamation" is almost exclusively being done by people on the autism spectrum. Autistic people are not the majority of the disabled community to whom that specific slur has been applied. The return of "r*tard" is a disgusting and alarming development. (13) It's as indicative of where we are on our horrible, reverse-Wonkavator journey into eugenics and fascist thought permeating every aspect of American society, even the "woke" ones. I grew up in the oh-so-woke 1980s, staring up at grinning portraits of Ronald Reagan until third grade, and a girl on my block had Down syndrome. I knew *by age 6* (1988) that anyone who uses that word is a bigoted asshole worth taking a swing at. Do not call sexual minorities—even bigoted ones—slurs, full stop. What one engages in when one does that is counter-reclamation.

Threats are rarely acceptable. They're appropriate if they're made in *response* to threats or aggression, but sending fascist sexual minorities threatening messages is still hate based on sexual orientation ***by definition***. If those messages include threats of sexual violence or wishful thinking about what these dorks' comrades will do to them come "the day of the rope," you've crossed a line that's hard to come back from. That sort of Grand Guignol approach to eliminationist rhetoric has never struck me as particularly satisfying or productive and doesn't speak well of the emotional health of anyone using it. It's not so much stooping to their level as it is outing yourself as someone whom I need to keep an eye on; someone whom I can't trust, in short.

Similarly, mocking someone for their appearance—specifically and especially, their gender presentation, weight, or evident disabilities—is just fucking heinous. Call me a wokescold if you want, but I'm an anarchist. We believe in dismantling hierarchies like the ones these types of insults are based on. "Fighting fire with fire?" Well, you don't put out a house that's going up in smoke by pouring on more fire with flamethrowers. I think it's safe to say that when it comes to hierarchy, artificial beauty standards, and the performance of masculinity or femininity, *none* of us should squander time on shit-talking non-passing right-wing trans women. That time is better spent on liberation work, community networking, and mutual aid.

We never know who's reading leftists' social media barbs. Dunking on someone, while it feels good, serves no good purpose if the arguments aren't *substantive*. Let's say a gay man in his 20s reads a post where someone calls Nick Fuentes "a twink." That man might get curious about the convergence of same-sex libidinal interest and Fuentes' brand of neo-Nazi fucknuttery. Suddenly, radicalization blooms. It's the chaos theory of social media; a BlueSky user posts a dark woke takedown in Tokyo, and in the American Pacific Northwest a violent homofascist is born. If anything encapsulates the "Everything Now" era of hyperreal politics, it's chaos. Please don't engage in homophobia, transphobia, misogyny, classism, or putdowns based on looks. To paraphrase a Batman-breaks-a-rifle-with-his-bare-hands panel from Frank Miller's *The Dark Knight Returns*: "these are the weapons of the enemy. We do not use them."

Am I tone policing? Maybe. Sexual minorities (including bisexuals, but not to the extent of trans women) have experienced horrible shit at the hands of bigots. It *feels* like justice to use every tool in the toolbox against them. ** But it's not strategic, it's not effective, and, dare I say it, it's not ethical. It's not strategic because it inevitably backfires. Nobody has ever been gay bashed into not being a Nazi. Attack someone's beliefs, sure, although I'd advise you only to do this if you're prepared to waste your time. Avoid leftist bigotry. It does nothing but make leftists look and seem like hypocrites.

It's also not effective. Any sexual minority can tell you that they get more "kill yourself" and "I'll kill you" and "I'll rape you" messages in a week than your average white, straight, cisgendered progressive person receives in their entire life, especially if that progressive is a man. (14) Finally, it's not ethical. Sure, fascists deserve to have their violence met with violence, and they deserve to know no happiness. But they deserve these things *for being fascists*, not for being queer. If you can't stay on target, you have no business on the range.

Overall, I've found that when I talk to sexual minorities who inhabit far-right spaces, the most effective tone is one of cool cordiality. If they say something funny that isn't racist or shitty, feel free to say so. You'd be surprised how easily disarmed people are by a sincere lack of hostility and slowness to anger these days. *** What's the point of "disarming' or charming these fucks, you might ask? Good question! I'll get to one reason in depth in a moment, but the first reason I'd cite is that this strategy deviates from the usual interaction script and disrupts the normal, mutually one-way conversation that almost always takes place between subscribers to opposed beliefs. However, I don't advise that you use a conversation as an opportunity to try to deradicalize anyone.

As my friend Scott said earlier, deradicalization from the outside isn't possible. What happens when people leave a hate movement is that the cracks start *within them*, not from the outside. (15) "Deradicalization" is the art of providing an off-ramp (more on that in a second), not the art of getting inside someone's brain and "fixing" it. More than that, most young people experimenting with fascism are just desperate to feel cool. And that's nothing more than a partially sublimated need to feel loved and accepted. If they can get a bit of that high, a dose of methadone if you will, from a non-4Chan interaction, or even an interaction *on* that board that's more or less devoid of racism? Great! That's a win and a form of saving souls from Adolf's undead clutches.

The moments when enemies can lower their metaphorical weapons and perhaps even share a joke, a smoke, and a meal are few and far between. Nor should you cede a single inch of ground to any pressure to haw-haw along with racist and anti-Semitic humor. The handshake has to come from *their* direction for the metaphorical ceasefire to take place, and that means it takes place on your terms. But here's the weirdest thing: it always does, in my experience. Not from influencers, who have a financial, not to mention possibly a legal, stake in fascism. From the rank and file. The lonely kids, the Nazi queers that everybody hates (and, admittedly, for at least half of a good reason). Many of the people who get sucked into shit like fascist femboy modeling are young. *Very* young, in some cases (18 or 19). If someone hasn't participated in a hate crime, directly driven someone to self-harm with targeted harassment (which amounts to the same thing), or sexually assaulted anybody, I fail to see why a wretched, inexcusable, but ultimately *mostly* stupid phase should ruin someone's entire life and haunt their every future moment. Provided that they extract themselves from the cult first, of course. That's why cover-up tattoos exist, and why so many shops are willing to do them pro bono for clients who want to put hate in the rear-view mirror. (16)

And on the subject of self-deradicalization and the gradual process of growth...

Provide Off-Ramps

Speaking with people on the verge of leaving hate is like speaking with people living in violent domestic arrangements or considering self-harm, and I use the same metaphor for both processes: the best strategy is to provide off-ramps. Provide off-ramps from self-harm, off-ramps from a journey with a monster, and provide off-ramps from far-right extremism. This does not mean that it's *your* responsibility to deradicalize anyone. For one thing, I've already said that the safest way to interact with these people is not to (unless they seem like they're in severe distress and you feel, with your personal ethical framework, that you should intervene). For another, a person always has to start the deradicalization process themselves. You *can* be there to listen to their doubts and affirm them. Help them feel like they're not crazy—because you'd better believe that if someone's thinking of leaving a neo-Nazi group, that group is going to gaslight the shit out of them.

Also provide affirmation that the information they're beginning to find for themselves is accurate. They *have* been duped and lied to. If they talk about how charismatic the figure who roped them into white supremacy or National Socialism is, listen politely, but *don't engage* (unless the tale is dark, in which case proceed as you think best in terms of your own safety—in fact, always put your own safety first). Focus on reinforcing the reality of their growing cognitive dissonance. Humans evolved to, in part, notice patterns and make connections. Fascist radicalization agents prey on this brain-machinery to promote "noticing" or "nooticing," a neo-Nazi online slang term for becoming enmeshed in conspiracy theories about Jewish world control. As Blue Square Alliance eloquently summarizes:

> In some cases, hateful actors will use words and phrases to carry hidden meanings online. These phrases will often be oddly worded or placed. One increasingly common example is "the noticing," a phrase extremists use to describe "noticing Jewish influence" without saying it directly.
>
> On social media, it often appears as a standalone post, a phrase or hashtag (#TheNoticing). Extremists will often play it off by saying they are just "pointing out a pattern" and calling it out, which has given rise to variations of the phrase like "impossible not to notice" or

"noticing will continue." (17)

A good response might be to ask if they've "nooticed" how often neo-Nazis are caught with vast treasure-troves of child sexual abuse material. (18) Have they "nooticed" how often fascists have turned State's Evidence and snitched on their Nazi comrades, (19) or engaged in murder of fellow white supremacists? (20) In some cases, all that deradicalization requires is that a person remove themselves from the foul atmosphere that's been keeping the infection alive. (21) Separated from a Discord or Telegram server, outcast for whatever reason from the core of their neo-Nazi friend group, sometimes people reach out to former enemies. Listen to them, if you have the patience, emotional bandwidth, and time to put on a sort of "therapist hat" for a moment. *Do not try to fix their problems.* Just listen.

Don't get played. Some "queer fascist" accounts are run by straight, cis Nazi pranksters. Did I get taken in by any of them in my interviews? No. A few tried, but when you've been doing this as long as I have, which is to say longer than some of these goons have been alive, it becomes relatively easy to determine who's authentic (even beneath a veneer of cool, ironic detachment) and who is not. It's even easier to establish who is actually queer and who is not. The terminology in the Appendix **B—Glossary** section of this book can help you to spot people who at least understand the bare bones of modern fascist queer slang. Beyond that, it's a simple combination of the smell test for bullshit regarding what they say about themselves and the depth of their knowledge of esoteric topics.

Providing an off-ramp from fascism can mean many things. It can mean listening when someone talks about losing an entire social group. When they decide to leave Adolf's flock of very woolly sheep, that's what will happen. This fear of a total loss of community is how religious cults keep members in line, too; from two-bit new religious movements (22) to mainstream Christian religious denominations. (23) Don't expect a person dealing with that loss of community—as well as the need to remap an entire world, ideologically speaking—to change overnight. Racist ideas are like parasites, and it takes time and the proper treatment to flush them out, *neither of which are your job*. You can direct them to a project like Recovering From Hate for resources on what to do next. It could very well mean that they hit on you, whether that's appropriate or not. React with kindness and firm refusal. Often, Nazi circles are intensely psychosexually abusive, and this person might be trying to recover from emotional distress by using sex with an internet stranger to cope (yes, this includes roleplaying online) (24). Don't do that. *Do* let them know you're there to listen and provide support—as long as you actually are.

Part of my repeated advice to use caution, I'm sad to say, is because Nazis like to honeypot sexual minorities and then rape, beat, and/or murder them, (25) and I value the safety of my precious, precious readers. I trust you to be discerning, but look after your security first. There are not enough of you (my precious, precious readers) for me to lose any of you to misadventure. Get an individual first aid kit (IFAK), a gun, and learn to shoot while we're on the subject. Not to seem paranoid, but keep the honeypot / empathy trap scenario in mind at all times when dealing with right wing folks online and off. They like to ambush and outnumber people, because it's virtually the only time that they win fights. Always put your own safety and the safety of your loved ones and community first. Deradicalization is nobody's responsibility.

There are some topics of discussion I'd suggest, especially if the person in question hates the cops and/or has recently (or not so recently) had dealings with them. One thing that I'd bring up is the prolific record of snitching the right wing has when compared to almost any other brand of criminal. They are untrustworthy, treacherous pieces of shit who love squealing to the fuzz. This fact in and of itself, ipso facto, makes them dorks and fuckwads. Enrique Tarrio's behavior alone warrants special mention, but many other examples of this phenomenon exist and can readily be cited (see my previous footnote (19). Remember: outside of MAGA "thin blue line" types, *nobody* actually likes the cops. The cops are the people who murder unarmed Americans, cost you time and money, and put your cousin behind bars for possession of a joint.

Most of all, especially if the person in question is young, emphasize that *this is not the end for them*. Or at least it doesn't have to be. Everyone goes through bad political phases: although, let's be honest, some are decidedly worse and more embarrassing than others. The important thing is, help this person picture life *outside* the hate cult, because it might seem impossible for them to imagine at that moment. Their future if they leave the hate cult most likely includes some form of love, even if not immediately. Tattoos can be removed or covered up. Internet identities can be deleted, new ones created, apologies given, and low profiles kept. Explanations will have to be made to potential employers, to prospective lovers, and to others. This full disclosure will make dating harder, because many members of the community of sexual minorities will justifiably not feel safe being with even an *ex*-fascist. But others almost certainly will. Life changes, constantly, provided that it goes on.

You can also direct them to stories that contradict the vision of heteronormative happiness projected by fascists. Don't attack Nazi treatment of queers: frankly, they already will know more about that than anyone this side of hell's fiery shores. Focus on how these supposedly mighty leaders don't live up to their *own* standards. Because some element of self-hatred or deep denial is already part of a queer fascist's identity, mention hate crimes but don't bring up slurs. Try to get them to wake up to the conduct of the straight members of the subculture. Their antics are both hypocritical and often filled with acts of chilling selfishness and violence.

People's choices are complex things. Many factors that go into them are pre- or unconscious. Others are barely perceptible to the decision-maker, or might be repressed from their own self-awareness. But life has taught me—and the literature agrees—that people's choices hinge on their ability to imagine a future that they can fit into. (26) That simple lifeline sometimes is the difference between someone dying beneath the boots of their supposed comrades after a brief career of inflicting the same sadism on minorities on the one hand, and that same person leaving that life behind and beginning to heal and thrive in a way that benefits the community at large on the other.

I'm not a pacifist. Once someone has drawn blood in the name of fascism, or spread sufficient hate, or even attained a long enough tenure in the movement, I don't necessarily consider them redeemable. But I can't say the same thing about a trans teenager who got turned the wrong way down a digital alleyway by the corporations and algorithms pummeling society to psychological splinters. That person is possible to redeem before a certain point.

Have I learned anything from my attempt to see the world through the viewpoint of these folks? Why yes, yes I have.

"The Internet Makes You Stupid?"

"The internet makes you stupid" is the motto of a website called Something Awful. I've mentioned the site and its forums a few times in this book. I used to frequent the site as a reader and forums regular back in the 2000s. From the beginning, SA was dedicated to finding the most (in their eyes) cringeworthy things on the internet and ruthlessly mocking them. †† The site served for a long time as a hothouse for the sort of chud-brained geek white-grievance culture for which 4Chan later became infamous (remember, OG 4Chan was mostly populated by former SA regs who left when the site owner got rid of the memorably-named anime subforum Anime Death Tentacle Rape Whorehouse). (27)

I don't think that the internet makes you stupid. Or at least, there was a time when it didn't. Now that AI has become integrated into everything from Google searches to social media platforms, it absolutely, provably is making people stupider every time they use it. (28) That's AI, though, not the internet itself. Increasingly, sacks of useless dough posing as "teachers" and "professors" require that students use AI to do everything from answer longform questions to compose essays. (29) The reasoning of these "teachers" doesn't matter. If they think they're preparing kids "for the world to come" by doubling down on cheating via AI, they should stop using ChatGPT for essays and start teaching kids how to scavenge food from picked-over supermarkets without falling pretty to tribes of cannibals. That's the future these "teachers" and "professors" are creating by using the intellectually and environmentally ruinous technology of AI. (30)

No, the internet doesn't make you stupid. Using it for certain mundane things is perfectly harmless, and often very beneficial. † Social media as a specific case of "the internet" is a different matter. An increasing body of evidence is growing regarding social media's effects on the human psyche, society, and politics. (31) My parents are old enough to remember the age when everybody smoked, pre-Surgeon General's warning style. Smoking was just a widespread societal thing that people didn't realize was horribly murdering them. The same thing's true of leaded gasoline, which one study demonstrated correlates with an era of widespread American violent crime that went into decline at the exact same time as the introduction of unleaded gas, which doesn't contribute to atmospheric lead. (32)

Social media is the smoking or the lead paint of our time. I don't think it needs to be abolished, but I do think significant reforms need to be worked into apps like Twitter and TikTok before they can be safe for users. I'm explicitly *not* talking about age restrictions here. Not because I think kids should have access to pornography but because I think they deserve access to information, which is all too easily labeled "pornography." This is done by malignant fascist actors like semi-notorious Florida church lady group Moms4Liberty. They are the group that spearheaded the removal of most materials that mention the existence of LGBTQIA+ people from first school, then public, libraries in Florida. (33) Young people, increasingly denied even basic sex education (let alone education that includes information for and about LGBTQIA+ people) (34) need a way to access information and perspectives they've been denied by fascist authorities from President to pastor to public school teacher.

From the antics of Moms4Liberty to 1st Trump term Education Secretary Betsy DeVos' plans for education; from the shadow network of rich fucks funding fascism to the very public fascist billionaires like Elon Musk reigning over social media platforms, the problem is the same. The supposedly anarchic, supposedly freewheeling age of communication we're currently living through is anything but. It's a carefully cultivated illusion (like the illusion that we've got everything now). The internet is not truly free, and hasn't been for decades. The reality is that online speech is pruned and fertilized, cultivated and curtailed by very, very right-wing, exceptionally wealthy pieces of shit, many of whom are open fascists. (35) In an environment like that, is it any wonder a minority of queer folks are turning out all fucked up, ideologically speaking?

Any solution seeking to address this problem—which, again, *involves only a tiny minority of fringe LGBTQIA+ people*—must address the root of the problem. Hate in America isn't just driven by personal bigotry or centuries of systemic racism, although those certainly play their part. The very people who've benefited most from systemic racism still control the message. All mainstream American media—not just social media—supports and reinforces white supremacy. (36) Since the dawn of mass media, including pamphlets and newspapers, white supremacy has always been the main narrative of American society. Until now, that message never was promoted with the technological tools and total domination technofascism has made possible. While there isn't a *unified* far-right, they're unified enough. Bitchy little slap fights between Nazi influencers aside, the domestic agenda for MAGA and the rest of American fascism couldn't be clearer. They aim to consolidate their power, brutalize the citizenry into compliance, then start to crack down on "undesirables:" a long list that includes immigrants, sexual or ethnic minorities, American anti-fascists, people opposed to AI and its attendant data centers, and even the tepid political opposition offered by the most radical members of the Democratic Party. (37)

That's the real root of the problem. Capitalists should be *expected* to treat us like this. Fascists should be *expected* to be violent, reactionary agents of genocidal destruction. Corporations will *inevitably* bend like willows in the political wind to accommodate whichever regime holds power at any given time. *It's the left that's fucking up*. Not the entire left, mind you. There are untold numbers of anti-fascist anarchists, communists, and others out there fighting the good fight. Not Jazzercising to combat ICE, which is utterly fucking ridiculous nonsense. (38) No, anti-fascists are out there getting pummeled—and taking risks. Taking more than risks, where justified. (39) That's the strong, fearless left (or post-left) that we need right now. The mainstream "left" has proven itself utterly without worth. The time for electoralism to fight fascism is past. In fact, that time has never existed. Fascism has quite literally never been voted out of power. Fascism must always be destroyed the same way: with justified and righteous violence.

One of the reasons I don't buy the idea that "the internet makes you stupid" is because it allows people to break out of ideological prisons. That's less true now than when the late, unlamented Richard "Lowtax" Kyanka struck the Something Awful motto. SA's idea of "stupid" was for someone to be a furry, or all too often trans, gender nonconforming, funny-looking, fat, too enthusiastic, disabled, or other things a suburban bully might decide are "stupid." SA was a proving ground for what would eventually become the so-called alt right; and a dumber fucking bunch of mythic history worshiping, Donald J. Trump-Stanning sacks of walleyed trout you'd be hard pressed to find. So Lowtax can suck my Juggalo balls from his spot in hell's pit next to Charlie Kirk.

The internet doesn't make you stupid. Hate cults do.

And their rise online was preceded by the early adoption of the internet by white supremacists like Louis Beam, a Vietnam vet turned hatemonger. Beam founded LibertyNet, one of the first internet forums ever and a valuable resource for online Klansmen, neo-Nazis, and the like, in ***1983***. That's so early in the internet's timeline that, though it pains me, I have to give Beam credit for his incredibly early and chilling foresight. Beam looked at internet communication and saw the future while hardly a Fortune 500 company did – and he was a shit-kicking Texas Klansman. (40) Not only that, in the beginning the internet was a lily-white phenomenon overall. (41) There were Black tech pioneers, of course, but the majority of users, programmers, coders, etc. were white and male for a long time before a course correction (since rescinded by the Trump Reich) attempted to correct this form of digital apartheid. (43)

The same virtual places that people have carved out to discover and express their sexual identity online were largely created, maintained, moderated, and tone-policed by white men. It's an inevitable consequence that white supremacy spreads there like a nasty and persistent rash. The fact that queer diversity thrives despite this handicap says nothing but good, beautiful things about the LGBTQIA+ community. Those members of the community who've chosen hate are, in some ways, victimizers, and in other ways they're victims. This makes dealing with them online extraordinarily strange and tricky. As I've said several times now, the winning move is not to play. However, we shouldn't exile those who've shown genuine remorse and course-correction from the queer online community permanently. They'll have bridges to repair, and (in some cases) tattoos to get removed or covered up. They'll have hate to un-learn, and years of indoctrination to jettison.

For those who make it out? In my experience, there are no fiercer fighters than those who've realized that fascism is based on lies, hatred, and betrayal. Especially if they're demonstrated real solidarity with other victims of fascism when they come back from the abyss. Time is running out, but there's still enough of it for them to change. To the extent we can, we should help in that process in whatever capacity we're best suited.

We're unlikely to collectively awaken anytime soon from a nightmare of a national fascist neon casino reigned over by a smirking pedophile king. While the nightmare still unspools around us, we must find love, happiness, and even grace wherever we can. Our consolation is that love amidst the fire and collapse can be the sweetest love of all.

* Rest in piss, bozo!

** Never, ever trust what "feels" like justice. Torture often "feels" like justice to the torturer. Death "feels" like justice to the executioner. I've come to the following conclusion: sadism is never ethical, never justified, and often what "feels" just is no more than thinly dressed-up sadism. Lex talionis, or the law of retribution (an eye for an eye) isn't real justice. It's the justice of bronze age monotheistic religion, not that of thinking people.

*** This takes practice, breathing exercises, and even after twenty years of doing this, I can still only manage it for maybe an hour at a time. My default online voice is very sweary and yelly.

† For example: I no longer trust colleges or universities for the most part, but individual professors can be great. When one comes to my attention, I check online. Their class syllabus is usually available, and sometimes they even post their lectures on YouTube. People arguably have access (if not direction) to more self-education through information, books, and journal articles than at any time in human history. AI has to go, one way or another, but I'd be sad if the internet went away. I'd have to loot a *shit-ton* of libraries to replace it.

†† Furries are a good example. When I was a lot younger and read Something Awful every day, I thought furries were hilarious because everyone on SA did. It was a shitty thing to think and say, and I regret participating in furry mockery. I've since come to learn that most furries (with the exception of Foxler and the other outliers I've covered) are extremely cool people.

1 Hashemi, Rhana & Vogel, Erin A. (2024). "Adolescents' perceptions of substance use

messaging in the age of social media: resolving cognitive dissonance". *Health Education Resources*. 39 (1). P1-11.

Crocetti, Elisabetta (2017). "Identity Formation in Adolescence: The Dynamic of Forming and Consolidating Identity Commitments". *Child Development Perspectives*. 88 (1).

Krettenauer, Tobias (2009). "The Role of Epistemic Cognition in Adolescent Identity Formation: Further Evidence". *Journal of Youth and Adolescence*. Vol. 34. P185-198.

2 Rothpletz, Peter (1/30/2025). "How do Democrats harness #DarkWoke?". *The Guardian*.

Press-Reynolds, Kiernan (3/13/2025). "Is 'Dark Woke' the Answer to Trumpism—or Just Liberal Cringe?". *GQ*.

Fox, Lauren; Ferris, Sarah (1/22/2025). "Democrats grapple with their own message in Trump 2.0." *CNN*.

3 Rodriguez, Mathew (11/17/2025). "'Blowing Bubba': The Epstein-Trump Email-Turned-Meme, Explained: Yes, we explain how Bill Clinton and Ghislaine Maxwell's horse are involved." *Them*.

4 https://www.youtube.com/shorts/AbVPee2UdJk

5 Lavietes, Matt (11/8/2024). "Some Democrats blame party's position on transgender rights in part for Harris' loss".

6 Staff (2013). "Growth & Opportunity Project". *Republican National Committee*.

7 Cheney, Kyle (3/4/2016). “Trump kills GOP autopsy”. *Politico*.

8 Staff (12/21/1993). “Department of Defense Directive 1304.26”. *Department of Defense*.

Staff (12/22/1993). “10 U.S.C. § 654(b)”. *United States Code*.

9 Relman, Eliza (6/4/2018). “These are the sexual-assault allegations against Bill Clinton”. *Business Insider*.

Off, Carol (11/16/2017). “Why the left is finally talking about the Bill Clinton sexual assault allegations”. *As It Happens – CBC Radio*.

Flanagan, Caitlyn (11/13/2017). “Bill Clinton: A Reckoning”. *The Atlantic*.

10 Koplowitz, Howard (1/30/2025). "Albertville anti-ICE protest 'deeply concerning,' Alabama official says: 'A game of dangerous rhetoric'". *AL*.

Salem, Iris & Fioresi, Dean (2/2/2025). "Protest erupts in downtown Los Angeles over surge in ICE raids, some demonstrators block 101 Freeway - CBS Los Angeles". *CBS*.

Li, Tom & Cheang, Ko Lyn (7/8/2025). “ Protestors cling onto ICE vehicle, get run over”. *San Francisco Chronicle*.

Ahn, Ashley (2/1/2025). "Protesters along Buford Highway condemn ICE arrests". *The Atlanta Journal-Constitution*.

Lee, Morgan (2/5/2025). "Thousands protest

Trump administration policies in cities across the US". *AP News*.

11 Owen, Tess (5/24/2024). "'A deranged fringe movement': What is MAGA communism, the online ideology platformed by Tucker Carlson?". *The Guardian*.

Steinberg, Julia (7/30/2024). "The MAGA Communists Launched a Party". *The Free Press*.

12 Vittar, Daniel (9/13/2024). “The strange communist group in the United States that supports Trump”. *LM Neuquén*.

Fernández, Celia (9/10/2024). "Trumpist communists: The anti-imperialist MAGA movement". *El País*.

Gravino, Michele (11/8/2024). “In America, they elected a communist. And he's a Trumpian.” *La Republica*.

13 Andrew, Scottie (5/31/2025). “The ‘r-word’ is back. How a slur became renormalized”. *CNN*.

Melendez, Pilar (5/8/2025). “The 'R-word,' embraced by Joe Rogan and Elon Musk, inches back into the mainstream”. *NBC News*.

Diament, Michelle (10/21/2024). “Resurgence Of ‘R-Word’ Alarms Disability Advocates”. *Disability Scoop*.

14 Alfonseca, Kiara (9/24/2024). “Hate crimes, particularly against LGBTQ community, on the rise: FBI data”. *ABC News*.

Staff. (1/4/2024). “2023 Year in Review: Anti-

LGBTQ Online Hate and Disinformation". *GLAAD*.

Bennett, Geoff et. al. (8/31/2023). "How the rise of anti-LGBTQ+ hate and violence is impacting the community". *PBS New Hour*.

15 Doosje, Bertjam et. al. (2016). "Terrorism, radicalization and de-radicalization". *Current Opinion in Psychology*. Vol. 11. P79-84.

Silke, Andrew (2011). "Disengagement or Deradicalization: A Look at Prison Programs for Jailed Terrorists". *CTC Sentinel*. 4 (1).

Brown, Bryan Andrew (2021). "What Do Former Extremists and Their Families Say About Radicalization and Deradicalization in America?" *RAND*.

16 White, Billy (Sep/Oct 2024). "I Cover up Racist Tattoos for Free: Being part of the process of human growth is better than anything." *Sojourners*.

Noe, Rain (6/17/2020). "Tattoo Artists Across the Country Offering Free Cover-Ups of Racist Tattoos: 'Let's get that shit off your body'". *Core77*.

Bloom, Deborah (2/5/2019). "Erasing the hate: the tattoo shop offering former white supremacists a fresh start". *The Guardian*.

17 Command Center Insights. (8/22/2025). "Antisemitic Dog Whistles: How Hate Spreads Through Coded Language". *Blue Square Alliance*.

18 Lamoureux, Mack (7/20/2023). "Why Do Neo-Nazis Keep Getting Arrested For Child Sexual Abuse Material?" *Vice*.

19 Staff. (1/27/2021). “Proud Boys leader ‘prolific’ snitch for law enforcement”. *Al-Jazeera*.

Winston, Ali & Hanrahan, Jake (8/1/2024). “He Was an FBI Informant—and Inspired a Generation of Violent Extremists”. *Wired*.

Sargent, Hilary (10/7/2020). “Snitches, cowards, and liars: white nationalists now hate Christopher Cantwell. The problem is they’re all just like him.” *The Informant*.

20 Schmaltz, William H. (2000) [1999]. *Hate: George Lincoln Rockwell and the American Nazi Party*. (Brassey’s, Washington, D.C.). P322.

Staff. (9/26/2011). “The murder of an American Nazi”. *60 Minutes*.

Sunshine, Spencer (2024). *Neo-Nazi Terrorism and Countercultural Fascism: The Origins and Afterlife of James Mason's Siege*. (Routledge, New York). P42.

21 Malthaner, S., & Waldmann, P. (2014). “The Radical Milieu: Conceptualizing the Supportive Social Environment of Terrorist Groups”. *Studies in Conflict & Terrorism*, 37 (12). P979–998.

Pilkington, Hilary (2022). “Radicalization as and in Process: Tracing Journeys through an ‘Extreme-Right’ Milieu”. *Studies in Conflict and Terrorism*. 48 (10). P380-398.

22Bailey, Shaquo & Shaw, Tori (2019). "Communities of Disrespect: What Happens When Personhood is Lost," *Episteme*. Vol. 30. P70-90.

Jackson, Sean (11/20/2023). “The Mental

Health Impact of Cults". *MenthalHealth.com.*

Hadding C, et. al. (2023) "Being in-between; exploring former cult members' experiences of an acculturation process using the cultural formulation interview (DSM-5)." *Frontiers in Psychiatry*. 13 (14).

23 Fenelon, Andrew & Danielsen, Sabrina (2016). "Leaving My Religion: Understanding the Relationship Between Religious Disaffiliation, Health, and Well-Being". *Social Science Research*. 8 (57). P49-62.

Björkmark, Maria et. al. (2021). "Suffering of Life after Religious Disaffiliation: A Caring Science Study". *International Journal of Caring Sciences*. 14 (1). P1-7.

24 Pittman, Delishia M. et. al. (2021). "Psychological Distress as a Primer for Sexual Risk Taking Among Emerging Adults". 33 (3). P371-384.

Anderson, Emily et. al. (4/18/2024). "Am I Using Sex to Cope?" *Sexual Wellness Institute*.

25 Luckhurst, Troy (3/21/2025). "Gang used social media to lure and attack gay people - Austrian police". *BBC*.

Habeck, Joachim Otto & Schröder, Philipp (2016). "From Siberia with Love or Angst in the City? On the Idea of Merging Research Projects in Novosibirsk and Co-Teaching in Hamburg and Berlin (editorial)". *Ethnoscripts*. 18 (1). P11–12.

Pierre, Dion J. (7/4/2024). "California Jury Convicts Neo-Nazi Who Brutally Murdered Gay Jewish Teenager". *The Algemeiner*.

Dmello, JR et. al. (2025). "LGBTQ+ Victimization by Extremist Organizations: Charting a New Path for Research." *PS: Political Science & Politics*. 58 (3). P447-455.

26 Vilhauer, Jennice (5/3/2025). "Why Thinking About the Future Makes Life Better Now". *Psychology Today*.

Gamble, Beau et. al. (2021). "The Futures We Want: How Goal-Directed Imagination Relates to Mental Health." *Clinical Psychological Science*. 9 (4), P732-751.

27 Wofford, Taylor (4/5/2017). "Fuck You And Die: An Oral History of Something Awful". *Vice*.

Langton, Jerry (11/22/2007). "Funny how 'stupid' site is addictive". *Toronto Star*.

28 Field, Matthew (6/17/2025). "Using AI makes you stupid, researchers find". *The Telegraph*.

Chen, Brian X. (11/6/2025). "How A.I. and Social Media Contribute to 'Brain Rot'". *New York Times*.

29 Sheffey, Ayelet (9/25/2025). "Teachers say AI has been a game changer for them, and they want their students to benefit — while still thinking for themselves". *Business Insider*.

Kelly, Mary Louise (1/26/2023). "'Everybody is cheating': Why this teacher has adopted an open ChatGPT policy". *NPR*.

Mok, Aaron (1/26/2023). "A Wharton business school professor is requiring his students to use ChatGPT". *Business Insider*.[a]

Chun, Caryolyn (4/2/2023). "Why some college professors are adopting ChatGPT AI as quickly as students". *CNBC*.[a]

[a]Far be it from me, a gutter academic with zero (0) undergraduate or graduate degrees, to hold anyone to a standard, but I firmly believe that *any* professor "adopting" or, especially, "requiring" AI in class should have their courseload handed to other instructors as *every piece of work* they handed in as part of their undergraduate and graduate degrees are thoroughly examined for AI plagiarism.

30 Mclean, Sophie (4/28/2023). "The Environmental Impact of ChatGPT: A Call for Sustainable Practices In AI Development". *Earth.org*.

Mazzucato, Mariana (5/30/2024). "The ugly truth behind ChatGPT: AI is guzzling resources at planet-eating rates". *The Guardian*.

31 Staff. (12/12/2024). "Effects of Social Media On Health." *Annie E. Casey Foundation*.

Shannon, Holly et. al. (2021). "Problematic Social Media Use in Adolescents and Young Adults: Systematic Review and Meta-analysis". *JMIR Mental Health*. 9 (4).

Ahmed, Oli et. al. (2024). "Social media use, mental health and sleep: A systematic review with meta-analyses". *Journal of Affective Disorders*. Vol. 367. P701-712.

32 Drum, Kevin (Jan/Feb 2013). "America's Real Criminal Element Is Lead: The hidden villain behind violent crime, lower IQs, and maybe even the ADHD epidemic." *Mother Jones*.

33 Craig, Tim (10/15/2021). "Moms for Liberty has turned 'parental rights' into a rallying cry for conservative parents". *The Washington Post*.

Bajagopal, Bulbul (9/28/2023). "Moms for Liberty attempts to restrict LGBTQ-plus books in local libraries". *NewTimes*.

34 *United States Department of Health and Human Services*. (8/26/2025). "Trump Administration Puts 46 States and Territories on Notice to Remove Gender Ideology Content from Sex Ed Material".

McKoy, Jillian (8/21/2025). "Only 37% of US States Require Sexual Education in Schools to Be Medically Accurate". *Boston University School of Public Health*.

Rogan, Ali et. al. (5/25/2024). "Sex education 'is under attack' by a wave of proposed legislation, advocate warns". *PBS News Weekend*.

35 Pascual, Manuel G. (10/11/2025). "Social media completes its shift to the right: 'TikTok is consequential'". *El País*.

Baker, Dean (10/10/2025). "Right-Wing Moguls Dominate Social Media. One Legal Fix Can Help Stem the Tide." *The Nation*.

Frenkel, Sheera (11/17/2024). "Liberals Are Left Out in the Cold as Social Media Veers Right". *The New York Times*.

36 Inwood, J. F., & Alderman, D. H. (2024). "The struggle against post-truth politics has always been about white supremacy: Lessons from the

informational praxis of SNCC." *Environment and Planning C: Politics and Space*. 43 (4). P783-801.

Smith, Marissa et. al. (2025). "Rooted in White Identity Politics: Tracing the Genealogy of Critical Race Theory Discourse in Identity-Based Disinformation". *Political Communication*. 42 (5). P815-837.

French, Howard (5/25/2016). "The enduring whiteness of the American media: What three decades in journalism has taught me about the persistence of racism in the US". *The Guardian*.

37 Langfitt, Frank (4/22/2025). "Hundreds of scholars say U.S. is swiftly heading toward authoritarianism". *NPR*.

Buerger, Cathy (9/25/2025). "Repression as Rescue: The Authoritarian Logic of Trump's Early Executive Orders". *Just Security*.

Paris, Gilles (7/29/2025). "Trump's second presidency is taking an authoritarian tone". *Le Monde*.

38 Smith, Corbin (11/11/2025). "Sweating Out the Fascism With Anti-ICE Aerobics". *Portland Mercury*.

39 Mallin, Alexander (10/15/2025). "DOJ charges alleged antifa followers with terrorism offense for attack on Alvarado ICE facility". *ABC News*.

Orenstein, Natalie (11/10/2025). "Anti-fascist protesters clash with attendees outside Turning Point event at UC Berkeley". *Berkeleyside*.

40 Abdelfatah, Rund (6/9/2022). “'Throughline': The Rise Of The Modern White Power Movement”. *NPR*.

41 Graham, Mark & Sengupta, Anasuya (10/5/2017). “We’re all connected now, so why is the internet so white and western?” *The Guardian*.

Perrin, Andrew & Duggan, Maeve (6/26/2015). “Americans’ Internet Access: 2000-2015”. *Pew Research Center*.

42 Mervis, Jeffrey (4/18/2025). “NSF starts to kill grants that violate Trump’s war on diversity efforts: Attracting women and minorities into science and studying misinformation are no longer priorities, agency says”. *Science*.

APPENDIX A

INTERVIEWS

Note

Some of my interviews included here are with right-wing extremists; some are not. I wanted to address some things about interviewing fascists up front. When conducting interviews for a project like this, the purposes of asking fascists questions isn't to debate them. I am, in fact, not keen on the concept of debate resolving anything with fascists. That said, I think that studying how they think, what they say, and what they believe—not to mention how they convey their beliefs—is important in order to both combat misinformation, and eventually (after deradicalization, if possible) help fascists walk out of the darkness and into a future worth living in. That last part is, I believe, both possible and worthwhile in a minority of cases. Even a handful of lives saved from fascism, both from perpetrating it and from future victims of it, would make this project worth pursuing.

You will see my interview participants boldly and

with their full chest say provable lies. I don't argue with or contradict them. That wasn't—and isn't—the purpose of this book. I will likely have a few fascist readers of this project, and I hope they think I've done justice to representing their perspectives here fairly. Not because I think their principles are worthwhile, but because honesty is something I stand by and think is the foundation of any progress with anything. Also, I told my interviewees that I would reproduce their words and let their voice be heard without interference, and I stand by my promises.

I've labeled each interview for references purposes. My fascist, far right, and fascist-adjacent interviews come first, followed by my interview with a sex worker on about anti-porn and otherwise anti-sex American approaches to sexuality and my interview with one of my friends, a former white nationalist and Stormfront moderator, and now an anti-extremism educator and researcher.

I'll let people speak for themselves from this point on.

Interview One: Jade Augustus AKA Sweeptypuss, Trans Nazi

Hello! First of all, thanks for agreeing to talk to me. Tell readers a little bit about yourself (nothing identifying, just any background that you think contributes to your perspective).

JA: Well, I'm a severely mentally ill tranny from the Midwest, born and raised in the twilight years of the old web before everything got cancerous and corporate. I have fond memories of Homestar Runner and frying my brain playing mostly classic Doom and other boomer shooters as a child. There's so much shit wrong with my head it isn't even funny.

I'm writing about sexual minorities in online far-right spaces. In the US, "sexual minority" includes gender nonconforming individuals as well as anyone who isn't traditionally heterosexual. How would you define your own identity in your own words?

JA: I define myself as a bisexual transgender woman. I'm about 6 months on HRT at this point. I was socially transitioned from 2019-2023 but never got access to HRT in that time. in dec 2023 I "detransitioned" [**Ed.: quotation marks hers**] and started repressing, but ultimately that went nowhere. That repressing was only to last about a year (throughout 2024).I got on HRT in February and despite the insane mood swings, I've felt a lot better about everything.

Speaking of online spaces, where do you spend time online? We encountered each other on Twitter. Have you spent time on 4Chan?

JA: Well as a child I spent most of my time on 8chan but these days, if I feel so inclined, I pop on over to the /LGBT/ board on 4chan to shitpost a bit and be the token racist tranny on a board full of retards. Against my better instincts I tripfag there. Attention is fun!

At about what age did you first get into those spaces? What led you there?

JA: When I started getting involved in those kinds of spaces, I was about 10 years old or so. What led me there was mostly curiosity invoked by the quasi-mythical status these places had attained. The magic of "lulz" drew me in. When I was 12 the whole "meme magic" thing started with Trump's 2016 campaign and that really interested and intrigued me.

Did spending time there help you figure out your identity? If so, how? (Example: did you meet other people like yourself, learn terms and concepts you didn't know about before, etc.?)

JA: The concept of transsexuality was inadvertently introduced to me through imageboards, but I did not readily identify anything about myself as "trans" until I was around 14 or so when I had met a trans person in the little majority-white rural town I lived in. It was quite interesting and their perspective really made me realize certain things about myself and explained things I would often do in the past (such as "pretending" to be a girl online). I was like 6-7 when I did that and I did it frequently.

Let's talk about your political identity, if that's okay. How do you self-identify, if you do? If not, what issues and topics are important to you and why?

JA: I'm straddling the line between a Strasserist and a literal National Socialist. Think the modern day CCCP but far more overtly Hitlerian and with more concentrated worker control of key industries. The topics and issues important to me include racial homogeneity, eradication/deportation of undesirables (browns, Jews, violent criminals, etc.), self-sufficiency, and effective propaganda. That being said, I am massively autistic about US presidential politics, so other issues that fascinate me are the economy, ongoing geopolitical conflicts (such as the Israel-Palestine conflict), income tax, income inequality, etc.

Do you view your gender / sexual identity as related to your political identity, and if so, how?

JA: Not really. I'm more so a National Socialist that just so happens to be a tranny, too. I don't really think the two are implicitly compatible, but they can be made to co-exist in a "stop indoctrinating kids and you get to live" kinda thing. I say if you want to advance the regime, you should be able to do so even if you're a tranny. i really do think Whiteness should be prioritized. Besides there are so many gorgeous White trans girls that i don't think they should be executed solely for being trannies. Once you get rid of interlopers, fetishists, and predators, there really is not a whole lot to complain about regarding the trans community.

This conversation was, in a way, spurred by a picture I saw of a trans girl holding a trans rights flag with a superimposed Schwarze Sonne (black sun) icon, a symbol from Esoteric Hitlerism. At first, I got it confused with the photoset you posted.

JA: When my new LARP came in the mail.

Could you explain what those images meant to you and what it was supposed to convey?

JA: Well, for me it is a pretty good summary of what I'm for: violent tranny revolution in the name of National Socialism. We are feral and severely ill individuals, it is highly likely most of us will snap anyway. Instead of killing ourselves, i advocate for going out in a blaze of glory. Of course, this is all purely hypothetical at this point and would require insane amounts of coordination, but I'm not that much different from the commies in this regard: motherfucking revolution. Far right tranny death squads will roam the streets. A cleansing is dearly required, or "the day of the rope" as *The Turner Diaries* put it.

What question should I have asked and didn't today? What am I missing or what do you feel like I left out of these questions, if anything?

JA: Personally, i would've asked "how the hell do you reach these conclusions? What's wrong with you?" And the answer is the data right in front of me along with what is happening in front of my very eyes. You don't need to be a weatherman to see which way the wind is blowing and I can tell that Blacks need to be in prison, Jews need to be deported/executed, and vast culls for every single motherfucker responsible for bringing all of these problems into our country. Hitler, even if I don't see completely eye to eye with him, was the only one to recognize this and do his damn hardest to rebel against it. For those 12-13 years, things were a hell of a lot better for Germany and I'm fairly confident it would've been so much better for the rest of the world had he won. You can look at everything around us and see it is *all* Jew-controlled. They're fucking everywhere. We live in an occupied territory, with Israel's dirty kosher fingers embedded in every single pocket of our society. Behind all of its ills, you will find Jewish hands rubbing together and scheming on ways to destroy us. None of this is a conspiracy and can be backed up by not just data trends, but simple observation. Follow the money. All you need to do is look.

And for me personally, I despise how the trans community is perceived as being inherently tied to leftist beliefs. I am not required to be a leftist just because I'm trans. That notion is also Jewish-made, especially when dysphoria was taken out of the DSM-5 and being "trans" was made to look cool even though dysphoria is a curse I wouldn't wish on fucking anyone.

Thank you for your time and responses—I really appreciate it. I think that at the very least, people from different perspectives should be able to understand what each other are saying. What do you think the biggest misunderstanding in discourse around issues of politics, gender identity, and sexuality is?

JA: The biggest misunderstanding is exactly what i said earlier: that gender identity and sexuality are inherently tied into politics. Sure, they may be big issues, and there are many moral arguments to be made, but nothing about being gay or trans inherently makes you lean any which way. i believe what I do because of the data in front of me, but I understand *why* most trans people tend to lean left and it's because the left is the only side that, on the surface, has promised some form of protection. I believe those promises are bullshit, but that's beside the point. I've been ostracized in a lot of right-wing communities purely because of the perception that trannydom is expressly verboten due to "left-wing tendencies," which is retarded.

However, you can get the exact same treatment in left wing communities if you don't completely adhere to the dogma. You really can't win. There is no understanding made on either side of the aisle, but I can tell you I've gotten *more* understanding on the right than I ever did on the left. I was a Democratic Socialist from 2019-2022 before evolving to a National Socialist in 2023. For the entire time i was a DemSoc, fully committed to the blue, I swear I always got shit on for the tiniest fucking things. It's absurd. Not to mention the fact that I'm majority White puts me high up on the progressive stack, meaning i didn't get as many "oppression points" as everyone else and thus was taken less seriously by the left. So even though I'm trans, poor, and crazy, my overwhelming Whiteness still made me evil. That's another big factor in why i "evolved" into a National Socialist in 2023; an inherent defiance of what my alleged in-group desired.

Interview Two: NonAnon, Bi Twink Nationalist

Hello! First of all, thanks for agreeing to talk to me. Tell readers a little bit about yourself (nothing identifying, just any background that you think contributes to your perspective). Knowing the general range of your age helps me sort responses, but don't feel obligated.

NA: 22 years old, university graduate but I don't work in the field I got my degree in, I live in a complete family of 4 with loving parents. I don't know what else to say here.

I'm writing about sexual minorities in online far-right spaces. In the US, "sexual minority" includes gender nonconforming individuals as well as anyone who isn't traditionally heterosexual. How would you define your own identity in your own words?

NA: By definition, I'm bisexual, but my attraction to men and women are not at all equal, I'd say 80% women and 20% men. Also, among men it's only towards the more feminine kind (twinks, femboys) as I am in that group as well. I'm not transgender, never was and never will be.

What do you think the biggest misunderstanding in discourse around issues of politics, gender identity, and sexuality is?

NA: Probably the biggest misunderstanding is that everyone thinks that people who heavily disagree with their opinions are subhumans that need to be eradicated.

Where do you spend time online? We encountered each other on Twitter. Have you spent time on 4Chan?

NA: I don't do a lot of chatting online nowadays,

usually Twitter, Instagram and formerly Discord. I've never in my life had a 4chan account, I despise that place with every fiber of my being. Also, I have never been on the likes of Telegram or VK either.

At about what age did you first get into those spaces? What led you there?

NA: Discord first in 2020 for online school, it branched into getting into random servers from there. On Instagram and Twitter maybe 1-2 years ago.

Did spending time there help you figure out your identity? If so, how? (Example: did you meet other people like yourself, learn terms and concepts you didn't know about before, see a particular aesthetic which spoke to you before you knew what it meant, etc.?)

NA: I guess you could say that. As you said that's where I first met people like myself, and I guess I just accepted that I like some people that are not women.

Forgive my crudity, but this has come up during my research on right wing sex culture. Have you heard of No Nut November? Related concepts might be the Proud Boys' "no wanks" and the anti-pornography movements of the right. Do you have an opinion on the idea of "sexual purity" with regards to masturbation and/or pornography? What about "sexual purity" in general?

NA: Yeah, I've heard of No Nut November, I haven't

heard of the Proud Boys' "no wanks". I think porn is inherently evil and people should make efforts to get away from it as far as possible, though I'm not really in a position to talk because I could definitely cut down on the amount of consumption I do. On the other hand, I think masturbation is a "necessary bad", as I see an increased difficulty for men to get partners, and self-relief can be a good way to get rid of sexual tension.

What question should I have asked and didn't today? What am I missing or what do you feel like I left out of these questions, if anything?

NA: Maybe if you're asking right wing people from sexual minorities, maybe you could ask how they think the two are compatible (ex. How is it compatible to be gay and far-right at the same time?) or something like that. I think here you'll always get some hypocrisy, like people cutting themselves some slack. For me this comes out as I'm conservative socially in basically everything except that I think people should be able to be attracted to their own sex without persecution or harassment UNTIL the boundaries of common normalcy. Therefore, I heavily dislike Pride and any large-scale display of sexual deviance.

Interview Three: Dutch Boykisser, Gay Fascist

Hello! First of all, thanks for agreeing to talk to me. Tell readers a little bit about yourself (nothing identifying, just any background that you think contributes to your perspective). Knowing the

general range of your age helps me sort responses, but don't feel obligated.

DB: I am a homosexual, Dutch teenager who comes from a generally left-wing family. My mother is a Social Democrat, and my dad is a Centrist, who generally supports the VVD [*Volkspartij voor Vrijheid en Democratie*, or People's Party for Freedom and Democracy, a Dutch center-right party. – Ed.].

I'm writing about sexual minorities in online far-right spaces. In the US, "sexual minority" includes gender nonconforming individuals as well as anyone who isn't traditionally heterosexual. How would you define your own identity in your own words?

DB: I think personal identity can be very complicated and difficult to define, but in the case of sexuality in specific, I am gay. I experience little-to-no attraction to women and am not interested in them romantically or sexually.

What do you think the biggest misunderstanding in discourse around issues of politics, gender identity, and sexuality is?

DB: The greatest misunderstanding people have in that area is definitely the belief in the so-called "2SLGBTQIAPP- Community." Such a demographic does not exist and to suggest otherwise is homophobic. Normies seem to believe that transsexuals and homosexuals are on the same team, when in reality, this could not be further from the truth. Transexuals are sexual groomers who target gay kids for their ideology. The only reason anybody thinks we're on the same side is because of Zionist propaganda. In fact, Transgender Ideology was created by the Jews to make the LGB Community look bad.

Where do you spend time online? We encountered each other on Twitter. Have you spent time on 4Chan?

DB: I primarily use X. It's where I go for activism and to find new friends I could add to my Discord server, where I hang out with my closest friends and allies. Right now, the server has 14 members and is called "Anticom," but I intend to change the name at some point. Also, I began my career on YouTube, where I met most of my friends. My channel had the same name as my X account and had 300 subscribers before it got banned, after which I relocated to X.

At about what age did you first get into those spaces? What led you there?

DB: I think I was 14 or 15 when I 1st began my "career" (for lack of a better term). In those days, I happened to leave a lot of comments on YouTube. In the comments section for the song; Ain't I Right, there was a sort of keyboard war going on between an alt-left troll group known as "DHAFC" and a few right-wing reactionaries. Because I commented a lot, I happened to get involved on the side of the right, eventually becoming the main, Reactionary figure in the comments section for Hava Nagila. I guess I'm just a natural leader like that.

Did spending time there help you figure out your identity? If so, how? (Example: did you meet other people like yourself, learn terms and concepts you didn't know about before, see a particular aesthetic which spoke to you before you knew what it meant, etc.?)

DB: I don't think the internet has helped me discover my sexual identity very much at all. As for my political identity, it has helped somewhat. For example, I never would've become anti-semitic were it not for the things I read online. However, I generally prefer to come up with my own concepts and terms than to use existing 1s.

Let's talk about your political identity, if that's okay. How do you self-identify, if you do? If not, what issues and topics are important to you and why?

DB: I am a Fascist. That is the most specific ideology you could accurately ascribe to me. I do not want to be called "a Nazi," a "Classical Fascist," "a Francoist," or any Fascist denomination in particular, as I feel that would make me feel obligated to agree with these systems completely, while "Fascism" is a much broader term that shouldn't be the source of false assumptions about me. Instead, think of my ideology as its own unique form of Fascism, which I would like some day to be called "Fascism with Dutch Characteristics."

I think the right-wing has a bad PR when it comes to that sort of thing. We need to be perceived as nicer people and right-wing spaces need to become more wholesome, especially so that femboys feel welcome.

Forgive my crudity, but this has come up during my research on right wing sex culture. Have you heard of No Nut November? Related concepts might be the Proud Boys' "no wanks" and the anti-pornography movements of the right. Do you have an opinion on the idea of "sexual purity" with regards to masturbation and/or pornography? What about "sexual purity" in general?

DB: #Nofap is gay and opposing masturbation is absurd. However, I do think that NNN is a fun challenge; a test of the will. As for pornography, that's a whole other story. Most pornography is extremely degenerate and Jewish.

What question should I have asked and didn't today? What am I missing or what do you feel like I left out of these questions, if anything?

DB: Well, I guess that depends on what your book is about, but I think we covered pretty much everything in my life. If you have any follow-up questions or things you feel like I should elaborate on more, feel free to ask away.

Thank you for your time and responses—I really appreciate it. I think that at the very least, people

from different perspectives should be able to understand what each other are saying.

DB: Of course! I'm always willing to share my perspective with intelligent normies.

*The People's Party for Freedom and Democracy, essentially the Dutch version of the Republican Party circa 1994 in the USA.

Interview Four: Sqeek McDohl, Fascist Furry

Hello! First of all, thanks for agreeing to talk to me. Tell readers a little bit about yourself (nothing identifying, just any background that you think contributes to your perspective). Knowing the general range of your age helps me sort responses, but don't feel obligated.

SM: Heya there, of course. I'm happy to talk with anyone who is chill. I'm Sqeek McDohl, a furry author and game developer. I won't give an exact age, but I have been in the furry fandom since 2007, so nearly two decades at this point!

I'm writing about sexual minorities in online far-right spaces. How would you define your own identity in your own words?

SM: I'm not too surprising on the Sexual front really. I'm Jewish, and somewhere between Straight and Asexual. The oddest part of me would probably be my interest in BDSM and snazzy uniforms.

I ran across you in the tabletop games space on X, where I encountered your project Iron Eagle. Could you tell readers about the setting, character design, and background lore?

SM: Of course. Iron Eagle is a Dieselpunk style universe inspired by stuff like Wolfenstein, GI Joe, and Iron Sky. The lore originated from a thought experiment of "What if America had absolutely zero involvement in WW2?" So, it leads to a world like our own in the Cold War, but if the European Union was a 3rd power composed of all fascist nations. Being a furry, I replaced all people with animals because this is primarily a personal project for me. It is a bit more fanciful and wacky than real life, as all the wonder weapon experiments from most nations ended up working. So, you'll have German UFO's, Japanese death rays, robotic soldiers, and weird magical spells.

How much of your love for the 1959 you designed for Europe is based on fashion and how much on ideology? I know that Nazi-controlled areas aren't the only setting in Iron Eagle, but I also recall some discussion I saw on your Discord server about Hugo Boss.

SM: That is the funny bit really. A large portion of it is a kind of uniform fetishism. The Nazi's had a really good sense of fashion and aesthetics, and I myself have a thing for women in officer clothes such as Lieutenant Fox from the anime "Squirrel and Hedgehog." As an Italian style Fascist, there is of course some overlap with mine and Nazism, but at the end of the day I simply tried to write a book from the perspective of the Germans because I felt that would be a unique selling point to help it stand out.

Where do you spend time online? Where have you found positive responses to the NatSoc aesthetic?

SM: Primarily I use Twitter, TheRPGSite, Discord, and Telegram to chat with friends. Most of the positive response comes from friends of mine on Telegram, who I had in mind when writing the book. Right-wing furries were my intended demographic, and they seem to like it because nobody else is really writing anything for people like us.

Was discovering your identity and interest in furry fandom separate related to your interest in the Third Reich and World War 2, or were they related (i.e., in the online spaces in which you'd encounter each)"

SM: Oh, most definitely they were separate. When I discovered the furry community, I mainly used websites such as Yiffstar, Yiffy.tk, and Furry 4 Life. The fandom was much more accepting and tolerant back then, so you could meet people of all types. We would all get along because we were just all there for the porn and community. My fondness of World War 2 things mainly comes from videogames. I like to joke that Iron Eagle is "War Thunder: The TTRPG" because it really is, but I also really like Red Orchestra 2. But there was always some overlap; the furry fandom was more or less founded by dudes from the military, so in old comic's you'll see anthros in uniforms with guns. Such as Albedo Anthropomorphics by Steve Gallacci or Stosstrupp by Ted Sheppard.

Let's talk about your political identity, if that's okay. How do you self-identify, if you do? If not, what issues and topics are important to you and why?

SM: I identify as a Classical Fascist more or less. I have to specify "Classical" because I'm not a fan of actual Nazism. If I had to pick a few important issues, I think everyone should have the right to be armed and speak freely, the state should offer free healthcare, I believe a permit should be required to have kids, and support a strong military who everyone should serve in at some point. I also oppose racism and discrimination except in the context of comedy.

Forgive my crudity, but this has come up during my research on right-leaning sex culture. Have you heard of No Nut November? Related concepts might be the Proud Boys' "no wanks" and the anti-pornography movements of the right. Do you have an opinion on the idea of "sexual purity" with regards to masturbation and/or pornography? What about "sexual purity" in general?

SM: Quite the unusual thing to bring up but of course I've heard of it. I personally think it's pretty dumb, and it's generally brought up as a joke in the circles I hang out in. I'm very anti-censorship, so oppose anything having to do with banning porn or masturbation. People should be free to enjoy whatever kinks they want as long as they aren't hurting someone (who doesn't want to be hurt, that is.) I do believe one shouldn't have sex outside of marriage, but that is just because I am religious.

What question should I have asked and didn't today? What am I missing or what do you feel like I left out of these questions, if anything?

SM: A thing you may miss just because you aren't a furry is how extremely Left and close-minded the furry fandom is nowadays. I do miss the days when we could all be friends regardless of differences.

Thank you for your time and responses—I really appreciate it. I think that at the very least, people from different perspectives should be able to understand what each other are saying.

Absolutely, it was my pleasure. I hope this was an alright interview, I don't do these often obviously. I share that belief, we should all be able to get along regardless of differences of beliefs. I will gladly be friends with anyone from the left or right so long as they are nice people, and oppose anyone hurting someone else because of these things.

Interview Five: Scott Kelley, Former Stormfront Facilitator

Hi, Scott! Thanks for taking the time. It has been quite the journey of friendship for us. Tell readers what forum you used to moderate before you became an antifascist and an extremism educator?

SK: I was a facilitator for Stormfont. A facilitator is a kind of mod meant to foment discussion. I was made a mod because I had created some secession petitions at White House dot gov and was put in charge of the secession forum. I didn't have the ability to ban people or anything like that, so I often helped keep an eye out for violations for the other mods. But I did my job well as a facilitator and was also known for being a good recruiter.

I remember you. I didn't have an active account—I had one to lurk and pick up on chatter there. What sorts of themes regarding sex did you notice in Stormfront's forum?

SK: Mostly Stormfront as a whole was very sex-averse. Most white nationalists are terrified of sex and those that aren't tend to be incels who are desperate for sex. Outside of Stormfront, white nationalists tended to be very predatory... no matter their age. I outed countless WNs for being child predators and even those not going after children tended to be abusively predatory towards women in general, and sometimes men and boys.

A sizable section of my book is about sexual minorities in far-right online spaces; gay Nazis, trans Nazis, and people like that. Fascist femboys,

Nazi furries. Did you see that (openly gay fascists) on Stormfront, and how did it go for them?

SK: Openly gay was not allowed on Stormfront, but as someone who was loosely closeted, I certainly noticed a lot of closeted gay activity. I walked in on quite a bit of that. In my view there was a direct link between the most virulent anti-gay bigots and being closeted.

What's your take on the phenomenon now and what might be driving it?

SK: Considering my view that white nationalists are almost all closeted, I don't really have any extra views.

With Nazi furries in particular, there's been a concerted effort (according to one Slate article) to deradicalize community members rather than ostracize or expel them. What are the potential benefits and potential risks of such a strategy?

SK: People can't deradicalize Nazis. Only Nazis can deradicalize themselves. Do I think it is a waste of time to reach out in such a way? No. People just need to be aware that those people will only deradicalize if they want to deradicalize. And if someone says they do, then by all means. But my organization Center for Extremism Prevention and Intervention does not actively pull people out. They come to us.

The furry fandom is majority-queer (heterosexuals make up 20%.) Do you think that may have something to do with this approach as opposed to the one embraced by, say, the punk music or metal

communities, which tend to violently expel fascists?

SK: I don't particularly oppose either method since deradicalization is a process the extremist has to go through. So there is nothing wrong with expelling them. Also, it really shouldn't be up to the furry community to deradicalize anybody anyway.

You yourself were once a white nationalist and now don't sexually identify the way you used to while moderating Stormfront. Can you tell me about that journey and what it has been like?

SK: Technically I do sexually identify as I did when I was at Stormfornt... mostly. I'm not sure if I ever explicitly said I was straight when I was on there. I may have on occasion, but those who knew me knew I was a bit more flexible on that, if not polysexual. It's complicated for me since I am solely attracted to femininity... so straight, polysexual, or bisexual... I prefer women and feminine men. I'm functionally close to being straight.

Thanks for your time, Scott, you're a credit to the fine people of the wide-open spaces of the American West.

SK: Sure!

Interview Six: E., Anarcha-Feminist Sex Worker

Hi! First of all, thanks for taking the time to talk to

me. I consider sex work real and legitimate work, as much or more so than most forms of employment in 2025. Would you tell readers a little bit about what you do and what it means to you?

E: Hey!! You're welcome, I'm happy to help. I'd call myself a content creator or a sex worker. Since my work, like many sex workers, doesn't necessarily fit into a neat box. I've done a bunch of different stuff over the years, but lately I've been more drawn to a sorta internet burlesque/ boudoir vibe. Sex work means quite a lot to me, I'm not the most successful sex worker, so not money. I just love it, it's made me feel extremely empowered and confident, I get to make a living off my art, and it's given me a platform to speak about things I care about.

In part, I'm writing about men who are anti-porn crusaders. What do you make of that phenomenon, and practices like "No Nut November" (the month-off-from-porn challenge many right-wing people participate in)?

E: I think no nut November is silly, but in general the widespread repression of sexuality to the point where one can't even pleasure themselves is dangerous. What I mean is that extreme sexual repression has a tendency to cause people to have an unhealthy relationship with sex & inappropriate sexual desires. Individuals having a healthy relationship with sex, keeps the community safe.

Between religion and government, it seems like

systems of control have a real problem with women (and men, and enbies) enjoying their own sexuality however they see fit. Why do you think that is?

E: When you control sex, you control a lot of aspects of someone's life. By restricting "acceptable sex" to cis heteronormative married couples and limiting sexual education, they can keep people in relationships which have a gendered power dynamic, accidentally pumping out babies, which benefits men and hierarchical structures. When women & queer folks are empowered sexually, we are much harder to control.

What do you think the biggest misunderstanding in discourse around issues of politics, gender identity, and sexuality is?

E: I wouldn't consider myself an expert in gender identity and I won't claim to know what the biggest misunderstanding on the subject is, I would just say that I think it's not that hard to be respectful of what people say their gender is. Concerning sexuality specifically, I would probably say it's that being sexual correlates with being immoral. That can definitely also be said about being trans or get as well, I just don't know if it's the biggest misunderstanding.

The COVID-19 pandemic seems to have played hell with certain aspects of young people's socialization, including when it comes to sex. Have you seen this reflected in your audience?

E: Hmm that's an interesting question, I do have a

large section of my audience that is younger & I've definitely had many younger clients who paid me just to teach them how to pleasure a woman. Many have expressed that it's because they feel embarrassed being 19-22ish and not really knowing because they didn't get the opportunity to learn and explore when they were younger. I can see & feel it more in the tone of the opposition to sex work & the general sex negative views going around, than in my audience.

What do you make of the "male loneliness epidemic" and increased tension between genders in the West lately?

E: If I'm being fair to the men that claim it's worse for them, I'd say maybe women are slightly better at being friends/community out of sheer necessity. We have to talk to each other about sex & our relationships in a vulnerable way, because we need each other's help to make sure we know things are healthy. We have to care about the drunk lady that we don't get along with when she talking to a bunch of random dudes, because caring for a moment could be the difference between her being raped or murdered or not. There is a level of community required in our existence that may be allowing us to have meaningful relationships outside of romantic ones, however men having shitty friendships isn't our fault or really our problem. Many women have offered men what we view as friendship and the outcome most of the time is her getting told she led him on, because most men only know how to be vulnerable with their sexual partners and mother. If dudes are so lonely I'd recommend they start by not constantly being cruel to their so-called friends and try being honest about their lives and emotions with each other, instead of relying on the two women society allotted them to handle their affairs.

Sorry if that sounds harsh, I'm not sure how to word it in a way that isn't a bit tough love vibes. I would like to say that I don't hate men or anything, I love men, my work is pretty much centered around them and I love my work, but I don't have a whole lot of sympathy for men specifically on this issue that effects everyone and is men's fault.

Last question: what question should I have asked but didn't?

I guess one thing I didn't touch on that I feel is important, is how restricting access to porn specifically is an attack on freedom of speech and art as a whole. It not only makes it harder for sex workers to have access to safer types of work, but also is part of a greater plan to restrict access to information and control speech and media. Everyone is free to have their own boundaries around sex, but when the state tries to regulate sexual interactions between consenting adults and media around it, they will not stop there.

Thank you for your time and your work!

APPENDIX B

GLOSSARY

Note: I've done my best here, but if any term I use is unfamiliar, search for it or, barring that, contact me.

AMAB/AFAB: Assigned male at birth and assigned female at birth, respectively; a person's birth gender (unless they are intersex or another nonmale, nonfemale gender).

Anthros: Anthropomorphic animal characters; what furries identify as, find sexy, and emulate.

Antinomian: Antinomianism is a descriptive term for beliefs or practice which deliberately go against moral, religious, or legal norms.

Armanen runes: Not runes. A set of symbols hallucinated by racist mountaineer Gudo von List when he temporarily went blind, and which were published as "the secret of the runes" in 1908.

Astroturf: A term that means "fake grassroots." When a corporation, PAC, political party, etc. attempts to folk-wash a policy push by funding and promoting common-man-level politics. A fairly standard practice with both major political parties and any energy or urban development company.

Autogynophiliac / AGP: In the wildly unscientific (and outdated) categorization of psychologist Ray Blanchard, men who are sexually excited by the idea of themselves as women. In Blanchard's typology, there are only AGPs—whom he believed could literally be spotted by physical characteristics—and HSTS, or "homosexual transexuals." (SEE: **Husstussie / HSTS**)

BDSM: Bondage, Domination, and Sadomasochism; the "bondage" portion of any kink scene. This includes everything from fairly vanilla stuff (being handcuffed in bed or engaging in playful spanking) to activities that require one to block out a weekend and invest thousands of dollars in equipment to make a "scenario" work.

Black Sun: (See **Schwarze Sonne**)

Blanchardism: A debunked and unscientific pseudo-taxonomy of trans women that divides them all into visibly-masculine "AGPs" (men with "autogynophilia," or sexual arousal at the idea of themselves as women) and "HSTS" ("homosexual transsexuals" or "extreme homosexuals," who could be identified by their feminine features and presentation). How this crude amalgamation of phrenology, physiognomy theory (both debunked!), and transphobia didn't disqualify Blanchard from holding a position at the University of Toronto, let alone to have sat on an advisory board for the DSM-V. Blanchard is also a member of the eugenicist, "race science"-promoting, anti-interracial-marriage, white supremacist Human Biodiversity Project.

Boymoding: A slang term born on 4Chan in /tttt/ and other niche spaces to refer to closeted trans women who "boymode" by dressing and acting as their assigned gender when they think it necessary to protect their secret.

Brick: Trans slang for a non-passing trans woman.

Chaser: A man (usually) who has a fetish for trans women.

Cisnormative: An adjective describing anything which portrays cisgendered identity as the "normal" or "desirable" or "good" way to live life. American society, for example, is cisnormative.

Comphet: A portmanteau of "compulsive heterosexuality." When a person transitions, they often feel societal and/or subconscious pressure to date members of the opposite gender, even if they are attracted to their own. Gender identity and sexual orientation have nothing to do with one another.

Cosplay: A practice in which a fan dresses up in costume as a character from comics, games, film, or, especially, anime. This can be done at conventions, for photoshoots, or to stream content.

Cuck / Cuckold: The term "cuck" is used derisively in modern slang to mean a person—especially a man—who is viewed as impotent and weak. It's a shortened version of the term cuckold, an antiquated term for a man whose wife cheats on him. A cuckold fetish—AKA a "hotwife" fetish—is when a couple, married or unmarried, invites a "bull" to have sex with one member of the couple (usually a woman in a hetero relationship) while her partner (usually the man / husband) watches. The arousal of the husband in this situation is linked to a sense of shame, humiliation, and un-manliness. If it seems strange that such an emotional cocktail can be sexually arousing, you probably have a very "normal" sex life. A cuck fetish is different in both form and mechanism of arousal from voyeurism (see **voyeur**).

Doll/s: A slangy way that trans women often refer to each other, the way a bro-ish dude might say "bro" or "dude."

Egg: Trans slang for a trans person who has not realized they are trans yet. When an egg begins to explore their gender identity more thoroughly, they are said to be "cracking."

Esoteric Hitlerism: A syncretic religious doctrine largely assembled by French-born Greek national and National Socialist Savitri Devi, who moved to India, "converted to Hinduism," and then wrote a body of very strange esoteric religious philosophy combining elements of German racial mysticism, misunderstood Hinduism, and National Socialist philosophy. Esoteric Hitlerism holds that Adolf Hitler was a living god, the avatar of the Hindu god Vishnu the Sustainer, and that we are currently living through an almost-endless cycle of war, strife, ignorance, and death called the Kali Yuga (that's a real term from Hindu philosophy having to do with cosmic eons and nothing whatsoever to do with Adolf Hitler), brought on by—one guess!—that's right, the Jews.

Ethnos: White nationalists borrowed this word from ancient Greece. It refers to a people defined and contained by, not just genetics/race, but a specific biome and homeland. Like other National Socialist concepts in both their original and modern use, there are mystical undertones to this idea that make it more than just a description of "ethnicity."

Fascism: An authoritarian, right-wing political movement that emphasizes a unified ethnos, demonizes an insidious internal and/or external enemy, embraces the cult of manly action, worships hierarchy, taxonomizes entire races of people as "inferior" or "superior" based on pseudoscientific claims, and other criteria. My definition is complex enough to encompass both Nazi Germany and MAGA, Mussolini and Andy Ngo.

Fascist Internationale: I used this term in *Black Sunrise on Piss Earth* to describe the international coalition of far-right idealogues who share ideas, tactics, and support online. It's why, for example, Great Britain's Tommy Robinson held a huge grief ritual spectacle for Charlie Kirk after Kirk sprung a leak. This support includes speaking gigs, paid think tank invitations, travel expenses, sometimes even language lessons, and the pooling of knowledge (and perhaps funds, though that hasn't been proven).

Femboy: A gender-nonconforming young man or nonbinary person whose gender expression is sometimes (or often) performed in feminine ways such as wearing makeup, skirts, thigh-high stockings, etc. Some femboys are cisgendered and a few are heterosexual; some might be boymoding (see: boymoding).

Fishy/Fishoid: "Fishy" is a venerable trans slang term

for a trans woman's ability to "pass" as AFAB (see: **AFAB**), or remain not visibly trans as a woman. The -oid suffix is a derogatory diminutive native to 4Chan that has infected other right-wing spaces online. -oid has its origins in incel slang, where "foid" was and is short for "female humanoid." Because women aren't actually human, in their eyes.

Gay Nazi Myth: The anti-historical assertion that the NSDAP in Germany was "run by homosexuals," which began in 1948 with the publication of *Germany's National Vice* by Samuel Igra, continued and amplified by Scott Lively and others in *The Pink Swastika* and countless other books, comics, films, games, etc.

Goon: From the late 90s until recently, slang for a member of the Something Awful forums. Now, a slang verb which means "to masturbate."

Great Replacement: A debunked conspiracy theory that originated in France and spread to the UK and the United States. It claims that sinister forces (Jews) are manipulating immigration to replace white people with imported people of color to destroy the West.

Gynesexuality / Gynesexual: A new term in sexual self-identification, this means that a person is attracted to femme-presenting people and effeminate traits, whether they appear in nonbinary people, women, or men.

Gynocracy: The very silly Men's Rights Activist version of the Patriarchy, this conspiracy theory presupposes that women secretly (or openly, depending on how ass-brained the MRA in question is) control society for and to their own ends.

Heteronormative: An adjective describing anything which portrays heterosexuality as the "normal" or "desirable" or "good" way to live life. American society, for example, is heteronormative.

Hon: The /tttt/ version of "brick:" a badly-dressing, non-passing trans woman. Derogatory. Strongly associated with—but not interchangeable with—AGP (see: **Brick** and **AGP**).

Husstussie / HSTS: Passing trans women, or "homosexual transsexuals" in the schema of washed-up psychologist Ray Milton Blanchard the Third.

Kawaii: From Japanese, literally "cute." A word popular in otaku culture that has also infested internet forums and social media platforms since time out of mind. The term is often used in otaku trans *and* otaku white supremacist circles, and also more broadly in anime-friendly groups in general.

Kleine-nihilism: "Perverse" or optimistic/joyous nihilism, or the nihilism of destruction. The nihilism of Nietzsche, as opposed to the pessimistic nihilism of Peter Wessel Zapffe, Arthur Schopenhauer, Phillip Mainländer, Eugene Thacker, or Thomas Ligotti.

Kulturkampf: German for "culture struggle" or "culture strife:" essentially, the first iteration of what would come to be called "culture war" in America.

LGBTQIA+: This acronym for non-heteronormative people stands for lesbian, gay, bisexual, transgender, queer, intersex, asexual, and anyone else we didn't include. For most queer people, it's unproblematic. To "LGB without the TQ" right-wing gay and lesbian people, it amounts to an attack on the rights they feel they've earned all by themselves (they didn't, as this book's description of the Stonewall Riot in Chapter One makes clear).

Male loneliness epidemic: According to some statistical data, men are increasingly isolated; from women, from their peers, and even from their family members. A great deal of ink has been spilled trying to explain this mystery while thousands of furious men on Twitter reply "DIE, RAPE U TRAITOR" to even the most tepid criticism of the Trump regime.

Meme: Originally, a unit of information (a rumor, a turn of phrase, a joke). Now, the same, but usually performed with text and image juxtapositions.

Normie: A normal person who does not spend an extraordinary amount of time thinking about these issues and is largely unaware of the more obscure facets of power in the world right now.

NSDAP: *Nationalsozialistische Deutsche Arbeiterpartei*, or National Socialist German Workers' Party—the long version of the political party abbreviated as the Nazis or the Nazi Party.

OC/s: Original character. It's not unusual these days for people to spend time crafting characters rather than complete works of fiction, games, etc. Part of this is that (especially for furries), creating an OC means that you can make art of that character yourself or commission it from other artists.

Paleoconservative: A form of old-school conservatism based on limited government, ruthlessly traditionalist moral values, and strict anti-interventionism in foreign wars.

Parasocial Relationship: While this phenomenon is

not new to the age of the internet (or even mass media), it has increased to the point where some sources claim most people have at least one parasocial relationship in their lives. It's simply this: a one-way relationship with someone in the media or popular consciousness who doesn't know you exist. This isn't the same as stalking—it's listening to that same podcaster who makes you feel safe and relaxed after a long day, and who tells you enough about their private life (often in a charming way) that you feel like they're practically part of the family, even if a distant relative. *They're not.*

Patriarchy: A traditional form of society in which males, and especially fathers and elders, have say over society. Modern patriarchy is intensively restrictive of men's and women's gender roles, and it doesn't always benefit men who aren't part of the elite. Patriarchy's male gender role, for example, "entitles" a man to spousal rape but also expects him to work so hard to support his stay-at-home mom wife and brood of kids that he has his first—and last—coronary at age 45. It's miserable for almost everyone.

Peeping Tom: A person who illicitly watches people without their knowledge or consent for sexual gratification. This often takes the form of "window peeping," but can also include taking photos of women unobserved while the women are partially exposed. It's a gross and unethical form of voyeurism.

PizzaGate: A long-debunked conspiracy theory that emerged during the Clinton vs. Trump campaign in 2015 and 2016. It holds that Comet Ping Pong, a pizza restaurant and family entertainment venue in Washington, D.C., is a front for a cabal of Satan-worshiping and possibly alien elites who rape (and, in some tellings, drain the adrenochrome from) innocent children. The theory became so inflammatory that in 2016 a man named Edgar Maddison Welch entered the restaurant with a rifle and demanded to be led to its basement. He got pissed off at one point and fired a shot into the ceiling to show them he meant business. Told there was no basement, Welch stormed around a little bit and, finding no children to free, he surrendered to the police. In 2025, after serving 4 years for his crime, Welch died in a shootout with police (seemingly unrelated to PizzaGate).

Poststructuralism: A school of philosophy that emerged in the 1960s. Poststructuralism calls into question the objectivity of the various interpretive structures (structuralism) in society. Critical textual analysis is an example of a technique employed by poststructuralist thinkers like Michel Foucault.

Pooner: A hate slur for a trans man.

PPG: The penile plethysmograph. A device that measures blood flow to the penis and therefore sexual response to various stimulus. Developed by Kurt Freund in Czechoslovakia in the 1950s so the Czech (read: USSR) military could tell who was faking homosexuality to avoid conscription.

Rapehon: /Tttt/ slang. A "hon" (see **Hon**) who desires access to female spaces to sexually assault females. Imaginary and derogatory.

SA: The shortened version of Sturmabteilung, or the "Stormtroopers" that served as Adolf Hitler's first street fighting troops against German communists and anarchists (among others), and then as his primary bodyguard and meeting security force. The SA was ruled over by Ernst Röhm, an openly gay man and one of Hitler's closest friends, until Hitler had him murdered and the SA was eclipsed by Heinrich Himmler's SS.

SS: The shortened version of Schutzstaffel, or the "Protection Echelon" that served early Nazis as bodyguards but grew into a larger organization, especially under the leadership of Henrich Himmler. The SS had two divisions: the Allgemeine (General) - SS, which was an administrative arm with some police capacities, and the Waffen (Weapons) -SS, which had entire divisions of troops that operated alongside—but separately from—ordinary Nazi military units. By 1934, they were one of Hitler's most important weapons.

Savitri Devi: See **Esoteric Hitlerism**.

Schwarze Sonne: The "Black Sun" of Esoteric Hitlerism and mystical neo-Nazism. A sunwheel consisting of twelve radial *sig* runes.

Sex Work / Sex Worker: A class of employment that includes strippers, Instagram and OnlyFans models, adult actors and actresses, and people who talk on the phone, DM, send personal pictures, or have sex for their income. A worker, just like you (assuming you're employed, and if not, congrats!).

Trans-Exclusionary Radical Feminist (TERF): A gender-essentialist "feminist" who does not view trans women as women, but rather as liars, frauds, and predators.

Trans-Exclusionary Compulsory Heterosexuality (TECH): The basis of the "natural family" espoused by fascists: one AMAB heterosexual man, one AFAB heterosexual woman, and as many healthy white kids as they can crank out.

Transmedicalism: The belief among some trans people, self-identified as “truscum” (a shortening of “true transsexual scum”), that the only valid way to transition is through gender reassignment surgery. This is an increasingly minority and bitter opinion in the trans community.

Transvestigate/transvestigation: An on- (and now, regrettably, off-) line phenomenon in which women are “investigated” to see if they were assigned female at birth based on ridiculous criteria like the shape of an actress’ jawline of the arms of a tennis player.

Troon: A hate slur for a trans woman.

Truscum: See **Transmedicalism**.

Völkisch: Of an ideology or movement: concerned with the “folk,” or race. So, for example, Ásatrú—the veneration of the ancient Norse pantheon—has two flavors. One claims you must be of “the blood” or “the folk” to worship: this movement is known as Völkisch Ásatrú (Nazi pagans). The other strand of Ásatrú, which is open to everyone and very based, does not.

Voyeur / Voyeurism: Voyeurism is a fetish where someone likes to watch. It doesn’t have to be their partner, and usually isn’t. Ethical voyeurism means all parties consent to the goings-on (see exhibitionism), which distinguishes a voyeur from a **peeping tom**. The fact that a voyeur is turned on by what they see and not by shame or humiliation distinguishes them from a cuck fetishist (see **Cuck**).

Woke: This has become a catchall term on the right, on the order of "political correctness," for any measure of treatment other than disdain and cruelty applied to sexual, racial, ethnic, or religious minorities. The word's origins make the meaning clear. In Black activist culture, to be "woke" meant that one had become awakened to the role of white supremacy in everyday life, influencing every aspect of American culture. That explains why the right will not stop whining about it, I suppose.

Wokescold: A slang term for someone who is overbearingly obsessed with performative wokeness; the "fun police" in the eyes of the right (and an apt description of a very annoying type of person, too).

AUTHOR BIO

Charles R. Bernard is a writer who lives in Salt Lake City, Utah. His work has been featured in publications like Thuggish Itch and Cosmic Horror Monthly and has appeared in anthologies like American Cult, Peaks of Madness, and Deadman Humour: 13 Fears of a Clown. He is the social media manager for Madness Heart Press, and has several books, fiction and nonfiction out through that press. He resides next to Salt Lake City Cemetery; a sprawling necropolis whose tombs and markers stretch out over a square kilometer of grounds. Charles is lively enough company, though. You can find him at https://www.charlesrbernard.com.

www.charlesrbernard.com

More Nonfiction From Madness Heart Press

Black Sunrise On Piss Earth by Charles R. Bernard
Ten Words for a Wicked Woman by Susan Snyder
Encyclopedia Sharksploitanica by Susan Snyder
The Book of Brilliance by Geoffrey Dennis

More from Charles R. Bernard

He Led Us Into the Wilderness and Spoke to Us
A Baptism for the Dead
Bound With Briars

www.ingramcontent.com/pod-product-compliance
Lightning Source LLC
Chambersburg PA
CBHW011349230926
51848CB00003B/515
9781967517305